always up to date

The law changes, but Nolo is always on top of it! We offer several ways to make sure you and your Nolo products are always up to date:

1 **Nolo's Legal Updater**

We'll send you an email whenever a new edition of your book is published! Sign up at **www.nolo.com/legalupdater**.

2 **Updates @ Nolo.com**

Check **www.nolo.com/updates** to find recent changes in the law that affect the current edition of your book.

3 **Nolo Customer Service**

To make sure that this edition of the book is the most recent one, call us at **800-728-3555** and ask one of our friendly customer service representatives. Or find out at **www.nolo.com**.

please note

We believe accurate and current legal information should help you solve many of your own legal problems on a cost-efficient basis. But this text is not a substitute for personalized advice from a knowledgeable lawyer. If you want the help of a trained professional, consult an attorney licensed to practice in your state.

3rd Edition

The Complete IEP Guide

How to Advocate for Your Special Ed Child

by Attorney Lawrence M. Siegel

THIRD EDITION	MAY 2004
Editor	LISA GUERIN
Illustrations	MARI STEIN
Book Design	TERRI HEARSH
Cover Design	TONI IHARA
Production	SARAH HINMAN
Index	ELLEN DAVENPORT
Proofreading	EMILY K. WOLMAN
Printing	DELTA PRINTING SOLUTIONS, INC.

Siegel, Lawrence M., 1946-
    The complete IEP guide: how to advocate for your special ed. child / by Lawrence M. Siegel.--3rd ed.
      p. cm.
    Includes index.
    ISBN 1-4133-0017-0
    1. Individualized education programs--Law and legislation--United States--Popular works. 2. Dispute resolution (Law)--United States--Popular works. 3. Special education--Parent participation--United States--Popular works. I. Title.

KF4209.3.Z9S57   2004
371.9'0973--dc22

371.90973
Sieg

2003064969

For information on bulk purchases or corporate premium sales, please contact the Special Sales Department. For academic sales or textbook adoptions, ask for Academic Sales. Call 800-955-4775 or write to Nolo, 950 Parker Street, Berkeley, CA 94710.

3 2530 60590 4927

Dedication

To the memory of Becky Luftig, my first client, and a remarkable young woman for whom "disability" was an attitude and nothing more

To my parents, and

To my wife Gail, for that first day on the Wheeler steps, and ever since, her joyous smile.

Acknowledgments

My appreciation to the entire Nolo staff which, to a person, has always been professional and friendly and never seemed to feel those two concepts were incompatible.

Special thanks to Marcia Stewart for her superb editing, her patience as we worked through and wrote about the complexities of the IEP process and her clear goal of making the IEP process friendly to and useful for families of children with disabilities. And thanks to Spencer Sherman for his work updating the 2nd edition.

Several other Nolo staff deserve special thanks:

Jake Warner, for his enthusiasm about the project

Robin Leonard, for her extensive editing and excellent work developing the list of resources for families of children with disabilities

Stanley Jacobsen, for his helpful research assistance

Terri Hearsh, for her terrific design work

Mari Stein, for her delightful illustrations

Toni Ihara, for her delightful cover (and patience)

Michele Crim, Jennifer Spoerri, Jennifer Macko and Kelly Rosaaen, for their kindness and marketing/pr expertise

Erin Douglass, for putting together clearly written cover copy and being a pleasure to work with, and

Karen Turk and Lisa Guerin, for their editorial assistance, especially on forms and checklists.

Thanks also to my colleagues and friends on the California Advisory Commission on Special Education.

Table of Contents

Appendixes

4 Sample IEP Form

5 Tear-Out Forms

Index

1

Introduction to Special Education

Some years ago, a parent came to my office to discuss the difficulties her teenager was having in school. The parent was a kind and thoughtful person, but looked overwhelmed. Her child had learning disabilities and increasing emotional problems, and the pain of the child was etched on the face of the parent. Her child was falling further behind, losing the confidence she once had, and missing the academic skills and emotional strength she would need for adulthood.

My client sat quietly for some time and then asked in a whisper, "What in the world can I do for my daughter?"

Whether you and your child are entering special education for the first time or the tenth time, you have probably asked the same question. You have a dozen concerns and a hundred fears. You don't know where to begin. The problems seem insurmountable. There are more than 5,000,000 children with disabilities in the U.S.— that's one out of every twelve children and teenagers. At some point their parents have felt the same way my client did—and you probably have, too.

Fortunately, Congress enacted a law called the Individuals with Disabilities Education Act, or IDEA, to assess children with disabilities and to provide special education programs and services to help them succeed in school. Before IDEA was enacted in 1975, public schools frequently ignored children with disabilities or shunted them off to inferior or distant programs. IDEA represents a long-overdue recognition that individuals with disabilities have the right to access public institutions and be served appropriately, with dignity and respect.

The detail and reach of IDEA are remarkable— no other law in this nation provides such clear and unique legal protection for children. Everything you do to help your child secure an appropriate education is connected to, and determined by, the legal requirements of IDEA.

A. What Is Special Education?

"Special education" is the broad term used to describe the educational system for children with disabilities. The term is used in this book to describe that portion of your child's school system that provides special services and programs for children with disabilities. There are three fundamental questions to consider as you begin the special education process:

- Where is your child now?
- Where do you want your child to be?
- What do you need to get your child there?

IDEA entitles your child to an "appropriate" education that meets his or her unique needs. You'll likely have a good sense of what is meant by an appropriate education as you read this book. Broadly speaking, an appropriate education involves the following educational components:

- The specific program or class (called "placement") for your child. Placement is more than just a classroom; it also includes characteristics such as location, class size, teacher experience, and peer makeup.
- The specific services (called "related services") provided your child, as well as the amount and frequency of those services and who provides them.
- Other educational components, such as curricula and teaching methods.

Special education provides a process for evaluating your child and developing an *individualized education program,* or IEP. The acronym IEP refers to several interrelated things:

- the meeting where the school district determines whether your child is eligible for special education (called the IEP eligibility meeting)
- the yearly meeting where you and school representatives develop your child's educational plan (called the IEP program meeting), and
- the actual detailed written description of your child's educational program.

"Disability" Is a Loaded Term

Webster's *New World Dictionary* defines disability as an illness, injury, or physical handicap that "restricts" or causes "limitations" and "disadvantages." Advocates in special education and disability rights understandably object to the term "disabled," preferring "child with disabilities"—this is the term we use throughout this book.

All human beings come into this world with a variety of qualities and characteristics. Having special education needs does not mean that your child should be treated as "different" or denied the care and respect that all children deserve. Human beings are complex, and a determination of who is able and "disabled" is an effort in futility. Franklin Roosevelt was president four times and could not walk. Stephen Hawking is severely disabled and understands the universe like few on this earth.

It is not a cliché to say that we all have some kind of disability, even as we realize that the difference in degree between one or another disability can be significant and life-altering. Defining terms should not be judgmental terms. I have many colleagues who are deaf. They are, to be sure, without hearing, but to consider them ineffective or incapable would be ludicrous. They cannot hear, but communicate in a beautiful, complex and effective way. In a meeting of deaf people, it is my halting sign language that is ineffective and disabling to me.

Special education laws give children with disabilities and their parents important rights not available to children in regular education and their parents. These include the right to:

- have the child assessed
- secure information about the child
- attend an IEP meeting
- develop a written IEP plan, and
- resolve disputes with the school district through an impartial administrative and legal process.

While the specifics of any one child's special education needs may vary—one child may need placement in a private school while another needs a one-to-one aide for full-time participation in a regular class (called "mainstreaming")—mastering the IEP process is central to securing an appropriate education for your child. But equally important, the IEP process is entirely individual. The program developed by you and the school district must fit your child, not the other way around. What works for other students is irrelevant if it won't work for your child. IDEA does not tell you or the school district specifically how your child will be educated. Rather, IDEA provides rules to govern the process the IEP team uses to decide what is appropriate for your child.

B. Being Your Child's Advocate

Advocating for your child is easy. You want the best for her. Still, there will be bumps along the way. The IEP process is maze-like, involving a good deal of technical information, intimidating professionals, and confusing choices. For some families, it goes smoothly, with no disagreements; for others, it is a terrible encounter in which you and your school district cannot even agree on the time of day. For most people, the experience is somewhere in between.

Don't fall into the trap of thinking that teachers, school administrators, and experts know everything and that you know nothing. Right now, you may not have all the information you need, and you may not know where to look for it. But the law states that you and your school district are equal decisionmakers, and that the school district must provide you with a good deal of information along the way.

You do not need to be a special education expert or a lawyer to be an effective advocate for your child. The general strategies for helping a child in the IEP process are not complex and can easily be mastered. The cliché that knowledge is power is absolutely true in the world of special education.

C. Using This Book

The purpose of this book is to help parents effectively proceed on their own through the IEP process, whether it's their first time or their fifth time. The book is for parents whose child has emotional difficulties, is deaf or blind, has other physical conditions, or has a multitude of disabilities. In other words, it's for every parent of a child with disabilities.

 If your child has learning disabilities: Nolo publishes a specialized version of this book just for parents of children with learning disabilities. *Nolo's IEP Guide: Learning Disabilities,* by Larry Siegel, addresses issues of particular concern for children with learning disabilities, including commonly used assessments, special eligibility requirements, teaching methodologies, and more. If your child has learning disabilities,

you'll want to use this more specific resource. Nolo will be happy to exchange this book for a copy of *Nolo's IEP Guide: Learning Disabilities.* Simply call 1-800-728-3555 Monday through Friday, 7AM to 7PM PST, and one of our customer service representatives will be happy to help.

Specifically, this book can help you:
- develop an understanding of special education law
- understand eligibility rules and the role of assessments
- gather current material and develop new information about your child
- determine your child's specific goals and educational needs
- gather current material and develop new information about various school programs, as well as options outside the school district
- prepare for the IEP meeting
- attend the IEP meeting and develop your child's IEP plan, and
- resolve disputes with the school district.

Mastering these tasks will require you to be generally organized (but not fanatically so), willing to ask questions and make use of resources that are widely available. The suggestions and forms in this book will help you get—and stay—organized throughout the IEP process.

Detailed appendixes provide invaluable information, including:
- copies of key federal special education statutes and regulations
- addresses and websites of federal and state special education agencies
- addresses and websites of national and state advocacy, parent, and disability organizations
- a bibliography of other helpful books, and
- two dozen tear-out forms, letters, and checklists to help you through every stage of the IEP process.

Some of the material will be very familiar to parents who have been through many IEPs—for example, you may already know too well the cast of characters and the basic legal requirements. Still, you should review each chapter, even the ones that cover familiar topics. You may find new insights or angles on old problems. Of course, you can skip material clearly not relevant—for example, if your child is already in special education, you don't need to prepare for an eligibility meeting.

If you are new to special education, very little in this book will be familiar to you. You might want to start by taking a quick look at the chapter titles and table of contents to become familiar with key ideas and how they relate to each other before you start reading. As you read, check the index and jump among chapters if that makes sense. Highlight points you want to remember.

The special education process has a discernible beginning and end. In general, it takes a year. There are similarities and differences between the first IEP year and subsequent years. For example, each year you will gather information and prepare for the yearly IEP program meeting, at which time you and the school district will determine placement and related services. But the first year always includes assessing your child and determining whether he or she is eligible for special education. In subsequent years, your child may or may not be assessed. Eligibility is rarely addressed after the first year, unless you or the school district feels a change is justified—for example, if your child no longer needs special education or may qualify under a different eligibility category.

There is a certain chicken-or-egg quality to the order of some of the chapters. For example, the chapter on assessments comes before the chapter on eligibility. You will soon learn that your child must be assessed before determined to be eligible, but you need to know how a child becomes eligible before you arrange an assessment. Which chapter do you read first? It really doesn't matter, as long as you read both.

What This Book Doesn't Cover

IDEA provides rights and procedures for children between the ages of three and 22. There is another procedure for children under three, but this book's fundamental focus is on children between three and 22. There are also certain IDEA issues that involve very complex and detailed procedures and are discussed only briefly in this book, such as transition services to help children over age 14 prepare for a job or college, including independent living skills. This book does not address in detail issues regarding discipline of special education students, including suspension and expulsion. This issue is complex; you should contact an attorney or at least a support group (see Appendix 3) regarding discipline issues. (20 U.S.C. §1415 (k); 34 C.F.R. § 3300.519-529; see Appendix 1.)

D. Icons Used Throughout This Book

The icons listed below appear throughout this book to help you along.

 Books or organizations that give more information about the issue or topic discussed in the text.

 Related topics covered in this book.

 Slow down and consider potential problems.

 You may be able to skip some material that doesn't apply to your situation.

 A practical tip or good idea.

A tear-out copy of the form discussed in the text is in Appendix 5.

 State law may vary on this issue.

E. Getting Help From Others

Other parents, local groups, and regional or national organizations can be of great help as you wend your way through special education. The amount of information these folks have can be amazing. Other parents and parent groups can be your best resource and certainly a source of support to help you through hard times. Others who have been through the process before can help you avoid making mistakes or undertaking unnecessary tasks. Most important, they can be a source of real encouragement. Chapter 15 provides further thoughts on making use of your local special education community.

Note: Reference is made throughout this book to parents, but the term is used to include foster parents and legal guardians. ■

2

Overview of the IEP and Special Education Law

As mentioned in Chapter 1, a federal law, the Individuals with Disabilities Education Act (IDEA), furnishes a formal process for assessing children with disabilities and providing specialized programs and services to help them succeed in school. Special education is unique because of the central role parents play in determining their child's educational program. Under IDEA, the program and services your child needs will be determined through the individualized education program, or IEP, process. The term IEP is used to refer to a meeting about and a written description of your child's program. Your ability to understand and master the IEP process is central to your child's educational experience. Indeed, the IEP is the centerpiece of IDEA.

This chapter discusses the specific mandates of IDEA and how they apply to your child. It provides an overview of your child's legal rights to special education and the IEP process, so you can effectively advocate for your child.

As you read this chapter, keep in mind the following:

- Don't let the word "law" throw you. The actual language of IDEA, and more important, its underlying purpose, can easily be mastered. The legal concepts in IDEA are logical and sensible.
- Developing a broad understanding of the law will help you when you review later chapters on eligibility, assessments, IEPs, and other key matters.
- The actual language of IDEA appears in the body of the book. While I provide plain English descriptions of special education law, you can find the actual law as passed by Congress in Appendix 1. IDEA is found in the United States Code starting at 20 U.S.C. § 1400. Key sections of IDEA's regulations (these are in the Code of Federal Regulations at 34 C.F.R. §§ 300.1-756) are also in Appendix 1. IDEA regulations are frequently referred to in this book because they include greater detail than the statutes.

A. What IDEA Requires

IDEA was enacted in 1975 and reauthorized and revamped in 1997; as this 3rd edition went to press, Congress was continuing its debate over the next reauthorization (see "Keeping Current on Special Education Law," at the end of this chapter). IDEA imposes a number of requirements on school districts—the most important are discussed below.

1. Eligibility and Assessments

Every school district has the legal duty to identify, locate, and evaluate children who may be in need of special education. This includes children who have no fixed address (such as migrant or homeless children) and children who may be advancing from grade to grade but nonetheless may need special education. (20 U.S.C. § 1412(a)(6)(B)(7); 34 C.F.R. § 300.125; see Appendix 1.) Once a child is identified and located, the school district must find him or her eligible for special education through an evaluation and IEP process before specific programs and services can be provided.

IDEA defines "children with disabilities" as individuals between the ages of three and 22 who have one or more of the following conditions (20 U.S.C. § 1401(3)(26); 34 C.F.R. § 300.7):

- mental retardation
- hearing impairment (including deafness)
- speech or language impairment
- visual impairment (including blindness)
- serious emotional disturbance
- orthopedic impairment
- autism
- traumatic brain injury
- specific learning disability
- ADD (Attention Deficit Disorder)
- ADHD (Attention Deficit Hyperactivity Disorder), and
- other health impairment.

For your child to qualify for special education under IDEA, it is not enough that he or she has one of these disabilities. In addition, there must be evidence that your child's disability adversely affects his or her educational performance.

Your child has a right to an initial evaluation or assessment, with subsequent evaluations at least every three years. If you are not satisfied with the initial evaluation or you feel that your child's disability or special education needs have changed, your child is entitled to more frequent assessments—and even outside or independent assessments—if you request them. (20 U.S.C. § 1414; 34 C.F.R. §§ 300.530-543.)

Eligibility for special education services is discussed in detail in Chapters 6 and 7. The very specific rules regarding the initial and subsequent assessments are described in Chapter 6.

2. Nature of the Education

Under IDEA, your child is entitled to the following fundamental educational rights (20 U.S.C. § 1401(8)(25)):

- **Free appropriate public education (FAPE).** Your child is entitled to an *appropriate* education at no cost to you.
- **Special education.** You child is entitled to an education *specially designed* to meet his or her *unique* needs.

Chapter 5 discusses how to develop a blueprint of your child's program and service needs.

IDEA fundamentally requires that the educational program should fit your child, not the other way around. For example, it is not appropriate for a school district to place a deaf child in a class for developmentally disabled children or a learning disabled child in a class of emotionally disturbed students. These would not be individually tailored IEPs. The classroom setting, teaching, and services provided would not be appropriate for the deaf or learning disabled child. "Appropriateness" is the standard for evaluating all IEP components—the goals, services, and placement.

Appropriate Does Not Necessarily Mean the Very Best

The law does not require that your school district provide the very best possible education, but an appropriate education. "Appropriate" is an elusive but tremendously important concept. It is used throughout IDEA and frequently in the IEP process. For one child, an appropriate education may mean a regular class with minor support services, while a hospital placement might be appropriate for another.

3. Educational Placement or Program

Your child's educational placement or program, along with related services (discussed in Section 4, below), will take center stage in the IEP process.

a. Least Restrictive Environment

IDEA does not tell you or the school what specific program or class your child should be in; that is a decision for the IEP team. IDEA does require school districts to place disabled children in the least restrictive environment (LRE) that meets their individual needs. What is LRE for a particular child, like what constitutes an "appropriate education," will depend on that child's abilities and disabilities. Although Congress expressed a strong preference for mainstreaming (placing a child in a regular classroom), it used the term LRE to ensure that individual needs would determine each individual placement decision—and that children who really need a more restricted placement (such as a special school) would have one.

Placement vs. Program

The terms placement and program are often used interchangeably, but there are some differences in meaning. As used in IDEA, placement refers to the various classrooms or schools where a child may be. Program has a broader connotation: It includes not only where the program is located, but also the components of that program, including the services, curricula, teaching methods, class make-up, and so on. Placement and program components should both be addressed in your child's IEP.

IDEA states that a child should be in the regular classroom "unless he cannot achieve satisfactorily even with the use of supplementary aides and services." (20 U.S.C. § 1412(a)(5); 34 C.F.R. § 300.550.) LRE further requires that a child should be educated as close to home as possible and in the class she would attend if nondisabled. (20 U.S.C. § 1412(a)(5); 34 C.F.R. §§ 300.550-552.) If a child will not participate with nondisabled children in the regular classroom and in other school activities, the IEP team must explain why. (20 U.S.C. § 1414(d)(1)(B)(iv).)

Is Mainstreaming a Requirement?

Court decisions interpreting the least restrictive environment rule have been as varied as the children in special education. Some court opinions have concluded that mainstreaming is a requirement of IDEA; other judges have ruled that it is "a goal subordinate to the requirement that disabled children receive educational benefit." *Doe v. Arlington*, 882 F.2d 876,878 (4th Cir. 1999).

A common example of the possible conflict between mainstreaming and an appropriate education setting occurs with a child who needs very specialized curricula, intense services, specialized staff, or a protected environment. The child's unique needs may conflict with the right to be mainstreamed.

What is clear from the court decisions and due process hearing decisions that have dealt with this issue is that there is no absolute right to a mainstreamed or alternative program. Whether the right to be mainstreamed is more powerful than the right to an appropriate education, or vice versa, will depend on the individual facts of each case.

b. Range of Placements

While IDEA expresses a preference for regular education, it recognizes that some children with disabilities should not be in a regular class. Individual need determines the appropriateness of a placement. If regular classroom placement is not appropriate, IDEA requires that the school district provide a range of alternative placements—called the Continuum of Placement Options—including the following:

- regular classes for part of the school day
- special classes in regular schools—for example, a special class for children with developmental disabilities
- special public or private schools for children with significant difficulties, such as a school for emotionally troubled students
- charter schools
- residential programs
- home instruction, and
- hospital and institutional placement.

If a child's unique needs dictate an alternative to a regular classroom, the continuum requirement ensures that the school district will make different placement options available. No matter where children are placed, however, IDEA requires every child to have access to the general curriculum taught in the regular classroom. The IEP must specifically address how this requirement will be met. (34 C.F.R. § 300.347.)

4. Support or Related Services

Support or related services are the additional help your child needs to meet her IEP goals. These services are not educational per se—they are the psychological, occupational, therapeutic, or practical assistance your child needs to succeed. IDEA requires schools to provide related services for two reasons:

- to help your child benefit from special education, and
- to ensure that your child has the chance to "achieve satisfactorily" in a regular classroom.

Under IDEA, related services include the following (20 U.S.C. § 1401(22) and § 1414(d)(1)(A)(iii); 34 C.F.R. § 300.24):

- speech-language pathology and audiology services
- psychological services
- physical and occupational therapy
- recreation, including therapeutic recreation

- social work services
- counseling services, including rehabilitation counseling
- orientation and mobility services
- medical services for diagnostic and evaluation purposes
- sign language or oral interpreter
- psychotherapy
- one-to-one instructional aide
- transportation
- art therapy
- technological devices, such as FM/AM systems or special computers, and
- nursing care.

This is not an exhaustive list. Because everything under IDEA is driven by a child's individual needs, the IEP team has the authority to provide any service your child needs, even if it's not listed specifically under IDEA.

Is a Medical Service a Related Service?

The question of what constitutes a related service has been debated since IDEA was enacted in 1975. One particularly difficult issue has been whether a medical service constitutes a related service, if it is needed for a child to benefit from special education. In 1999, the U.S. Supreme Court confirmed that a medical service is a related service if it is limited to "diagnostic and evaluation purposes." (20 U.S.C. § 1401(a)(17).).

The court also ruled, however, that other medical services might constitute related services under the rules of the IDEA if they can be performed by a nonphysician. In the case heard by the court, the child needed and was granted the services of a nurse to provide, among other things, daily catheterization, suctioning of a tracheotomy, and blood pressure monitoring. *Cedar Rapids Community Sch. Dist. v. Garret F., by Charlene F.,* 119 S. Ct. 992 (1999).

5. Assistive Technology

IDEA requires that a child be provided with assistive technology services. These services include:

- evaluating how the child functions in her customary environment
- leasing or purchasing assistive technology devices
- fitting, maintaining, and replacing assistive technology devices
- using and coordinating other therapies, interventions, or services in conjunction with such technology, and
- training and technical assistance for the child, the child's family, and the educational staff.

Technological devices are defined as any item, piece of equipment, or system acquired, modified, or customized to maintain, increase, or improve the functional capabilities of a child with a disability. An assistive technology device or service might be an augmentative communication system, a computer, an FM trainer, computer software, pulmonary devices, a touch screen, a calculator, a tape recorder, a spell-checker, books on tape, and even items such as oxygen tanks. (20 U.S.C. § 1401(1)(2), 34 C.F.R. §§ 300.305, 306; see Appendix 1.)

6. Transition Services

IDEA requires that the IEP team consider, for a child who is 14 or older, vocational and advanced-placement needs and courses, including noneducational agencies that provide vocational and other support services for individuals with disabilities. (20 U.S.C. § 1414(d)(1) (A)(vii); 34 C.F.R. §§ 300.29, 300.347(b).) (See Chapter 11, Section D, for more information.)

7. Due Process

In law, "due process" generally refers to the right to a fair procedure for determining individual rights and responsibilities. Under IDEA, and as used in this book, due process means your child's right to be evaluated, receive an appropriate education, be educated in the LRE, have an IEP, and be given notice of any changes in the IEP.

Due process also refers to your specific right to take any dispute you have with your child's school district—whether a disagreement about an assessment, eligibility, or any part of the IEP, including the specific placement and related services—to a neutral third party to help you resolve your dispute. These rights are unique; children not in special education do not have them. (20 U.S.C. § 1415; 34 C.F.R. §§ 300.500-517.)

There are two options for resolving disputes through due process: mediation and a due process hearing. Mediation is a process in which you and the school district meet with a neutral third party who helps you come to an agreement. The mediator has the power of persuasion, but, no authority to impose a decision on you.

If you cannot reach an agreement in mediation (or prefer to skip mediation altogether), you can request a fair hearing, in which you and the school district present written and oral testimony about the disputed issues before a neutral administrative judge, who will decide who is right and issue an order imposing a decision. If you or the school district disagree with the decision, you can appeal to a federal or state court, all the way to the U.S. Supreme Court. But before you conjure up images of walking up the marble stairs to the highest court in the land, you should know that most disputes with school districts are resolved before a hearing and certainly before you find yourself in a courtroom.

 Chapter 12 discusses in detail how to resolve disputes through mediation or a fair hearing.

If you believe that your school has violated a legal rule—for example, by failing to hold an IEP meeting—you should file a complaint (discussed in Chapter 13). The complaint process is quite different from due process. A due process matter involves a factual dispute between you and the school district. A complaint involves a failure by the district to follow the law.

8. Suspension and Expulsion

Some children with disabilities have trouble behaving themselves in school. Like all other kids, children with disabilities sometimes act out, try to get attention in the wrong ways, or are more interested in their friends than their schoolwork. But sometimes, these children have behavioral problems that are directly related to their disabilities. A child with ADD who can't pay attention in class, a child whose developmental delays lead to immense frustration, or a child whose autism makes it hard to follow a teacher's instructions can create disciplinary problems. A child who has secondary emotional difficulties because of a disability may be disruptive or even get into fights. How can schools balance their responsibility to maintain order with their duty to provide an appropriate education for children with disabilities?

Most states have laws and procedures about disciplinary action—including suspension and expulsion—quite separate from the special education laws and procedures. These disciplinary rules apply to all students within a school district. For special education students, however, these rules must be applied in conjunction with the laws and procedures of IDEA, including specific protections that apply when a child with a disability is subject to suspension or expulsion. Like all children in school, your child must follow the rules; if she does not, she may be suspended or expelled. Before the school district can take this type of action, however, IDEA requires a very careful analysis of whether her disability played a role in her behavior and, if so, whether suspension or expulsion is really justified.

When IDEA was reauthorized in 1997, Congress included many new rules regarding the suspension and expulsion of special education students. Although these rules provide specific rights and procedures for children in special education who are subject to discipline, Congress clearly intended to allow school districts to remove students who misbehave or are dangerous.

Get some help. The IDEA rules and procedures applicable to suspensions and expulsions are pretty complicated—and the stakes for your child in these situations are potentially very high. This section provides an overview of this area of the law, but you'll probably want to contact a parent support group or special education lawyer if your child faces serious disciplinary action. This is one situation in which you shouldn't try to go it alone.

a.   IDEA and Disciplinary Action

IDEA provides that a student with an IEP cannot have his program, placement, or services changed unless the school district and the child's parents agree to the change. Absent such an agreement, the child is entitled to remain or "stay put" in the current program until either a new IEP is signed or a hearing officer decides that the child's program can be changed. (20 U.S.C. § 1415(j); 34 C.F.R. § 300.514.) The school district cannot remove your child or unilaterally change your child's program—if it tries to do so, you can assert your child's stay-put right to maintain the current placement until a new IEP is in place or a hearing officer approves the change. This very broad rule is intended to prevent a school from moving a child without parental approval.

A proposed suspension or expulsion clearly constitutes a change in placement, and this is where state laws on suspension and expulsion run directly into IDEA requirements. Can a school district suspend or expel (remove the child from school) without violating the stay-put rule? The answer is, as you probably expected, yes and no. The law clearly states that a child with disabilities can be suspended or expelled, but the suspension or expulsion cannot take place unless certain IDEA procedures are followed. (20 U.S.C. § 1415(j)(k); 34 C.F.R. §§ 300.520-529.)

Congress created different rules depending on the length of the suspension or expulsion. This part of IDEA is fairly complex, but generally, children who are facing more than ten days out of school have more procedural protections under the law.

b. Suspensions or Expulsions for Up to Ten Days

Any special education child removed from school *for up to ten consecutive days* is not entitled to the IDEA procedures and protections. Because such a removal does not constitute a "change in placement," the child cannot claim the right to stay put. Because many suspensions are for fewer than ten consecutive days, most special education students who are suspended do not have the right to contest that removal based either on IDEA's stay-put rule or on IDEA's specific disciplinary procedures. In short, a child with disabilities can be suspended from school for up to 10 days just like any other student.

c. Suspensions and Expulsions Exceeding Ten Days

If a school district intends to suspend or expel a special education student for more than ten consecutive days, that *might* constitute a change in placement. In these situations, additional IDEA procedures kick in before the child can be removed. These procedures might also apply to a child who is removed from school for more than ten nonconsecutive days, if the removal repre-

sents a "pattern." What is meant by a pattern? The law isn't entirely clear, but essentially you have to look at whether the frequency and length of the removals—and the total time the child is out of school—create a change in placement similar to that caused by a removal for more than ten consecutive days. Courts have begun to issue some decisions on what constitutes a pattern, but this is still a vague and uncertain part of the disciplinary process—and one good reason why you will probably want to talk to an expert and/or attorney if your child is in this situation.

Once a special education student is to be removed for more than ten days (whether consecutively or over a longer period of time), specific IDEA procedures kick in to protect the child. Before the removal takes place, an IEP team must hold a "manifestation review" to decide whether the student's behavior was a manifestation of his disability. If the IEP team determines that the behavior was a manifestation of the child's disability, then the student's placement cannot be changed except through an agreed-to IEP (signed by the school district and the parents) or a fair hearing decision. The child can remain in his current placement and assert his stay-put right (no change without an IEP agreement or fair hearing decision). The student cannot be suspended (for more than ten days) or expelled unless the school follows IDEA procedures for a change in placement.

If the IEP team determines that the behavior was not a manifestation of the disability, the child has no stay-put rights and can be removed. To reach this conclusion, however, the team must decide that all three of the following statements are true:

- in relationship to the behavior that led to the disciplinary action, the IEP placement and services were appropriate and behavior intervention strategies were provided consistent with the IEP
- the child's disability did not impair his ability to understand the impact and consequences of the behavior, and

- the child's disability did not impair his ability to control the behavior subject to the disciplinary action.
(34 C.F.R. § 300.523.)

d. Dangerous Behavior

IDEA makes an exception to the ten-day rule for disciplinary problems involving weapons or drugs. If a special education student brings a weapon to school or possesses, uses, sells, or solicits the sale of drugs at school or during a school function, she can be removed for up to 45 days without parental agreement. This means the student cannot assert her stay-put right and argue that she is entitled to remain in her current placement pending the conclusion of the required IDEA disciplinary procedures. The student is entitled, however, to an "interim alternative placement" as determined by the IEP team.

e. Related Requirements

As a general rule, IDEA requires the IEP team to develop a "behavioral intervention" plan for students whose behavior "impedes his or her learning or that of others." (34 C.F.R. § 300.346(a)(2)(i).) It would not be surprising if a special education student facing suspension or expulsion had such a plan in his IEP. If a student is removed for more than ten days, IDEA also requires the IEP team to do a "functional behavioral assessment" and implement a "behavioral intervention plan" if one is not already in place.

For a child whose disability impairs his ability to relate to others or behave appropriately, the plan should address those needs and provide strategies for helping that student improve his peer relationships and/or his school behavior. For example, a child who takes out the frustration of her disability by lashing out at other students might be taught alternative methods to express her frustration, such as talking to a counselor, tak-

ing a "time out," or expressing her anger more constructively ("I don't like it when you interrupt me when I'm speaking in class").

For lots of great ideas on dealing with disciplinary and behavior problems, as well as detailed information on drafting behavioral intervention plans, check out the website of the Center for Effective Collaboration and Practice (a group dedicated to helping students, teachers, and parents address emotional and behavioral concerns) at http://cecp.air.org.

9. Additional IDEA Rights

IDEA provides for many rights, including the following additional mandates.

a. Summer School

IDEA requires that your child be provided summer school or an "extended school year" if necessary to meet his needs or if, without summer school, his skills will be affected by the pause in program and services. (20 U.S.C. § 1412 (a)(1), 34 C.F.R. § 300.309; see Appendix 1.)

b. Private School

IDEA gives your child the right to be placed in a nonprofit or private (including parochial) school if your school district cannot provide an appropriate program. (34 C.F.R. §§ 300.302, 349, 403, 450-462.)

There must be an IEP agreement or due process or court ruling that the private school is appropriate before the school district is required to pay for a private school placement. If you place your child in a private school unilaterally—on your own—your school district is not required to pay.

IDEA does, however, require school districts to offer special education and related services in a public program to a child in a private school. IDEA further states that the school district can actually provide those special education services at a private (including a parochial) school if it so chooses—with limitations on how much money the district has to spend on such special education and services. (20 U.S.C. § 1412(a)(10).) However, while most courts have ruled that a district must make related services available to a child placed in private school by her parents, they have also generally ruled that the services need not be provided *at* the private school. Instead, the services must be made available at an appropriate public school site. You should pay particular attention to the differences in regulations between school-placed and parent-placed private school children. (34 C.F.R. §§ 400.400-403, 450-462.) This part of IDEA is complicated. If your child is in private school in this type of situation, contact a special education attorney or one of the support groups listed in Appendix 3.

IDEA Notice Requirements and Private School Placements

If you plan to remove your child to a private program, you must notify the school district of your intent either:

- at the most recent IEP meeting you attended prior to removing your child from public school, or
- at least ten business days before the actual removal.

(20 U.S.C. § 1412(a)(10)(C).)

If you don't provide this notice and then pursue due process to seek reimbursement for your child's placement in a private school, reimbursement may be denied, or you may receive only partial payment.

---

c. Special Education in Prison

Imprisoned children between the ages of 18 and 21 who were identified and had an IEP prior to incarceration are also entitled to a free, appropriate public education. (34 C.F.R. § 300.311.)

B. Individualized Education Program

IEP may seem complicated—it is a meeting, a document, and a description of your child's entire educational program. While the IEP is discussed in detail in Chapters 10 and 11, here are a few introductory concepts:

- By law, you are an equal partner in the IEP process. As a general rule, no part of the IEP can be implemented without your approval.
- Your child's first time in special education will follow an initial eligibility IEP. Thereafter, IEP meetings will be held yearly, focusing on the specifics of your child's current educational program and what next year's IEP will look like. While the procedures for these two kinds of IEPs (called eligibility and program IEPs) are the same, there are some important differences—see Chapters 7, 10, and 11.
- You and the school district must agree to and sign an IEP before your child either begins special education initially or begins a new school year.
- Whenever you or your child's school district wants to change your child's current IEP, the district must schedule a new IEP meeting and develop a new written IEP.
- You are entitled to an IEP meeting whenever you feel one is needed—for example, if you have concerns about your child's progress, there are classroom problems, or the related services or placement is not working.

- The IEP, once signed by you and the school district, is binding; the school district must provide everything included in that IEP.

The written IEP and IEP meeting are discussed in detail in Chapters 9, 10, and 11. Appendix 4 includes a sample IEP form.

This section provides details about the written IEP. Every IEP, in every school district in every state, must include the same information (although forms will vary).

1. Current Educational Status

The IEP must include a description of your child's current status in school in the areas of cognitive skills, linguistic ability, emotional behavior, social skills and behavior, and physical ability. (20 U.S.C. § 1414(d)(1)(A)(i)(I); 34 C.F.R. § 300.347(a)(1) and (2).) Current functioning may be reflected in testing data, grades, reports, or anecdotal information, such as teacher observations. IDEA calls this the "present level of educational performance." This part of the IEP must describe how your child's disability affects her involvement and progress in the general curriculum. Formal testing or assessments of your child will provide a good deal of information.

Chapters 6 and 8 cover assessments and other ways to develop useful evidence of your child's educational status and needs.

2. Goals and Objectives

Goals and objectives are the nuts and bolts of your child's daily program as detailed in the IEP. They generally refer to academic, linguistic, and other cognitive activities, such as reading or math. IDEA calls these "measurable annual goals, including benchmarks or short-term objectives" re-lated to your child's specific educational needs and involvement in the general curriculum, if appropriate. (20 U.S.C. § 1414(d)(1)(A)(ii); 34 C.F.R. § 300.347(a)(2); 34 C.F.R. § 300.347(a)(1).)

Example:

Goal: John will increase his reading comprehension.

Objective: John will read a three-paragraph story and answer eight out of ten questions about the story correctly.

While goals and objectives are usually academic and cognitive in nature, there is no restriction on what goals and objectives may cover or say. They should reflect whatever the IEP team determines is important to your child's education. Goals and objectives can relate to physical education, how your child socializes with peers, even how your child will move about the school.

Whether your child is receiving a free appropriate public education (FAPE) may depend on whether the program offered by the school district can help her achieve her goals and objectives. If you and the school district disagree about whether a specific placement or service is appropriate, one key issue will be whether your child's goals and objectives can be met without it.

Chapter 9 shows you how to write goals and objectives that support the placement and service needs of your child.

Congress may change the rules for goals and objectives. As this book went to press, Congress was discussing the possibility of reducing or even eliminating part of the goals and objectives requirement of IDEA. Whether this change (or some version of it) will make it into the final reauthorization of the IDEA is anybody's guess. You'll need to find out whether the law has changed before you begin working on your child's IEP. Check Nolo's website (www.nolo.com) for updates on the law, or the website of the National Dissemination Center for Children with Disabilities (formerly the National Information Center for Children and Youth with Disabilities), at www.nichcy.org (click on "IDEA").

3. Instructional Setting or Placement

The IEP must include information about the appropriate instructional setting or placement for your child. Section A3, above, discussed various placement options; here are a few examples of specific IEP placements:

> Examples:
> - A child with significant physical disabilities or learning disabilities might be placed in a regular classroom with support services.
> - A child with significant language and cognitive delays might be placed in a special class.
> - A child who is terrified of large spaces and crowds could be placed in a small, protected nonregular school.
> - A child with serious emotional difficulties might be placed in a residential program.

4. Related Services

As mentioned in Section A4, above, related services are developmental, corrective, and other supportive services necessary to facilitate your child's placement in a regular class or to allow your child to benefit from special education. These must be included specifically in the IEP.

Once the IEP team determines the appropriate related support services, the team should specify the nature of each service, including:
- when it begins
- the amount (such as all day, once a day, twice a week, once a week, once a month)
- the duration (such as 15, 30, 45, or 60 minutes per session)
- the ratio of pupils to related service providers, and
- the qualifications of the service provider.

5. Other Required IEP Components

As part of the 1997 reauthorization of IDEA (20 U.S.C. § 1414(d)(3)(B)(i)-(v); 34 C.F.R. § 300.347), the IEP must specifically address:
- how your child's disability affects her involvement and progress in the general curriculum used in the regular classroom
- how your child's need to be involved in general curriculum will be met
- how special education and related services will help your child advance toward attaining annual goals; be involved in general curriculum, extracurricular, and nonacademic activities; and participate with children with and without disabilities
- how parents will be regularly informed of their child's progress
- how your child will participate in any district or statewide assessment of student achievement used for the general education population, and whether he needs any modifications or accommodations in order to take the assessment
- how your child's transition services will be provided, and
- how your child's need for assistive technology will be met.

For blind and visually impaired students, the IEP team must provide for instruction in Braille and the use of Braille, unless the IEP determines that Braille is not appropriate. (20 U.S.C. § 1414 (d)(3)(B)(iii); 34 C.F.R. § 300.346(a)(2)(i).)

In addition, IDEA requires that the IEP team "consider" the following:
- strategies, including positive behavioral interventions, to address the needs of

children with behavior difficulties (20 U.S.C. § 1414(d)(3)(B)(i))

- the language needs of children with limited English proficiency (20 U.S.C. § 1414(d)(3)(B)(ii)), and
- the communication needs of deaf and hard of hearing children, including opportunities for direct communication with peers and staff, and instruction in the child's language and communication mode. (20 U.S.C. § 1414(d)(3)(B)(iv); 34 C.F.R. § 300.356(a)(2)(i).)

For more details, contact your school district, your state department of education (Appendix 2), or a disability group (Appendix 3). See Appendix 4 for a sample IEP that includes these provisions.

6. Optional Components

The IEP may include other components, such as specific teaching methods, particular class subjects, or anything else the IEP team agrees should be included. (20 U.S.C. § 1414(d)(1)(A).)

**More Information:
Special Education and Local Schools**

Your school district is required by IDEA to provide you with a copy of federal and state statutes and regulations, and any relevant policies. Be sure to request this information, along with the school's IEP form. Most school districts have some kind of parent guide, as do most states. Contact your school district for a copy.

Examples:
- An autistic child may be instructed in a method called Lovaas.
- A deaf child may be taught in American Sign Language.

C. State Special Education Laws

IDEA is a federal law, binding on all states. The federal government provides financial assistance to the states to implement IDEA; in exchange, states must adopt laws that implement IDEA.

State laws generally parallel IDEA and often use identical language. State law can provide children with more, but not fewer, protections than IDEA does. IDEA is always your starting point, but you should check to see what your state law says about special education—it may provide more rights.

Each state's educational agency is responsible for making sure local school districts comply with the federal law. The federal government allocates billions of dollars a year to the states for special education. The pressure on states to come up with special education funding is significant, particularly given competing interests for education dollars. Moreover, while Congress promised when IDEA was passed to provide approximately 40% of its cost to states, it has actually provided only between 8% and 13%, which has created significant shortfalls for states and the local school districts. The funding process varies from state to state, but it is often complex. No matter how your state funds special education, it is most important that you remember this general rule: Money (and how it gets from Washington to your state to your district to your child) should not determine what is in your child's IEP—but in reality, financial constraints affect almost all school districts.

Budgetary Constraints Are Getting Worse

Cost should not be a factor in determining the appropriate educational program for your child. If a school district says "we can't afford it," you can rightfully respond that the law requires the IEP team to make decisions based on your child's individual needs—not on the school's budget.

However, the sad truth is that state governments are facing rising deficits, which means that funding for schools is on the chopping block. As spending for education decreases, many schools will have to cut back on educational programs and staff. Unfortunately, this means that some districts will make IEP decisions based on budgetary constraints rather than on educational need. While you need not be swayed by arguments about funding, don't be surprised to hear them.

This problem will only get worse until federal and state governments start funding education and special education commensurate with their importance in our society. Even as laws that impose stricter standards for students, teachers, and classroom size go into effect, schools aren't given the funding they need to implement these new requirements. As a result, many educators are leaving the profession. Until parents and professionals unite to address this funding problem, legislators will continue to give education the short end of the fiscal stick.

D. Working With Your School District

Most, if not all, of your dealings will be with your local public school district, which has the legal responsibility for your child's IEP. Sometimes, however, special education programs are the responsibility of a larger educational unit, such as a county office of education. This is often the case when a school district is small or there are not enough children to establish a specific special education class.

The term used to describe the appropriate local educational agency can vary from state to state. Always start with the school district in which you reside. It has the ultimate responsibility for your child, even if there is a larger, area-wide agency involved. As used in this book, the term "local school district" refers to whatever educational unit is involved.

1. Key Players in the IEP Process

The key participants in the IEP process are:
- you (the child's parents)
- your child (if appropriate)
- your child's teacher (potentially the best ally or worst enemy you have in the IEP process), whether a regular teacher or a special education teacher
- a school administrator with responsibility for special education—a site principal or special education administrator
- specialists, such as a school psychologist, speech or occupational therapist, communications specialist, or physical education specialist, and
- anyone else you or the school wants to attend, such as your child's physician, your lawyer, the school's assessor, or an outside independent assessor you selected.

Chapter 10 covers the IEP participants in detail, including who has the critical roles, who has authority, and who should attend the IEP meetings. Chapter 10 also covers how to prepare yourself and your IEP participants for the IEP meeting.

More Information: State Special Education Laws

State special education laws (statutes) are normally found in the education code of each state. State departments of education often have their own regulations implementing the law.

Appendix 2 includes addresses, phone numbers, and websites of state departments of education. We highly recommend you get a copy of your state laws and any publications explaining your legal rights from your state department of education (many are online). Ask about the state special education advisory commission—IDEA requires that each state have one, composed of educators and parents.

Because laws and policies change, it is important to keep up to date, especially if you are involved in a dispute with your school. For more information on legal research, see Chapter 14.

2. The Realities of Schools and Special Education

School districts and their special education administrators are as varied as parents. Their programs, services, and budgets will differ, as will their personalities. All of these factors influence the kind of programs school districts offer and how they deal with children and parents. Depending on the population breakdown in the district, there may be many special education programs or only a few. Philosophical differences may have an impact on programs and services. Some administrators believe very firmly that most, if not all, children with disabilities should be mainstreamed or in regular education. Some administrators believe with equal vigor that special programs are important and children with disabilities, more often than not, belong in special classes.

Finding out what programs are in your district, and what personalities and philosophies you'll face, is important. Ask around. Talk to your child's teacher and other parents; go to a PTA meeting. Many school districts have community advisory committees for special education; the parents involved in that group can be invaluable resources and will likely know the specific programs and approaches in your school district.

Demonizing the "Other" Side

It is not uncommon for parents to view school administrators and other staff as impediments rather than partners in the special education process. Sometimes school personnel return the favor by viewing parents as unreasonable and difficult.

While there are times when such viewpoints are justified, remember that a majority of educators are passionate, hard-working, and caring individuals. They teach in a complicated environment with too much paperwork, too many requirements, and not enough support or pay. Demonizing all teachers or administrators does little more than polarize everyone—and your child is the one who will suffer from these strained relationships. Viewing everyone associated with the school as an enemy is a poor strategy for getting your child's needs met. And in most cases, it's simply not fair.

Of course, you should be vigilant and stick up for your rights, but remember that most folks on the other side of the table are there because they believe in your child. In return, you should expect those hard-working educators to see you as the determined, loving, and concerned parent that you are.

Chapter 8 provides detailed advice on how to explore available school programs. Chapter 15 discusses parent groups.

E. Some Overriding IEP Principles

In any endeavor, the details—particularly technical matters and legal language—can be overwhelming: IEP, due process, least restrictive environment, goals and objectives, related services. What do these words really mean, and how do you use them to help your child?

As you go through this book and the IEP process, you will become more familiar and comfortable with IEP terms. Particularly in the early stages of your planning, keep your focus on the following key factors.

1. Your Child's Needs Dictate the Contents of the IEP

IDEA uses the term "unique" to describe your child's needs. As emphasized in this chapter, the IEP must fit the child, not the other way around. Practically speaking, this means that if your child needs a small class (fewer than ten children), a teacher with specific skills, and a variety of support services, then your local school district is required to provide them. Always ask whether a particular goal, service, placement, or other IEP component is providing your child with a free appropriate public education as required by law, and is serving her unique needs.

2. Factors Determining Individual Need

Your child's age, disability, and specific needs—academic, social, linguistic, emotional, cognitive, and physical—are key elements in determining his IEP. Of course, other factors may come into play, including necessary educational strategies, methodologies, and curricula.

3. Specific Classroom and Instructional Services

Your child's needs must translate into specific support or related services and a specific class or program. All the discussion in the world about unique needs will be meaningless if you and the IEP team don't eventually discuss (and come to terms on) services and placement.

4. Broad Discretion in Determining the IEP

It is human nature to want specificity. At some level, we may have liked Congress to have said exactly what should be part of a special education program, and what should go into the IEP. But in passing IDEA, Congress knew it could not say specifically what should be in an IEP for child #1 or #999 or #99,999. There are too many variables and too many individual considerations.

That is why IDEA does not say that a child with disabilities will be placed in a particular program with particular services. Instead, the unique needs of each child must determine what specific program and services are required. Thus, the IEP team has broad discretion. This flexibility is good for you, but also requires hard work and preparation on your part.

Section 504 of the Rehabilitation Act of 1973

Separate from any rights under IDEA, your child may also qualify for special services under the Rehabilitation Act of 1973 (29 U.S.C. § 794), more commonly known as Section 504. This is essentially an access law that prohibits a school district from denying your child access to an educational program or educational facilities. For more information on Section 504, see Chapter 7, Section F2.

Keeping Current on Special Education Law

IDEA, like many laws, is always in a state of change. As new (and old) issues come to the forefront and are addressed in courts or through new legislation, IDEA is reinterpreted and given new meaning.

Congress has the right to change IDEA. In 1997, for example, Congress added new rights and rules to IDEA. These rules, and the new regulations implementing them, are included in Appendix 1 and incorporated throughout this book.

As this book went to press, Congress has been vigorously debating further changes to the law. Advocates anticipate that IDEA will be reauthorized in 2004, which gives Congress the opportunity to make amendments. Among other things, Congress has considered making changes to the rules for goals and objectives, discipline, assessments, and attorney fees for parents who win a due process dispute.

You can find the most current IDEA regulations online at www.gpoaccess.gov/cfr/ index.html. You can also get a copy from the U.S. Department of Education, Office of Education, or from your state department of education (see Appendix 2 for contact information). Check Nolo's website (www.nolo.com) for updates on the law, or the website of the National Dissemination Center for Children with Disabilities (formerly the National Information Center for Children and Youth with Disabilities), at www.nichcy.org (click on "IDEA"). If you have questions as to how any new regulations will affect your child, contact your local school district.

3

Getting Started: Tips for All Parents

I f your child has had a disability since birth or from a young age—perhaps he is in a wheel-chair and needs support to access a regular classroom, is developmentally disabled, has difficulty writing, or has a hearing loss or reduced vision—you've probably known for a while that your child would need special education.

If you've just recently realized that your child is having difficulty in school—from a simple problem with reading or math to a profound problem involving cognitive functioning or emotional difficulties—you may not have given much thought to special education. Perhaps a teacher, pediatrician, neighbor, or friend has pointed something out to you. The recognition may come as surprise or even a shock. What does this mean for your child's immediate educational experience? What does it mean for the future? Will your child now be labeled—as learning disabled, visually impaired, emotionally disturbed?

The process you are about to embark on can be hard and frustrating. There may be times when the school makes life tough. Your child's difficul-ties may persist or even get worse. At times, the problems may seem insurmountable. There may be a teacher shortage, insufficient school funds, or awful program options. For all your prepara-tion, you may feel like you're getting nowhere. We know how difficult and frustrating the IEP process can be.

There may be times you ask yourself why this happened to your family. But if you plan, organize, and persevere, if you take small, daily steps (rather than try to solve the problem in one fell swoop), you will help your child. You may not make the school experience perfect, or even always tolerable, but your child will benefit from your efforts.

Whether you, your child's teacher, or another professional discovers the difficulty, your school district has a clear legal responsibility under IDEA to ensure that all children with special education needs within the district are identified, located, and evaluated (see Chapter 2, Section A1). Usu-ally, this means (or should mean) that your child's teacher or the school principal, or perhaps the

school psychologist, will contact you, indicate the areas of initial concern, and perhaps suggest a meeting to discuss these concerns. The school will then likely recommend an assessment by a specialist in your child's disability. The assessment is the first major step toward special education eligibility and the development of an IEP. (Chap-ter 6 discusses assessments in detail.)

Parents of Children Between Three and Five Years Old

If your child is between ages three and five and is not yet enrolled in school, contact the local school district if you believe your child has a disability. Your child may be entitled to ser-vices under IDEA even though he or she hasn't started school. To be eligible, your child must be experiencing delays in physical, cognitive, communication, social, emotional, or adaptive development. (20 U.S.C. § 1401(3)(B)(i).) If your child is found eligible, the IDEA rules and IEP procedures outlined in this book will apply to your child.

Even though your school district has the re-sponsibility to start the process, you shouldn't wait for the school to contact you if you have concerns. If you suspect that your child has spe-cial education needs and you haven't heard from the school district, get in touch with them. This chapter will help you get things started.

➡️ If your child has already been found eligible for special education or you have had experience with the IEP process, you can skip Section A. Even if you have been through the IEP process, however, be sure to read the dis-cussion on securing your child's records in Sec-tion B. Many intelligent and determined parents who have been through numerous IEPs have not taken this important step.

A. First Steps

What's the first thing you should do if you believe your child is eligible for special education? There's no number to look up in the phone book. This section provides some suggestions on how to get started.

1. Recognize Your Child's Special Needs

It is very common for parents to realize that their child has unique needs and simply not know what to do about it. It may be that your child's problems can be isolated and addressed very specifically, or the problems may be more serious. But don't assume the worst; let the information you gather determine how serious the matter is and what you should do about it.

Start by focusing on your child's specific difficulties. Think back and consider whether your child has experienced any of the following:

- academic problems in reading, spelling, or math
- delays in developmental areas, such as language or fine motor skills
- difficulties processing or retaining information, such as understanding simple instructions or problems with short- or long-term memory
- social or emotional problems
- trouble sleeping, eating, or getting along with the family
- sustained difficulties in paying attention or staying focused
- inappropriate or hyperactive behavior, or
- delays in physical milestones or other physiological difficulties, such as hearing loss, sight problems, difficulties with mobility, or handwriting problems.

Write down what you can remember about your child's past behavior or what you've observed recently. Try to think clearly, focusing on specific behavior patterns. You may feel some emotional upheaval or fear; you may even worry that you have done something wrong. These feelings are normal. Almost everyone who has had a child in special education has felt exactly as you do right now.

A child who is having difficulty in school will not automatically qualify for special education. There may be interim steps or nonspecial education solutions for your child. Those steps are discussed below, in Section A3.

At this stage, you may also want to contact the school principal to request information about special education.

A sample letter requesting information on special education is below; a blank, tear-out copy is in Appendix 5.

Get into the habit of writing. You can request information about special education by calling the school principal, who is likely to either provide the information or refer you to the district's special education administrator. Better yet, make your request in writing. A letter is more formal, won't be forgotten as easily as a phone call, and creates a record of your contact with your school district. In this book, you will be reminded frequently of the importance of putting things in writing.

2. Make a Formal Request to Start the Special Education Process

At any time, you can formally ask to begin the process of special education evaluation. To start:

- Call your school and ask for the name and phone number of the special education administrator.
- Call the special education administrator and ask about the eligibility assessment process in the district.
- Follow up your phone call with a written request (and keep a copy for your records).

Request for Information on Special Education

Date: February 20, 20xx

To: Ronald Pearl, Principal

Mesa Verde Elementary School

123 San Pablo Ave.

San Francisco, CA 94110

Re: Amber Jones, student in second-grade class of Cynthia Rodriguez

I am writing to you because my child is experiencing difficulties in school. I understand there is a special process for evaluating a child and then determining eligibility for special education programs and services. Please send me any written information you have about that process. Please also send me information about how I can contact other parents and local support groups involved in special education.

Thank you very much for your kind assistance. I look forward to talking with you further about special education.

Sincerely,

Mary Jones

Mary Jones

243 Ocean Ave.

San Francisco, CA 94110

Phones: 555-1234 (home); 555-2678 (work)

A sample letter making a formal request to start the special education process and conduct an assessment is below; a blank, tear-out copy is in Appendix 5. Other sample letters in this chapter make slightly different requests. You can combine some or all of these requests into one letter, if you wish.

3. Gather Information

Whether you plan to begin the formal assessment process right away or wait a bit, you should start gathering information on your child's situation. Here are some good ways to start.

a. Talk to Your Child's Teacher

Find out what your child's teacher thinks is going on and recommends as a possible solution. Here are a few specific questions to ask:

- What are the teacher's observations? What are the most outstanding and obvious problems, and how serious are they? Is it a problem with math, reading, or broader cognitive issues (processing information or memory lags)? Does the problem have social or emotional manifestations?
- Would some adjustments in the classroom help, such as extra attention from the teacher, after-school tutoring, or measures to address behavioral problems?
- What recommendations might be useful at home? Does the teacher think that you need to spend more time on homework, walking your child through certain subject matters?
- What are the observations, conclusions, and recommendations of other school personnel?
- Are your child's difficulties serious? Do they require more formal special education involvement? If so, what are the next steps?

If you and the school agree to go ahead with interim, nonspecial education steps, be sure to monitor your child's progress closely so you can determine whether they are working. Chapter 8, Section B, provides suggestions about tracking your child's progress.

b. Talk to Your Child's Pediatrician

Your child may have an organic or medical problem. Although most pediatricians are not experts in special education, they can discuss a child's developmental stage; other health-related matters that will affect the educational experience; and cognitive, physical, linguistic, and emotional factors that might impact special education eligibility and possible educational solutions.

c. Talk With Other Parents

The local PTA should have information on parents with special education children, and most school districts have advisory committees of parents with children in special education. Call the school principal to find out about these.

Chapter 15 explains how to find or start a parents' group. Appendix 3 has information on various national special education support groups.

d. Do Some Research

Look for written materials on special education and your child's area of difficulty. A wealth of information is available online.

Appendix 3 has information on special education materials and organizations, both general and disability-specific.

Request to Begin Special Education Process and Assessment

Date: _February 20, 20xx_

To: _Ronald Pearl, Principal_

Mesa Verde Elementary School

123 San Pablo Ave.

San Francisco, CA 94110

Re: _Amber Jones, student in second-grade class of Cynthia Rodriguez_

I am writing to you because my child is experiencing difficulties in school. _As I mentioned to you over the phone this morning, she is way behind in reading [or other specific difficulties your child is exhibiting]._

I am formally requesting that the school immediately begin its special education process, including initial assessment for eligibility. I understand that you will send me an assessment plan that explains the tests that may be given to my child. Because I realize the assessment can take some time, I would appreciate receiving the assessment plan within ten days. Once you receive my approval for the assessment, please let me know when the assessment will be scheduled.

I would also appreciate any other information you have regarding the assessment process, how eligibility is determined, and general IEP procedures.

Thank you very much for your kind assistance. I look forward to working with you and your staff.

Sicerely,

Mary Jones

Mary Jones

243 Ocean Ave.

San Francisco, CA 94110

Phones: 555-1234 (home); 555-2678 (work)

B. Obtain Your Child's School Records

As a part of your information gathering, it's important to find out what is in your child's school file and what effect it will have on the IEP process. You'll need this information to assess the seriousness of your child's difficulties and the possible need for special education. If your child is found eligible for special education, reviewing the school file will help you determine the services and programs that may be appropriate.

Whether you are new at this or have been through many IEPs, whether you anticipate a major change in your child's educational program or no change at all, and even if you're not sure that you want your child in special education in the first place, it is important to secure copies of your child's school file on a yearly basis. New and important items may be added each year.

While the contents of your child's file may vary, it is likely you will find:

- report cards and other progress reports
- medical data (immunization records, health reports)
- attendance records
- disciplinary reports
- testing data
- assessments and other testing material
- teacher comments and other observations, and
- pictures of your child (it's fun to see the kindergarten picture, the second grade picture with the missing teeth, and so on).

1. Your Right to Access Your Child's School File

You have a legal right to inspect and review any education records relating to your child. If your child is already in the special education system,

you have this right under IDEA. (20 U.S.C. § 1415(b)(1); 34 C.F.R. §§ 300.501, 560-577.) The rules in this section refer to children already in the special education system.

If your child has not yet been found eligible for special education, you still have a legal right to his or her file under the Family Educational Rights and Privacy Act (FERPA). (20 U.S.C. § 1232(g).) State law may also provide a right to your child's file, separate from IDEA or FERPA rights. State law can vary, however, and you may want to find out the specifics—such as how requests should be made and how long the school has to provide you the file. Call your state department of education or your school district for information regarding these rules.

2. How to Get Copies of Your Child's File

When seeking a copy of your child's school file, make a written request for *everything*. The written request should go to the administrator in your school district who is responsible for special education. That may be the school principal or a person in your district's central office. The site principal can refer you to the appropriate person.

A sample letter requesting your child's school file is below; a blank, tear-out copy is in Appendix 5.

IDEA requires that your child's school grant your request without unnecessary delay and before any IEP meeting. The school must send you the file within 45 days, although it can and should send it more quickly. (34 C.F.R. § 300.562(a).) (The Family Educational Rights and Privacy Act includes the same 45-day deadline.)

If you have any problem getting a copy of your child's school file in a timely manner:

- Call and write the appropriate administrator, indicating that the law requires the school to provide the records without "unnecessary delay."
- If the principal or administrator does not respond to your request, contact the school district superintendent and your state department of education. Failure to provide you with your child's records is a violation of the law. Chapter 13 covers procedures for handling legal violations by your district.

Your state special education law may give schools a shorter deadline for schools to provide copies of your child's record than the 45-day limit provided by IDEA. California schools, for example, must provide copies of the record within five days of a parent's request. Get a copy of your state's special education laws from your department of education early on so you know your rights—and cite the law when you request your child's file.

3. Cost of Getting Files

The school may charge a fee for making copies of your child's records, as long as the fee "does not effectively prevent you from exercising your right to inspect and review those records." (34 C.F.R. § 300.566.) This means that you cannot be charged an excessively high fee—or *any fee at all*, if you can show you cannot afford it. In addition, the school cannot charge a fee for searching and retrieving records.

If your child is not in special education, any fee for records might violate the Rehabilitation Act of 1973 (29 U.S.C. § 794) and the federal Freedom of Information Act. At least one court (*Tallman v. Cheboygan Area School*, 454 N.W. 2d 171 (Mich. Ct. App. 1990)) has said that charging a fee for search and retrieval would violate the Freedom of Information Act.

While some districts can be very uncooperative about providing free copies of your child's file, others provide them as a matter of course. If your district charges you an excessive fee for searching and retrieving the file or charges you when you can't afford to pay a fee, write a letter to your administrator.

Request for Child's School File

Date: _____ March 3, 20xx _____

To: _____ Ronald Pearl, Principal _____

_____ Mesa Verde Elementary School _____

_____ 123 San Pablo Ave. _____

_____ San Francisco, CA 94110 _____

Re: _____ Amber Jones, student in second-grade class of Cynthia Rodriguez _____

I would like a copy of my child's file, including all tests, reports, assessments, grades, notes by teachers or other staff members, memoranda, photographs—in short, *everything* in my child's school file. I understand I have a right to these files under _____ IDEA, specifically _____

_____ 20 U.S.C. § 1415(b)(1) and 34 C.F.R. § 300.562 [or the Family Educational Rights and _____

_____ Privacy Act (FERPA) (20 U.S.C. § 1232 (g)) if your child has not yet been found eligible _____

_____ for special education]. _____

_____ .

I would greatly appreciate having these files within the next five days. I would be happy to pick them up. I will call you to discuss how and when I will get the copies.

Thank you for your kind assistance.

Sincerely,

Mary Jones

_____ Mary Jones _____

_____ 243 Ocean Ave. _____

_____ San Francisco, CA 94110 _____

_____ Phones: 555-1234 (home); 555-2678 (work) _____

Request for Reduction or Waiver of Fee Charged for Child's School File

Date: March 20, 20xx

To: Ronald Pearl, Principal
Mesa Verde Elementary School
123 San Pablo Ave.
San Francisco, CA 94110

Re: Amber Jones, student in second-grade class of Cynthia Rodriguez

On March 3, 20xx, I requested copies of everything in my child's school file. Your secretary called me on March 19, 20xx, and stated that there would be a fee for the copies [or an excessive fee, or a fee for searching and retrieving]. IDEA (34 C.F.R. § 300.566) specifically states that you cannot charge a fee if it prevents me from exercising my right to inspect and review my child's file. I am on a fixed income and I cannot afford the fee you are charging.

[or: IDEA prohibits you from charging such a high fee. A fee of 15¢ a copy seems fair, not $1 a copy.]

[or: IDEA specifically prohibits you from charging a fee for searching for and retrieving the files.]

Therefore, I would appreciate it if you would send me copies, at no cost, at once. Thank you for your kind attention to this matter.

Mary Jones
Mary Jones
243 Ocean Ave.
San Francisco, CA 94110
Phones: 555-1234 (home); 555-2678 (work)

Go for the Copies

IDEA allows you to inspect and review your child's school file as well as receive copies. (34 C.F.R. § 300.562.) These are two different rights—and you should exercise them both. You should always get copies of your child's file. If you can, you should also go to the school and review the original file, just to make sure the school district gave you everything.

4. What to Look for in Your Child's School File

Items that you are likely to find in your child's file are listed at the beginning of this section. As you review those documents, look for any information about your child's performance and needs, as well as comments from teachers and other professionals.

 Chapter 4 discusses in greater detail how to organize your child's records.

5. Amending Your Child's File

You have the right to request that any false, inaccurate, or misleading information, or information that violates the privacy or other rights of your child, be amended or removed from your child's school file. (34 C.F.R. § 300.567.) You also have the right to an explanation of the records. (34 C.F.R. § 300.562(b)(1).)

If the school refuses to amend or remove the information, you have the right to a due process hearing on the issue. (See Chapter 12.)

 A sample request to amend the child's school file is below; a blank, tear-out copy is in Appendix 5.

Request to Amend Child's School File

Date: _April 1, 20xx_

To: _Ronald Pearl, Principal_

Mesa Verde Elementary School

123 San Pablo Ave.

San Francisco, CA 94110

Re: _Amber Jones, student in second-grade class of Cynthia Rodriguez_

I recently reviewed a copy of my child's file and would like to have a portion of the file amended, specifically:

The assessment/memorandum from the school psychologist, Ms. Taylor, stating that

my child had severe emotional problems, is inaccurate and inappropriate because

Ms. Taylor did no testing and only briefly observed my child. This is insufficient to sup-

port the conclusion she reached.

IDEA gives me the right to request that all information that is "inaccurate or misleading, or violates the privacy of [my] child" be amended. (34 C.F.R. § 300.567.) I feel that this is just such a case and, therefore, request that you rectify the situation immediately.

Please notify me in writing as soon as possible of your decision regarding this matter. Thank you.

Sincerely,

Mary Jones

Mary Jones

243 Ocean Ave.

San Francisco, CA 94110

Phones: 555-1234 (home); 555-2678 (work)

4

Getting Organized

Whether you are entering special education for the first time or preparing for your child's tenth IEP, you will be dealing with many issues and tasks, and vast amounts of written material. This chapter will help you organize the information you'll need throughout the IEP process. It also explains how to most effectively plan your IEP year.

Gathering information, getting organized, and figuring out what should go into your child's program are all related. If you haven't yet read Chapter 3, be sure to review Section B on securing your child's school file before proceeding. And when you get to Chapter 5 on developing an IEP blueprint for your child's ideal program and services, you will use much of the information from this chapter.

Use the Forms in This Book

Nearly two dozen sample forms, checklists, and letters appear throughout this book, with tear-out copies in Appendix 5. You can simply photocopy (make as many copies as necessary) and insert the relevant forms into your IEP binder—either as a separate section or folded into one of the major sections we list below. The IEP Blueprint (discussed in Chapter 5) is one key document you should include as a separate section in your binder. Another is the IEP Material Organizer form (discussed in Chapter 10), which you'll use to highlight key information in your binder and easily access your materials during the IEP meeting. These and other forms have spaces for far more information than you'll be ready to provide right now. That's okay. You're just getting started. It's perfectly fine to leave many of the form sections blank. You can fill them in later, as you read this book and get into the IEP process.

A. Start an IEP Binder

Many parents have found a simple three-ring binder with clearly labeled sections to be an invaluable organizing tool. A binder allows you to keep everything in one convenient location—from report cards to IEP forms.

Include every important document in your IEP binder. What's an important document? Anything containing substantive information about your child or procedural information concerning how and when things happen in the IEP process. While certain items can probably go into a file drawer, if you have any doubt, add them to your binder.

Listed below are some of the most important materials for your binder. Make as many sections as necessary to help you easily locate the information you'll need throughout the IEP process.

1. Your Child's File and Relevant School Materials

Your child's school records will play a key role at the IEP meeting, in developing the IEP itself, and possibly at any due process mediation or hearing. As emphasized in Chapter 3, Section B, make sure to secure copies of *everything* in your child's school file, including report cards, attendance and disciplinary records, assessments and testing data, and teacher comments. Review the documents carefully and put important items in your binder.

You can put everything in one large section of your binder labeled "school records," or you can divide the material into several sections. You'll probably have an easier time locating the information if you break it down into categories.

In addition to your child's file, your binder should include other relevant school materials, such as:

- assessments
- samples of your child's work

- notes from your child's teacher and other staff members
- correspondence to and from the school
- past IEPs
- your notes and information on available programs and services, including the qualifications of particular teachers or service providers within the school district (Chapter 8 discusses how to develop information on available school options), and
- forms and informational materials sent to you by the school district, such as the school's IEP form and copies of key statutes and regulations on special education. (As mentioned earlier, the school is required by IDEA to provide you with a copy of federal and state statutes and regulations.)

It's never too early to secure a copy of your school's IEP. If you're new to the IEP process, be sure to get a copy of the local IEP form (this varies from district to district) and any school guidelines on the IEP process. Keep the form and related materials in your binder.

Binder Versus File Drawer

As your child progresses in school, your binder could quickly become unwieldy. Consider developing a new one each year. You can keep a file drawer or box of dated material—for example, "2002 assessment" or "2003 report cards." Include in your binder only information that is relevant to the current IEP year.

---

2. Your Child's Health and Medical Records

Your child's school file will probably include some medical information, such as the results of hearing or vision tests done at school. Be sure your binder includes these as well as medical records and important letters from your child's pediatrician and other health professionals.

3. Independent Assessments

As explained in Chapter 8, an independent assessment or evaluation may be the most important document supporting what you want for your child. You'll definitely want to keep a copy of all independent assessments in your binder.

4. Information on Programs and Services Outside the School District

If you're exploring private programs or service options, such as a specialized school for children with autism, be sure to include details in your binder, such as suggestions made by other parents, school brochures, and notes of your conversations and visits. (Chapter 8 explains how to develop information on programs and services outside of your school district.)

5. Special Education Contacts

You'll want to have a list of the names, mailing addresses, phone and fax numbers, and email addresses of people you will deal with on a regular basis, such as your child's teacher, the district's special education administrator, your child's physician, the school nurse, staff members who provide related services, parents or parent groups, and the like.

Keep this list of contacts in a prominent place in the front of your binder. Also, keep a copy with you, should you need to phone or write any of your contacts when you're away from home.

A sample Special Education Contacts form is below; a blank, tear-out copy is in Appendix 5. Make as many copies as you need.

Special Education Contacts

Name, Address, Phone and Fax Numbers, and Email Address

School Staff

School: Lewis Elementary, 123 Rose St., Chicago, 60611; 555-1234 (main phone), 555-5678 (fax)

David Werner, Principal, 555-9876, DWE@aol.com

Charlene Hanson, District Special Ed. Administrator, 4444 Main, Chicago, 60611; 555-4201 (phone), 555-7451 (fax), chsed @dusd.edu

Thayer Walker, Carrie's teacher, 567 Elm Ave., Chicago, 60611 (home); 555-0111 (classroom), 555-0114 (home)

Dr. Judy Goffy, school psychologist, 555-4333 (phone); 555-7455 (fax), drjg@aol.com

Outside Professionals

Dr. Hugh Maloney, independent assessor, 780 Spruce Lane, Chicago, 60612; 555-5169 (phone), 555-5170 (fax), drhm @compuserv.com

Martha Brown, tutor, 2229 Franklin, Chicago, 60612; 555-1490

Other Parents

Kevin Jones (son Robert in Carrie's class), 7 Plainview Dr., Chicago, 60614; 555-5115, kj@aol.com

Melaney Harper, District Community Advisory Chair, 764 Rockly, Chicago, 60610; 555-7777 (phone), 555-9299 (fax)

Support Groups

Chicago Learning Disabilities Association (contact: Mark Kelso), 775 Kelly Rd., Chicago, 60610; 555-6226 (phone), 555-7890 (fax), chldas@aol.com

State Department of Education

Special Ed. Office (contact: Dr. Hillary Casper), State Department of Education, 88 Capitol Row, Springfield, 61614; 217-555-8888 (phone), 217-555-9999 (fax), ilsped@worldnet.att.net

Other

Dr. Joan Landman, Carrie's pediatrician, 32 Ashford Rd., Chicago, 60611; 555-2222 (phone), 555-0987 (fax)

Illinois Special Ed. Advocates (Steve Miller, Esq.), 642 Miller Dr., Chicago, 60611; 555-4511 (phone), 555-8709 (fax), spedatt@netcom.com

6. IEP Journal

The importance of keeping a record of all conversations, visits, and information-gathering activities, whether on the phone or in person, cannot be overemphasized. In particular, you want to note the following in an IEP journal:

- the date and time of the conversation or meeting
- the names and positions of all people who participated in the discussion, such as your child's teacher, other school staff, the special education administrator, your pediatrician, or another parent
- what was said by whom (this is *really* important), and
- any necessary follow-up actions (for example, a person you should call).

You'll want to fill in your IEP journal just as soon as possible after a conversation or meeting has ended. The longer you wait, the more likely you are to forget certain details or confuse dates, times, and statements or promises made. Don't be shy about taking notes when you meet or talk with someone. To establish written verification of what you've been told, you'll want to send a confirming letter soon after your conversation. Confirming letters are covered in the following section.

A sample IEP journal page is below; a blank, tear-out copy is in Appendix 5. Make several copies and keep a few with you—to use if you make phone calls from work, for example. Use the Class Visitation Checklist in Chapter 8, Section C, to keep detailed notes on visits to school programs.

IEP Journal

Date: _11/3/03_   **Time:** _4:30_   a.m./p.m.

Action: ☒ Phone Call _201-555-0105_   ☐ Meeting _____

☐ Other: _____

Person(s) Contacted: _Dr. P. Brin (Sp. Ed. Administrator)_

Notes: _I explained that Steve is having problems in reading, comp., and spelling, plus some_
social difficulties.

I said Steve needs an aide.

Dr. B: "We can't do that now; wait until the IEP."

I said we need IEP at once.

Dr. B: "We just had one; can't schedule another for at least two months."

■■■

IEP Journal

Date: _11/5/03_   **Time:** _2:10_   a.m./p.m.

Action: ☐ Phone Call _____   ☒ Meeting _Washington School_

☐ Other: _____

Person(s) Contacted: _Met w/ T. Walker (teacher)_

Notes: _T. Walker said, "Steve will need at least two hours per day of a 1:1 aide next year."_

I asked if he needs an aide now.

T. Walker: "Probably."

7. Confirming Letters

Confirming what someone has said to you creates some proof of that conversation. A confirming letter can provide useful evidence—of what was said, by whom, and when—for an IEP meeting or a due process hearing.

To be sure the school district receives confirming letters, send them certified mail, return receipt requested.

Example:
Your son needs a good deal of one-to-one help. You believe that a qualified aide should sit with him to work on reading, math, and spelling at least half of the school day. Your child's teacher tells you during a classroom visit that he agrees that your son needs one-to-one help for much of the day. In addition, the special education administrator admits to you that the current amount of aide time your son is receiving is not enough. You note both of these conversations in your IEP journal and send the administrator a confirming letter. Later, at the IEP meeting, the administrator balks at providing your son with more aide time. Your confirming letter will be quite helpful in establishing that both your son's teacher and the school administrator told you your son needs more aide time.

Sample Confirming Letter

Date: May 14, 20xx

To: Salvador Hale, Special Education
Administrator
Coconut County School District
1003 South Dogwood Drive
Oshkosh, WI 50000
Re: Rodney Brown,
fourth grader at Woodrow Wilson School

I appreciated the chance to speak with you yesterday regarding Rodney's current problems with reading comprehension. I agree with your comment that he will need at least half of the day with a one-on-one aide. I look forward to our IEP meeting next week and resolving Rodney's current difficulties in school.

Sincerely,

Martin Brown

Martin Brown
145 Splitleaf Lane
Oshkosh, WI 50000
Phones: 555-4545 (home); 555-2500 (work)

8. Calendars

Section B, below, describes the tasks and events that typically take place during the yearly IEP process, and Section D explains how to keep track of these tasks and events on a monthly calendar. To stay organized, keep a copy of your calendar in your binder.

B. The Yearly IEP Cycle

Part of successful organizing is having a clear sense of when things happen in the IEP cycle. Once your child is assessed and found eligible for special education, the yearly IEP process will involve three broad considerations:

- Review—how are things currently going?
- Reassess—what additional information is needed?
- Rebuild—will the program be the same next year, or does it need changing?

IDEA requires that an IEP be in place before your child begins the school year. (34 C.F.R. § 300.342.) To develop a complete IEP, you'll need to gather information, deal with assessments, prove that your child is eligible for special education, prepare for the IEP meeting, attend the IEP meeting, and work out any disagreements you might have with the school. This means you'll have to start planning well in advance to make sure everything gets done in time.

The best way to think about the IEP cycle is to start from your final goal—an IEP in place by the start of the school year—and work backward.

1. Finish Before Summer

To make sure that all special education issues are resolved before the school year begins, you will want an IEP meeting in the spring of the preceding year. This will give you time to resolve any disputes before the next school year starts. Because school personnel are usually gone during the summer, plan for the IEP meeting in May—or better yet, April—in case there is a dispute that has to be resolved through due process.

2. Request Your Meeting During the Winter

To ensure that your child's IEP meeting takes place in the spring, put the school district on notice by submitting a written request in February or March stating that you want the annual IEP meeting in April or May.

3. Begin Planning in the Fall

You'll need to be well prepared for the spring IEP meeting. Don't start collecting information a few weeks or even a month or two in advance. You'll need much more time than that. Start in the fall or early winter of the preceding year.

4. The Cycle Isn't Set in Stone

Let's say you've just discovered that your child's problems in school make her a candidate for special education. It's October. You didn't participate in the IEP cycle the previous year because it wasn't an issue. You'd prefer not to wait until the spring to have an IEP meeting to develop a plan for the following year, as your child would lose almost a whole year of school. Or, you went through the IEP cycle the previous year, but the current program is not working. It's November, and you don't want to wait until spring for a new program. What do you do?

Speak up. Don't wait until spring to raise issues that need immediate attention. Start gathering information, and request an assessment and IEP meeting ASAP. The IEP cycle is an ideal, but you should request an immediate IEP meeting if you need one.

Midyear IEP meetings are a bad idea. Many students' IEP meetings take place in December or January. While you can request an IEP meeting at any time (and you should when there is an immediate concern), it is not generally a good idea to have your yearly IEPs after school starts. Otherwise, you'll be making decisions after your child is already in a program. The easiest way to get back on schedule is to indicate at the midyear IEP meeting that you want another one at the end of the school year, preferably in April or May. Follow up your request with a confirming letter.

C. Sample Year in the Life of Your Child's IEP

Let us assume you are planning for the school year that begins in the fall of 2005. Ideally, by starting your preparation a year ahead of time, in the fall of 2004, you will have enough time without rushing or facing last-minute problems.

The sections below follow the general IEP yearly calendar and are intended to give you an introduction to the IEP year. Specific tasks are listed in each section; you'll find the details in Chapters 5 through 11.

1. Information Gathering: Fall (September–December)

No matter how many times you have been through the special education process, the fall months are generally a good time to gather information and develop a sense of what your child's program should be. The specific tasks include the following:

- Talk to teachers, school staff, and other parents (Chapter 3, Section A3).
- Request copies of your child's school records (Chapter 3, Section B).
- Request an assessment of your child as appropriate (Chapter 6).
- Begin drafting your child's blueprint (Chapter 5).
- Schedule visits to your child's class or other programs you think might be viable (Chapter 8, Section C).
- Gather other information, such as letters from your pediatrician and your child's tutor (Chapter 8, Section F).

2. Assessment: Winter (January and February)

After the first few months of school, the key issues for your child should begin to crystallize

for you. You will know that your child needs to be in special education or, if already eligible for special education, what programmatic components make sense. Now is the time to assess what information you have or need to make a strong case for eligibility. Steps to take include the following:

- Assess the current information in your child's record and decide whether it supports your IEP goals for your child.
- Monitor the progress your child is making under the current program.
- Complete additional assessments, if you need more supporting information (discussed in Chapters 6 and 8). Depending on who will be doing any additional assessments and their calendars, you may need to plan for those assessments earlier in the year.
- Continue developing your child's IEP blueprint (Chapter 5).

3. IEP Preparation and IEP Meeting: Spring (March–May)

Spring is when you focus on working toward getting an IEP program in place for your child. This may be the most labor-intensive time of the whole cycle. Tasks include the following:

- Finalize your child's IEP blueprint of program and service needs (Chapter 5).
- Draft your goals and objectives for your child's IEP program (Chapter 9).
- Prepare for the IEP meeting and invite participants who will speak on your child's behalf (Chapter 10).
- Attend the IEP meeting (Chapter 11).

4. Dispute Resolution: Spring–Summer (June–August)

If you did not reach an agreement with the school administrators on your child's IEP program, then

you can, as discussed earlier, go to a due process mediation or hearing. It is important that this process is completed before the beginning of the new year. See Chapter 12.

5. School Begins: Fall (September)

You've been through your first (or another) IEP cycle. You'll want to monitor your child's progress in school and see if the IEP program is working. Remember: If it's not, you can request another IEP meeting and try to come up with some changes that make sense.

D. Keep a Monthly Calendar

We cannot overemphasize the importance of writing down details of IEP tasks (such as drafting goals and objectives) and events (such as assessments, school visits, and the IEP meeting).

Write down all details on a monthly calendar (your own or the form we provide here), including dates on which:

- you were told things would happen—for example, "Scott's school file should be mailed today"

- you need to schedule a meeting—for example, "Request IEP meeting no later than today"
- you need to call or meet with someone such as a teacher, a pediatrician, or another parent, or
- you need to start or complete a particular task, such as develop an IEP blueprint.

A sample Monthly IEP Calendar is below; a tear-out copy is in Appendix 5. Make copies for each month of the year.

E. Track Your Child's Progress

Whether your child is just entering special education or already has an IEP in place, it's vitally important that you keep track of his or her progress in school. Gauging how well your child is doing will help you in several ways:

- It will provide you with a basis for comparing one semester or year to the next, and one subject to the next. If you don't keep close tabs on your child's progress, you won't know whether he or she is improving or getting worse, whether certain subjects are posing more difficulty than others as time goes by, or whether a particular classroom, service, or teaching methodology is having a positive effect.
- It will help you make your case for eligibility. If your child is not yet in the special education system, you can use the materials you gather to show that your child's academic achievement is not what it should be, or that certain subjects are posing particular difficulty.
- It will help you draft effective goals and objectives. When you sit down with the IEP team to write goals and objectives for your child, you will know exactly what subjects give him or her trouble—and where he or she needs to work especially hard to see

Monthly IEP Calendar

Month and Year: Oct '03

1	2	3 Call Dr. Brin (Request visits)	4	5 Follow-up assessment request if not received	6	7
8	9 Meet w/ Janice re: her son's experiences	10	11	12 Call Dr. Pearl re: recomm. on auditory problem	13	14
15	16	17 Call at 4 p.m. T. Walker to discuss Steve's sign reading problem	18	19 Send school written request for assessment	20	21
22	23 Call J. Brown of parent group	24	25 4:15 meet w/ T. Walker	26	27	28
29	30	31 Begin Steve's IEP blueprint				

improvement. This will help you tailor the goals and objectives to your child's particular needs.

- It will help you argue for a particular placement or service. If your child is not making appropriate progress, you can argue that the current placement or related services need to be changed. Keeping track of how your child is doing in every subject will give you the information you need to evaluate your child's educational program.

- It will help you develop a positive relationship with your child's teacher. Most teachers welcome parents who want to play an active role in their child's education, as long as the parents are respectful of the teacher's time and experience. By keeping in touch with your child's teacher and weighing in on issues of special concern, you'll help the teacher do a better job educating your child. And there's a lot parents can learn from teachers, too—including which teaching methods might be appropriate, or what exercises or activities you can do at home to reinforce classroom lessons.

Get into the habit of reviewing all of your child's homework, classroom assignments, tests, and teacher reports. (Be sure to keep any that seem to really illustrate your child's difficulties or successes for your IEP binder.) Plan to visit your child's classroom often—volunteer your time, serve as a class parent, or participate in planned activities for parents. This will give you a chance to see how your child does in the classroom environment.

Talk to the teacher to set up a reasonable schedule for a brief update or conversation about your child. Remember, most teachers have more work to do than they have hours to do it in, so don't expect to hear from the teacher every day or every week. Instead, ask for some communication twice a month or so, on a day and time that's convenient. Some teachers find it easiest to send parents a brief email report of their child's progress; others would rather have a phone conversation. (If the teacher prefers a conversation, make sure to take notes.)

Create a section in your IEP binder for documents relating to your child's progress. Save copies of written updates from the teacher and samples of your child's schoolwork here. For more information on keeping track of your child's progress with an existing IEP, see Chapter 8, Section B.

■

5

Developing Your Child's IEP Blueprint

At some point in the IEP process, you'll need to describe in detail what you believe your child's educational program should look like, including the placement and support services your child needs. We call the specifics of this program a blueprint. Despite the fancy name, a blueprint is just a list of items or components that you want in your child's program.

Why create a blueprint? Primarily to help you be an effective advocate for your child. To convince others that your child needs particular services or assistance, you must first be able to articulate exactly what you want for your child and why it's appropriate.

There are a few other reasons for creating a blueprint:

- It forces you to be specific. For example, stating that your child needs help in reading is not as effective as saying your child needs a one-on-one reading specialist one hour per day, four days per week.

- You'll know exactly what documentation you will need to support your request at the IEP meeting. For example, if your blueprint includes a one-on-one reading specialist one hour per day, four days per week, you'll need information from your child's school record or a person at the IEP meeting to support that position.

- IDEA requires that the program fit the child, not the other way around. Just because the school district offers a particular class or program doesn't necessarily mean that it is appropriate for your child. A blueprint helps you determine what may be missing from the program suggested by the school.

- The blueprint serves as a standard against which you can evaluate your child's existing program and options currently available to you.

- The blueprint provides you with a continual reference point as you talk with others about your child's needs and move toward the IEP meeting.

In essence, the blueprint represents your ideal IEP program. It is your starting point—a sort of "druthers" test. That is, if you had your druthers, if you could be the special education administrator for your school district for one day, this is the IEP program you would design for your child.

You may think it's too early to draft a blueprint. Perhaps your child was just assessed and found eligible for special education, but hasn't been in special education yet. Or maybe your child has been in special education for some time, but is scheduled for a new assessment in another month. It's possible a new special education administrator will take over in the spring, with promises of new program options about which you know little. In any of these situations, you may think you don't know enough. In truth, there's always more information you can gather. But you have to start sometime, and now is as good as any. Don't worry if your blueprint is skeletal at first; it's for your use only.

Even parents new to special education usually have some intuitive sense of what their child needs. Take a moment to think about it. By the time you finish this chapter, you'll have the beginnings of a useful blueprint, not just vague notions of what might help. And as you go through other chapters and gather information on your child's needs, you'll be able to develop a more complete blueprint.

A. Begin at the End: Define Your Child's Needs

It's the first day of school in the upcoming school year. Close your eyes and picture what your child's classroom will look like. Is there a tutor? A sign language interpreter? No more than ten kids in the room? Is it a regular classroom? A special education class in a neighboring school district? A special private school? Don't hold yourself back.

Sit down with a pad of paper and pen or in front of your computer, and write out the ideal program and services for your child. Remember that your blueprint is your wish list for your ideal IEP. Don't dwell on the fact that you fought over the IEP last year or you're expecting a fight again. Don't draft your blueprint to follow the school district's program if you think it's not appropriate.

B. Preparing an IEP Blueprint

This section covers the seven key components of a blueprint, the items you want included in your child's IEP. You can use the blueprint to develop your IEP form, although the two documents won't be identical. (Chapter 11, Section C, explains how to do this.)

Some components are quite general, such as ideal classroom setting; others are very specific, such as a particular class. Some of these seven components may not be relevant to your child's situation and may be ignored. You may not have enough information to complete each section now. As you know more, you can fill in the gaps.

A sample IEP Blueprint is below; Appendix 5 includes a blank tear-out copy. Be sure to put your blueprint draft into your binder, along with supporting information and documents. (See Chapter 4.)

1. Classroom Setting and Peer Needs

In this section, specify the type of classroom you'd like for your child, including the kinds of peers she should be with. Specific items to identify (when relevant) include:

- regular versus special education class
- partially or fully mainstreamed
- type of special education class (for example, for learning disabled students)
- number of children in the classroom
- ages and cognitive ranges of children in class
- kinds of students (with similar or dissimilar disabling conditions) and what behaviors might or might not be appropriate for your child—for example, a child with attention deficit disorder may need a classroom where other children do not act out, and
- language similarities—for example, a deaf child may need a class of children who use the same sign language.

2. Teacher and Staff Needs

Use this section to identify your desires concerning teachers and other classroom staff, such as:

- number of teachers and aides
- teacher-pupil ratio—for example, your child may require a ratio of no more than four students to one teacher
- experience, training, and expertise of the teacher—many special education classes are set up for children with specific disabilities; if your child has communicative disabilities or emotional problems, a class with a teacher for the learning disabled may not be appropriate, and
- training and expertise of aides.

IEP Blueprint

The IEP Blueprint represents the ideal IEP for your child. Use it as a guide to make and record the educational desires you have for your child.

Areas of the IEP	Preferred Situation for Your Child
1. Classroom Setting and Peer Needs— issues to consider:	
☐ regular versus special education class	
☐ partially or fully mainstreamed	
☐ type of special education class	
☒ number of children in the classroom	A class of no more than 10 students
☒ ages and cognitive ranges of children in class	Age range 9-10; same cognitive range as Mark
☒ kinds of students and behaviors that might or might not be appropriate for your child, and	No behaviorally troubled students No mixed "disability" class
☐ language similarities.	
2. Teacher and Staff Needs—issues to consider:	
☒ number of teachers and aides	1 teacher; 1 full-time aide or 2 half-time aides
☒ teacher-pupil ratio	10:1 pupil-teacher ratio
☒ experience, training and expertise of the teacher, and	Teacher with specific learning disability training, experience, credentials
☒ training and expertise of aides.	Aide: previous experience working with L-D students
3. Curricula and Teaching Methodology— be specific. If you don't know what you *do* want, specify what you *don't* want.	Slingerland method Large print material Teaching strategies that include significant repetition

Areas of the IEP	Ideal Situation for Your Child
4. Related Services—issues to consider: ☒ specific needed services	1:1 aide two hours per day
☒ type of services	Speech and lang. therapy three times/week, 40 min. per session, 1:1
☒ frequency of services, and	
☒ length of services.	30 minutes of psych. counseling once a week with psychologist experienced with children with learning disabilities and emotional overlay
5. Identified Programs—specify known programs that you think would work for your child and the school that offers them.	Special day class (5th grade) for learning disabled at Washington School (Ms. Flanagan)
6. Goals and Objectives—goals are long range in nature, while objectives are more short term.	Improve reading fluency and comprehension: Read three- paragraph story with 80% comprehension; complete reading within 10 minutes. Improve peer relationships: Initiate five positive peer in- teractions/week.
7. Classroom Environment and Other Features—issues to consider: ☒ distance from home	No more than five miles and less than 30-minute bus ride to neighborhood school
☐ transition plans for mainstreaming	
☐ vocational needs	
☒ extracurricular and social needs, and	Involvement in afterschool recreation and lunch-time sports activities
☒ environmental needs.	Small school (no more than 250 students); quiet class- room; protective environment (school procedures to ensure students do not wander); acoustically treated classroom

3. Curricula and Teaching Methodology

In this section, identify the curricula and teaching method or methods you feel are appropriate for your child. You may have no idea right now. As you gather information, however, you will begin to learn about the various teaching methods, materials, strategies, and curricula used with children with disabilities.

Be as specific as possible. If you don't know what you *do* want, specify what you *don't* want. For example, an autistic child will require very different curricula and teaching methods from a child with a learning disability. A child in a regular classroom may require only a minor adjustment to the regular classroom curriculum.

Is There a Right to a Specific Methodology?

While IDEA does not specifically require that a methodology or curriculum be included in the IEP and provided to the child, there is no prohibition against it. If a child needs a specific methodology to benefit from special education, then it is required; if he does not have or you cannot prove the need, then the school district need not follow your preference.

---

4. Related Services

Include in your blueprint a list of necessary services, including the type and amount of services (such as number of times per week and length of time per session).

 Chapters 2 and 8 provide details on related services, such as speech therapy, aide support, physical therapy, transportation, and psychological services.

5. Identified Programs

In Section 1 of the blueprint, you may have stated whether you want your child in a regular classroom or special education classroom. If you know about a program in a particular school that you think would work best for your child, be it in a regular classroom or a special education classroom, public or private, identify that here.

6. Goals and Objectives

As discussed in Chapter 2, goals are long range in nature, while objectives are more short term.

Examples of goals include:
- improve reading comprehension or other academic skills, such as math, spelling, or writing
- improve social skills
- resolve a serious emotional difficulty that impedes school work
- improve fine or large motor skills
- develop greater language and speech skills
- develop independent living skills, or
- improve auditory or visual memory.

Objectives tie in specifically to the goals identified above. For example, if your goal is to improve your child's reading skills, then a specific objective may be to improve reading comprehension from the third to the fourth-grade level or to master specific speech sounds.

 Chapter 9 discusses how to prepare goals and objectives.

7. Classroom Environment and Other Features

Use your blueprint to identify any other features of the program you want for your child, such as:
- distance from home
- transition plans for mainstreaming

- vocational needs
- extracurricular and social needs, and
- environmental needs—protective environment, small class, small campus, acoustically treated classroom, or the like.

C. Other Sources of Information for the Blueprint

Developing your blueprint is an important part of gathering information and developing a sense of what your child needs. As you learn more about your child's needs from professionals and others, and find out what services and programs are available, add to or change your blueprint as appropriate.

People who are trustworthy and know your child—such as other parents, your pediatrician, the classroom teacher, or a tutor—are excellent sources of information for your blueprint. Pose your question like this: "Terry is having some problems with reading (math, cognitive growth, language development, social issues, emotional conflicts, mobility, fine or gross motor activities, or whatever), and I'm wondering if I should look for a new program (or different related services). Do you have any suggestions of people I might talk to, or programs or services I might consider?"

Chapter 8 contains important information about gathering facts, visiting school programs, and developing supportive material, such as an independent assessment. This information will help you work on your blueprint.

D. What's Next?

If you are new to special education, the next step is to learn about the assessment and eligibility processes—how your child is evaluated and becomes eligible for special education. Review Chapters 6 and 7 carefully.

If you are not new to special education, your next step will depend on your child's situation. Your child may need an assessment before the IEP meeting—if so, be sure to read Chapter 6. If your child does not need an immediate assessment and has already been found eligible for special education, move on to Chapter 8. ■

6

Assessments

Assessments are important tools that help you and the school district determine what your child's needs are and how they can be met. For children new to special education, an assessment provides information the IEP team will use to determine whether or not the child is eligible for special education by evaluating the child's current ability levels and potential areas of need. (20 U.S.C. § 1414(a)(1); 34 C.F.R. §§ 300.320, 527, 531-535.) This kind of assessment is called the initial assessment.

For children previously found eligible, re-evaluation assessments take place at least once every three years (more often if the parent or child's teacher requests) to review ability levels and potential areas of need. (20 U.S.C. § 1414(a)(2); 34 C.F.R. §§ 300.321, 536.)

In either situation, a good assessment report also makes recommendations as to needed programs and services for your child.

If you are new to special education, you will quickly learn that assessments and eligibility are closely related. Should you read the assessments chapter before Chapter 7 on eligibility, or vice versa? While it ultimately doesn't matter as long as you read both, you might better understand eligibility if you read this chapter on assessments first.

Special Education Assessments vs. General Assessments

Most (if not all) states require schools to administer a variety of tests to measure how children are doing in school and whether they are meeting certain state standards. These tests—often called general assessments—measure a child's mastery of specific subject matter, such as American history or algebra. Most children also take tests to graduate from high school and qualify for college. While special education assessments often measure similar abilities or aptitudes, they are intended to be used for a different purpose: to determine whether a child is eligible for special education and which special education services will be helpful to a particular child.

Since 1997, IDEA has required that children in special education be included in state- and district-wide assessments, with appropriate accommodations for the child's unique needs. (20 U.S.C. § 1412(a)(17)(A); 34 C.F.R. § 300.300.138.) Not all of these tests are sensitive to special education test-takers, however. For example, California requires high school seniors to pass an "exit exam" before they graduate—but the State Board of Education has generally ignored the needs of special education students and failed to make appropriate exit exam accommodations or modifications. The state was recently sued for this inexcusable oversight. You should carefully review any state or district tests in which your child participates to make sure that the test is appropriate and that your child receives the accommodations necessary to take the test.

The assessment report will be a key factor in decisions made at an IEP meeting about your child's program and services. Ideally, the assessment report will support what you want included in the IEP. For example, if you feel your child needs placement in a specific special education program, your chances of securing that placement are increased, if the assessment report recommends it.

 This chapter covers assessments done by local public school districts. You also have the right to have your child assessed by someone outside of the school district, often referred to as a private or independent assessment. As discussed in Chapter 8, such independent assessments are very valuable when you disagree with the school district's assessment or feel that an independent assessor will provide an evaluation supportive of your child's blueprint.

A. When Assessments Are First Done

There are two kinds of assessments: an initial assessment to determine whether you child qualifies for special education, and subsequent or follow-up assessments to get up-to-date information on your child's status and progress. The initial assessment must be done *before* your child can be found eligible for special education.

While you can wait for the school district to initiate the initial assessment process, you don't want to delay unnecessarily. If you haven't heard from the school, make a formal request for an assessment.

 A sample Request to Begin Special Education Process and Assessment is in Chapter 3, Section A2; a blank, tear-out copy is in Appendix 5.

The Assessment Process, Step by Step

Here is how an assessment process typically proceeds:

1. You request an assessment, or the school identifies your child as possibly needing special education. (See Chapter 3.)
2. The school presents you with an assessment plan listing all testing to be done on your child in order to determine eligibility for special education, or to assess your child's current status if already in special education.
3. You approve the assessment plan (or ask that certain tests or evaluation tools be added and/or eliminated).
4. You meet with the assessor to discuss specific concerns and your own evaluation of your child's problems, based on your personal observations, physician reports, and the like.
5. The school assesses your child.
6. You receive a copy of the school's assessment.
7. You schedule independent assessments if necessary. (See Chapter 8.)
8. You attend the IEP eligibility meeting (or the yearly IEP meeting, if your child is already in special education), where the assessment results are discussed.

IDEA does not require that your school district submit an assessment plan to you or complete the assessment within a specific time limit; it requires only that the school complete the assessment within a reasonable time after receiving your request or your consent to an initial assessment.

States may have their own timelines. For example, California requires the school to give you an assessment plan within 15 days of your request for an assessment, and to develop an IEP program within 50 days of your request. Contact your state department of education to see if your state laws include more specific timelines than IDEA.

B. Assessment Components

Assessments almost always include objective tests leading to numerical conclusions about a child. Depending on your child's disability, many tests are available—including ones to evaluate general intelligence, reading comprehension, psychological states, social development, and physical abilities. You may have already heard of some of them, such as the Wechsler Test, Kaufman Assessment, and Draw-a-Person. For each test, the assessment report should include an explanation of the test and the test's results.

An assessment need not be made up of only formal tests. It can also include supportive material that provides information or recommendations about your child's educational status, such as:

- a general description of your child
- teacher and parent reports
- full-scale evaluations by experts specializing in your child's disability
- letters from a family doctor or counselor
- daily or weekly school reports or diaries, and
- other evidence of school performance, including work samples.

Finally, the assessment report should draw a conclusion about your child's eligibility for special education and make specific recommendations about strategies, curricula, interventions, related services, and programs needed for your child.

Legal Requirements for Assessments

IDEA guarantees every child certain rights in the assessment process An assessment must:

- use a variety of assessment tests or tools, and strategies to gather information about your child
- not be racially or culturally discriminatory
- be given in your child's native language or communication mode (such as sign language if your child is deaf or hard of hearing)
- validly determine your child's status—that is, it must include the right test for your child's suspected areas of disability
- be given by trained and knowledgeable personnel, in accordance with the instructions provided by the producer of the tests
- not be used only to determine intelligence
- if your child has impaired speaking or sensory skills, accurately reflect your child's aptitude or achievement level—not just your child's impairment
- assess your child in "all areas of suspected disability," including health, vision, hearing, social and emotional status, general intelligence, academic performance, communicative status, motor abilities, behavior, and cognitive, physical, and developmental abilities, and
- provide relevant information that will help determine your child's educational needs. (20 U.S.C. § 1414(a)(6); 34 C.F.R. § 300.532.)

In addition, the assessment process must include other material on your child, such as information you provide (a doctor's letter or a statement of your observations), current classroom assessments and observations (objective tests or subjective teacher reports), and observations by other professionals. (20 U.S.C. § 1414(c)(1,2,4); 34 C.F.R. § 300.533.)

C. Assessment Plans

Before the school district begins the formal assessment process—either an initial assessment or a re-evaluation assessment—it must send you a written assessment plan and receive your written approval (20 U.S.C. § 1414(a)(1)(C); 34 C.F.R. § 300.505.)

The assessment plan must include:
- specifically named tests
- a section where you can request additional tests or other methods of evaluation, and
- a place for you to provide your written approval.

1. Evaluating the Assessment Tests

In almost all cases, a person in your school district who is knowledgeable about special education will determine which tests are to be given to your child. There's a very good chance that this person will also administer the assessments or supervise whoever does the assessments. How will you know if the proposed tests are appropriate for your child?

The best source of information is people who are familiar with special education testing. Likely candidates include the person who developed the assessment plan, your child's teacher, other parents, and your pediatrician. Other possibilities include independent special education assessors you've worked with or school special education personnel you trust. You may also want to talk to organizations that represent the specific disability of your child, such as the Council for Exceptional Children or a state association for learning disabilities.

Chapter 8 discusses independent assessments. Appendix 3 provides a list of advocacy, parent, and disability organizations you might consider contacting for information on different types of assessments. Appendix 3 also references books on testing and assessments.

Here's what you want to find out:
- whether the proposed tests are appropriate to assess your child's suspected disability
- what the tests generally measure, such as general cognitive skills or language abilities
- whether the tests' results are usually numeric scores or more descriptive statements about your child's performance (or both)
- whether the tests' results will provide a basis for specific recommendations about classroom strategies, teaching methods, and services and programs for your child
- how the tests are administered—for example, are they timed, are they oral or written
- the assessor's expertise, training, and experience in doing this kind of assessment, and
- how the results are evaluated—for example, will your child score in a certain percentile ("Mary is in the 88th percentile," meaning she scored better than 87% of the children taking the test) or will your child be given a different type of rating ("Mary scored at the second-grade level").

2. Adding to the Assessment Plan

If you have concerns about the assessment plan submitted to you, you have every right to ask for changes. IDEA states that the assessment process should include evaluations and information provided by the parents. (34 C.F.R. § 300.533(a)(1)(i).) You can request that specific tests be administered to your child, or that certain information (such as a formal interview with you, a review of your child's school work, a teacher's observations, or a pediatrician's report) be used to evaluate your child and be included as part of the assessment report. Be as specific as possible in your request. For example, if your child has limited fine motor skills and problems with handwriting, ask that the assessor analyze his handwriting samples.

How do you know what "other information" should be included in the assessment plan? By this time, you have probably gathered information about your child—secured his school file and talked to his teacher, other parents, or experts—and have some sense of the key issues. Be sure to take a look at your blueprint, no matter how incomplete it may be. See Chapter 5.

Many special education assessors are not comfortable evaluating testing and other data that don't produce a numerical result. The assessment plan you receive may consist primarily of standardized tests. The school district may object if you ask for an evaluation of subjective reports or anecdotal observations. Nevertheless, you have the right to insist that this information be included in your child's assessment. Subjective reports and anecdotal observations may be key in coming up with the ultimate IEP program.

If the assessor refuses to make the changes you request, send a letter to the school district's special education administrator. Explain that you are exercising your right under IDEA, 34 C.F.R. § 300.533(a)(1)(i), to request that additional materials be added to your child's assessment plan, and that the assessor refused to do so. Describe exactly what you want included and the reasons the assessor gave you for the refusal. As always, keep a copy of your correspondence.

3. Approving or Rejecting the Assessment Plan

Ultimately, you must sign the assessment plan, indicating whether you accept or reject it. Signing the assessment plan need not be an all-or-nothing proposition. You can:

- accept the plan
- accept the plan on condition, or
- reject the plan.

a. Accepting the Plan

If you accept the plan as submitted to you, mark the appropriate box—most assessment plans have approval and disapproval boxes—sign and date it, and return it to the school district. If there is no acceptance box, write "plan accepted," sign and date it, and return it. Be sure to make a photocopy of the assessment plan and add it to your IEP binder.

b. Accepting the Plan on Condition

There are two possible reasons why you might accept the plan with a condition. First, you might accept the tests proposed, but want additional tests administered or additional information considered. In this situation, try to get the assessor to agree informally, or ask for help from the school district. (See Section C2, above.)

Second, you may not want certain proposed tests administered to your child—perhaps you believe that they aren't reliable or that they test for a problem that your child doesn't have. Whatever the reason, indicate your partial acceptance of the plan on the form as follows:

> I approve only of the following tests:
> _Wrat, Kaufman_
>
> Date: _March 1, 20xx_
>
> Signature: _Jan Stevens_

c. Rejecting the Plan

You have every right to reject the assessment plan and force the assessor or school district to work with you to find an acceptable plan. Your reasons for rejecting will probably fall into one or more of the following situations:

- the tests are not appropriate
- you want additional tests and materials as part of the evaluation, or
- the assessor is not qualified.

Evaluating the Assessor

Your child's assessment must be "administered by trained and knowledgeable personnel in accordance with any instructions provided by the producer of the tests." (34 C.F.R. § 300.532(c)(ii).) How can you judge the qualifications of the assessor?

- Ask the special education administrator for the credentials of the assessor. If the administrator refuses, assert your right to know under IDEA.
- Ask other parents and your child's teacher what they know about the assessor.
- If you are working with an independent assessor (see Chapter 8), ask her if she knows the school's assessor.
- If possible, meet with the assessor prior to the testing (see Section D, below).

Can a School District Force Your Child to Be Assessed?

The short answer is yes. You are entitled to receive an assessment plan, and to approve or reject that plan or to say that you don't want your child assessed at all. Your disagreement will be noted, but if the district feels that the child should be assessed against your wishes, it can use due process procedures to secure an order requiring assessment (see Chapter 12 for more on due process).

There have been a number of decisions in which an assessment was ordered over the objection of a parent. The due process hearing judge will consider evidence as to why or why not the assessments should proceed, including whether there is already sufficient data and/or whether your child might be harmed by the assessment. (34 C.F.R. § 300.505(b); see Appendix 1.)

To reject the assessment plan, check the disapproval box, sign and date the form, and return it to the school district. If there is no box, write "assessment plan rejected," sign and date the form, and return it. Keep a copy.

If the assessment plan is not clear or does not give you enough room for your objections, you should attach a letter to the assessment plan. A sample letter is below. Use this as a model and adjust it depending on your specific situation.

Sample Letter Rejecting Assessment Plan

Date: December 14, 20xx

To: Carolyn Ames, Administrator, Special Education
       Central Valley School District
       456 Main Street
       Centerville, Michigan 47000

Re: Assessment Plan for Michael Kreeskind

I am in receipt of the November 21, 20xx, assessment plan for my son Michael. I give my permission for you to administer the Vineland, PPVT-III, and Wechsler tests, but not the rest of the ones on your list. I have investigated them and feel they are too unreliable.

In addition, I am formally requesting that the assessment plan reflect:

- that the assessor will meet with me and my husband to review Michael's entire history and will include the issues raised during that meeting in the assessment report, and

- that the assessor will evaluate samples of Michael's work and letters from professionals who have observed Michael.

I have one final concern. I have reviewed the credentials of Brett Forrest, the assessor selected by the district to evaluate Michael. I am concerned that Mr. Forrest has no prior experience evaluating children with Michael's disability. Specifically, I do not believe he is trained or knowledgeable about the specific tests to be administered, as required under IDEA, 34 C.F.R. § 300.532(c)(ii). Therefore, I do not approve of the assigned assessor, Brett Forrest. I request that an appropriate one be assigned and that we be provided proof of the assessor's qualifications.

Thank you very much.

Michelle Kreeskind

Michelle Kreeskind
8 Rock Road
Centerville, Michigan 47000
Phones: 555-9876 (home); 555-5450 (work)

After you submit your rejection (partial or complete) of the assessment plan, the assessor or school district will probably attempt to find a plan that meets your approval. If the district feels the assessment should proceed under the plan you've rejected, it has the right to proceed to mediation or a due process hearing to force this issue, although this is rarely done (see Chapter 12).

D. Meet With the Assessor

After you accept the assessment plan proposed by the school district, the assessor will contact you to schedule the testing of your child. Now is the time to think ahead. In a few months, when you are at the IEP meeting planning your child's IEP program, the school district will pay the most attention to the evaluation done by its own assessor. Therefore, you will want to take some time to establish a positive relationship with the assessor before testing begins.

A good relationship is one in which the parties don't have preconceived ideas or view each other with hostility. Try to put aside negative comments you've heard about the assessor from other people (or any bad experiences you've had with the assessor in the past). Start with the assumption (or new attitude) that the assessor is there to help your child get an appropriate education. Of course, this may not be an easy task. The assessor may not be easy to talk to or may be put off by parents who want to play an active role in the assessment. No matter what attitude the assessor adopts, you should try to remain rational and pleasant.

Reality Check: The Assessor Works for the School District

While you should assume that the assessor wants to develop a good and appropriate educational plan for your child, don't lose sight of the fact that the assessor is an employee of the school district. The assessor probably knows what the school district will offer regarding your child's eligibility for special education or in terms of an IEP program, and the assessor's report may very well reflect the school's position. Some assessors know exactly what a school district can provide and, unfortunately, tailor their assessment reports accordingly, rather than prepare a report based on what a child truly needs.

On the other hand, just because the assessor's report doesn't support what you want, it doesn't necessarily follow that the assessor is acting against your child's best interests. Her conclusions may be well reasoned and supported by the data. Be objective. Are her recommendations consistent with or contrary to the data? If you conclude that the assessor is biased against you, request a new one. Remember, you always have the right to an outside or independent assessment (see Chapter 8).

Your job is to educate the assessor about your child. She'll have test results to evaluate and reports to read. But she doesn't live with your child or stand before your child in a classroom. To the extent possible, help the assessor see your child from your perspective, particularly as it relates to the academic programs and services you feel are necessary for your child. Ideally, you want the assessment report completed by the assessor to recommend eligibility and the specific program components you want for your child, as articulated in your blueprint (in Chapter 5).

So how do you go about getting your points across to the assessor? If possible, meet with the assessor before the testing is done. The law doesn't require an assessor to meet with you, but the law does not prohibit it, either. Call up and ask for an appointment. State that you'd appreciate the chance to talk, are not familiar with all the tests, would like to find out how they are used, and would just feel a lot better if you could meet for 10 to 15 minutes. If the assessor cannot meet with you, ask for a brief phone consultation or consider sending a letter expressing your concerns.

Whether you meet in person, talk on the phone, or state your concerns in a letter, you'll want to be clear and objective.

Eligibility assessment. Let the assessor know the specific problems your child is having in school, the material you have documenting those problems, and why you believe those problems qualify your child for special education.

Example:

"Carl has had a terrible time with reading. He's only in the second grade, but he is way behind. His teacher agrees—I have some notes of my conversation with her from last October. I could provide you with a copy of them if that would help. I'd greatly appreciate it if you could focus on Carl's reading problem in your assessment."

IEP program assessment. If your child is already in special education or is likely to be found eligible, let the assessor know of the IEP program components you believe are important. Here are a few examples.

Examples:

"Billy needs a small class where none of the children exhibit behavioral problems, with classroom strategies and methodology geared for children with his learning disability."

"Howard needs the Lovaas method for autistic children. I would like you to evaluate the reports done by his doctor, his teacher, and the classroom aide, and address their suggestions in your recommendations section."

Letter Requesting Assessment Report

Date: _____ November 1, 20xx _____

To: Harvey Smith, Assessment Team

Pine Hills Elementary School

234 Lincoln Road

Boston, MA 02000

Re: Robin Griffin, student in first-grade class of Sean Jordan

I appreciate your involvement in my child's assessment and look forward to your report. Would you please:

1. Send me a copy of a draft of your report before you finalize it. As you can imagine, the process can be overwhelming for parents. It would be most helpful to me to see your report, because the proposed tests are complicated and I need time to evaluate the results.

2. Send me your final report at least four weeks before the IEP meeting.

Again, thank you for your kind assistance.

Sincerely,

Lee Griffin

Lee Griffin

23 Hillcrest Road

Boston, MA 02000

Phones: 555-4321 (home); 555-9876 (work)

Be careful about how specific you get. The assessor may think you're trying to do his job and might not appreciate being told exactly what to include in the assessment report. For example, a straight out, "Please recommend that Mary have a full-time, one-on-one aide" or "Please write that Tom should be placed in the learning disability program at Center School" may be met with hostility. You may need to be less direct, such as, "The teacher wrote that Mary cannot learn to read without constant one-on-one attention. Please address that need in your report." Remember, your blueprint is a good guide here.

This part of the process is not easy. Don't be disappointed if the assessor doesn't agree fully or even partially with what you are requesting. The best you can do is be clear about what your child's problem is, what you feel your child needs, and what materials support your conclusions. The rest is up to the assessor. Ultimately, if the assessor does not address your questions and you have good evidence to support those concerns, the value of the school's assessment may be diminished.

E. Reviewing the Assessment Report

After your child is evaluated, the assessor will issue his report. Some assessors issue their reports in two stages: a *draft* report and a *final* report. Ask the assessor how and when he plans to issue his report. Ideally, the assessor will issue a draft report that you can review before he submits his final report prior to the IEP meeting.

Even if the assessor will issue only one version of the report, it is imperative that you see it before the IEP meeting. Under IDEA, the school district must provide you with a copy of the evaluation report and with information documenting eligibility. (34 C.F.R. § 300.534(a)(2).)

By asking to see the report (preferably a draft of the report) ahead of time, you convey to the school district your intention to carefully review the assessor's work. This will help you keep a sense of control over the assessment process and prepare for the IEP meeting. It will also keep you from wasting valuable time at the IEP meeting.

A sample letter requesting the assessment report is included here; a blank, tear-out copy is in Appendix 5.

If the assessor shows you a draft of the report and you disagree with anything in it or feel something is missing, ask the assessor to make a change or add the missing information. Be prepared to point to material outside the assessment report that supports your point of view. If the assessor refuses, put your request in writing, with a copy to the special education administrator.

If the assessor won't make the changes—or sends you only the final version—what can you do if you disagree with the final assessment report? You can reject it. While you can express your disagreement before the IEP, it might be strategically wise to wait for the meeting and prepare your counterarguments with the evidence you have, including existing material and your independent assessment (if any).

Don't forget independent assessments. You have the right to have your child assessed by someone outside of the school district, often referred to as a private or independent assessment. As discussed in Chapter 8, such independent assessments are of value when you disagree with the school district's assessment. The independent assessor can analyze the district's assessment and perhaps point out its shortcomings. ■

7

Who Is Eligible for Special Education?

Eligibility is the process the school district uses to determine whether or not your child qualifies for special education. This is a two-step process. First, your child is assessed. Then, you meet with school administrators at an IEP meeting where the school actually determines whether or not your child is eligible for special education. This IEP eligibility meeting is different from the IEP program meeting, where your child's annual academic program is developed, although they may be combined (see Section D, below).

Eligibility, like assessments, IEP meetings, and other aspects of the special education process, is bound by the rules of IDEA. And like those other procedures, eligibility is frequently the source of disagreement between parents and a school district.

 If your child has already been found eligible for special education, skip ahead to Chapter 8.

Your child may be found eligible for special education for any number of reasons—for example, because she has a learning disability, has sensory or physical impairments, or has psychological problems. To qualify, your child will have to meet the criteria discussed in Section A, below.

Eligibility Is Not an Annual Event

Once your child is found eligible for special education, she won't need to requalify each year. There are only three situations when your child's eligibility might be redetermined:

- she dropped out of special education and wants to reenter
- you or the school district proposes a change from one eligibility category to another, or
- there is evidence that your child no longer qualifies for special education.

A. Eligibility Definitions

In order to qualify for special education, your child must meet two eligibility requirements: (1) he must have a disabling condition, as defined in IDEA, and (2) that condition must have an adverse impact on his education. In other words, it is not enough to show that your child has a disability—you must also show that your child's disability is causing enough problems to warrant special education help.

1. Disabling Condition

IDEA provides a list of disabling conditions that qualify a child between the ages of three and 22 for special education. The list includes:

- hearing impairments, including deafness
- speech or language impairments, such as stuttering or other speech production difficulties
- visual impairments, including blindness
- multiple disabilities, such as deaf-blindness
- orthopedic impairments caused by congenital anomalies, such as a club foot
- orthopedic impairments caused by diseases, such as polio
- orthopedic impairments caused by other conditions, such as cerebral palsy
- learning disabilities (see "Emotional Disturbance as a Disabling Condition," below)
- serious emotional disturbance (see "Emotional Disturbance as a Disablinng Condition," below)
- autism
- traumatic brain injury
- mental retardation, and
- other health impairments that affect a child's strength, vitality or alertness, such as a heart condition, tuberculosis, rheumatic fever, nephritis, asthma, sickle cell anemia, hemophilia, epilepsy, lead poisoning, leukemia, diabetes, Attention Deficit Disorder (ADD), and Attention Deficit Hyperactivity Disorder (ADHD).

You can find the legal definition of each of the above disabilities at 20 U.S.C. § 1401(3) and 34 C.F.R. § 300.7. (See Appendix 1.)

If your child has learning disabilities, see *Nolo's IEP Guide: Learning Disabilities,* by Larry Siegel, which explains in detail the eligibility requirements for children with learning disabilities.

Fitting your child's condition into a disability covered by IDEA and finding data to prove that your child's disability is causing academic problems can be tough—and emotionally trying. But it's a necessary part of qualifying for special education. If you find yourself in a muddle, remember these tips:

- **Take it slowly.** Some of the qualifying conditions have multilayered definitions. Don't try to take it in all at once. Breaking down a definition into manageable parts will help you figure out what evidence you need to show that your child meets all of the eligibility requirements.

- **You're not a doctor and you don't have to become one.** Don't be put off by some of the complicated terminology. For now, you need a basic understanding of your child's condition and how it affects his or her educational experience. Ask your pediatrician, the school nurse, or the assessor. Contact other parents and local or national support

or advocacy organizations (Chapter 15 discusses parent organizations, and Appendix 3 lists useful resources.)

- **Focus on key portions of each definition.** Pay attention to words such as "severe" or "significant." These are clues that a minor disability may not qualify your child for special education. If your child doesn't fall under one of the delineated conditions, take a look at the catchall category, "other health impairment." If your child's strength, vitality, or alertness is limited because of a chronic or acute health problem, he or she may qualify under this category.

- **The IEP team has flexibility in finding eligibility.** The list of qualifying disabilities is long, but not exhaustive. If your child exhibits the characteristics of any of the disability categories, he or she may very well be deemed eligible for special education, even if there hasn't been a formal diagnosis. In addition, the IEP team has some discretion in determining eligibility. If your child has been diagnosed with a mild condition, it's up to the IEP team to decide whether it's serious enough to justify a finding of eligibility.

A Word About Labels

This list of disability categories asks you to define your child as "this" or "that." Labeling is one of the difficult and unpleasant parts of the IEP process. Many people feel that labels are unnecessary, even harmful—and from a psychological perspective, they may be right. From a legal perspective, however, your child will be eligible for special education only if he or she fits into one of these categories. If you can, focus on the specifics of your child's condition rather than the label. Remember, your goal is to secure an appropriate education for your child; proving that your child qualifies for special education under one of the eligibility categories is part of the process.

There's a fine line, however, between acknowledging the label for the purpose of meeting the eligibility criteria and making sure your child does not become defined by that label. For example, Bill has dyslexia, which causes him some significant problems in school and qualifies him for special education. But Bill is also a terrific center on the basketball team, he hates to clean up his room, at times he frustrates you and certainly worries you, he has a good heart, and, most important, he is quite determined to make his way in the world. These are the qualities that label him.

Emotional Disturbance as a Disabling Condition

A child who has an "emotional disturbance" (this is the term used by IDEA) qualifies for special education. Although this term can conjure up images of bizarre behavior and institutionalization, children with a wide range of emotional difficulties can qualify for special education in this category. When you look at the actual defining language in IDEA, you'll see that it encompasses issues that might affect most human beings at some point in their lives, and certainly could arise for children who have a disability.

IDEA defines an emotional disturbance as a condition that has existed over a long period of time and adversely affects your child's educational performance (20 U.S.C. § 1401(3)(A)(i); 34 C.F.R. § 300.7(c)(4)), resulting in:

- inability to learn that is not explained by intellectual, sensory, or health factors
- inability to build or maintain satisfactory interpersonal relationships with peers and teachers
- inappropriate behaviors or feelings under normal circumstances (for example, extreme frustration, anger, or aggression over minor setbacks or disagreements)
- general pervasive mood of unhappiness or depression, or

- tendency to develop physical symptoms or fears associated with personal or school problems (for example, a child might get a stomach ache before tests or oral reports).

A child who is only socially maladjusted will not qualify for special education, although a child who is emotionally disturbed under IDEA can, of course, be socially maladjusted. Like any other disability, emotional disturbance must adversely affect your child's educational performance in order to make him or her eligible for special education. If your child qualifies for special education in another disability category but also shows some signs of emotional disturbance, the IEP team still can (and should) address those emotional difficulties in the IEP by developing goals and objectives and providing services to meet those emotional needs. Rather than label the behaviors as an "emotional disturbance," simply have the IEP team address them as one of many aspects of your child's disability. For example, the IEP might describe how the teacher, teacher's aide, school counselor, and written goals and objectives could address how your child might deal in a concrete and helpful way with peers who make fun of his or her disability.

2. Adverse Impact

It is not enough to show that your child has a disabling condition; you must also demonstrate that your child's disability has an adverse impact on his or her educational performance.

IDEA does not say how "adverse impact" is measured, but your child's grades, test scores, and classroom or other behavior will provide important evidence of adverse impact. While grades can most directly show whether a disabling condition is adversely affecting educational performance or achievement, they don't tell the whole eligibility story. A parent can (and should) argue that a child who receives As, Bs, or Cs but cannot read at age level, follow instructions, or relate to peers is not benefiting from his or her education, and therefore that his or her disability is directly affecting educational performance, regardless of grades.

If your child is getting passing grades, you will need to make the connection between your child's disability and school performance in some other way. Factors to consider (other than grades) include:

- limited progress—for example, little or no improvement in reading, math, or spelling even though the teacher does not fail your child; high school students might have significant difficulty in social studies, algebra, or English
- difficulties in cognitive areas, such as mastering basic concepts, memory, or language skills—forgetting to turn in homework, trouble with reading comprehension, or difficulty grasping abstract concepts in math or history might demonstrate these problems
- discrepancy between performance and ability—for example, the child is developmentally and chronologically ten years old, but reads at a six-year-old's level; your eighth-grader has an above average IQ but is performing at the sixth-grade level on math and spelling tests

- evidence of emotional, behavioral, or social difficulties, or
- physical difficulties, such as handwriting, hearing, or coordination problems.

The IEP team has a lot of discretion in determining whether your child is eligible for special education. If your child has passing grades, the team may have to exercise that discretion to find that his or her disability has adversely affected educational performance in other ways.

3. Eligibility: What's Not in the Law

Almost as telling as what IDEA requires is what it doesn't. Contrary to what school district representatives may tell you, none of the following is required by IDEA.

a. Requirement of Numeric Proof

IDEA does not require that your child score at a certain level on specific tests to qualify for special education. Numeric information is important and may prove a key element in determining eligibility, but a test score is not the end of the story.

Some state laws do include specific numeric requirements, particularly for a finding of eligibility based on a learning disability. Check with your school district or your state department of education to find out whether your state has a law on eligibility. (Appendix 2 includes information on how to contact your state department of education.) For information on eligiblity requirements for children with learning disabilities, see *Nolo's IEP Guide: Learning Disabilities,* by Lawrence Siegel.

b. One Test as Sole Determinant

Eligibility cannot be determined based on the results of one test. IDEA specifically requires that any evaluation to determine eligibility include information provided by the parents of the child. (34 C.F.R. §§ 300.533(a)(1)(i) and 300.535(a)(1).) Furthermore, IDEA requires that the school district draw upon information from a variety of sources, including aptitude and achievement tests, teacher recommendations, and the child's physical condition, social or cultural background, and adaptive behavior.

c. Eligibility Based on Environment, Cultural or Economic Status

IDEA specifically states that a child cannot be determined eligible for special education solely because of limited English proficiency or environmental, cultural, or economic disadvantage. (34 C.F.R. §§ 300.7(c)(10)(ii) and 300.534(b)(1).) These factors may be considered, however, as part of the overall picture.

B. Preparing for the IEP Eligibility Meeting

After your child is assessed, the school district will schedule an IEP meeting to discuss your child's eligibility for special education. Depending on the circumstances of your case, your school district may hold off scheduling the IEP program meeting until after your child is found eligible. But if eligibility seems likely, the school district may be prepared to hold the IEP program meeting immediately after the eligibility meeting; otherwise, it must do so within 30 days of determining that your child is eligible for special education. (34 C.F.R. § 300.343(b)(2).)

The strategies for a successful IEP eligibility meeting are the same as for a successful IEP program meeting. In preparing for the IEP eligibility meeting—or the possibility of a joint IEP eligibility and program meeting—review Chapters 10 and 11.

To prepare for the eligibility meeting, follow these tips:

- **Get a copy of your child's school file.** If you don't already have a copy, see Chapter 3.
- **Get copies of all school assessments.** Assessments are covered in Chapter 6. A sample letter requesting the assessment report is in Chapter 6, Section E.
- **Know the school district's position in advance.** If the assessment report recommends eligibility, call the special education administrator and ask if the district will agree with that recommendation. If the answer is yes, ask if the IEP eligibility meeting will go right into an IEP program meeting. If the assessment report is not clear about eligibility, call the administrator and ask what the district's position is on your child's eligibility. If the assessment recommends against eligibility, be prepared to show that your child is eligible. Here are a few suggestions:
  - ▲ *Review the school file and assessment report.* Cull out test results and other information that supports your child's eligibility.
  - ▲ *Organize all other reports and written material that support your position on eligibility.* Observations from teachers and teacher's aides are especially important. Ask anyone who has observed your child and who agrees that he should be in special education to attend the IEP eligibility meeting. If a key person cannot attend, ask for a letter or written observation report.
- **Consider having your child assessed by an independent assessor.** An independent assessor may be necessary if the school district's assessment report concludes that your child is not eligible for special education. Even if your child is found eligible, you may disagree with the school's recommendations regarding services and programs—many times these are spelled out in the school district's assessment report.

- **Get organized.** Get your documents together before the eligibility meeting so you can immediately find what you need.

Chapter 8 provides tips on how to best organize existing material—and develop new information—to make your case at an IEP eligibility or program meeting. Chapter 8 also discusses how to use an independent assessor.

C. Attending the Eligibility Meeting

Many of the procedures and strategies used at the IEP eligibility meeting are similar to those used at an IEP program meeting. Chapters 10 and 11 explain how to prepare for, and participate in, an IEP meeting. This section highlights some issues that are particularly important for eligibility meetings.

1. Who Should Attend?

Who should attend the eligibility IEP meeting depends a great deal on whether you anticipate a debate about eligibility. If your school district appears ready to find your child eligible for special education, then you probably don't need anyone at the meeting other than you and your child's other parent. If the school district does not agree that your child is eligible, or you don't know the district's position, you may want to ask people who can support your position to attend the meeting. Such people might include:

- an independent assessor
- your child's current teacher, and
- other professionals who know your child.

Whether you ask any of these people to attend the IEP eligibility meeting may depend on their availability, the strength of their point of view, and cost. Sometimes, a letter from your pediatrician or another professional might be just as effective—and is certainly less expensive—than paying your pediatrician to attend in person. As a general rule, do not pay someone to attend the IEP eligibility meeting unless you are certain that there will be a disagreement and that you will need that person to support your position. In most cases, an independent assessor is your most effective advocate.

2. Preparing Your Participants

Make sure your participants are prepared to:
- describe who they are, their training, and how they know your child
- discuss their conclusions about your child's eligibility for special education and the basis for those conclusions—observation, long-term knowledge of your child, or testing, and
- contradict any material concluding that your child is not eligible for special education.

3. Submitting Your Eligibility Material

As you prepare for the IEP eligibility meeting and accumulate material (such as an independent assessment) supporting your child's eligibility, you will have to decide whether to show the material to the school district before the meeting. IDEA does not require you to do so, but consider the kind of relationship you want to establish with the school district. If you ask for the school district's assessment in advance, it is only fair to offer the district a copy of yours. Granted, you will give the school a chance to prepare a rebuttal. On the other hand, if you submit an independent assessment or other material at the IEP meeting, the school may ask to reschedule the meeting in order to review your material. In the long run, your best bet is to treat the school district as you want to be treated. If you have favorable material not in the school district's possession, submit it in advance, or at least call the administrator and ask if he wants your information ahead of time.

4. Meeting Procedures

An IEP eligibility meeting generally proceeds as follows:

- general introductions
- review of school material
- review of any material you want to introduce, and
- discussion of whether your child qualifies for special education and, if so, on what basis.

Learning Disabilities: Special Requirements for Documenting Eligibility

When an IEP team finds a child eligible for special education based on a learning disability, the team must provide a written statement supporting the determination. The statement must include the following:

- basis for making the determination
- relevant behavior noted during observations of the child
- relationship of that behavior and the child's academic functioning
- degree of discrepancy between achievement and ability that cannot be corrected without special education, and
- effects of environmental, economic, or cultural conditions on the child.

Each member of the IEP team must state whether the determination of eligibility reflects her own conclusion. If it does not, that member must submit a separate statement presenting her conclusions. (34 C.F.R. § 300.543.) The purpose of this requirement is to ensure that the IEP team does not qualify a child as learning disabled based on the wrong reasons—such as economic disadvantage.

For more information on eligibility requirements for children with learning disabilities, see *Nolo's IEP Guide: Learning Disabilities,* by Lawrence Siegel.

5. Outcome of Meeting

If the school district determines that your child is eligible for special education, then it will prepare for the IEP program meeting—to happen immediately after the eligibility meeting (see Section D, below) or on another date. If the school district finds that your child is not eligible for special education, see Section E, below.

D. Joint IEP Eligibility/ Program Meeting

The school district may combine the IEP eligibility and program meetings into one. In such a situation, your child would be found eligible for special education, and then the IEP team would shift gears and immediately begin developing the IEP program—goals and objectives, program, placement, services, and the like. Holding one meeting may save you time and scheduling headaches, but it also requires that you do a lot of preparation up front. If you're not ready to discuss the IEP program at the IEP eligibility meeting, ask for another meeting to give yourself time to prepare.

On the other hand, if you'd like to combine the meetings (assuming your child is found eligible), ask the school district to do so. Make your request well before the scheduled eligibility meeting so everyone will have enough time to prepare.

A sample Request for Joint IEP Eligibility/ Program Meeting is below; a blank, tear-out copy is in Appendix 5.

E If Your Child Is Not Found Eligible for Special Education

You may attend the IEP eligibility meeting, point out significant information supporting your child's eligibility, and argue your point in a manner worthy of Clarence Darrow—all to no avail. What then? You have two options.

1. Exercise Your Due Process Rights

As explained in Chapter 2, due process is your right to take any dispute you have with your child's district—whether a disagreement about an assessment, eligibility, or any part of the IEP—to a neutral third party to help you resolve your dispute. Due process is covered in Chapter 12.

2. Seek Eligibility Under Section 504 of the Rehabilitation Act

Section 504 of the federal Rehabilitation Act (29 U.S.C. § 794) is a disability-rights law entirely separate from IDEA. It requires all agencies that receive federal financial assistance to provide "access" to individuals with disabilities. Historically, Section 504 has been used to require public agencies to install wheelchair accessible ramps, accessible rest rooms, and other building features, and to provide interpreters at meetings. Section 504 also requires school districts to ensure that children with disabilities are provided access to educational programs and services through physical modifications (such as ramps, widened doorways, and accessible restrooms and other school facilities) and assistance from interpreters, note takers, readers, and the like.

Your child may be entitled to assistance under Section 504 even if he or she is not eligible under IDEA. The first step in the process is to refer your child for Section 504 services—this simply means asking the school to consider your child's eligibility under Section 504. Some school districts automatically consider children who are found ineligible under IDEA for Section 504 services; if yours does not, request—in writing—that it do so.

Once a child has been referred, the school will evaluate his or her eligibility. It will look at:

- whether the child has a physical or mental impairment
- whether the child's impairment substantially limits the child's "major life activities," including learning, and
- what types of accommodations the child needs in order to receive a free, appropriate public education.

If your child is found eligible for help under Section 504, the school must develop a written plan, describing the modifications, accommodations, and services your child will receive. Like an IEP, the Section 504 plan must be individually tailored to meet your child's needs. Many schools have developed a standard form for Section 504 plans; ask your school if it has one.

Because Section 504 tries to achieve the same result as IDEA—to give your child the help necessary for academic success—many of the tips and strategies described in this book will be useful to you as you develop a Section 504 plan for your child. The eligibility, procedural, and other requirements of Section 504 are different from IDEA's requirements, however. Because this book focuses on the IEP process, you'll need to get more information on Section 504 if you decide to proceed.

 For more information on Section 504, contact the U.S. Department of Education, Office of Civil Rights (contact information is in Appendix 2), your school district, your local community advisory committee, or one of the disability groups listed in Appendix 3. You can find a copy of the Section 504 regulations in Appendix 1.

Request for Joint IEP Eligibility/Program Meeting

Date: __March 10, 20xx__

To: __Valerie Sheridan__

__McKinley Unified School District__

__1345 South Drive__

__Topeka, KS 00078__

Re: __Carl Ralston, student in fourth-grade, Eisenhower School__

I believe there is sufficient information for us to discuss both my child's eligibility for special education and the specifics of my child's IEP at the same meeting. I would appreciate it if you would plan enough time to discuss both those important items at the __April 14, 20xx__ IEP meeting. I would also like to see any and all reports and other written material that you will be introducing at the IEP meeting, at least two weeks before the meeting.

Thanks in advance for your help. I hope to hear from you soon.

Sincerely,

Albert Ralston

__Albert Ralston__

__78 Elm Drive__

__Topeka, KS 00078 Elm Drive__

__Phones: 555-1111 (home); 555-2222 (work)__

8

Exploring Your Options and Making Your Case

Once your child is found eligible for special education, the IEP team must decide what type of instruction and assistance your child will receive. This chapter will help you develop material supporting your child's special education needs. By now, you should have a copy of your child's school file and the school district's assessment report. You should also have developed a rudimentary IEP blueprint for your child. In addition, you may have spoken to other parents, your child's teacher and classroom aide, your child's pediatrician, and others who have recently observed your child. In other words, you may have a mountain of information available—and you may not know exactly how to put it to use.

The key to a successful IEP meeting is developing and using information that supports your position regarding your child's educational needs. This chapter will explain how to:

- review your child's school file and the school district's assessment report (Section A)
- keep tabs on your child's current progress in school (Section B)
- look into available special education programs and services—both in and out of the school district—that may be appropriate for your child (Sections C and D)
- figure out whether available programs and services fit your child's education needs and whether you need additional information to make your case (Section E), and
- make a list of other materials you might generate to support your position, such as an independent assessment, a statement from your child's teacher, or a statement from your child's pediatrician or other professional (Sections F and G).

Key Elements for Child's Program

Child: William Smith		
Date: June 1, 20xx		
Desired IEP Components	District Material	District Position
Placement in regular class	4-4-98 Assessment	Agrees, p. 4
1:1 aide for regular class	4-4-98 Assessment	No position
	3-12-98 Biweekly Teacher Report	Teacher agrees
Adaptive Physical Ed.	5-2-98 Adaptive P.E. Assessment	Disagrees (but see comment on p. 5)

Chapter 10 provides a system for organizing all of your materials—positive and negative—to best make your case at your child's IEP meeting.

A. Review the School District's Information

Your first step in preparing for the IEP program meeting is to figure out what position the school will probably take, and whether you can use any of the school district's own documents and statements to show that your child needs a particular program. Start by reviewing all of the information you've received from the school district. As you look over your child's school file, assessment report, and other school district items, there are several issues to consider.

1. Read Between the Lines

Can you figure out what position the school district will take simply by reading your child's file and assessment report? Sometimes it's easy—for example, if the report says "Martha qualifies for special education as a student with specific learning disabilities," or "Henry needs speech therapy twice a week," you'll know exactly where the school district stands. Sometimes it's not so clear. For example, the report might say, "Henry has difficulty in producing the 'th' and 's' sounds" but not mention needed services. Don't be surprised to find more vague statements than definitive ones.

2. Where to Look for the School District's Position

You can find the school district's position in a variety of material. It is most likely to come up in an assessment report, but you may also find the school district's position in a letter, teacher report or memo, your child's report cards, or another written item in your child's file. Your child's teacher, the school assessor, or another district employee may even have stated the school district's position in a conversation.

If the school district employee's statement supports your position, be sure to send a confirming letter (see Chapter 4, Section A7).

3. Sources of the School District's Data

It's important to figure out who is saying what in the school district's material. These speakers are the district's experts, and their opinions will greatly influence the IEP process. Specifically, you'll want to know each person's:

- name and position—for example, a teacher, teacher's aide, or assessor
- training and expertise, and
- first-hand experience with your child.

4. Keeping Track of the School District's Statements

Once you've reviewed all of the information available from the school district, make a chart like the one shown to highlight key elements of your child's program (see your blueprint for ideas), whether the school district agrees or disagrees with your position, and where in the school district's materials the issue is addressed. Note where the school district's data supports or opposes your position, and where you have gaps to be filled—little or no information to show that a particular program or service is necessary for your child to receive an appropriate education. Finally, note the source of the information—was it in writing, or did someone say it to you?

5. Changing a Report or Assessment

If there is something in your child's school file or the assessment report that is inaccurate and harmful to your child, find out whether the school district is willing to change the statement. Start with a phone call. For example:

"Hello, Mr. Crandel, I'm Vickie Jones's father. I read your assessment, and I appreciate your help in evaluating Vicki's needs. I did want to ask you a question. You say on page 4 that Vickie does not need help with her reading comprehension. Did you see the teacher's report, which says that she needs one-on-one reading help?"

To make a formal request for a change, see Chapter 3, Section B5 (changing something in a school file) and Chapter 6, Section E (changing a draft assessment report).

B. Keep Tabs on Your Child's Progress

As you prepare for an IEP program meeting, take some time to learn how your child is currently doing in school—in regular or special education. If your child is doing poorly in school and you're preparing for an IEP eligibility meeting, you'll want to describe at the IEP meeting exactly how your child is floundering. If you are preparing for an IEP program meeting, be ready to explain why the current program is right for your child or why it needs changing.

Here are a few suggestions for getting current information about your child:

- Ask the teacher, teacher's aide, and service provider for periodic reports focusing on key areas of need for your child—reading, behavior, language development, social interaction, spelling, physical mobility, and the like.

- Ask the teacher for samples and reports of your child's work.
- Visit your child's class (see Section C, below).
- Set up periodic meetings with your child's teacher. If your child already has an IEP, ask the teacher whether the current IEP goals and objectives are being met.

Example:

One of your child's current IEP objectives is to read a three-paragraph story and demonstrate 80% comprehension by answering questions. Ask the teacher if your child can read a three-paragraph story. Then ask about your child's reading comprehension level. If it's not up to 80%, where is it—60%? 40%? 20%?

To easily organize this material, you can create a chart for your child's teacher to complete on a regular (such as monthly) basis, updating your child's progress in key areas such as math, reading, behavior, and motor development, as well as emotional and psychological issues and self-help skills.

A sample Progress Chart is below; a blank, tear-out copy is in Appendix 5. You can tailor this chart to your child's particular goals and objectives. This form will help you track your child's general progress, as well as whether your child is meeting the IEP goals and objectives. (See Chapter 9 for more details on developing goals and objectives.)

C. Explore Available School Programs

To prepare for the IEP program meeting, you will want to gather information about your child's existing program and other possible programs that may be appropriate for your child.

Program possibilities include:

Progress Chart

Student: Mary Hamilton

Class: Ms. Frank's 3rd Grade

Date: February 23, 20xx

Key Goals and Objectives	Current Status	Comments
Math	Progressing appropriately? [X] yes [ ] no	On schedule to complete goals and objectives.
Reading	Progressing appropriately? [X] yes [ ] no	On schedule to complete goals and objectives. Needs to improve reading fluidity.
Writing	Progressing appropriately? [X] yes [ ] no	On schedule to complete goals and objectives.
Spelling	Progressing appropriately? [ ] yes [X] no	Reversals continue to be problem.
Social-behavioral	Progressing appropriately? [ ] yes [X] no	Still problems with focus; hard time not teasing others.
Language development	Progressing appropriately? [X] yes [ ] no	On schedule, but some problems going from specific to general.
Motor development	Progressing appropriately? [ ] yes [X] no	Small motor problems affecting handwriting.
Other	Progressing appropriately? [ ] yes [X] no	When struggling with spelling and handwriting, seems to feel high level of stress.

- placement in a regular classroom, perhaps with support services—ask about local options, including your child's neighborhood school
- placement in a program designed specifically for children with learning disabilities, difficulties with communication, or other disabling conditions—ask about special day classes at your neighborhood school, nearby schools, or other schools in the area, or
- placement in a specialized program, such as a private school or residential program— ask about the existence and location of any such programs.

1. Ask About Available Programs

Contact your child's teacher, the school assessor, the district special education administrator, other parents, your PTA, and your local community advisory committee. Ask about programs generally used for children with similar needs.

The school administrator (or even the classroom teacher) may be reluctant to tell you about programs. You may hear, for example, "It is way too early to be looking at programs for next year, Mr. and Mrs. Smith. We've just started this year." Or "We don't think it is appropriate to discuss programs until the IEP team meets and drafts goals and objectives. Then we can talk about programs."

Although school personnel may have reasons for making assertions like these, you have every right to find out about available program options. Emphasize that you are not looking to change programs or force an early IEP decision—you are merely trying to gather information. You might respond, "I appreciate what you are saying, Ms. Casey, but it will really be helpful to me and my child to begin as early as possible, so we can plan ahead. I am not looking for a change in programs or for a commitment on your part. Is there some

reason why I shouldn't gather information about programs in the district?"

2. Visit Programs

The best way to find out what a particular school or program has to offer is to spend some time there. However, while a school administrator may provide you with some information about existing programs, she may be reluctant for you to actually visit a program before the IEP meeting. Although the IEP team may not know which program will meet your child's needs until after you have the IEP meeting, nothing in IDEA prevents you from visiting potential programs before the meeting, as long as your requests are reasonable.

If the administrator refuses to let you visit programs, put your concerns in writing.

A sample Program Visitation Request letter is below; a blank, tear-out copy is in Appendix 5.

If the administrator still refuses your request, don't give up. Indicate that you understand her concerns, but feel that you could not possibly make a decision in the IEP about placement without some basic information about available programs. Make it clear that you are more than willing to visit programs again after the IEP meeting.

If you get nowhere, contact the administrator's superior. If that fails, you can file a complaint with your state department of education or other appropriate educational agency, as discussed in Chapter 13. The complaint might not be processed until after the IEP meeting. If this happens, you'll have to decide whether to postpone the IEP or ask (at the IEP meeting) to see the programs after the meeting. In that case, you may not be ready to sign the IEP. (See Chapter 11, Section E, for information on signing the IEP.)

Program Visitation Request Letter

Date: _April 6, 20xx_

To: Mr. John White, Special Education Administrator

Carlson Unified School District

8709 Fourth Street

Helena, MT 00087

Re: Elizabeth Moore

I appreciate the concerns you have, and I realize that you can't know what programs are appropriate for my child until after the IEP meeting. Nonetheless, I think it would be very helpful for me to see existing programs so I can be a more effective member of the IEP team. I do not feel I can make an informed IEP decision without seeing, firsthand, all possible options. I want to assure you that I understand that by giving me the names of existing programs, you are not stating an opinion as to their appropriateness for my child.

I assure you that I will abide by all rules and regulations for parental visits. If those rules and regulations are in writing, please send me a copy.

Thanks in advance for your help. I hope to hear from you soon.

Sincerely,

Arnette Moore

Arnette Moore

87 Mission Road

Helena, MT 00087

Phones: 555-3334 (home); 555-4455 (work)

Obviously, you don't need a school administrator's permission to visit private programs in the area. Simply call and schedule your own appointments.

a. When to Visit Programs

Ideally, you will want to visit programs in the fall of the school year. While it may seem logical to visit right before the IEP meeting, checking out possible program options earlier offers these advantages:

- The sooner you see a particular program, the sooner you'll have a sense of whether or not it is appropriate for your child.
- If you can't judge whether a particular program is a good fit for your child, there will be time for others, such as an independent assessor, to take a look and give you an opinion.
- You'll have time to visit a program more than once, if necessary.

b. Visitation Guidelines

The purpose of your visits is to gather information. As you plan your visits, keep in mind these points:

- Ask to visit *all* program options.
- Follow the policies and rules established by the school district, school site administrator, and teacher.
- If an independent assessor or other professional will attend the IEP meeting, it is a good idea to have him visit with you. Be sure to inform the school district ahead of time.
- Do not ask for any personal information about the students, such as names of individual children. A teacher should *not* give you this information. You can (and should) talk with any parents you know who have children in the programs.
- Secure as much detail as possible about each program or class. Include the same catego-

ries of information you use in your blueprint (see Chapter 5):

- ▲ student description (number of students in the program; students' disabilities, age, cognitive range, and language range)
- ▲ staff description (details on teachers and aides)
- ▲ teacher-student instruction (teacher-to-class, small group, or individual)
- ▲ curricula, methodology, and other teaching strategies used
- ▲ classroom environment (behavior problems, noise level, number of teachers and teacher aides, and how much time teacher aides spend in class)
- ▲ related services (how many children leave the class to go to another program and how often; how many children receive related services in the class), and
- ▲ any other comments you have on the program.

IDEA does not require that the teacher provide you with this information, so you should ask in a pleasant, matter-of-fact way. If the teacher balks, indicate that the information you seek is important and noncontroversial, and should be made available.

Write down your observations and the answers to your questions. You can write as you watch the class and talk to the teacher. If you "interview" the teacher with notebook in hand and pencil poised, however, the teacher may be intimidated. By saying, "I have a poor memory; do you mind if I take notes while we talk?," you may put the teacher at ease. If not, try to take notes in an unobtrusive way, or wait until you're outside and write down what you remember as soon as possible.

A sample Class Visitation Checklist is below; a blank, tear-out copy is in Appendix 5. Be sure to keep copies of this important form in your IEP binder.

Class Visitation Checklist

Date: 9/11/04   Time: 9:00-10:15   a.m./~~p.m.~~

School: Jefferson School, Chicago

Class: Third-grade Special Day Class for Learning Disabled (Teacher: Sue Avery)

Student Description:

Total students: 17   Gender range: 12 boys, 5 girls

Age range: 7 - 10 (ten kids are nine or younger; seven ten-year olds)

Cognitive range: "Wide range, probably from pre-K through 5th-grade skills," says S. Avery (teacher)

Language/communication range: Two students with hearing impairment, two other students with delayed communication skills (1st-grade level)

Disability range: 12 students have specific learning disability, three are borderline retarded, one has emotional disturbance, and one autistic-like behavior

Behavioral range: Five students acting out throughout class, four other students constantly demanding of teacher. Two students sent to principal because of behavior. Rest of class generally cooperative, quiet.

Other observations: Overall impression was of a class of children with varied needs and behavior, which made it difficult for the teacher to focus on any one group of children for very long.

Staff Description:

Teachers: Sue Avery has four years' experience working with learning disabled children. She was generally very patient with students (less so with the behaviorally troubled children), but she seemed easily distracted.

Aides: In class two hours per day; worked with all children, no one child more than few minutes. Seemed mostly to check in with students superficially, but not provide any sustained 1:1 help. Aide has no specific training working with learning disabled children.

Other observations: Neither teacher nor aide seemed fully comfortable with curriculum, particularly given varied needs of students. Both were very nice to students.

Curricula/Classroom Strategies:

Curricula: "Using Mathematics," (Book 2) for math, teacher-developed materials for spelling, and "Project Explore" for science lessons.

Strategies: Teacher/aide when working 1:1 in reading divided words into simple sounds using much repetition; no overall strategy or specific curriculum designed for learning disabled children.

Classroom Environment:

Description: Classroom had tiled floor so sound echoed. Quite loud; no other apparent acoustical treatment to reduce noise; all added to a noisy room. Various work stations and cubicles set up so students can work 1:1 or by themselves. Somewhat effective, but noise was distracting to all students. Classroom situated near playground, so much visual stimulation outside classroom window and noise from outside.

Related Services:

At least four students received their related services in class, one had speech therapy, another had a special aide who worked with her in the corner.

Other Comments:

School site principal (Lee Parsons) is interested in special education but has no training or expertise in the field. She did express reservations about excessive mainstreaming of children with disabilities into regular classrooms. Visited one mainstreamed class; teacher seemed interested, but expressed concern that the school had not provided any support or training for dealing with special education students in her regular class.

How This Program Relates to IEP Blueprint:

Program does not meet Tara's blueprint:
- Cognitive and behavioral range of students too wide
- Teacher unable to provide individual attention
- Aide not trained for working with L-D kids
- Question about curriculum

D. Find Out About Related Services

Classroom programs are only one component of your child's IEP program. Related services, such as occupational, physical, or speech therapy, are also very important (see Chapter 2).

Gathering information about related services will be a little different from gathering information about programs. You'll still want to talk to your child's teacher, the school assessor, the district special education administrator, other parents, your PTA, and a local parent group for disabled children to find out about related services for children with similar needs. But the similarities end there.

Service providers, such as physical therapists, usually work one-on-one with individual children or in small groups. So visiting these specialists in action may not be possible. Instead, when you talk to people about the services available, ask about the background, training, and experience of the specialists. Candid conversations with other parents should be most helpful.

Keep detailed notes of your conversations and include them in your IEP binder.

E. Compare Your Blueprint With the Existing Programs and Services

Once you have information about your school district's programs and services, compare what's available to what you believe your child needs. Obviously, if the school provides services you feel will meet your child's needs (as described in your blueprint), the IEP process should be relatively simple. On the other hand, if there is a gap between what your child needs and what is available, you face the task of convincing the IEP team that the school options are inappropriate.

You'll need to detail the shortcomings of the programs and services offered by the school district. Be as specific as possible: Is the problem the frequency or location of a service, the pupil-teacher ratio, the qualifications of the teacher or service provider, the specific work to be done with a service provider, the class makeup, the teacher methodology, the curriculum, or other important features?

Make a comprehensive, side-by-side comparison of your blueprint and what you know about the school's options, and put the details on the bottom of the Class Visitation Checklist.

F. Generate Additional Supporting Information

Once you've reviewed your child's school file, developed your blueprint, reviewed the school assessment, evaluated your child's progress, and gathered information about program and service options, you may need further data to support your goals. This material will be invaluable in preparing for the IEP meeting.

1. Help From School Personnel

Contact any teachers, assessors, or service providers who are likely to support your position. You can do this by phone or in person. Explain what programs and services you want for your child (your blueprint), and why you feel they are appropriate. Note any discrepancy between what you want and what you believe the school district has available. Explain why you want what you want for your child and ask for their ideas and opinions.

Ask if the teacher, assessor, or service provider would be willing to write a statement supporting what you want for your child or to state his position at the IEP meeting.

If you talk to someone who supports your point of view but doesn't want to put anything in writing, follow up the conversation with a confirming letter (see Chapter 4, Section A), such as, "Thank you for the chance to chat today. I appreciate your frankness and was glad to hear that you agree that Max needs an aide in order to function effectively in the regular class."

Be aware that a confirming letter can put the teacher in an awkward position. If the teacher says one thing to you (and you confirm it in a letter) and then says another thing at the IEP meeting, the letter may be important proof of what was originally said—but this may lead to some friction between you and the teacher. If the teacher will not speak frankly at the IEP meeting, however, the confirming letter will be valuable proof of what was said earlier—and might discourage the teacher from changing her tune.

No matter what, be sure to keep notes of what was said, including the date, time, and place of the conversation, in as much detail as possible. This is your record in case the school representative changes his mind later.

2. Help From People Outside the School

Anyone who knows your child or has some expertise in special education or your child's disability may be of value. This includes your child's doctor, tutor, therapist, or other specialist.

Ask each person to write a letter to the IEP team stating:

- how she knows your child
- her expertise
- any specific comments on your child's condition and educational experience, and
- her recommendation for your child in terms of programs, services, or other IEP components.

Example:

"Teresa needs extensive help with small and large motor skills, and should work with an occupational and physical therapist at least three times a week."

G. Independent Assessments

An independent assessment may be the most important document supporting what you want for your child. An independent assessment, like the school district's assessment, can be as comprehensive or as narrow as your child's needs dictate. In most cases, an independent assessment will use a variety of tests to evaluate your child's needs.

Chapter 6 discusses assessments in general, and Chapter 11 covers how to present an independent assessment at the IEP meeting.

Under IDEA, you have an absolute right to have an independent assessment of your child. Moreover, your school district is required to provide you with information on where you can get an individual assessment. (34 C.F.R. § 300.502(a).)

While IDEA requires the school district to consider the results of the independent assessment in making any decision regarding your child's education, it does not require that your school district agree with the results. While an independent assessment may include persuasive information, your child's school district can reject the conclusions. (You do have the right to go to due process (mediation session or hearing) to prove the district is wrong. See Chapter 12.)

1. When to Use an Independent Assessment

You may want an independent assessment because you need more information about your child or because the school district's assessment does not support what you want. If the district's position is clear—and you disagree with it—an outside assessment may very well be needed.

2. Finding Independent Assessors

Independent assessors generally work in private practice or are affiliated with hospitals, universities, or other large institutions. How do you find a qualified independent assessor? Here are a few tips:

- Ask parents of children with similar disabilities. Check with the PTA or your school district's advisory committee of parents with children in special education.
- Get recommendations from the school. A trusted teacher, aide, service provider, or other school employee may be able to give you the names of independent assessors.
- Talk to your child's pediatrician.
- Call a local hospital, particularly a university medical hospital. A department that employs experts in your child's disability may be able to do the assessment or refer you to an independent assessor.
- Contact an organization that specializes in your child's particular disability. (See Appendix 3.)
- Call local private schools for disabled children. Private schools often work with credible independent assessors.

How Not to Find an Independent Assessor

Assessors are often psychologists. If you look in the phone book, you will see a long list of psychologists. But choosing randomly from the phone book is a poor method for selecting a reputable and knowledgeable assessor. The only thing you really know about these people is that they could afford to pay for a listing.

3. Selecting the Right Assessor

Speak to various independent assessors, and ask the following questions for each person:

- Does the assessor have significant expertise, training, and experience in dealing with your child's disability?
- Is the assessor affiliated with a well-respected institution?
- Were you referred by someone who actually worked with the assessor?
- Do you trust the person (or institution) who recommended the assessor?
- Will the assessor give you references?
- Did the assessor's references like the results of the assessor's work and find the assessor easy to work with?
- Is the assessor impartial? (An assessor who has previously done work for—and been paid by—your child's school district may not be truly independent.)
- Can the assessor complete the assessment and written report well in advance of the IEP meeting?
- Can the assessor attend the IEP meeting, if necessary?

The answers to these questions, your own sense of the assessor, and recommendations from others are key factors in making your decision. It is also important that the independent assessor be able to clearly articulate her position, professionally and vigorously.

4. Getting an Independent Assessor on Your Side

The reason you are hiring an independent assessor is to support your educational goals for your child. Be very clear on your plans and perspectives.

Examples:

- You have very specific desires (your blue-print) concerning the related service you believe is best for your child—you know what you want in terms of type, amount, and duration of service; type of service provider; and teacher-pupil setting. Be sure the assessor makes recommendations that support the program and services you want for your child: "Given Michelle's need to develop expressive speech, she requires speech therapy four times a week, each session of 50 minutes. She also needs one-to-one work with a qualified speech thera-pist experienced in working with children who have an expressive language delay."
- You want your son placed in a school for children with emotional disturbances. Ideally, the assessor will write, "Philip requires placement in a program with no more than ten children, a full-time aide, a teacher qualified to work with emotionally troubled children, and a class where there are no behavioral problems. The Woodson School in Boston is the only program that can meet Philip's needs."

If the assessor can't or won't name a specific school or program, then make sure she will name the specific components of an appropriate program. Continuing the example above, if the independent assessor won't say Philip needs to be placed in the Woodson School, she should say that he needs placement in a program that has the characteristics of the Woodson School.

It is of course possible that your goals may not be supported by the data. A good assessor will not write something he disagrees with or make a recommendation he does not believe in. A good assessor will tell you when the evidence—the testing data—does not support what you want.

You want an assessor who will:

- show you a draft assessment report
- consider your concerns about the draft report

- make specific recommendations about your child's educational status and appropriate programs and related services to meet your child's needs, and
- provide a written rationale for these recommendations.

5. How an Independent Assessment Proceeds

Most independent assessors will meet with you and review your child's school file, the school district's assessment, and other district material. The assessor will then explain what testing will be done, secure your approval, do the testing, and prepare a report. Depending on your child's characteristics and needs, the assessor may also want to observe the child in class.

6. When to Submit the Independent Assessment

Just as you want to review the school district's assessments before the IEP meeting, the school district will likely want to see your independent assessment before the IEP meeting. Of course, the more time the school has to review the independent assessment, the more time the administration will have to find data to counter its conclusions. Does this mean you should delay giving the school district your assessment? While such a strategy has its attractions, the bottom line is that the school district is entitled to the same courtesy that you are.

Holding off on giving the district a copy of your assessment could ultimately prove counter-productive. The district may distrust you and your assessment. The delay may be grounds for post-poning the IEP meeting. And your relationship with the district may be affected. Because you will likely be working together for many years, you should maintain a positive relationship, if possible. If one party will be nasty, unfair, or un-trustworthy, let it be someone other than you.

While there is no hard-and-fast rule here, providing the independent assessment (and other key material) a week before the IEP meeting is usually appropriate.

7. Cost of an Independent Assessment

Independent assessments can be quite costly, anywhere from several hundred dollars to several thousand dollars.

But you may not have to pay for the assessment. Under IDEA, a parent has the right to an independent educational evaluation of her child (by an assessor of your choosing) at public expense if you disagree with an evaluation obtained by the school district. The school district must pay for that independent assessment unless it exercises its due process rights under IDEA and convinces the hearing officer that the school district evaluation was appropriate. (34 C.F.R. § 300.502(b).)

While a school district rarely proceeds to due process on the issue of paying for an independent assessment, that doesn't mean your school district won't. To win, the district has to show only that its own evaluation was appropriate, the appropriate tests were used, the assessor was properly trained and knowledgeable, and your child was evaluated in all areas of suspected disability. The district must either pay for the independent assessment or initiate due process "without unnecessary delay." (34 C.F.R. § 300.502(b)(2).)

So the real problem for parents is how to get the district to pay for the assessment, particularly because IDEA does not require the school district to pay in advance or provide assurances that it will pay for the independent assessment. If you want the school district to pay, you will probably have to pay the assessor yourself and seek reimbursement from the district.

Here are some ideas on getting the district to pay:

- Ask the assessor to bill the school district directly. Because the assessor wants to be paid, she may not be willing to do this. But there's no harm in asking.

- If the assessor won't bill the district, pay her bill and submit a copy to the district, with a cover letter explaining that IDEA requires the district to pay unless it pursues due process. Refer to the law, too. (34 C.F.R. § 300.502.)

- If the district doesn't go to due process and still won't pay, file a complaint (as discussed in Chapter 13). ■

9

Writing Goals and Objectives

Goals and objectives are the nuts and bolts of your child's education: the academic, cognitive, linguistic, social, and vocational aims you have for your child (goals) and the specific things your child will need to accomplish (objectives) to reach those goals. Objectives might be the skills your child will need to master to achieve a particular goal, or they might be benchmarks you can use to determine whether a goal has been met. An IEP program may include one or many objectives for each broad goal.

Examples:

Goal. Tim will improve his reading comprehension.

Objective. Tim will read a four-paragraph story and demonstrate 75% comprehension using objective classroom tests.

Goal. Ellen will improve her peer relationships.

Objective. Ellen will initiate three positive peer interactions each day, per teacher observation.

Goal. Juan will master all third-grade math skills.

Objective. Juan will identify sets of ones and tens with 90% accuracy, using appropriate textbook tests.

Goal. Jane will improve her writing skills.

Objective. Jane will write a three-sentence paragraph with subject and predicate sentences, per teacher evaluation.

Goal. Mark will improve short-term auditory memory.

Objective. Mark will be able to listen to a set of ten related items and list them with 75% accuracy.

IDEA requires that an IEP program include a statement of measurable annual goals, including benchmarks or short-term objectives, for two reasons (34 C.F.R. § 300.347(a)(2)):

- to ensure that the child is involved and progressing in the general curriculum, and
- to meet the child's other educational needs that result from the child's disability.

Because IDEA requires the school district to provide an appropriate education for your child, the question underlying many IEP decisions is, "Can this child's goals and objectives be met in a specific program or with a particular related service?" Your child's ability to meet the goals and objectives may very well determine whether the school district is providing an appropriate education.

What Goals and Objectives Are Not

- Goals and objectives are not used for students who are in regular education. They are written for special education students—even special education students who are mainstreamed into regular classes.
- Goals and objectives are not part of a contract between you and the school district—that is, the school is not legally liable if your child does not meet the goals and objectives. Goals and objectives are a way to measure your child's progress.
- Goals and objectives are not the totality of your child's instructional plan. They are important aims to be accomplished during the school year.

A. Areas Covered by Goals and Objectives

Goals and objectives can cover a wide variety of skill or need areas. If your child is not having difficulties in certain areas, however, the IEP team typically will not develop goals and objectives in those areas.

Goals and objectives can cover a wide range of areas, including:

- academic skills, such as math computation, reading comprehension, spelling, and writing
- cognitive skills, such as abstract thinking and memory
- emotional and psychological issues, such as overcoming fears or improving self-esteem
- social-behavioral skills, such as relating to peers
- linguistic and communication skills, such as expressing oneself effectively
- self-help and independent living skills, such as using money, dressing, using transportation, or using the toilet
- physical and recreational skills, such as improving fine and large motor skills
- vocational skills, such as work skill development, and
- transition skills, such as exploring work or college options.

Congress may change the rules that apply to goals and objectives. Congress is likely to reauthorize IDEA in 2004—which gives our elected officials an opportunity not only to appropriate funds for the law, but also to amend it. One possible change that has been widely discussed is eliminating (or modifying) the requirement of goals and objectives. To find out whether Congress has taken action, check with your school district, state department of education, or local support group. You can also check Nolo's website, www.nolo.com, for information on any changes to IDEA.

B. Developing Goals and Objectives

IDEA does not specify how to write goals and objectives, what subjects to cover, how many to include, or how to implement or measure them. The details are up to the IEP team. This flexibility allows you to develop goals and objectives that will be useful in conjunction with the programs and services you want for your child.

This section describes the typical elements of goals and objectives.

A sample Goals and Objectives form appears later in this chapter. Also, see the section on goals and objectives in the sample IEP in Appendix 4.

1. Child's Present Level of Performance

The IEP program should spell out your child's current level of skill in each particular goal-objective area. For example, for a reading comprehension goal and objective, a child's present level of performance may state, "Beth's current reading comprehension is at the mid–fourth-grade level. She enjoys reading but requires help in maintaining focus."

2. Who Implements Goals and Objectives

Your child's classroom teacher is usually responsible for implementing your child's goals and objectives. Depending on the goal and objectives, however, an aide or support professional may also be involved. For example:

- A child's language goals and objectives may be the responsibility of a speech therapist.
- Physical education or motor goals, such as handwriting improvement, may be the responsibility of an occupational or physical therapist.

- Emotional goals and objectives may be covered by a school counselor or therapist.

3. Completion Dates for Goals and Objectives

Goals and objectives are normally written for a one-year period, but this is not set in stone. In fact, because objectives are concrete, bite-sized, manageable tasks, they may be completed in less than a year.

Example:

Lily is in a special day class with no mainstreaming in a regular classroom. Her IEP reading goal and objective have a completion time of one year. Lily's parents feel that she could reach her reading goal and objective more quickly if she were in a regular classroom. Establishing a shorter period may help her parents convince the school that Lily should be mainstreamed.

4. Measuring Goals and Objectives

IDEA requires a child's goals and objectives to be "measurable." There are a number of ways to measure goals and objectives, including objective testing, teacher or other staff observation, assessment of work samples, or any other method agreed to by the IEP team. Many IEP goals and objectives include a quantifiable accomplishment level, such as "Mia will read a four-paragraph story with 90% reading comprehension as measured by the Woodcock Reading Mastery Test."

Don't Set Your Objectives Too Low

Be wary if an IEP team member from the school district suggests setting your child's objectives fairly low. The district may want to set low standards so your child can achieve them without too much help from the school. If the school wants to eliminate a particular support service (such as a one-on-one aide) or keep your child in a special day class rather than mainstreaming him or her in a regular class, it might propose objectives that your child can meet without this extra help.

IDEA does not require goals and objectives to be quantifiable—that is, capable of being measured in numbers. Although numbers can be of value, not everything of value can be reduced to numbers. For example, how does one measure numerically whether goals and objectives were met in areas relating to emotions, psychology, self-help, or vocational skills?

Example:

As a part of Sue's IEP program, Sue will explore whether she wants to go to college or begin work right after high school. As goals and objectives, these are stated as follows:

Goal. Sue will explore at least five areas of vocational interest.

Objective. Sue will read about five areas of vocational interest, write a brief explanation of each, and visit local examples of each.

The best ways to "measure" Sue's achievement may be teacher observation or Sue's completion of a personal diary.

C. When to Draft Goals and Objectives

While specific goals and objectives are approved at the IEP meeting and included in the IEP program, it makes sense to draft them ahead of time.

In fact, it is not uncommon for school representatives to write goals and objectives in advance. Under IDEA, the school cannot simply present its goals and objectives at the IEP meeting, insist that you accept them, and refuse to discuss alternatives. That would violate a basic tenet of IDEA—that the IEP team makes all IEP decisions as a group, at the meeting. Still, you should anticipate that the school district might draft goals and objectives in advance. Prepare for the IEP meeting by asking the school district (in writing) for a copy of any predrafted goals and objectives at least two weeks in advance.

You, too, should draft goals and objectives in advance of the IEP meeting. You do not have to give a copy to the school district before the IEP meeting unless it asks you to, which would be unlikely. However, even if you aren't asked for a copy, you can give your goals and objectives to the school district in advance. Some advocates might argue against doing this because it gives the district time to counter your goals and objectives. Others argue that if you present your goals and objectives for the first time at the IEP meeting, the school district might need time to review them—and have to postpone the meeting.

In general, it is best to be open and provide the school district information in advance, unless the element of surprise is necessary in your particular situation.

D. Writing Effective Goals and Objectives

Writing goals and objectives for the first time may seem as foreign to you as writing a medical prescription or nuclear physics equation. But don't worry—you'll get the hang of it. Like much of the IEP process, writing goals and objectives requires information gathering, asking questions, and a little practice.

1. Get Your School's IEP Form

Every school district has its own form on which the IEP program is written. As mentioned earlier in this book, you should get a copy and any guidelines that accompany it. As you begin to draft your child's goals and objectives, refer to the school's current IEP form for guidance.

2. Gather Your Information

Your dining room table or desk may be overrun with special education papers. If they are not already organized in a binder (as recommended in Chapter 4), take some time to gather them together. Make sure you have:

- your child's school file
- all assessment reports
- written reports from professionals, and
- your blueprint.

Start with your blueprint—your desires for your child's education. The goals and objectives should support what's in your blueprint. While the blueprint won't show you how to write specific goals and objectives, it will help you think about what you ultimately want for your child. The goals and objectives you create will be the stepping stones your child uses to achieve these ultimate ends.

3. Talk to Professionals

Talk with your child's teacher, other support staff, your independent assessor, service providers, and others who know your child. They might be willing to suggest specific goals and objectives, or at least to review yours.

If this is your child's first IEP, ask the professionals what areas your goals and objectives should cover and how to make them as specific as possible. Be sure to explore with them all the areas that you feel require goals and objectives.

If this is not your child's first IEP, ask professionals the following questions:

- What previous goals and objectives should be retained?
- If previous goals and objectives are carried over, why were they not accomplished before? What can be done to better ensure completion this year? Using the Progress Chart in Chapter 8, Section B, will help you monitor goals and objectives throughout the year.
- What new goals and objectives should be developed?

By talking with your child's teacher and other staff members about goals and objectives, you may learn their opinions about your child's placement and services. You may also develop an informal agreement on goals and objectives before the IEP meeting.

4. Talk to Other Parents

If you know other special education families, ask to see their IEPs, particularly if their child's needs are similar to your child's. Even if the needs are not the same, other parents may have very valuable information about how to draft goals and objectives; many are probably old pros at writing them.

Also, check with the PTA or school district's local advisory committee on special education for written material on goals and objectives, advice, and the names of any local individuals or organizations that provide help to special education parents. (Chapter 15 discusses parent organizations.)

Finally, check Appendix 3 for support organizations you can contact for help.

5. List Your Goals and Objectives Areas

Your job is to develop general goals and specific objectives for each skill area that relates directly to your child's needs. Eight such areas are listed in Section A, above. Be as precise as possible. For example, don't simply state "academic achievement." Specify reading, writing, math, cognitive, spelling, and the rest. Under social-behavioral, you might specify peer goals and objectives as well as self-control goals and objectives.

A sample Goals and Objectives Chart is below; Appendix 5 includes a blank, tear-out copy. This chart is intended to give you a feel for what goals and objectives look like and provide you with language often used for different types of goals and objectives. Also, be sure to see the sample IEP form in Appendix 4.

6. Connect Goals and Objectives to a Specific Program and Services

The best goals and objectives don't only state your immediate expectations for your child's performance, but also provide support for the program and services you want for your child. In fact, the goals and objectives in our sample form do just this. In the case of Leah, the sample is very descriptive—a "small and protected educational environment" and "a quiet and safe school environment." While not all goals and objectives are written this way—schools often argue that goals and objectives are not the place to mention programs or services—IDEA does not prevent such added language. You should argue for it and, at a minimum, include it in your draft goals and objectives.

When referring to a specific program or service, be as precise as you can. If you can mention the name of a special school or the details of the service, so much the better. If you don't have the exact information, then add something that will support your broad IEP program goals.

Goals and Objectives Chart

Skill Area	Annual Goal	Short-Term Objective (or Benchmark)	Present Performance Level	How Progress Measured	Date of Completion
Reading	Ted, in a special day class of no more than 10 students, will improve reading comprehension.	Ted will demonstrate 90% comprehension of three-paragraph stories from the fourth-grade reading text.	Ted demonstrates 50% comprehension of a two-paragraph story from the fourth-grade reading text.	End-of-chapter questions in the reading text.	June 20xx
Math	Bob, in his mainstreamed class, will master fourth-grade math skills.	Bob will subtract a one-digit number from a two-digit number with 90% accuracy.	Bob subtracts a one-digit number from a two-digit number with 25% accuracy.	Teacher material.	June 20xx
Emotional and psychological	Leah, in a class of no more than 12 students in a small and protected educational environment, will reduce her outward anger.	Because Leah is adversely affected by acting out behavior of others, she will, in a quiet and safe school environment, develop a better self-awareness of her anger and reduce her angry outbursts from five to two a day.	Leah averages five daily angry outbursts as observed.	Teacher and therapist observation and recording.	June 20xx

Skill Area	Annual Goal	Short-Term Objective (or Benchmark)	Present Performance Level	How Progress Measured	Date of Completion
Social-behavioral	Sara will improve her peer relationships.	With the support of her aide and in a class of no more than ten students, Sara will initiate three positive peer interactions per day.	Sara is unable to initiate positive peer interactions.	Teacher-aide observation and recording.	June 20xx
Linguistic and communication	Adam, in his triweekly, 45-minute, one-to-one speech therapy sessions, will improve articulation.	Adam will produce the s, sh and c sounds.	Adam produces the s, sh and c sounds irregularly.	Speech therapist observation and recording.	June 20xx
Self-help and independent living skills (transition services	Nina will develop independent living skills.	Nina, with the support of her regular classroom peers, will be able to purchase her lunch in the school cafeteria, make change, locate her school bus, and take that bus home.	Nina cannot make change and is unable to ask for help in locating her bus.	Teacher and other staff observation and recording.	June 20xx

The key is to write the goals and objectives so that an objective person will conclude that your child will need the particular program or service to meet the goals and objectives. Even if the school district doesn't include the language in the final goals and objectives, you can use your draft as a reminder of what you want.

Write a variety of goals and objectives for each skill area, incorporating specific language and referring to the desired program and services. Then write a second set, omitting references to the program and services, but describing the programs and services you want. For example, assume you want your child in a regular classroom with a one-to-one aide in order to improve her reading comprehension. The ideal goal would be, "Mary, in Ms. Jones's regular third-grade class at Spencer School, will improve her reading comprehension, using her full-time one-to-one aide." The alternative would be, "With the assistance of her one-to-one aide and by modeling her regular peers, Mary will improve her reading comprehension." If the school district disagrees that Mary should be mainstreamed, suggest implicit, instead of explicit, language, such as "modeling her regular peers."

■

10

Preparing for the IEP Meeting

Now that you've gathered information and figured out what kinds of help your child will need, it's time to get ready for the IEP meting, where you and the school district will hammer out the details of your child's special education program. Preparing for the IEP meeting will make you a better advocate for your child, allow you to influence the IEP meeting agenda effectively, and reduce your own anxieties. In short, preparation increases your chances of success.

If you are attending your first IEP meeting, be sure to read this entire chapter. If you've done IEPs before, you'll want to at least skim this chapter. You might find some new ideas that you can put to use.

While this chapter will help you prepare for the IEP meeting, everything that you've done to this point—gathering your child's school records, having your child assessed, drafting a blueprint, and so on—will be crucial to the success of the meeting. If you've skipped any earlier chapters, you should go back and read them before reading this chapter.

A. Schedule the IEP Meeting

IDEA sets out rules about scheduling the IEP meeting (34 C.F.R. §§ 300.343, 300.349):

- It must be held at a time and location convenient for all parties, especially the parents. The school district cannot simply schedule a meeting on a morning when you must be at work or pick a time without your input.
- It must be held at least once a year.
- It must be long enough to cover all issues.

Do You Need an Interpreter?

The school district must take necessary steps to ensure that you understand the IEP proceedings, including hiring an interpreter if you are deaf or hard of hearing, or if your first language is not English. Be sure to let the school district know in advance if you need an interpreter at the IEP meeting. (34 C.F.R. § 300.345(a)(e).)

1. Date of the IEP Meeting

As discussed in Chapter 4, the best time for the IEP meeting is in the spring preceding the school year for which you are developing the IEP plan. Before you choose a date, you may have to make several calls to the district administrator and your attendees to make sure everyone can attend. Make sure to give yourself at least a month to prepare for the meeting.

2. Length of the IEP Meeting

IDEA does not require that the IEP meeting last for a specific length of time. Before the meeting, ask the school administrator to find out how much time has been put aside. Two or three hours is common. If the administrator has allotted less time than you think is necessary, explain why you think a longer meeting is needed, particularly if it may eliminate the need for a second meeting. If the administrator insists that the time allotted is enough, put your concerns in writing and send a copy to the superintendent of schools. If you're really concerned, you can file a complaint (see Chapter 13), but there is no legal rule setting a minimum length for the IEP.

Sample Letter Requesting More Time for IEP Meeting

Date: September 28, 20xx

To: Ms. Julia Warner
Director of Special Education
Monroe School District
892 South 4th Street
Salem, OR 97307

Re: Karen Jamison, student in first-grade class of Drew Bergman

You indicated that we had one hour for my daughter Karen's October 14th IEP meeting. As I mentioned on September 27, I believe the issues we have to discuss will require at least two hours. It would be a hardship on our family to attend two meetings.

I will be calling you within the next few days to discuss this. I appreciate your understanding in this matter.

Sincerely,

Denise Jamison

Denise Jamison
909 Hanson St.
Salem, OR 97307
Phones: 555-3090 (home); 555-5000 (work)

cc: School Superintendent Phyllis Bander

The initial IEP meeting must be held within 30 days after the school district determines your child is eligible for special education. (34 C.F.R. § 300.343(b)(2).) If this is your child's first IEP meeting and the administrator doesn't set aside enough time, point out that you might have to schedule a second one, which could fall more than 30 days after the eligibility determination and, therefore, violate IDEA.

B. The IEP Meeting Agenda

Knowing the IEP meeting agenda in advance will help you tremendously as you prepare for the meetings. Although IDEA does not require the district to provide you with an agenda, it does require that you be given the opportunity to participate in and understand the proceedings. (34 C.F.R. § 300.345(a)(e).) It would not be unreasonable, therefore, to know what issues will be discussed.

Most IEP meetings cover the following issues:
- your child's current status—how he or she is doing, whether or not previous goals and objectives were fulfilled, and what the current assessments state
- specific goals and objectives
- specific support or related services, and
- specific program, including the type, makeup, and location of the class.

Ask the school district special education administrator for an agenda or a description of the specific issues that will be discussed at the meeting. After you receive it, check it against your blueprint to make sure that the issues you've flagged will be covered at the meeting. If a crucial item is not on the agenda, let the administrator know, preferably in writing.

C. Organize Your Materials

Having access to key material is vitally important in an IEP meeting. You don't want to be fumbling about, looking for that one report or quote that could really help. Following these steps will help you organize the mountain of material.

1. Review Your Blueprint and All Written Material

Your starting point in getting organized is your blueprint. You should also gather all written material, such as assessments, previous IEPs, notes, and reports from your child's teacher and other staff members, work samples, and letters to and from your child's school district. These should all be in your IEP binder, clearly labeled and organized for easy reference.

Review all of these documents. Plan to bring to the meeting everything that supports your blueprint. Also bring any materials that counter the negative points school district representatives might raise.

2. Highlight Supportive Material

Go through your binder and highlight or underline every important positive and negative statement. You may want to tab certain key statements for easy reference. How do you know what statements to highlight? Focus on the following:

- Test results, staff observations, reports, and other information on your child's current educational status. Highlight descriptive statements, such as "Tom scored at the first-grade level on the Brigance Test, Counting Subtest" or "Sheila has difficulty staying focused in class; any activity beyond three to five minutes can be quite taxing for her."
- Recommendations regarding program placement, related services, goals and objectives, and methodology. Look for statements such as "Carla would benefit from 30 minutes of speech therapy a week" or "Jim needs to be in a small classroom in which there are minimal disturbances or acting out behavior."
- The consequences of providing or not providing specific placements, services, methodology, and other program components—for example, "Teri has significant fears about large groups and open space; placing her in a large class on a big campus will increase those fears and put her at risk for serious emotional difficulties."

As you go through all your IEP-related information, you will probably highlight a lot of what you read, making the task of organizing the material seem overwhelming. To make it manageable, use different colored highlighters or tabs to differentiate the important from the less important statements or items—such as yellow for very important, green for somewhat important, and blue for less important. You can also make second copies of all significant items and keep them in a separate section in your IEP binder.

3. Use an IEP Material Organizer Form

Once your material is highlighted, you should take the time to create an additional document that will help you organize and access important information. I call it, for want of a more creative term, an IEP Material Organizer form.

A sample IEP Material Organizer is below; Appendix 5 includes a blank, tear-out copy. Use one page for each major issue.

An IEP Material Organizer divides your written information, notes, and reports into important topics (such as related services or methodologies), keyed to your blueprint. As you can see from the sample, the IEP Material Organizer form allows you to find specific information—such as an assessment report, a pediatrician letter, or key statements made by a teacher or other potential witnesses—that support or dispute your blueprint items.

You can divide the IEP Material Organizer into subtopics that track your child's specific needs. For example, under "placement," you might have subtopics like class size, peer needs, type of class, location of class, and the like. Under the related service of a one-to-one aide, you might add the

IEP Material Organizer Form

Use this form to track documents and persons that provide support for or opposition to your goals.

Issue: _Related Service: 1:1 Aide_

Document or Witness* Name(s):	Binder Location (if applicable)	Helps You	Hurts You	Key Supportive or Oppositional Information	Rebuttal Document or Witness Name(s) (If hurts) (If none, what will you say at meeting?)
Lee Portaro (District) 3/1/xx assessment	1C		✓	Recomm. #s 3, 6, 8, 10 (p.8)	Brown Assessment
Suzanne Brown 2/4/xx Assessment (Independent)	1B	✓		Narrative (p. 3, ¶s 4, 5). Recomm. #s 1-7, p. 12	
Weekly Teacher Reports	1F	✓	✓	9/6/xx, 10/4/xx, 1/17/xx Support 10/14/xx, 11/5/xx, 2/2/xx Against	Portaro Report: No IEP Agreement on Aide
5/2/xx IEP	1A	✓	✓	Narrative (¶s 7, 8) Against Narrative (¶s 2, 5) Support	Portaro p. 3 (¶2)
Dr. Baker (Pediatrician) 1/22/xx letter	1G	✓		P. 2, Concerns for psychological impact if no aide	
Phil Anderson (tutor) 12/6/xx letter	1H	✓		Reports positive results with direct work, 1:1 work	
Karla Jones (District Psychologist)	1M		✓	Sees Steve once/month Reports no adverse psych. impact	Brown, p. 3, ¶s 6, 9
Student Work	1P	✓		Steve on 10/5 assignment writes "Don't understand, who cares."	

* A "witness" is someone (teacher, doctor, assessor, tutor, psychologist) who gives an oral or written opinion regarding your child's needs at the IEP meeting.

length and number of sessions, the qualifications of the aide, and what the aide will do. Under a curricula/methodology issue such as a reading program, you might include when the reading work is done or at what pace.

Feel free to use the IEP Material Organizer form to subdivide issues in whatever way works for you.

4. Identify Negative Material and Prepare Rebuttals

Keeping in mind your blueprint and goals for your child, what materials hurt your position? Do test results, staff observations, or assessor recommendations state that your child doesn't need what you want for him or her? Do lines such as "Ben does not need any special education services now" or "Leo should be provided one hour of aide time a week" (when you believe he needs one hour per day) or "Nicole cannot function in a regular classroom at this time" (when you're in favor of mainstreaming) appear in the written materials?

Some negative material is less direct. For example, a test result may not reflect the difficulties your child is actually experiencing. If an assessment concludes that "Sandy is at age level for reading," you might face an uphill climb in convincing the school district she needs additional help. Or, a teacher's observation may undermine a placement or service you want. A teacher's statement that "Steven frequently acts out and disrupts classroom activities" may make it very hard for you to have Steven mainstreamed.

Here are some ways to counter negative material:

- Look for anything that directly or indirectly contradicts a troublesome statement or report. For example, an aide's statement that "Steven's behavior is erratic, but with help he can control his behavior and focus effectively and quietly on his work" might help you convince the school that Steven can be mainstreamed.

- Look for professional opinions contrary to the school's position. Usually, statements in an independent assessment can counter school data.

- Are the qualifications of the person who wrote the unfavorable statement appropriate? If a psychologist completed the school assessment, find out if he or she has expertise in the specific areas to which the negative comments refer.

- Is the negative statement crystal clear? For example, what exactly does this observation mean: "While Jane does not need a small class, there is some indication that she has a difficult time in a large school environment"? The reference to a large school environment may indirectly support a small class placement.

- Is the unfavorable statement supported by data, testing results, or anecdotal information? If not, be prepared to point that out.

Use the IEP Material Organizer form to identify negative statements and rebuttal information. While you should be prepared to address or rebut a troublesome statement, conclusion, or recommendation, this may simply not be possible. As a general rule, don't bring up negative statements unless the school district raises them first.

5. Provide Documents Before the IEP Meeting

In preparation for the IEP meeting, have everything in your binder marked, tabbed, highlighted, and referenced in your IEP Material Organizer. Also, make copies of material you want to show to school district representatives at the IEP meeting. This includes anything that supports your blueprint or rebuts negative information. The material can be in any form—a letter, report, independent assessment, teacher's report, or work sample. You may want to make a copy for each person who will attend the meeting.

Provide the school district with a copy of all material you've generated, such as an independent assessment. Give these to the district a week before the meeting. This way, school representatives can't argue that they need more time to review your material and must postpone the meeting.

As mentioned earlier, there may be a reason to surprise the district at the IEP meeting by introducing a particular item for the first time. As a general rule, however, it is best to play it straight and provide material ahead of time.

D. Draft Your Child's IEP Program

IDEA requires you and the school district to develop the IEP program together. This does not mean, however, that you cannot—or should not—draft key portions of what you want to see in the IEP program beforehand. Drafting some language ahead of time can help you organize your arguments and recognize any potential roadblocks to getting what you want for your child.

Can Your School District Write the IEP Before the Meeting?

All IEP members, including you, must have a full opportunity to discuss all aspects of your child's IEP. This means that the district can't just present you with a completed IEP at the start of the IEP meeting and tell you to take it or leave it. Like you, however, the district can prepare draft statements ahead of time. School district representatives will probably have discussed the IEP agenda and their thoughts on your child's needs before the meeting as well—and they have every right to do so.

The key portions of the IEP program are:

- goals and objectives
- specific programs and placement
- related services, and
- other items, including curricula, methodology, and a description of the placement.

Writing out your IEP program will not only help you learn your material, but it will also force you to think again about how to make your case for the key issues. When you prepare your program you can either fill out a blank school district IEP form—you should get a copy early in the process—or write out your statements so you're ready to discuss them at the IEP meeting. As the IEP team proceeds, bring up the specific components you want in the IEP program.

Your blueprint and IEP Material Organizer form will help you draft an IEP and participate effectively in the IEP meeting. Chapter 11 explains how the IEP form and blueprint work together and how to get as much of your blueprint as possible included on the IEP form.

1. Goals and Objectives

Goals and objectives refer both to the broad goals for your child—usually involving reading, math and language skills, social development, motor skills, behavioral issues, and other cognitive areas of need—and to the specific tasks your child will have to complete in order to reach those goals. Chapter 9 covers goals and objectives in detail.

2. Specific Programs and Placement

Program and placement refer to the exact school, class, and classroom characteristics you want for your child.

Examples:
- Placement in the special day class for learning disabled students at Hawthorne School.
- Placement in a special day class for children with developmental delays, no more than 12 students, and a qualified teacher; SDC at Laurel or Martin Schools is appropriate.
- Placement in Tina's home school, the regular third-grade class.

3. Related Services

Related services are developmental, corrective, and other supportive services (such as transportation) that your child needs to benefit from special education or to be placed in a regular class.

Examples:

- Jason needs three speech therapy sessions per week, each session for 30 minutes, one-on-one with a qualified speech therapist.
- Maria needs a full-time one-on-one aide in order to be mainstreamed in a regular fifth-grade class, the aide to be qualified to assist Maria specifically in the areas of reading comprehension, spelling, fifth-grade math, and developing positive peer relationships.

4. Other Components

Other components of the IEP program include:
- curricula, including how your child will be involved and progress in the general curriculum found in the regular classroom, and whether specific related services or special education are needed to assure your child's involvement and progress
- teacher methodology
- transition plans, including vocational needs, and
- extracurricular activities such as after-school clubs, lunchtime activities, and sports.

 Chapter 2 provides details on each of these components of the IEP.

Child Profile

The school district might balk if you present them with a fully drafted IEP program or a blueprint. As an alternative, you might prepare a statement for the IEP meeting that incorporates important information without necessarily triggering school district opposition. Instead of emphasizing goals and objectives, placement, and services, emphasize your child and her needs.

Example:

Sally has a learning disability with specific difficulties with auditory memory, spelling, and reading comprehension. She has some emotional difficulties because of her learning disability, which appear in the forms of anxiety, fear of other children, and concern with safety. She has on a few occasions run off campus. When placed in a large classroom her fears can be increased.

Sally needs a program in which the environment is not overly active, with no behavioral problems; she should not be on a large campus, which might overwhelm her. She needs to be in a classroom of no more than 15 children; she benefits from the Slingerland method and requires instruction in simple, small steps. She needs one-on-one help with reading for at least two hours a day, and does best when this help is provided in continuous segments that are at least 30 minutes long.

This child profile combines parts of the blueprint with a description of your child and her needs. It is not unlike a school district's assessment, which normally includes a narrative section describing your child. Although you will want to draft the child profile for the meeting, do not give it to the school district in advance. Focus on:

- describing your child (quiet, kind, determined, afraid)
- your child's areas of need, including academic, social, and environmental, and
- weaving in references to specific service and placement needs.

E. Establish Who Will Attend the IEP Meeting

Under IDEA, any person with knowledge or expertise about your child may attend the IEP meeting. This includes the following people (34 C.F.R. § 300.344):

- you and your child's other parent
- your child, if appropriate (see Section 2, below)
- a representative of the school district who is qualified to provide or supervise your child's special education and is knowledgeable about the general curriculum
- your child's special education teacher
- your child's regular classroom teacher if your child is or may be in a regular class
- a person who can interpret the assessments and their impact on instructional strategies
- at your discretion or the discretion of the school district, other people who have knowledge or expertise regarding your child or her needs, and
- if your child is 14 or older, someone who knows about transitional services.

Representatives From Noneducational Public Agencies

Sometimes, representatives from other public agencies may attend an IEP meeting, particularly if responsibility for certain IEP services is entrusted to an agency other than the school district. In California, for example, mental health services are provided by the county mental health department, and therefore a representative from that agency will often be present. In Vermont, a representative of an agency other than the school district will attend to discuss transition services. If the child has been involved with the juvenile authorities, a probation officer may attend, depending on the laws in your state.

Prior to the IEP meeting, talk with any of these additional folks and find out why they are attending the meeting, what they will do there (such as report on your child), and what position (if any) they plan to take on your child's needs.

1. Representing the School District

Knowing who will attend the IEP meeting on behalf of the school district will help you prepare. The school district should give you a written list of attendees, but if you are not told at least two weeks before the meeting, write the district and ask for the following information for each person who will attend:

- name
- reasons for attending
- qualifications and specific title, and
- whether or not he or she knows your child and, if so, in what capacity.

Prepare a list of all participants, including the positions they are likely to take on your child's needs.

A sample IEP Meeting Participants form is below; Appendix 5 includes a blank, tear-out copy.

IEP Meeting Participants

Name	Position/Employer	Purpose for Attending	Point of View
Fred Brown	Third-grade teacher, Kentington School District	Gene's teacher	Supports Gene's placement in regular class; does not think Gene needs aide
Diana Hunt	Psychologist, Kentington School District	Did assessment	Recommends placement in special day class
Violet King	Psychologist, independent assessor	Did independent assessment	Supports regular class and aide
Jane Gough	Speech therapist, Kentington School District	Representative of school district	Agrees with need for speech therapy, but not on amount
Phil Chase	Administrator, Kentington School District	Representative of school district	No stated position

a. Your Child's Teacher

If your child is in a regular class, then his or her current teacher must attend the IEP meeting. (34 C.F.R. § 300.344(a)(2)(3).) Your child's teacher has the most information about your child's education and the most experience with your child. The teacher may write reports about your child's progress, help write goals and objectives, be responsible for seeing that these goals are met, and make recommendations for the next school year.

The teacher can be your best ally or your worst enemy in the IEP process. Either way, the teacher is often the most convincing team member. The teacher's opinion may carry the most weight and influence how far your school district will pursue a dispute. If the teacher supports your position, you have a better chance of success. If the teacher does not, the school district may feel it would win any due process dispute and, therefore, may decide to stand its ground at the IEP meeting.

Making sure the teacher understands your concerns and is prepared to speak frankly about them is crucial, but not always easy to achieve. Teachers work for their school districts, and may face subtle or not-so-subtle pressure to make recommendations that fit within the school's budgetary or other constraints. A teacher who speaks frankly regardless of what a school administrator thinks is invaluable—but not always easy to find. It is therefore vital that you keep in contact with the teacher, ask his or her opinion, and indicate your specific concerns. Be specific, direct, fair, and always conscious of the teacher's time.

Chapter 8, Section B, discusses the importance of keeping in regular contact with your child's teacher and talking with teachers and other school personnel before the IEP meeting.

b. School Administrator

In most cases, someone representing the school district will attend the IEP meeting. This may be the district special education coordinator, student services director, county or regional office of education administrator, or school principal. There are all kinds of administrators, just like there are all kinds of parents. The administrator may be a kind, cooperative, and terrific advocate for your child—or may be burned-out, unpleasant, and remarkably bureaucratic.

You will be working with the administrator a good deal and will want to know where he or she stands on your child's IEP. Your inclination might be to ask the administrator in advance of the meeting what his or her position is regarding the key issues for your child. Is it a good idea to do so? Many a wise administrator will let you know when he or she agrees with you, but will not let you know in advance about disagreements. That doesn't mean you can't ask, but it does mean you should consider the pros and cons of asking the administrator's position prior to the IEP meeting.

Pros
- You will find out if the administrator agrees with you.
- If you get an honest answer, you'll know what the administrator thinks and how strong his or her feelings are.
- If you disagree with the answer, you may convince the administrator to change his mind, or you will better know how to prepare for the IEP meeting.
- You may learn about options you like.

Cons
- The administrator will learn your goals and be able to counter them.
- You may put the administrator on guard, making it difficult for you to communicate with staff, visit programs, and the like.

If you decide to ask and the administrator opposes your goals for your child, consider the following:

- If the administrator will not support you on a particular item, he or she may have violated IDEA—that is, made a decision before the IEP meeting. This may be the basis of a formal complaint against the school district (see Chapter 13). This doesn't mean you should trap the administrator into making a decision outside of the IEP meeting. But if it happens, be aware of your rights.
- If the administrator has not made a decision, you may want to share the materials you have that support your position. You might give the administrator some ideas as to why the district can agree with you. On the other hand, you may help the administrator prepare to rebut you at the IEP meeting. You'll have to judge the chance of making the administrator into an ally rather than a well-prepared adversary.

c. School Psychologist and Other Specialists

Depending on your child's condition and needs, other professionals may be involved in the IEP meeting, such as a school psychologist, speech therapist, occupational therapist, physical therapist, adaptive physical education specialist, or resource specialist. They may provide assessment reports and other information regarding your child, and are likely to have opinions about goals and objectives, services, and placement. Like your child's teacher, these specialists may be great allies or formidable foes.

As with the teacher or administrator, speak with the specialists ahead of time to find out their positions on key issues.

d. Limits on School Representatives

Are there limits to who can attend the meeting? Federal policy states that a school may not invite so many people as to make the IEP intimidating. State laws and policies may also cover who may attend IEP meetings. California, for example, requires that the IEP meeting be "nonadversarial"—and having ten district employees may make the IEP meeting feel very adversarial indeed.

IDEA regulations say that people who attend the IEP meeting at the invitation of a parent or the school district must have knowledge or special expertise about the child. (34 C.F.R. § 300.344(a)(6).) If it seems inappropriate for a particular person to attend based on this standard, notify the school in writing (even if you initially call) of your concern. State why the individual is not qualified to attend, or why his or her attendance is not necessary or helpful. If the school insists that the person attend, see Chapter 13 on filing a complaint. And at the IEP meeting, state for the record, without being personal, that you feel so-and-so should not be there. When it's time to sign the IEP plan, reiterate your objection.

Sample IEP Meeting Attendance Objection Letter

Date: May 15, 20xx

To: Dr. Sean Gough

Hamilton School District

1456 Howard Ave.

Little Rock, AR 72212

Re: Amy Crane, student in third-grade class of Carol Smith

I understand that Joan Green, the district's psychologist, will be at Amy's IEP meeting. Joan Green knows nothing about Amy and appears to have no knowledge that might be of use to the IEP team. I am formally requesting that Ms. Green not attend, unless there is some clear reason that makes Ms. Green's attendance appropriate and necessary for the development of Amy's IEP plan. As you know, IEP meetings can be particularly difficult for parents. We are already anxious about ours and would prefer that you not take action that will heighten our stress level.

If you insist on Ms. Green attending without any reason, then we will file a complaint with the state and federal departments of education.

I will call you in a few days to find out your decision on this issue. Thank you for considering my request.

Sincerely,

Eva Crane

Eva Crane

88 2nd Street

Little Rock, AR 72212

Phones: 555-1998 (home); 555-8876 (work)

A sample letter objecting to a particular person attending the IEP meeting is above; a blank, tear-out copy is in Appendix 5.

One Teacher Too Many

I once represented a child at an IEP meeting where there were a dozen school representatives, including several administrators; the school nurse; and Bruce, the "teacher of the day." I asked Bruce if he knew my client, Laura. The answer was no—he had neither met her nor knew anything about her. I asked him why he was there. Without hesitation he said he was there to "represent the teachers of the area." The involvement of someone like Bruce—or anybody else with no knowledge of your child or the relevant educational issues—would be contrary to federal policy and the underlying purpose of the IEP meeting.

---

2. Representing the Parents

While some of the people representing the school district may support your goals for your child, you may want some or all of the following people to attend the IEP meeting on your behalf:

- your spouse or partner
- your child
- others who know your child, such as a relative or close family friend
- independent assessors or other professionals who have worked with your child, and
- an attorney.

Contact these people well in advance to let them know the date, time, location, and likely duration of the meeting. Make sure they understand the key topics that will arise during the IEP meeting, and the issues and solutions they are there to discuss. Let them know the positions of the various school representatives on the key issues, and be sure to show them copies of materials that both support and are contrary to your goals.

Remind your attendees that the IEP meeting is informal and that points of view should be stated in a positive but firm way. Disagreements can be spirited, but should remain professional and respectful.

Some of the people you ask to attend—such as an independent assessor, a pediatrician, another specialist, or a lawyer—might charge you a fee. Find out the cost ahead of time. If you can't afford to have the person stay for the entire meeting, let the school administrator know in advance that you will have someone attending who needs to make a statement and leave. Before the meeting, ask the administrator to set aside a specific time for that person to speak.

Some people you want to attend might not be able to, or you might not be able to afford to pay them to attend. In either situation, ask the person to prepare a written statement for you to read at the meeting. Some people's testimony may actually be better in writing than it would be in person—for example, someone who is timid or reluctant to strongly state a position in person might come across better in writing.

Chapter 8, Section F, discusses items to include in a written statement from your child's doctor or other people from outside the school.

a. Parents

While work schedules or living arrangements may make attending the IEP meeting difficult, it is generally best if both parents attend, even if you are divorced or separated. If you have differences of opinion, resolve them before the IEP meeting. If you argue with each other during the IEP meeting, you could damage your credibility and chances of success.

If one of you cannot attend, prepare a strong and emotional statement for the other to read.

Can an IEP Meeting Be Held Without You?

Your school district has a duty to ensure that you are present at the IEP meeting. It can hold an IEP meeting without your involvement only in unusual situations, and only after following very specific procedures, including:

- notifying you early enough of the meeting to ensure you have the opportunity to attend
- scheduling the meeting at a mutually convenient time and place, and
- finding ways of including you—including individual or conference telephone calls— if you cannot attend.

The district can proceed without you only if it can prove that it took specific steps to convince the parent to attend, by showing records of attempts to arrange a mutually agreeable time and place, detailed phone records, correspondence, and even visits to the parent's home or workplace. (20 U.S.C. § 1414(d); 34 C.F.R. § 300.345.) See Appendix 1.

Sample Statement to IEP Team

To: Marilyn Haversham's IEP Team

From: Claudine Haversham (Marilyn's mom)

Date: March 1, 20xx

I cannot attend the March 15th IEP meeting, but I wanted you to know that I am very concerned that Marilyn might be removed from her regular program. She is such a happy child now that she is mainstreamed. As her mother, I see the joy in her eyes when she gets up in the morning to get ready for school. A placement in a more restrictive environment would be devastating to my daughter. I must be frank and tell you that we will vigorously oppose any efforts to remove Marilyn from her current program.

I greatly appreciate your sensitivity to Marilyn's needs and your past assistance in making her educational experience a positive one.

Sincerely,

Claudine Haversham

Claudine Haversham

b. Your Child

IDEA says that the student shall attend the IEP meeting if it is appropriate or if the IEP team is considering transition services for a child. (34 C.F.R. §§ 300.344(a)(7).) (See Chapter 2, Section A, for a discussion of transition services.)

When is it considered appropriate for a child to attend? A child who can speak about his or her hopes and needs may be a compelling self-advocate. But be careful—if your child is unpredictable or unsure of the importance of the meeting, you may not want to risk the possibility of a "wrong" answer. For example, you want your child to remain in his mainstreamed program. A school district representative says, "Tell me, Tommy, do you want to stay in your class?" You're not going to be happy if Tommy responds, "Nope."

If your child does attend, focus on his or her feelings and hopes. You probably want to avoid referring to the written materials, unless your child is older—perhaps a teenager. In that case, you can ask something like, "Carl, the school assessor says you had a hard time in Ms. Shaver's class, particularly with other students. Why do you think that was so?" Be sure you know what his answer will be.

c. Relatives, Friends, and Child Care Workers

It is important to limit the number of people who attend the IEP meetings—the more people in attendance, the longer the meeting can drag on. Therefore, you'd normally not bring a relative, friend, or child care worker to the meeting. But if someone can present a view of your child that wouldn't otherwise be told, you might want that person to come. For example, if your child's regular babysitter can describe how your otherwise shy and reserved child talks for the first 30 minutes after she gets home about how she loves being in a regular class, it may be powerful testimony.

Generally, a sibling or peer of your child, particularly a young one, should not attend unless he or she is the only person who can speak to an issue or has a really powerful presence. Preparing young attendees will be very important, with focus on the sibling or peer's "feelings" about your child, rather than more formal information.

Bring Someone to Take Notes

Ask a friend or relative to attend the IEP meeting and take notes for you—paying careful attention to who says what regarding important items. A notetaker can be invaluable, particularly if you anticipate a controversial meeting.

d. Independent Assessors and Other Professionals

Because the conclusions reached by any independent assessor who tested your child will probably be instrumental in helping you secure the right services and placement, it is crucial that the assessor attend the IEP meeting. The assessor must be able to clearly articulate his or her professional opinion on the key blueprint items and on all assessment data. The assessor must also be prepared to rebut contradictory information presented by the school district.

Other professionals, such as a pediatrician, private tutor, therapist, or psychological counselor, can be important witnesses on your behalf if they know your child and can speak to key issues affecting the IEP plan. Prepare these individuals as you would prepare an independent assessor.

e. An Attorney

If you hire or consult an attorney during the IEP process, that person can attend the IEP meeting. You can also hire a lawyer just for the IEP meeting. (See Chapter 14 for information on working with lawyers.) As a general rule, you may want an attorney at the IEP meeting if your relationship with the school district has deteriorated and you anticipate a complicated and difficult IEP meeting.

If you bring an attorney to the IEP meeting, school representatives are more likely to be on guard and less likely to speak frankly. On the other hand, if the school administrators haven't been cooperative and you feel the plan that will emerge from the IEP meeting will be harmful to your child, bringing an attorney shows you mean business. You're much better off not using an attorney—it does change the entire experience—but if you must, then find one who is reasonable and cooperative.

If you plan to have an attorney at the IEP meeting, you should notify the school district reasonably in advance. Except in unusual situations, you will be responsible for paying your attorney, with little chance of reimbursement. (See Chapter 14, Section D, for information on when you might be reimbursed for lawyer's expenses.)

F. Final Preparation Concerns

As you finish your IEP preparation, consider these additional recommendations.

1. Taping the IEP Meeting

You (and the school district) have the right to tape record the meeting. While a tape recording may be the best proof of what was said, it may have an inhibiting effect. People don't always want to make a particular statement "on the record." In addition, tape recordings are not always of great quality; participants are not always audible, and it can be hard to discern what was said and who said it.

If you decide to tape record, bring a good-quality recorder. Bring extra tapes and batteries in case an outlet is not accessible. The school district can tape record even if you object—just as you can tape over the objections of school representatives. If the school district tapes the meeting, you are entitled to a copy of the tape, and it becomes part of your child's file—just as the district can ask for a copy of your tape.

You should notify the district in advance that you want to tape record the meeting.

School Resistance to Tape Recording

The U.S. Department of Education, Office of Special Education Programs, has issued several statements reinforcing the right of parents to tape record IEP meetings. If, once you get to the meeting, the special education administrator says you cannot tape record, ask to reschedule the meeting. You can also state that this affects your ability to function at the IEP meeting, that it is against the law, and that you will file a complaint. (After the meeting, follow up with a letter to the school administrator; see Chapter 13 for advice on filing a complaint.)

2. Reducing Your Anxiety

It is a given that you will be nervous at the meeting, so don't worry about being anxious. But do give some thought to what you might do before the IEP meeting to relax. It may be taking a walk or jogging, soaking in the bathtub, going out for breakfast, or any other activity that helps you settle your nerves. If you need to get a babysitter or take time off from work, set it up well in advance, so you're not scrambling the day before the meeting.

By preparing—knowing your material, completing your IEP blueprint, drafting your IEP plan, and talking to your IEP participants ahead of time—you will do much to reduce your anxiety.

IEP Preparation List

Things to do before the IEP meeting:
- Find out the date, time, and location.
- Get a copy of the school's agenda.
- Make your own agenda.
- Prepare your IEP Material Organizer.
- Draft IEP plan.
- Find out who is attending on behalf of school district.
- Invite and prepare your own IEP participants.
- Give the school a copy of the following:
  - ▲ independent assessments
  - ▲ documents such as formal reports and work samples
  - ▲ names and titles of people attending IEP, and
  - ▲ notice of intent to tape record IEP meeting (if applicable).
- Create meeting reminder list of items you want to be sure to remember:
  - ▲ "Make sure we read statements of Dr. Wilson and Rona (babysitter), who can't attend."
  - ▲ "Make sure Dr. Ramirez covers Lydia's physical therapy needs."
  - ▲ "Remember we don't have to sign all of the IEP—we can object."

11

Attending the IEP Meeting

Your IEP meeting is soon. You'll enter the room, sit down, put your binder on the table, take a deep breath, and do just fine. You'll do fine because being nervous is natural, the school administrator probably feels the same way and, most important, you are prepared for this meeting. You've developed your child's blueprint and drafted an ideal IEP, supported by various documents. You're familiar with the school's IEP form, policies, programs, and services. You know who will attend the meeting and where each person stands on key issues. You have people with you who are prepared to help you make your case.

Chapter 10 provides valuable advice on preparing for the IEP meeting. Chapter 7 provides tips on preparing for and attending an IEP eligibility meeting.

A. Getting Started

IEP meetings can take a lot of time. Therefore, it's very important that you be on time. In fact, you'll want to be at least ten to 15 minutes early so you can get the lay of the land, see the meeting room, and perhaps say a few words to the teacher or school administrator. More important, being early will give you the chance to talk to your participants and make sure everyone is clear about their roles at the meeting.

1. What to Bring

Bring your IEP binder and the written material you've gathered, including assessments, letters, reports, and your IEP Material Organizer form. Make sure you have extra copies of key documents, such as an independent assessment.

2. Get the Notetaker Organized

It's a good idea to bring someone to take notes, particularly if you anticipate a controversial meeting. Make sure you provide your notetaker with paper and pens (or a laptop computer). Remind your notetaker to take detailed notes regarding important items, particularly those that relate to your blueprint—what was said and who said it are especially important. These notes, particularly for items that you and the school district dispute, will be extremely important should you end up filing for due process (see Chapter 12) or making a formal complaint (see Chapter 13). If you do not have a notetaker, make sure you give yourself time to jot down important statements.

3. Set Up the Tape Recorder

If you're planning to tape record the meeting, set up the equipment and check that it's working.

Chapter 10, Section F, explains how to notify the school district in advance of your intent to tape record the IEP meeting and how to deal with any dispute that arises about taping the meeting.

4. How the Meeting Will Begin

The IEP meeting is typically led by the school administrator responsible for special education programs, although it may be led by the school site principal, the school district assessor, or even a teacher.

Most IEP meetings begin with the introduction of all participants. School representatives will explain their roles at the meeting. You should do the same with your participants. If, for example, a friend will take notes or an outside assessor will explain her report, make that clear.

After introductions, the administrator will probably discuss the agenda and then explain how the meeting will run, and how decisions will be made.

 Obtaining the agenda in advance is discussed in Chapter 10, Section B.

If the agenda is different from what you anticipated or omits issues you want to cover, bring up your concerns at the beginning of the meeting. You have the right to raise any issue you want at the IEP meeting. Also, if the agenda appears too long for the allotted time, explain that you don't think there will be enough time to cover everything, and ask that certain items be discussed first. If your request is denied, do your best to keep the meeting moving forward.

While most IEP meetings follow a certain pattern (discussed in Section D, below), don't be surprised if yours seems to have a life of its own, going in directions you did not anticipate. Just make sure your key issues are covered before the meeting ends.

IEP Meeting Basic Dos and Don'ts

Is there an etiquette to the IEP meeting? There should be. As in any potentially difficult encounter, try to proceed in a positive way.

Dos
- Do respect other opinions.
- Do try to include all IEP team members in the process.
- Do ask questions in a fair and direct way.
- Do state your position firmly, but fairly.
- Do explore ways of reaching consensus.

Don'ts
- Don't interrupt.
- Don't accuse.
- Don't make personal attacks.
- Don't raise your voice.
- Don't question another's motives.

You might begin by saying that you appreciate everyone's attendance, the time and energy they're giving to your child, and their professional dedication. Emphasize that you are determined to discuss all issues in a fair and thorough way, and that you are looking forward to a challenging but ultimately positive meeting in which everyone's point of view is respected.

B. Simple Rules for a Successful IEP Meeting

Several simple rules can help you get the most out of the IEP meeting.

1. Know Your Rights

IDEA was created for your child and provides for:
- a free appropriate public education (FAPE) in the
- least restrictive environment (LRE), based on an
- individualized education program (IEP).

Parents are coequal decisionmakers—just as important as everyone else at the IEP meeting.

Chapter 2 explains your child's legal rights under IDEA. Appendix 1 includes the relevant statutes and regulations.

2. Don't Be Intimidated

You have special knowledge of your child's needs. School personnel are not the only experts. If you have documents to support each item you want in the IEP plan, you may be even better prepared than school representatives.

At the same time, don't automatically assume that teachers or other school officials are wrong. There are many dedicated teachers and school administrators who want to provide the best education for your child, have expertise in educating children with disabilities, and have been through this process numerous times before. This doesn't mean you won't encounter opposing opinions or

---

How to Deal With Intimidating or Nasty Comments

For many parents, dealing with teachers and school administrators in an IEP meeting can be intimidating. You don't want to (but may) hear:
- *I'm sorry, Mr. Walker, but you're wrong.*
- *I'm sorry, Ms. Richards, the law doesn't say that.*
- *Your assessment report is incorrect.*
- *Our policy precludes that.*
- *Maybe they do that in another school district, but we don't.*
- *I will not agree to that!*
- *That's enough on that subject!*

In most cases, you can ignore these kinds of comments or make a simple response. (Section B5, below, discusses how to challenge blanket assertions.) Try to determine whether the comment is anything more than just an impolite or negative remark. If it is unimportant, say your piece and move on.

"I don't appreciate your tone of voice, Ms. Hanson. I have treated you with respect and expect the same from you. Even if we disagree, we can do it in a civil way. More important, your statement is not correct (or reasonable or produc-

tive or conducive to a positive IEP meeting)."

If the comment seems important, you may need to be more assertive.

"Ms. Hanson, I resent your comment and believe you are undermining this IEP meeting. Please understand, I will do what is necessary to ensure my child receives the program she needs and bring your behavior to the attention of the appropriate individuals."

If you don't feel calm and your voice is shaky, that's okay, too. Just don't yell or get overly aggressive. If necessary, you may want to raise the possibility of filing a formal complaint regarding something that seems illegal—for example, if the district won't allow you to discuss your independent assessment. (Chapter 13 covers complaints.) But don't make a threat without first thinking it through. Do you really have grounds to file a formal complaint? Is there any validity to the school representative's comment? Is it worth alienating the school district and changing the atmosphere of the IEP meeting? In most cases, you can make your point without threatening to file a formal complaint.

perhaps even run up against someone who is just plain nasty or incorrect. But as a general rule, most of the folks are in special education because they want to help.

3. Focus on Your Child's Needs—Not Cost or Administrative Constraints

IDEA recognizes that each child's needs are unique and, therefore, that each individual program will be different. If you can show that your child needs a specific service, such as a one-to-one aide or two hours of occupational therapy each week, then the law requires it.

If the school district does not have the staff to provide the related service your child needs, such as a speech therapist, then the school should pay for a private therapist.

A child's needs—not cost—should dictate all IEP decisions. For example, the school administrator cannot refuse to discuss or provide a service or placement because it "costs too much." An administrator may try to get the point across indirectly, by saying something like "If we provide that service for your child, another child will not get services she needs." Don't argue the issue; simply respond with something like this:

> *Mr. Keystone, it is wrong for you to make my child responsible for your budgetary difficulties. I won't be put in the position of making a choice between my child's needs and the needs of other children. The law is clear that we should be discussing an appropriate education for my child, not the cost.*

If you can't reach agreement, and the school district representatives continue to admit that there is an administrative or budget problem, be sure you (or your notetaker) has written this down in case you end up in due process.

This is not to say that cost is never an issue. Let's say you want your child in Program X and the school offers to put your child in Program Y, which is less costly for the district. You're unable to reach an agreement and decide to resolve the matter through due process. If the district can prove Program Y is appropriate for your child, it will likely prevail at the due process hearing.

Remember: IDEA does not require the best education for your child, but an appropriate one. You won't win a fight for the ideal program when an appropriate one is available.

 Don't describe the program you want as "the best," "optimum," or "maximum." The school district might use these descriptions as evidence that you want more then the "appropriate" education to which your child is entitled under IDEA. If you feel that a program or service offered by the school isn't right, characterize it as "inappropriate"—this will signal that you don't think the school district is meeting its legal obligations.

4. Know When to Fight— and When Not To

It is important to realize when you don't have a case. Understanding the IEP process and having a clear step-by-step strategy does not mean that all problems will always be resolved in a manner you think best. You may be fully prepared, do a superb job in the IEP meeting, and still not have enough evidence to support your position. Knowing the strength of your case will help you know when to fight and when to concede.

Fight for the crucial issues and be more flexible on others. For instance, goals and objectives and test protocol may be important, but, ultimately, the related services, placement, and methodology are what matter in your child's education. Fighting for 30 minutes over the wording of one goal or objective is probably a waste of time; spending 90 minutes on a major issue like placement is probably worth it.

5. Ask Questions

You should always feel comfortable asking questions—and there will undoubtedly be times during the IEP meeting when you need more information or clarification. There are several very good reasons to ask questions: to obtain basic information, to persuade someone of your position, or to question a blanket assertion.

a. Obtain Basic Information

During the IEP meeting, many technical terms will be used. If you don't understand something, ask what it means. It's better to ask—even for the tenth time—than to proceed without understanding.

Most important, find out what these terms mean for your child. Knowing that your child scores at the 42 percentile on the Wechsler is useless unless it tells you something about your child's abilities and opportunities for improvement.

b. Persuade

Asking questions can be an effective way of persuading others that your position is right and theirs may be wrong. State your questions positively, such as "Do you [IEP team members] agree with the recommendations on page eight of Dr. Calderon's report?" or "Ms. Porter, do you agree that Amy should be placed in a regular eighth-grade class with a one-to-one aide?"

Sometimes you may need to establish agreement on preliminary matters before asking these kinds of big questions.

> Example:
> You want a particular IEP member to agree with you on placement. You realize that you must first establish agreement on the assessment supporting that placement. You first ask, "You read Dr. Harper's report. She states that Carolyn needs, and I am quoting, 'a quiet environment in which there are no behavioral problems or acting out by other students.' Do you agree with Dr. Harper?" The IEP member agrees and you follow up by asking, "Given Dr. Harper's report and our desire that Carolyn be placed in the special day class at the Manning School, do you agree with that placement?"

Someone may chafe at being asked such a pointed question and may feel cross-examined. One good way to respond would be to say, "I certainly don't mean to cross-examine you and appreciate you reminding me of that. Please understand that I am not a lawyer but a parent. What is important to Carolyn is not the nature of the question but the answer. I will certainly try not to be too formal; would you like me to try to put it another way?"

c. Challenge Blanket Assertions

Nothing is more frustrating for a parent than hearing lines like the following:
- *"Unfortunately, we are not allowed to discuss that issue."*
- *"We don't provide that service."*
- *"That's not our policy."*
- *"Sorry, but you can't do that."*
- *"That's not the law."*

If an assertion seems illegal or illogical, ask what it's based on. If the administrator says something vague like "It's our policy," "It's the law," "It's our best judgment," or "It's the way things are," keep asking why. Request a copy of the law or policy.

If possible, refer to your documentation. For example, the district administrator says that as a general rule, the district doesn't provide more than two hours of a related service per week. An assessment states that your child needs three hours. Point that out and ask how the district's rule complies with IDEA, which requires that the specifics of a service be determined by the IEP team.

The administrator may say something like "Mrs. Wasserman, that is just the way it is and I won't respond any further to that question." You'll want to follow up with something like "I'm sorry you won't answer my question; it is a fair question, and I plan to ask your superintendent or the school board to answer it." If the issue is key, you may want to file a complaint, as discussed in Chapter 13.

Or the school district may not agree with you on an important IEP component. For example, you feel there is clear support for a specific placement, but the administrator disagrees. Ask her to explain why and to provide you a detailed explanation supported by appropriate material.

6. Pay Attention to What's Written on the IEP Form

Make sure you know what statements are entered onto the IEP document, and voice any objections immediately—whether it's about a particular goal or objective, or a general statement made on the narrative page of the IEP form. (Section D, below, discusses the narrative page.)

7. Keep Your Eye on the Clock

Whether the school has allotted two hours or five hours for the IEP meeting, keep track of time. If you are 45 minutes into a 90-minute meeting and the IEP team is still talking in generalities, you should say, "We need to move on to a specific discussion of Cora's goals and objectives, placement, and related services."

A good school administrator will keep the meeting on schedule. If the administrator is not

doing so, take the lead. Be ready to suggest moving on to the next issue when the discussion on a particular topic has gone on long enough.

8. Don't Limit Your Options to All or Nothing

At some point during the IEP meeting, you may realize that you will not reach agreement on all issues. For example, you feel your child needs at least two sessions of speech therapy a week, 30 minutes per session. The district offers one 30-minute session. You've done your best to persuade them, to no avail. What do you do?

The school district cannot present you with a "take-or-leave-it" position—for example, "We've offered speech therapy once a week. You want it twice a week. You can either agree with us and sign the IEP or disagree and go to a hearing." Furthermore, the school district cannot insist that you give up your right to due process—for instance, "We've offered speech therapy once a week and that's all we'll offer. We'd advise you to sign the IEP form and not make waves."

Your best bet is to make sure the IEP document specifically states that you agree that a specific service is needed—or that a particular placement is appropriate—and that your child will receive at least what the school district has offered. Then make sure your opinions are reflected on the parent addendum page.

You can agree to the lesser amount of a service such as speech therapy and indicate on the IEP form that you believe your child needs two sessions of speech therapy, but will accept the one session so he or she will have something while you pursue due process. Or you agree on placement and related services, but not certain goals and objectives (or vice versa).

Section F, below, discusses how to prepare and use a parent addendum page, which is a very important IEP tool for any disputed items.

9. Don't Be Rushed Into Making a Decision

If you're on the fence about a particular issue, don't be rushed into making a decision. Ask for a break and go outside for a few minutes to think about what the school has offered. If you are concerned that pausing on some issues may mean delay on others, ask for a day or two to make up your mind on a particular issue so that the IEP team can proceed with other items. This may require a second IEP meeting, unless you eventually agree with the rest of the IEP team on the issue. If an item is that important, however, then a second meeting is worth the time.

C. Become Familiar With Your School's IEP Form

As I've already suggested, you should get a copy of your school district's IEP form before the IEP meeting. While forms vary, they will almost always have sections on the following:

- present level of educational performance
- goals and objectives (and evaluation procedures)
- related services
- placement/program
- effective dates of the IEP
- attending summer school or an extended school year, and
- a narrative page or pages for recording various important statements, such as comments on assessments, or keeping a running account of the meeting discussion. This important part of the IEP is described in Section D, below.

In addition, IEP forms typically include the following types of information:

- identifying information, such as your child's name, gender, date of birth, grade, school district, and parents' names and addresses
- the type of IEP (eligibility or annual review) and date of IEP meeting

- your child's eligibility status and category of disability
- the amount of time your child will spend in a regular or mainstreamed program, if applicable
- your child's English proficiency, and
- signatures of IEP team members and parents.

The IEP team may include other important information in the IEP, such as a specific curricula or teaching methodology, a specific classroom setting, peer needs, or a child profile.

 You can find a sample IEP form in Appendix 4.

The IEP Form and Your IEP Blueprint

The IEP form and your blueprint (your list of desired program components) will have similar categories but will not be identical.

Most of your blueprint items, such as related services and placement, have a corresponding section in the IEP. But in some cases, you may find that the IEP form does not have space for all the details you included on your blueprint. For example, the IEP form will allow you to specify the kind of program or placement—such as a regular class or special day class—but might not provide space for the details of the placement—such as peer numbers and makeup, the classroom environment, and the school environment. Other blueprint items, such as methodology and curricula, may not have a corresponding section on the IEP form. And the school administrator may not be familiar with a blueprint like yours.

As you prepare for the IEP meeting, keep in mind that while the IEP form may not reference all of your blueprint items, IDEA allows the IEP team to discuss and agree on any element it feels is necessary for your child. These types of details can go on the IEP narrative page (see Section D, below) or, if the school disagrees, a parent addendum page (see Section F, below).

D. Writing the IEP Plan

Usually, someone from the school district will write the IEP plan as the meeting progresses, by filling in specific sections, checking off boxes on the IEP, and completing the narrative or descriptive page.

You should ask frequently to see what has been written, to make sure it accurately reflects what was discussed or agreed upon. You may want to check every 30 minutes or so, with a simple "Excuse me, but can we break for just a few minutes? I want to see what the IEP looks like so far." If 30-minute breaks seem forced, ask to review the form each time you complete a section. Pay special attention to the narrative page—this will be more subjective than other parts of the IEP.

How does the IEP team make an actual decision on IEP components? IDEA establishes no set method for reaching agreement. The school administrator may not even raise the question of how agreement is reached. You can request voting, but, in most IEP meetings, the team tries to reach consensus through discussion. No matter how the administrator proceeds, make sure your objections are heard and no one assumes consensus when there isn't any.

How items are recorded on the IEP plan is equally important. From the beginning to the end of the IEP meeting, you want to be sure that the IEP's narrative page, goals and objectives, placement, and related services reflect your point of view.

1. Child's Current Educational Status

If your child is presently enrolled in school, the IEP team will review your child's current IEP's goals and objectives, program, and related services. Your child's current status may be reflected in testing data, grades, and teacher reports or observations. If this is an eligibility IEP meeting, the team will review assessment data; it will do the same every three years when your child is re-

assessed. Discussion of your child's current status may be broad or specific. It may occur at the beginning of the IEP meeting or as you review specific items, such as goals and objectives, for the upcoming year.

Watch what you—and others—say about your child's current situation. For example, if you are concerned about the current program, you won't want the IEP narrative page to state that "Sam's placement has been highly successful this past year." If such a statement is made and entered onto the IEP document—perhaps on the narrative page—be sure to object, with something like "I'm sorry, but I don't think that statement is accurate, and I certainly cannot agree with it. It should not be on the IEP as reflecting our consensus."

2. Assessments

A school district representative (most likely the assessor) will either read or summarize the school district's assessment. If the assessor starts reading the report, ask him or her to synthesize the salient points, rather than spend precious time reading the assessment verbatim—especially if you reviewed a copy before the meeting.

This may be the time to use your IEP Material Organizer (see Chapter 10) to point to other documents—such as previous IEP plans, an independent assessment, other reports, teacher notes, and the like—to support or contradict the school assessment.

If you haven't already introduced the independent assessment, you will do so once the district has finished presenting its assessment. You or your assessor should provide a synopsis of the report, focusing on:

- the assessor's credentials
- the reason for the assessment
- the tests used
- the key conclusions regarding the testing, and
- the specific recommendations.

Be sure to highlight the test results and recommendations not covered in the school assessment. This is also the time to introduce any other supporting material, including letters, work samples, and other professional opinions.

On most IEP forms, the narrative page refers to the assessments. The IEP plan might specify the sections, results, or statements in the assessments on which you all agree. Even if there is only one statement in the assessment you all agree on, be sure it gets into the IEP document if it is essential to your child's needs. If the person drafting the IEP plan includes something from an assessment with which you disagree, make sure your objections are noted.

Sometimes, the assessments are attached to the IEP document. This can work in your favor if you agree with the assessment.

If an assessment is not attached, or there is some disagreement over the assessment, the narrative page should specify what parts of the assessments are included or excluded.

Examples:

- The IEP team agrees with Sections 1, 2, 4, 6, and 8 of the school assessment and Sections 3, 5, 9, 10, and 12 of the independent assessment, and incorporates them into the IEP.
- The IEP team disagrees with the rest of both assessments and does not incorporate them into the IEP.

You can use the parent addendum page to state the reasons for your disagreement (see Section F, below).

3. Goals and Objectives

If this is not your child's first IEP, the IEP team will next review the previous year's goals and objectives. This discussion is likely to lead to one of four different outcomes:

- You and the school district agree that the goals and objectives were met.

- You and the school district agree that certain goals and objectives were met, but others were not. You may also agree that an objective was met, but not the larger goal. For example, if John met the objective of successfully adding two-digit numbers 75% of the time, it does not necessarily mean that John achieved the larger goal of doing third-grade math or that John understood the process.
- You and the school district agree that the goals and objectives were not met.
- You and the school district disagree on whether the goals and objectives were met.

Although you won't be working on placement and services during this part of the meeting, keep in mind that your child's success or failure in meeting the goals and objectives will likely affect whether the placement and services are changed. If your child met the goals and objectives, perhaps it means the placement is correct and should continue. Or maybe it means your child is ready to be mainstreamed. If the goals and objectives weren't met, your child may need a smaller class. Or maybe the placement is fine, but more tutoring (a related service) is necessary.

Once you finish reviewing the previous goals and objectives—or if this is your child's first time in special education—it's time to write goals and objectives for the coming year. Chapter 9 explains how to draft goals and objectives—and recommends that you do so in advance. It's possible the school representatives have also prepared some ahead of time.

Remember, your goal is to have the IEP team agree on goals and objectives that support the placement and related services you want for your child.

What if you disagree with each other's goals and objectives?

- Do your best to convince school members of the IEP team that your goals and objectives are consistent with the recommendations made by others, such as the assessor, the classroom teacher, or your child's aide.

- Ask school members what they specifically disagree with in your goals and objectives.
- If you can't agree on all goals and objectives, try to reach consensus on some—half a loaf is better than none.
- If attempts to compromise fail, suggest dropping all predrafted goals and objectives and coming up with something new.

If you and the school representatives disagree about past or future goals and objectives, be sure the IEP document clearly states that. At the very least, record your concerns on your parent addendum (see Section F, below).

4. Transition Services

If your child is 14 or older, the IEP team must discuss transition services regarding her course of study, including advanced courses and vocational classes.

The IEP team should consider strategies to assist your child in assessing, securing information about, and taking steps regarding vocational, employment, independent living, and post–high school educational plans. Your child can look into transition in a variety of ways, including looking at potential jobs, learning how to function in the community, accessing other agencies that will provide support for adults with disabilities, and researching college opportunities.

Once your child reaches the age of 14, the IEP must include a statement about his or her transition needs, as those needs relate to your child's courses of study. (34 C.F.R. § 300.347(b)(1).) This means that the team must indicate what advanced placement or vocational courses or classes are necessary to meet your child's unique educational and career needs. For example, if your child wants to go to college, do clerical work, or look into computer jobs, then his or her studies must provide for ways to explore these possibilities.

If your child is at least 16, the IEP must also include a statement about necessary transition services. This means that the IEP must provide for services that will help your child develop the skills necessary to meet his or her vocational, academic, or independent living plans for the future (after high school ends). Such transition services might include help in developing the skills to create a resume, perform certain jobs, access and use community services (such as public transportation), and find out about job training or college programs. The IEP must also indicate whether there are noneducational agencies that might provide additional support to your child (such as the department of health or job training agencies), and how your child can access the services these agencies provide.

As you prepare for the IEP meeting, talk to your child's teacher and other professionals about his or her vocational, college, and independent living skill needs. If your child wants to go to college, what skills will that require, and what institutions or agencies might be available to help your child develop those skills? If you child plans to look for work after high school, what are his or her vocational interests, and how can your child get the training and experience necessary to get into those fields? If your child needs help developing independent living skills, such as using transportation, balancing a checkbook, or keeping house, what kinds of school activities will help?

5. Related Services

Your discussions regarding related services (and placement, covered in the next section) are likely to generate the most debate. You and the school district may have very different notions of the type and amount of related services that are appropriate for your child.

Under IDEA, related services are developmental, corrective, and other supportive services, including transportation, that a child with disabilities needs to benefit from special education. They also include the services your child needs to be educated in a regular classroom. Remember, the burden is on the school district to show that your child cannot achieve satisfactorily in a regular classroom, even with the use of some related services (see Chapter 2, Section A).

Independent assessors and others supporting your position should be prepared to state their opinions in detail—for example, "Given Gavin's severe difficulties in articulation, he needs a minimum of three 30-minute sessions each week, one-to-one with a speech therapist who has a lot of experience in articulation work." If someone is not there to make this statement, be prepared to point to written materials that show your child's need for the particular related service.

The related services section of the IEP document requires more detail than any other. It's not enough to say, "Gavin will receive speech therapy." The IEP team should specify how often (three sessions per week), how long (30-minute sessions), the ratio of pupils to related service provider (one-to-one), and the qualifications of the service provider.

The more vague the description, the more flexibility the school district has to give your child something less than (or different from) what he or she needs. Speech therapy two to three times a week is very different from speech therapy three times per week. Try to avoid terminology such as "or," "about," "to be determined" or "as needed." When in doubt, be specific; it's that simple.

The school district cannot deny your child related services because of budgetary or administrative constraints. See Section B3, above.

> ### Some Related Services May Be the Responsibility of Other Agencies
>
> In some states, certain related services, such as mental health services, are the responsibility of a noneducational public agency. Still, these services should be discussed at the IEP meeting, and the school district is responsible for making sure representatives of those other agencies attend the meeting. Those noneducational agencies have the same responsibilities as the school district—and therefore the same role to play at the meeting—regarding the services they must provide.

6. Placement or Program

Placement or program refers to both the kind of class (such as a regular class, special day class, or residential placement) and the specific location of the program (such as a regular fifth-grade class at Abraham Lincoln School). Placement or program, sometimes referred to on the IEP form as the instructional setting, is central to a successful IEP and an effective educational experience. IDEA requires your child's school district to offer a continuum of placement options. (34 C.F.R. §300.551.) Placement or program is most often some kind of public program, but IDEA requires placement in a private school if there is no appropriate public option. Placement or program is generally the last item discussed at the IEP meeting.

As explained in Chapter 2, IDEA requires that your child be educated in the least restrictive environment. This means that to the maximum extent appropriate, children with disabilities are to be educated with children who are nondisabled. Special classes, separate schooling, or other removal of children with disabilities from a regular class should happen only if the nature or severity of the disability is such that your child cannot receive a satisfactory education in a regular class, even with the use of supplementary aids and services.

Despite the LRE guideline, there is no absolute rule that your child must be mainstreamed. IDEA prefers a mainstreamed placement, but many courts have ruled that a child's individual needs determine the appropriateness of a placement.

If you don't want your child mainstreamed, point out that although the law favors regular classroom placement, individual need determines whether a particular placement is appropriate for a particular child. Courts have clearly stated that there is no prohibition to placing a child in a nonregular class. In fact, if a child needs such a placement, it is by definition the least restrictive environment. (See *Geis v. Board of Education,* 774 F.2d 575 (3d Cir. 1985) and *Stockton by Stockton v. Barbour County Bd. of Educ.,* (4th Cir. 1997) 25 IDELR 1076.) (For more on court cases and legal research, see Chapter 14.)

If you want your child mainstreamed, emphasize your child's basic right to the least restrictive environment. You should also emphasize your child's right to be educated as close to home as possible, in the school the child would attend if not disabled. Ultimately, the burden is on the school district to prove that your child should be removed from a regular classroom.

School representatives may be prepared to discuss a specific program in a named school. Or, they may propose a kind of class, such as a special day class, but want to leave the specific location up to the school administration. If the school representatives suggest this latter option, object. The IEP team should decide both the kind of class (such as a special day class for language-delayed children) and the specific location (such as a regular class at King School).

You and the school administrator will probably know before the meeting where each of you stands on placement. Still, an open-minded IEP team should fully discuss your child's placement needs. The school administrator will probably state that the IEP team has reviewed your child's record, agreed on goals and objectives, resolved related services, and decided that a particular placement is called for.

If you disagree with the administrator's conclusion, state your preference and refer to supportive materials—particularly items that are very persuasive about placement. Then ask (or have your independent assessor ask) pointed questions, such as:

Ms. Parton, you said Betsy should be placed at Johnson School in the special day class. We believe Betsy should be placed in the regular class at Thompson School with a one-to-one aide. The assessment by Dr. Jones is specific about that, and Betsy's current teacher agrees. Can you explain why you disagree?

If the school administrator is not persuaded or does not answer your question adequately, be direct and frank:

With all due respect, I think your answer is vague and does not address the specifics in Dr. Jones's report and your own teacher's comment about Betsy's readiness for a regular classroom. I feel very strongly about this, and we will go to due process on the issue of placement if we have to. I also think that with the documentation and the law on mainstreaming, we will be successful in due process. I really feel that going in that direction is a bad use of school resources and will only make the ultimate move that much more expensive for you. I just don't understand—given the evidence—why you want to put me and my wife, your district personnel, and, most important, our child through that.

7. Narrative Page

The narrative page is the place to record information that can't be conveyed by checking a box or won't fit in the space provided on the form. The narrative page can include information on any other topic covered, whether covered by the IEP document or not. Here are some examples of narrative page statements.

Examples:

- The IEP team agrees that the school district and outside assessments are complete and appropriate, and are incorporated into the IEP.
- The IEP team incorporates the child profile provided by Steven's parents into the IEP.
- The IEP team agrees that Melissa needs a school environment in which there are no behavioral problems.
- The IEP team agrees that Henry is beginning to show signs of emotional distress; the classroom teacher will report on a weekly basis to the family about any signs of such distress. The district psychologist will observe Henry in class. The IEP team agrees to meet in three months to review this matter and to discuss the possible need for more formal assessment or the need for additional related services.
- The IEP team agrees with the recommendations made by Dr. Jones on page 4 of her report.
- Ms. Brown, Steve's teacher, is concerned about Steve's lack of focus.
- The IEP team agrees with recommendations 1, 2, 5, 7, and 9 made by Dr. Jones on page 4 of her report.
- Carolyn's parents expressed concern about class size.

Sometimes, the person recording the IEP document may write something that you and the school district don't agree on. Make sure the narrative is changed to reflect your disagreement or to indicate that the statement reflects only the point of view of the school personnel. Basically, you don't want the narrative to imply agreement when there is none.

Include a Child Profile in the IEP Plan

In Chapter 10, Section D, I suggested that you create a child profile to give school officials a perspective on your child beyond numbers and test results. The school administrator may question whether law or policy allows a child profile to be included in the IEP document. IDEA does not prohibit it, so nothing prevents the IEP team from discussing and including a child profile.

Emphasize that your statement about your child will help the school staff implement the goals and objectives, and for that reason it should be included in the IEP document. If the school administrator disagrees, ask why. Try to convince the team of the importance of the profile. If the administrator continues to refuse, use the parent addendum to include it.

E. Signing the IEP Document

At the end of the IEP meeting, the school administrator will ask you to sign the IEP document. School officials will be signing the form as well. You don't have to sign the IEP document on the spot. You may want to take it home and return it the next day. This will give you time to decide whether you agree or disagree with each aspect of the plan. It will also give you time to record your disagreements coherently on a parent addendum (discussed in Section F, below).

Of course, if you agree with the school representatives on all issues and don't need time to mull anything over, then go ahead and sign. Read the document carefully, however, to make sure the statements and information are correct and reflect the IEP team's intentions. Also, make sure that everything on your agenda was covered and that all important issues have been resolved.

If you do take the IEP document home, be sure that all other participants have signed off on each item to which they agreed.

Every IEP form has a signature page with a variety of checkboxes, including:

- a box to indicate you attended
- a box to indicate that you were provided your legal rights
- a box to indicate your approval of the IEP document, and
- a box to indicate your disapproval.

There may also be boxes to indicate partial approval and whether or not you want to initiate due process.

Take care in checking the appropriate boxes. If you partially agree, check the partial agreement box or, if there is no partial agreement box, check the approval box—*but* carefully and clearly write next to it: "Approval in part only; see parent addendum." (Section F, below, discusses the parent addendum.)

You must state your position clearly on the IEP. There are no legally required phrases to use—plain and direct English will do fine.

1. Full Agreement

Congratulations! Check the correct box and sign the form.

2. Nearly Full Agreement

It's possible that the IEP team will agree on all important items concerning related services, methodology, and program or placement, but disagree on some secondary issues, such as goals and objectives or statements in an assessment. In this situation, you have two choices:

- You can check the box to indicate your approval and sign your name. This might make sense if the issues on which you disagree are minor and you want to foster a good relationship with the school district.

- You can check the box to indicate partial approval, list the items you dispute (on the signature page if there's room or on the parent addendum), and sign your name.

Sample

Date: April 24, 20xx

Signature: *Lucinda Crenshaw*

I agree with all of the IEP except for:

- items 3, 4, and 6 on the district's assessment
- goals and objectives numbers 2 and 5.

You Don't Have to Accept "All or Nothing"

The school district cannot present you with an "all or nothing" choice. For example: "We're offering two sessions of occupational therapy. Either agree with the two sessions or there will be no occupational therapy for your child." You can agree to the two sessions without giving up your right to seek more. See Sections B8 and F for examples.

3. Partial Agreement

In this situation, you agree on some, but not all, of the big issues (related services, methodology, and program or placement). You can check the box to indicate partial approval, state that your disagreements are on the parent addendum, spell out your disagreements on the parent addendum, and sign your name.

Sample

> Date: April 24, 20xx
>
> Signature: *Lucinda Crenshaw*
>
> I agree with all of the IEP except for those items listed on the parent addendum page, designated as "Attachment A" and attached to the IEP.

4. Nearly Total Disagreement

In this case, you don't agree on any of the major items concerning related services, methodology, and program or placement, but do agree on certain goals and objectives, parts of the assessment, and minor items. Again, you can check the box to indicate partial approval, state that your disagreements are on the parent addendum, spell out your disagreements on the parent addendum (see Section F, below), and sign your name.

5. Total Disagreement

In some instances, there is total disagreement. If so, sign your name after checking both the box acknowledging that you attended the meeting and the disapproval box. You could also refer to the parent addendum page.

At this stage, your options are informal negotiations, mediation, or a fair hearing.

See Chapter 12 for information on due process, including your child's status when there is no IEP agreement.

F. Parent Addendum Page

When you disagree with the school personnel and cannot reach a compromise, make sure to state your position clearly. You or your notetaker should keep a list of all issues you dispute on a separate piece of paper.

A parent addendum page is an attachment to the IEP where you can record these disagreements and give your point of view. There is no IDEA requirement for an addendum page, although your district's IEP form may have one. The addendum page need not be a formal document—a blank piece of paper will do.

You will most likely complete the addendum page at or near the end of the meeting. The content of the addendum page is vastly more important than its format. Your statement should:

- relate to issues concerning your child's education—don't use the addendum to state general complaints
- be in plain English, and
- state your point of view on all key items of dispute.

As shown in Section E, above, you should indicate on the signature page that you disagree with part of the IEP document and refer to the attached addendum page for the detail of the disagreement.

> Date: _____
>
> Parent Signature**: _____
>
> ** See Addendum page (designated as "A") for a statement regarding what we are agreeing to and not agreeing to. My signature above is to be read only in conjunction with the statement on "A."

If your school's IEP form includes an addendum page, use it; otherwise, mark "Attachment A" at the top of a blank piece of paper and write something like the following:

> Parent Addendum Page of Carol and Steven Stack
> IEP for Beatrice Stack
> March 12, 20xx

You have an absolute right to state your position, but if, for some reason, the school district does not allow you to attach an addendum, indicate on the signature page that you do not agree with everything in the IEP document, that you want to attach an addendum, and that the school administration will not let you. Then file a complaint (see Chapter 13).

Example Addendum Statements:

- The district does not agree with the recommendations of Dr. Jones's independent assessment but has refused to state why. We believe that her assessment is valid and should be fully incorporated into the IEP as representing useful and valid information about Tonya.
- We do not agree with recommendations 3, 6, 9, and 14 of Dr. Lee's assessment of January 21, 20xx. We do agree with the rest of her report.
- The IEP team agrees with sections 3, 7, 8, and 9 of the school's report and all of Dr. Friedman's assessment, but the school will not put this agreement into the IEP. We believe those agreed-to sections should be incorporated into the IEP.
- Dr. Pentan of the school district stated that we have no right to include a child profile in the IEP. IDEA does not say that, and if the IEP team agrees, the profile can be part of the IEP. We believe the profile provides valid and important information regarding Fernando.
- While the teacher reported that Stanley increased his reading comprehension (this relates to goal #4 on page 2), we have observed at home, over a long period of time, that his reading comprehension seems substantially below the test results.

- We don't agree that Sandy's goals and objectives were met because the evaluation of the goals and objectives was inaccurate.
- The district offered speech therapy one time a week, 20 minutes per session. Moira needs three 40-minute sessions per week, each session to be conducted one-to-one with a licensed speech therapist. This is supported by the May 2, 20xx report of Dr. Shawn Waters. We accept the one session and give permission for that to begin, but this acceptance is not to be construed as agreement about the amount of the related services, only agreement as to the need.
- The IEP agrees that Nick be placed in the regular fifth-grade class at Kennedy School. We agree with placement in the regular fifth-grade class at Kennedy School, but we believe Nick needs an aide to allow him to achieve satisfactorily in that regular class.
- We believe that the regular seventh-grade class at Roosevelt School is the only appropriate placement for Tony. We believe placement in the special day class at Roosevelt as offered by the school district is inappropriate. We agree to placement in the regular classroom at Roosevelt for three periods a day, although such agreement is not to be construed as agreement on partial mainstreaming. We will proceed to due process on the issue of full-time mainstreaming in the regular seventh-grade class at Roosevelt.

■

12

Resolving IEP Disputes Through Due Process

The purpose of this book is to help you successfully develop an IEP plan for your child, and thereby make this chapter irrelevant. But the nature of the IEP process is such that disagreements arise, and some cannot be resolved informally.

Under IDEA, you have the right to resolve these disputes with your school district through "due process." (20 U.S.C. § 1415; 34 C.F.R. §§ 300.500-517.) There are two ways to resolve disputes through due process: mediation and a hearing.

In mediation, you and representatives of the school district meet with a neutral third party, who tries to help you reach a compromise. The mediator has no authority to impose a decision on you.

If you cannot reach an agreement in mediation, or if you prefer to skip mediation altogether, you can request a due process hearing—sometimes called a "fair hearing"—where you and school district personnel present written evidence and have witnesses testify about the disputed issues before a neutral third party, called a hearing officer. Much like a judge, the hearing officer considers the evidence, makes a decision, and issues a binding order within 45 days after you formally request due process. (34 C.F.R. § 300.511.) If you or the school district disagree with the decision, you can appeal to a state or federal court.

Due process is available to resolve factual disputes—that is, when you and your child's school district cannot agree on eligibility or some part of the IEP plan. If the school district has ignored a legal rule—by failing to hold an IEP meeting, do an assessment, meet a time limit, or provide an agreed-to part of the IEP—you must file a complaint rather than pursuing due process. (Complaints are covered in Chapter 13.)

Don't Delay Filing for Due Process

In almost all kinds of legal disputes, states have something called a statute of limitations, which establishes a time limit for taking legal action. Depending on the state and the kind of case, this may be anywhere from a few months to several years. If you fail to bring your legal action within your state's time limit, you will likely be barred from taking any legal action at all.

IDEA does not establish a time limit for filing for due process, submitting a complaint, or appealing a due process decision to a court. Numerous courts have ruled, however, that state statutes of limitations apply to IDEA matters. To avoid losing your right to file for due process, it is therefore very important that you check with your state department of education or a local lawyer regarding your state's statute of limitations—and be sure to file for due process well before the deadline.

Alternatives to Informal Negotiations and Formal Due Process

Informal discussions with the school district and formal due process aren't the only ways to resolve disputes. Other methods, such as building parent coalitions and becoming involved in the local political process, can also be effective. These options are discussed in Chapter 15.

In addition, IDEA provides that a state or local school district can establish alternative dispute resolution (ADR) procedures for parents who choose not to use due process.

In ADR, you meet with a neutral third party who is under contract with a parent training center or community parent resource center, or who is from an appropriate alternative dispute resolution entity. The purpose of the meeting is for you to explore alternative ways to resolve your dispute and for the third party to explain the benefits of mediation. This ADR meeting is intended to be nonadversarial, while mediation is the first step in formal due process. Be aware, however, that using ADR may delay resolution of the dispute—so if you need immediate action or the time limit for pursuing due process is coming up, you might want to skip this step.

If you're interested in ADR, call your school district or state department of education (see Appendix 2) to find out if ADR is available.

A. Before Due Process: Informal Negotiations

Before invoking due process, you may want to try to resolve your dispute through informal discussions or negotiations with the school. While resolving some problems might require formal action, many issues can be settled informally.

In addition, some disputes may not even qualify for due process. (See Section B, below.) For ex-

ample, you and the school principal may disagree over when you can visit the classroom or why the assessor had to reschedule your child's testing. Because you can't take these issues to due process, you'll have to hash them out informally or not at all.

1. Pros and Cons of Informal Negotiation

Informal negotiation is useful for several reasons. Ultimately, it may save you stress, preparation time, and money. It will also help you maintain a more positive relationship with the school district, and will keep problems from escalating. Finally, informal negotiation is easier to pursue than due process.

Even if you eventually pursue your due process rights, it might be a good idea to start with informal negotiation. This will show that you are reasonable and fair-minded, and don't immediately look to an adversarial method of settlement. Informal negotiations will also help you understand the school district's position, which will be valuable if you end up in mediation or at a fair hearing.

In limited situations, however, there may be reasons to go immediately to due process. For example, skip the informal negotiations if:

- You need an immediate resolution because the issue affects your child's well-being, safety, or health. For example, if you think that your child needs psychological counseling for depression, but the district disagreed, you may not have time for informal meetings.
- The school administrator is so unpleasant or inflexible that you just don't want to deal with him or her.
- The IEP meeting made it clear that it would be a waste of time to try to resolve things informally.

2. Basics of Informal Negotiation

To begin informal negotiations, call or write your child's teacher, school principal, or special education administrator and ask for a meeting to discuss your concerns. You can raise the issues in your phone conversation or letter, but ideally you'll want an appointment to discuss the problem face to face.

Before the meeting, prepare a brief and clear written description of the problem and a recommended solution. Also, find out if any school personnel support you. If so, ask them to attend the meeting or ask for permission to present their opinions at the meeting.

During the meeting, emphasize problem solving, not winning. Try to structure the negotiation as a mutual attempt to solve a problem. Avoid personal attacks on school personnel. Respect the school's point of view even if you disagree. Acknowledge the school representatives' concerns. Even if you strongly disagree, you don't lose anything by saying, "I understand your concerns, but I think we can address those by doing ...."

Finally, be respectful, but firm—for example, you can say, "It is clear we disagreed at the IEP meeting. I am not adverse to trying to solve this informally, but I will not hesitate to pursue my due process rights if we cannot."

Good Books on Negotiation

Getting to Yes: Negotiating Agreement Without Giving In, by Roger Fisher and William Ury (Penguin Books). This classic book offers a strategy for coming to mutually acceptable agreements in all kinds of situations.

Getting Past No: Negotiating Your Way From Confrontation to Cooperation, by William Ury (Bantam Books). This sequel to *Getting to Yes* suggests techniques for negotiating with difficult people.

---

3. After Meeting Informally

If you do not resolve your dispute informally, send a letter briefly stating the problem, the solution you think makes sense, and what you are considering next, such as contacting an attorney, pursuing mediation or fair hearing, or filing a complaint with your school board or the state department of education.

If you resolve your problem informally, it is very important to follow up the meeting with a confirming letter.

A sample letter confirming the results of your informal negotiation is below; a blank, tear-out copy of this form is in Appendix 5.

Use the Law to Make Your Case

As you try to persuade your school district—in writing or in person—that you are correct, cite the legal authority for your position if possible. Referring to a section in IDEA or even a court decision may help you convince the school district. See Chapter 14, Section F, for tips on legal research.

If the meeting does not resolve the problem to your satisfaction, then you may proceed to due process (either mediation or a fair hearing) or file a complaint.

B. Typical Due Process Disputes

Remember, due process (mediation or fair hearing) is used to resolve only factual disputes, not disagreements over what the law requires or allows. Here are some due process disputes:

- eligibility for special education
- results of an assessment
- goals and objectives

Sample Letter Confirming Informal Negotiation

Date: ___June 1, 20xx_____

To: Michael Chan, Principal_____

Truman Elementary School_____

903 Dogwood Drive_____

Paterson, NJ 07506_____

Re: Tasha Kincaid, student in second-grade class of Marlene Walker, Truman School

I appreciated the chance to meet on ___May 28, 20xx_____ and discuss

Tasha's placement_____. I also appreciated your

point of view and the manner in which we solved the problem.

I want to confirm our agreement that ___Tasha will be placed in the regular third-grade___

class at Truman School for the upcoming school year. [If you have already requested

due process, add: Once you have confirmed this in writing to me, I will formally withdraw

my due process request.]_____ .

I greatly appreciate the manner in which you helped solve this problem. ___Please tell the___

third-grade teacher, Ms. Solarz, that I would be delighted to meet with her before

school starts to discuss effective ways to work with Tasha._____

_____ .

Thank you.

Sincerely,

André Kincaid_____

André Kincaid_____

4500 Fair Street_____

Paterson, NJ 07506_____

Phones: 555-3889 (home); 555-2330 (work)_____

- specific placement or program
- related services
- proposed changes to your child's current IEP program, and
- suspension or expulsion of your child.

Several kinds of disputes are *not* eligible for due process, including:

- requesting a specific teacher or service provider by name for your child
- hiring or firing school staff
- assigning a different school administrator to your case, or
- requesting a specific person to represent the school district in the IEP process.

These concerns may be addressed through non-IDEA activities, such as parent organizing (see Chapter 15) or informal negotiations with the school.

C. When to Pursue Due Process

Due process is hard; it takes time, energy, and sometimes money, and it can be quite stressful. When you consider whether to go forward, think about these factors:

- **The precise nature of the problem.** You will have to pinpoint exactly what your dispute is, and make sure it is a factual dispute. For example, if you feel your child's education is generally not working (and you have not yet gone to an IEP meeting), or you object to the attitude of the school administrator, your concern is not yet ready for due process. If, however, your child has fallen behind in her regular class, you feel she should be in a special class, and the IEP team did not agree, you have a problem that qualifies for due process resolution.

Don't File for Due Process Until After the IEP Meeting

Many parents make the mistake of requesting a fair hearing before the issue is considered at an IEP meeting. Unless there are very unusual circumstances—for example, your child's health or well-being is threatened—you must go to an IEP meeting and reach an impasse there before you can request due process. However, if your school district has been dragging its feet about holding the IEP meeting or otherwise failing to address your child's needs, filing for due process before the IEP meeting can get things moving.

- **The importance of the issue to your child.** Placement or related service disputes are often central to your child's educational well-being. On the other hand, a dispute over goals and objectives or assessment conclusions may not be significant enough to go to due process, because it does not directly impact your child's placement and related services.

- **The strength of your case.** Can you win? What evidence do you have to support your position? What evidence exists against it? What are the qualifications of the people making supportive or contrary statements? Remember that the district is required to provide your child with an appropriate education, not the best possible one. After the IEP meeting, review and update your IEP Material Organizer form (discussed in Chapter 10) to evaluate the evidence for and against you. If you want other opinions on the strength of your case, consider these sources:

  ▲ Nonschool employees, your independent assessor, an outside tutor, or an attorney. Describe the disputed issue, your evidence, and the evidence against you, and ask whether you have a good chance of winning.

▲ Other parents, particularly those who have been through due process with your school district. How does the school district react? Is the school likely to take a hard line position, or might it offer a compromise after you show you are determined to go forward?

▲ Local parent and disability organizations. (Chapter 15 discusses how to find and work with a parents' group.) If you need help finding a local group, start by contacting a national organization (see the list in Appendix 3).

• **The bottom line concerns for the school district.** For any disputed issue, the school district will have some bottom-line concerns—notably the cost and administrative difficulty of providing what you want. For example, the school administrator may be willing to compromise on a dispute between two public school program options, rather than pay for costly private school placement. The school's bottom line may affect your bottom line—and how far you'll go to get it.

• **The cost of going forward.** Due process witnesses (including independent assessors) and attorneys will charge for their time. If you prevail at a fair hearing, you are likely to be reimbursed for those costs, but not if you lose. (See Chapter 14 for information on using an attorney and attorney's fees.)

D. Your Child's Status During Due Process

While you are in dispute with the school district, your child is entitled to remain in her current placement until you reach an agreement with the school, settle the matter through mediation, receive a fair hearing decision rendered that neither you nor the school district appeal, or get a final court decision. This is called the "stay put" provision. (34 C.F.R. § 300.514; 20 U.S.C. § 1415(j).)

"Stay put" can be a complicated legal right. If you are concerned about whether your particular situation involves a "stay put" issue, see an attorney at once or contact a nonprofit disability rights organization.

Example:
Your child is in a regular sixth-grade class with a one-to-one aide, two hours a day. At the IEP meeting, the school district offers a special day class, not a regular class, for seventh grade. You want your child to continue in a regular class. You are unable to reach an agreement at the IEP meeting. You initiate due process, during which time your child is entitled to remain in a regular classroom with the aide until the matter is resolved.

Exceptions to the Stay Put Rule

IDEA entitles your child to remain in his or her current placement pending due process unless your child carries a weapon to school or a school function, or knowingly possesses, uses, sells, or solicits illegal drugs while at school or a school function. In situations involving weapons or drugs, the school district can change your child's placement to an appropriate interim alternative educational setting for up to 45 days, or suspend your child for up to ten school days. See Chapter 2A for more information on discipline for students in special education.

E. Using a Lawyer During Due Process

Using an attorney in due process certainly escalates the adversarial nature of the dispute, but by the time you've reached due process, that is probably not your primary concern. Using an attorney may also speed things along and increase your chances of success.

In mediation, an attorney will present your case and counter the school district's arguments. In a fair hearing, an attorney should prepare witnesses, submit exhibits, make the opening statement, and direct the proceeding. An attorney can also play a less active role, such as providing advice and helping you organize your case material, without attending the proceeding. Your attorney will contact the district to let them know that he or she is involved in the case.

Not surprisingly, legal costs can be considerable. To prepare for and attend a one-day mediation session, an attorney will likely charge from $500 to $1,000—sometimes less, sometimes more. The cost for a two- to three-day fair hearing may range from $1,500 to $7,500 or more. It is not unusual for an attorney to use ten to 25 hours to prepare for a three-day hearing. If you use an attorney for advice only—for example, to help organize your case—your legal costs will be lower.

 See Chapter 14 for a thorough discussion of attorneys and legal fees.

Check Out Free or Low-Cost Legal Services

The school district must provide you with a list of free or low-cost legal services available in your area. See Chapter 14, Section C, for advice on finding and working with an attorney.

---

1. Attorney Fees in Mediation

During mediation, you should ask the school district, as part of your proposed settlement, to pay your attorney fees. Your legal fees are one of many bargaining chips you can use to negotiate a settlement in mediation. However, the school dis-

trict doesn't have to pay your fees, just as it doesn't have to agree to any other particular settlement term. Because mediation (and any settlement you reach as a result of it) is voluntary, the school district may or may not agree to pay your fees. Remember, a mediation is usually a settlement in which neither party gets everything it wants; attorney fees my be one of those things you are willing to forgo in order to get something more important.

The school district's decision will depend largely on how strong your case is and how motivated the school district is to settle. The school district may try to avoid having to reimburse you by agreeing to provide the education you want, if you agree to drop your demand for attorney fees. You will have to assess the strength of your case to decide whether you are willing to forgo your legal fees. If your case is very strong, the school district may decide that they are better off paying your fees now rather than later, when you will have run up a higher legal bill. Your attorney can advise you of the pros and cons in this situation.

SO MUCH FOR THE SMALL TALK! HOW MUCH DO YOU CHARGE?

2004 IDEA Reauthorization and Attorney Fees

As Congress debated reauthorization of IDEA in 2003, it considered changing the way attorneys are reimbursed when a parent prevails in due process. Currently, IDEA governs the payment of attorney fees—for example, it states that the attorney will receive an hourly rate based on the general rates in the area where the attorney practices and the child lives.

Congress is considering changing this provision to give each state the right to set rates for attorneys in special education matters. Under this proposal, states would not be prohibited from setting low rates of compensation, which might discourage attorneys from taking these cases in the first place.

While one can fairly feel some skepticism when attorneys complain that they don't earn enough, the truth is that special education lawyers earn fairly modest incomes, especially compares to attorneys who practice in other areas of law. If Congress changes this provision, it could have a real impact on your ability to find a lawyer. Check Nolo's website (www.nolo.com) for updates on the law, or the website of the National Dissemination Center for Children with Disabilities (formerly the National Information Center for Children and Youth with Disabilities), at www.nichcy.org (click on "IDEA").

2. Attorney Fees in Fair Hearing

If your case goes to fair hearing and you win, you will be entitled to reimbursement of your attorney's fees. If you lose the hearing, you're responsible for your own attorney's fees, but you will not have to pay the school district's attorney's fees.

If you win on some issues but not on others, you will be reimbursed for the time your lawyer spent on the winning issues (but not on the losers).

3. Other Legal Advocates

There are nonattorney advocates who can be quite skilled in due process. Their fees are usually lower than a lawyer's fees, but you are not entitled to reimbursement of an advocate's fees if you settle in mediation, prevail in a fair hearing, or prevail after representing yourself.

Special education attorneys, nonprofit law centers, and disability and parent support groups may know the names of special education advocates in your area.

F. Requesting Due Process

You must formally request due process in order for a mediation or fair hearing to be scheduled. Different agencies are responsible for due process in different states. Your school district must provide you with the name, address, and phone number of the appropriate agency. Call the agency and ask how to initiate due process. Usually, you will have to either complete a form provided by the agency or send a letter providing the following information:

- your name and address
- your child's name and grade
- the name of your child's school and the address of the school district
- a description of the disputed issues
- your desired resolution—not only what you want for your child's education, but also that you want to be reimbursed for your due process costs, such as attorney's fees, witness fees, and independent assessment costs, and
- whether you want to mediate or to go directly to a fair hearing.

This information is required under IDEA. (34 C.F.R. § 300.507(c)(2).)

Keep a copy of your completed form or letter for your records.

A sample letter requesting due process is below; a blank, tear-out copy is in Appendix 5. Your school district is required to have a model due process request letter for you to use. (34 C.F.R. § 300.507(c)(3).)

G. Preparing for Due Process

While a mediation session and a fair hearing are different, preparing for the former will help as you get ready for the latter. In addition, the preparation you did for the IEP meeting will be of enormous help as you go through due process. The recommendations in this section apply to both mediation and the due process hearing.

1. Organize Your Evidence

First, pull out your child's file, and the reports, assessments, and other documents in your IEP binder (see Chapter 4), your blueprint (see Chapter 5), and your IEP Material Organizer form (see Chapter 10).

Make a list of the disputed issues. Using a blank IEP Material Organizer form, write next to each disputed issue the witnesses, documents, or facts that support your point of view—and those that oppose it. You should make a separate list of your potential witnesses and people who might testify for the district.

Now find every piece of evidence you have to support your position. Review your binder, original Material Organizer forms, and notes from the IEP meeting. Focus not only on reports and assessments, but also on comments made at the meeting. Gather all your supportive evidence together, or tab it in your binder and highlight key statements. Make photocopies of all written materials that support your point of view to have available during the mediation or hearing.

Now work on the school district's case—that is, figure out what evidence contradicts your point of view. Think about any evidence you can use to rebut the district's likely arguments.

2. Make a List of Expenses

Once you've gathered evidence, make a list of expenses you've incurred throughout the IEP process, such as the costs of:

- independent assessments
- tutors
- lost wages for attending IEPs
- private school or private related service costs
- personal transportation costs, such as those incurred driving your child to a private school
- attorney's fees
- costs for other professionals (such as a private speech therapist or counselor), and
- photocopying.

Note the date a payment was made or cost incurred, the name of the payee, and purpose of the expense. Attach all receipts.

There are no IDEA rules on how you must prepare or present these expenses. At mediation or the fair hearing, you will want to request payment for the expenses; if the district agrees to pay some or all of them, or if the hearing officer rules in your favor, the receipts will be your proof that you really spent this money.

3. Prepare an Opening Statement

At the beginning of a mediation session or fair hearing, you will need to make an opening statement explaining why you're there and what you want. Some people are comfortable making notes and then talking extemporaneously; others write out a complete statement and read it. Do what's easiest for you. The opening statement should include the following:

Description of your child. Briefly describe your child, including his or her age, current educational program, general areas of educational concern, and disabling conditions. Give a short explanation of your child's educational history.

Letter Requesting Due Process

Date: March 1, 20xx

To: Philip Jones   **Sent Certified Mail**

Due Process Unit

Wisconsin Department of Education

8987 Franklin Ave., La Crosse, WI 54601

Re: Steven Howard

Our son, Steven Howard, is a fourth-grader at Clinton School in La Crosse. His school district is the Central La Crosse Elementary School District, 562 5th Ave., La Crosse, WI.

We are formally requesting due process, beginning with mediation. We believe Steven requires a full-time, one-on-one aide in order to be fully mainstreamed in next year's regular fifth-grade class at Clinton School. The school district has refused to provide that aide.

We believe an appropriate solution would include, but should not be limited to, the following:

- a qualified full-time academic aide, to work one-on-one with Steven in the regular fifth-grade class at Clinton School for the coming school year.

- reimbursement for all attorney's fees, witnesses, independent assessments, and other such costs as accrued by us for the February 14, 20xx IEP meeting and subsequent due process.

We understand IDEA (34 C.F.R. § 300.511) requires that a fair hearing decision be rendered within 45 days after your receive this request. We would appreciate it if you would contact us at once to schedule the mediation.

Sincerely,

William Howard   *Kate Howard*

William and Kate Howard

1983 Smiley Lane

La Crosse, WI 54601

Phones: 555-5569 (home); 555-2000 (work)

Description of items in dispute. Briefly describe the specific items in dispute—for example, the amount of a related service or the placement.

Description of what you want and why. Summarize what your child needs—for example, speech therapy three times a week, in a one-to-one setting with a therapist qualified to work with students with language delays, placement in the Smith School, or the use of the Lindamood-Bell program or the Orton-Gillingham method.

Description of your evidence. Often, you'll close with a strong statement briefly summarizing the evidence you have for your position. In some mediations, however, you may decide not to reveal all of your evidence right away. You will have to judge the best approach considering the situation, the personalities involved, and even your intuition. (See "How Much Evidence Do You Reveal in Mediation?," below.)

H. Mediation Specifics

Mediation is the first official step in due process. It is less confrontational than a fair hearing, and is intended to explore ways to compromise and settlement of your dispute. The IDEA requires that all states offer mediation. (20 U.S.C. § 1415(e); 34 C.F.R. § 300.506.)

The mediator is a neutral third party, usually hired by the state department of education, who is knowledgeable about IDEA and special education matters. The mediator has no authority to force a settlement on you. If you reach settlement, however, your agreement will be put into writing and will be made binding on you and the district—you both must abide by and follow the written settlement.

While mediation is fairly similar from one place to another, the way sessions proceed will vary depending on the style of the mediator and the rules established by your state.

Contact your state department of education to find out the details of your state's laws on mediation. See Appendix 2.

Mediation must be made available to you at no cost. Mediation is completely voluntary. If you don't want to mediate, you don't have to. If you prefer, you can go straight to a fair hearing and skip mediation.

If mediation is not successful, any settlement offers and other comments made during the mediation cannot be used as evidence at the fair hearing or any subsequent legal proceedings. This rule allows you to discuss matters in a frank manner without fear that your statements will later be used against you. (34 C.F.R. § 300.506(b)(6).)

1. Pros and Cons of Mediation

You may be asking yourself why you would try mediation, particularly because it ends in compromise, rather than a clear victory for one side or the other. There are some compelling reasons to go to mediation:

- **Know thine enemy.** Mediation gives you a chance to understand more fully the school district's arguments. Of course, the school district gets the same opportunity to hear about your case, but sharing information in this way may bring you closer to a solution.
- **The school district may be motivated to compromise.** Mediation takes the school district one step closer to a fair hearing and the possibility of a ruling against the school, with all the attendant costs, including possible attorney's fees. The school administrator may be far more flexible in mediation than at the IEP meeting, feeling that a compromise now is better than an expensive loss later.
- **Mediation is constructive.** Mediation encourages the parties to work out disagreements. Thus, you may retain a more

positive relationship with your school district by mediating the dispute. You also keep control over the outcome—you must agree with any mediated solution. When you go to fair hearing, the decision-making power is out of your hands.

- **Mediation is cheap.** As a general rule, you will have few or even no costs at mediation; fair hearings can be expensive, particularly if you use an attorney.

- **Mediation can provide a reality check.** Even if you don't settle the case, mediation gives you a chance to have a neutral party assess your case and point out its strengths and weaknesses.

- **You get two bites of the apple.** By going to mediation, you give yourself two chances at success. If the mediation is unsuccessful, you can move on to a fair hearing.

There are also downsides to mediation:

- **Half a loaf can be disappointing.** Ideally, you can settle in mediation and get everything your child needs. In reality, however, mediation usually involves compromise, meaning you will probably settle for less than what you would have received if you had won at fair hearing.

- **Mediation may delay resolution of your dispute.** The IDEA requires that a fair hearing decision be issued within 45 days after the date you request due process, whether you go through mediation or go straight to fair hearing. In reality, however, extensions of that 45-day rule can be granted if you spend time in mediation. Unless you have a real time problem—your child must be placed in a specific program by a certain date or will suffer dire consequences—most cases can stand the delay.

- **You do things twice.** If you go to mediation and then a fair hearing, you will have been involved in two procedures, doubling the time, inconvenience, stress, and some costs.

Try mediation. Although there are some downsides to mediation, they are almost always outweighed by the benefits. Unless there is a compelling reason to go straight to a hearing—like a serious time crunch or a truly entrenched opponent—you should give mediation a try.

2. Mediators

The mediator's job is to help you and the school district reach a settlement. The mediator will not decide who is right and who is wrong. A good mediator will:

- put you and school representatives at ease
- try to establish an atmosphere in which compromise is possible
- be objective
- give you and the school district a frank assessment of the strengths and weaknesses of your positions, and
- go beyond your stated positions to explore possible settlements that may not be initially apparent.

Some mediators play a more limited role—they simply present everyone's positions and hope that the weight of the evidence and formality of the process will lead to a settlement.

3. Mediation Logistics

Mediation sessions must be held at a time and place convenient for you. They are often held at the school district's main office, but they can be held elsewhere. Some people are concerned that having the mediation at a school office gives the district an advantage, but I have found it usually does not matter.

The length of the mediation can vary, but sessions generally take many hours and often a full day. Expect the mediation session to take more time than you would think.

While districts vary, most will send the special education administrator and perhaps another person who has direct knowledge of your child to the mediation. While you can bring outside assessors, aides, tutors, and any other individuals you want, including a lawyer, you will usually want to save them for the fair hearing.

Bringing in experts might make mediation more expensive and difficult to schedule. Whether you include experts will depend on:

- how forceful the experts can be
- whether there is any chance to change the district's mind, and
- the risks of revealing some of your evidence prior to the fair hearing.

If you expect a fair hearing and don't want to put all your cards on the table at mediation, don't bring the experts. On the other hand, if you want to settle quickly and your experts can aid in that process, bring them along.

4. The Mediation Session

You, the mediator, and the school representatives will gather in a conference or meeting room. After brief introductions, the mediator will explain how the mediation process works, stressing that mediation is a voluntary attempt to resolve your disagreement.

a. Your Opening Statement

You begin by briefly explaining your side of the dispute. (Section G, above, shows how to prepare an opening statement.) Do not hesitate to express your feelings. Your child has important needs, and his or her well-being is at stake. Say that. Express how worried you are. Explain why you feel the school district has not effectively served your child by failing to provide an appropriate education. It's important to show the mediator how imperative the matter is to you and your child. This does not mean tirades or irrational, unfocused

monologues. Give your opinion, but don't question the honesty, professionalism, or decency of the school representatives.

Your opening statement should not go on and on or discuss every possible problem. It should be clear and succinct, and run from five to 20 minutes.

If the school has committed any legal violations, you can raise these in your opening statement. While legal violations are subject to the complaint procedure (see Chapter 13), evidence of a legal violation may be a powerful addition to your case, showing the school district's disregard or lack of understanding of the law, and possibly the district's lack of reliability. Nothing in IDEA prevents you from raising legal issues in the mediation. While the mediator cannot remedy legal violations, the mediator can say to district personnel, "You are in trouble because you clearly violated the law; you might want to think about settling this case now."

How Much Evidence Do You Reveal in Mediation?

Section G, above, suggests that you describe your evidence as a part of your opening statement. But you may not want to reveal all your supporting evidence at mediation. By telling all, you may help the school prepare for the fair hearing. On the other hand, if your evidence is very strong, revealing it may lead to a settlement in your favor. If you're not sure what to do, ask the mediator's opinion in your private meeting. If the mediator feels that the school realizes its case is weak or for some other reason is close to settling, then it may be wise to share everything. On the other hand, if the mediator feels the school is rigid and unlikely to settle, then it may be better not to reveal all of your evidence.

In either case, you'll want to provide at least a synopsis of your evidence, noting where a professional (teacher, related service provider, administrator, doctor, outside assessor, or private tutor) has made a clear statement about the disputed issue. Also note the credentials of the person, particularly if he or she is well-known, is loaded with degrees, and has a lot of experience. Highlight all documents or statements by school district representatives that support your position.

b. School District's Opening Statement

After you make your opening statement, the school district's representative presents the district's point of view, perhaps responding to what you have said. Don't interrupt or respond, even though the school's version of the dispute may be very different from yours. Take notes of their main points.

After the school representative finishes, the mediator may invite you to add anything you forgot or to respond to the school's statement. If you respond, make it brief and to the point, focusing on why you disagree with the school's position.

c. Private Sessions With the Mediator

After you and the school representatives make your opening statements, the mediator will meet privately with you, then with the school representatives, then back with you, then back with the school representatives, continuing back and forth as necessary. When you meet privately with the mediator, speak frankly. The mediator cannot disclose anything you say to the school representatives, unless you give the mediator permission. Be sure of this by clearly telling the mediator what you want conveyed to school district and what you want kept between you and the mediator.

In your first meeting, the mediator may want to clarify issues and begin exploring whether you're willing to compromise.

As the mediator shuttles back and forth, specific evidence may come up related to a disputed issue. For example, you and the school district may have very different views on the validity of the district's assessment versus your independent assessment. You can say to the mediator something like "Please convey to Mr. Roberts that my assessor is a recognized expert and is clear in her recommendations; the district's expert has limited knowledge of my child's disability."

After a few of these private sessions, the mediator should be able to tell you how far the school will go to settle the dispute. At this point, you will have to think about your bottom line. Hopefully, you thought about this before the meeting. Think about what is essential, what you can give up, how strong your case is, and how hard a line the school is taking. Make use of the mediator by asking direct questions, such as:

- What do you think the school will do on the placement issue?
- Do they understand that Dr. Parnell said Victor needs placement in the private school?
- What is their bottom line?
- Do you think we have a case if we go to a fair hearing?

The strength of the evidence and the work of the mediator will convince the district to settle (or not). If the district has moved from the position it held at the IEP meeting, but some issues remain unresolved, you'll have to decide what to do. You'll have to weigh the importance of the outstanding, nonresolved issues, your willingness to go to a fair hearing, and the likelihood of ultimate victory.

Tips on Bargaining in Mediation

Bargaining is part of mediation. When presenting what you want, make your list as strong and inclusive as possible. Put in everything you could possibly want, including your expenses and even minor items. But know your priorities, including what you can live without and can therefore use as bargaining chips.

Example:

You feel your child should be in a private school, which costs $15,000 per year. You also want the school district to pay for your private assessment, which was $1,000. You also have some reimbursement costs, including a tutor, totaling several hundred dollars. Your case is strong enough to go after all of these items. But to compromise, you may have to forego the assessment and other costs.

---

d. Wrapping Up the Mediation Session

After various private meetings with the mediator, there will be four possible outcomes:

- full settlement of all issues
- partial settlement—you agree on some issues and disagree on others
- no settlement, but you agree to try again with the mediator at a later date, or
- no settlement and no further mediation sessions scheduled.

A mediation settlement can contain anything you and the school district agree to—including that the school will provide all or part of what you want for your child and, if you have an attorney at mediation, pay your attorney fees.

Whatever the outcome, you will all return to the meeting room, and the mediator will complete a mediation form. The mediator will write down what the parties agreed to (if anything), what issues are unresolved (if any), and what the next steps will be if full agreement was not reached.

If you don't reach a settlement on all or some issues, you have three options:

- go to a fair hearing
- drop the matter—this may make sense if only minor issues remain unresolved, or
- go directly to court—this highly unusual approach requires you to prove that the problem is so serious you can't spend time at a fair hearing and need a judge to look at the matter immediately; you will need a lawyer's help (see Chapter 14).

Once you and the school district sign the mediation form, both of you are bound by whatever agreement you reached.

I. Fair Hearing

A fair hearing is like a court trial, although it won't be held in a courtroom. You and the school district submit evidence in the form of written documents and sworn testimony from witnesses. A neutral third party, called a hearing officer, reviews the evidence and decides who is right and who is wrong. That decision is binding on you and the district. The hearing officer has the authority to act independently of you and the school district—in essence, as a judge. The hearing officer cannot be an employee of the school district or the state educational agency if either agency is involved in the education of your child. (34 C.F.R. § 300.508.)

Although IDEA establishes specific rules for fair hearings (34 C.F.R. §§ 300.507-511), states can vary some of the procedural details. For example, Ohio provides that attorneys will act as hearing officers; other states specify qualifications, rather than require that officers be members of particular professions. In most states, the department of education provides a list of hearing officers or contracts with a qualified agency to do so. For instance, in California, the state department of education has contracted with a law school, which in turn hires the hearing officers.

Contact your state department of education to find out the details of your state's laws on fair hearings. See Appendix 2.

A fair hearing is used to resolve factual disputes between you and your child's school district, including disagreements about placement, a related service, curricula, or methodology. Section B, above, lists typical IEP due process disputes.

Often, a factual dispute contains a legal dispute. For example, you want your child in a private school, and the school district offers a special day class in the public school. The factual dispute involves which placement is appropriate for your child. The legal issue is whether IDEA allows a private school placement when supported by the facts (it does).

Or, the school district wants to place your child in a special school 15 miles from your home; you want your child placed in a regular class at the local school. Again, the factual dispute involves finding the appropriate placement. The legal issue is IDEA's requirement that your child be placed in the least restrictive environment.

You may be thinking at this point, "I thought legal problems were subject only to the complaint process." Here's how it works: In a fair hearing, there may be legal issues that shape the factual analysis and outcome. In a complaint, you are only claiming that the school district broke the law—there is no factual dispute regarding an IEP issue (as there is in a fair hearing).

In some cases, you may simultaneously file a complaint and due process, as discussed at the end of Chapter 13.

A witness may testify about a legal issue, or you or the school district may raise a legal issue in your opening statements. In most cases, however, legal issues are addressed in a post-hearing brief (see Section 6, below). Discussing legal issues at the hearing or in a brief may seem quite daunting. If you anticipate major legal disputes, see Chapter 14 on lawyers and legal research, or contact an attorney for help on this part of the process.

Fear of Fair Hearings

It's natural to be afraid of a fair hearing—after all, it's like a trial and can be difficult and complicated. But many parents conduct fair hearings. So how do you get through one with your nerves intact?

- Be organized.
- Take some time to think through the issues and your evidence.
- Know that everybody else is nervous, too.

Never doubt that you can do it. Lots of parents have had these same fears—and done just fine. In preparing for the IEP meeting (and perhaps mediation), you already did a good deal of the hard work.

1. Your Fair Hearing Rights and Responsibilities

IDEA sets out several rights and responsibilities you *and* the school district have during the fair hearing process. (20 U.S.C. § 1415(h)(i); 34 C.F.R. §§ 508-511.) These include the following:

- You have the right to be advised and accompanied by an attorney or another person with special knowledge or training.
- At least five days before the hearing, you and the school district must provide each other with a list of your witnesses and copies of all written evidence you will submit at the hearing, including any assessments. The hearing officer can exclude the testimony of anyone not on the witness list or any document not exchanged before the hearing.
- Before the hearing, you can subpoena witnesses to ensure that they will attend. (Most state educational agencies have subpoena forms.)
- Before the hearing, you have the right to declare the fair hearing closed or open to the public. An open hearing gives access to the public, including the press, which you may want. But an open meeting may also increase the stress and invite district employees to come and go.
- At the hearing, you can present written evidence in the form of exhibits and ask witnesses to answer questions.
- After the hearing, you are entitled to a verbatim record of the hearing (in a written or electronic format). This means that the hearing officer will tape the proceedings.
- After the hearing, you're entitled to a written decision, including findings of fact, within 45 days of when you first requested due process.
- You have the right to appeal a fair hearing decision to a state or federal court.

 Check your state laws and regulations for any different or additional rules. For example, California requires each party to a fair hearing to submit a statement of issues and proposed resolutions at least ten days before the hearing. (Cal. Educ. Code § 56505(e)(6).)

2. Pros and Cons of a Fair Hearing

There are several good reasons to request a fair hearing:

- If you win, your child will receive the education he or she needs.
- If you win, it's unlikely you will have to fight the battle again.
- If you win, your attorney's fees and other costs will be reimbursed for every issue you prevail on.
- Whether or not you win, you buy time. If your child is currently in a placement you want to maintain, your child is entitled to remain there until the issue is finally resolved —either through the fair hearing decision or a final court decision, if you appeal. (Section D, above, discusses this "stay put" provision.)

There are also disadvantages to going to a fair hearing:

- Fair hearings are difficult, time-consuming, emotionally draining, and contentious.
- You might lose.
- Your relationship with your school district will likely be strained and formal. Future IEPs may be hard. If you lose, the school district may feel invincible.
- If you lose, you won't be entitled to reimbursement for your costs and attorney's fees (you won't have to pay the school district's attorney's fees in any event).

3. Fair Hearing Logistics

A fair hearing must be at a time and place convenient to you. Normally, fair hearings are held at the school district office and last anywhere from one to several days.

Once you request a fair hearing, you will be sent a notice of the date and location of the hearing, as well as the name of the hearing officer. You will also be given the name, address, and phone number of the school district representative. This information is important—you must send your exhibits and witness lists to this representative, as well as to the hearing officer.

4. Preparing for a Fair Hearing

If you go to mediation first, much of your preparation will be done by the time you go to fair hearing. But you still have some very important and time-consuming work to do. Give yourself several weeks to prepare, more if you skip mediation and go straight to fair hearing.

a. Know Your Case

Review your child's file (see Chapter 3), your binder (see Chapter 4), and your IEP blueprint (see Chapter 5). Be clear on the disputed issues— what you want, what the school district is offering, and how you disagree. Don't confuse personality conflicts with disputes over your child's needs.

b. Determine Your Strategy

At the hearing, you must clearly state your position on each disputed issue and offer evidence to support it, in the form of witnesses and documents.

Example:
You want your child mainstreamed with a one-to-one aide, but your school district offers a special class. At the hearing, you will have to show that:

- the school district failed to offer mainstreaming placement
- an aide will help your child function in the classroom
- your child will do well socially because her friends are in the class, and
- a special class will be detrimental to your child because it will not address your child's unique needs and is contrary to IDEA's least restrictive environment requirement.

c. Prepare Exhibits of Written Material

You can submit any written document that contains supportive evidence or provides information that the hearing officer will need to make a decision as an exhibit. But be choosy—you don't necessarily want to turn over your entire IEP binder. The issues in dispute will guide you. Review all of your documents, looking for everything that supports your position, such as an assessment or teacher's report. Note the specific place in each document where the supportive statement is made—that is, the page number and paragraph. You have probably done much of this work with the Material Organizer form you developed for the IEP meeting.

⚠ **Do not submit material that damages your case or reveals private information you don't want known.** The school district may submit evidence that harms your case or points out the gaps in your evidence; obviously, you should not. Remember that the school district and hearing officer will get to examine the exhibits you submit— if they contain personal or confidential information that you don't want to reveal, you should try to find a different way to make your point.

Example of exhibits typically presented at fair hearings include:
- IEP documents
- assessments and evaluations

- letters or reports from your child's teacher or physician
- articles about your child's disability, appropriate teaching methods, or any other issues in your case
- witnesses' résumés and articles they've written that relate to the issues in dispute, and
- your child's classroom work or artwork.

If in doubt, include the item. You never know when you might want to refer to something during the hearing. If you don't include the item when you prepare your exhibit exchange (at least five days before the hearing), you will probably be barred from using it at the hearing.

Arrange your exhibits in an order that makes sense to you, such as the order in which you think you'll introduce them or alphabetical order. Place them in a folder or binder with tabs and a table of contents. Be sure to page number each individual exhibit, too, so you can find specific statements easily.

You'll refer to these exhibits in your own testimony and when you question witnesses. At this stage, it is unlikely that you will have to develop new evidence. But if you do not yet have support for a disputed item, you may need new material—for example, a supportive letter or even an independent evaluation.

d. Choose and Prepare Witnesses

Witnesses are crucial to the outcome of a fair hearing. Choose and prepare your witnesses with care.

i. Choosing Witnesses

Double-check your list of *all* potential witnesses, both people who support you and people who might testify for the school district (including participants at the IEP meeting). Try to anticipate what each witness can testify about. One witness may be able to testify about several issues, while others may focus on only one disputed matter. In choosing your witnesses, look for the following:

- The strength of the witness's testimony.
- The witness's experience, training, education, and direct knowledge of your child.
- The witness's willingness to testify under oath. You must make sure a person is willing to testify at the hearing before you put him or her on your witness list. A favorable or supportive report won't help if the witness equivocates at the hearing. In that case, submit the person's written material and have other witnesses refer to that report.

In some cases, you may need to subpoena a reluctant witness to testify at the hearing. A subpoena is an order that requires the witness to appear. Ask your state's education agency where to get subpoena forms.

ii. Preparing Witness Questions

Write out a list of questions for each witness. The following is a general outline:

- Ask the witness to identify him- or herself—for example, "Please state your name, occupation, and place of employment."
- Ask about the witness's experience, education, training, and specific expertise in the area of dispute—you can refer the witness to the résumé or written articles that you included in your exhibits.
- Establish the witness's knowledge of your child—for example:
  - *"Have you met my son, Philip Jones?"*
  - *"Please tell us when, for how long, and for what purpose."*
  - *"Did you also observe him in school?"*
  - *"Please tell us when that was and for how long."*
- Ask questions to elicit your witness's opinion about the issues in dispute, for example:
  - *"You stated that you tested Philip. What tests did you administer?"*
  - *"What were the results?"*
  - *"What do those results mean?"*
  - *"What conclusions did you draw regarding Philip's reading difficulties?"*
  - *"How severe are his difficulties?"*

▲ *"In your professional opinion, what is the appropriate way to help Philip improve his reading?"*

▲ *"Do you have any specific recommendations regarding Philip's reading needs?"*

▲ *"What is your professional opinion regarding Philip's prognosis as a successful reader if he is not provided the help you recommend?"*

Keys to preparing your witnesses. As a general rule, witnesses must be able to clearly state what your child needs and why, the consequences if those needs are met, and the detriment to your child if they are not.

iii. Preparing Your Witnesses

Before the hearing, meet with your witnesses and go over your questions. Their answers may lead to new questions you'll want to ask, trigger a new strategy or approach, and help you and your witnesses prepare for the hearing. Explain that after you're done asking questions, the school district representative will cross-examine the witness by asking additional questions.

Some witnesses, particularly any school employees who agree to testify for your child, may be unwilling to meet during school hours. You may have to arrange to meet them at their home. Others may not want to meet at all. What should you do about witnesses who can help your case but won't talk to you ahead of time? If you can't discuss the case before the hearing, you won't know exactly how the witness will testify. Taking this kind of risk may backfire. One strategy is to leave the person off your witness list and hope the district calls him or her so you can cross-examine. Of course, if the witness is the only person who can testify about a certain element of your case, then you'll probably need to take a chance and use the witness, even though you didn't talk in advance of the hearing.

Another strategy is to include the person on your witness list but don't ask him or her to testify during your presentation. Then, either cross-examine if the school calls the witness, or use him or her as a rebuttal witness to counter something said by a school district witness.

Just before the hearing date, get back in touch with your witnesses to tell them:

- the date, time, and location of the hearing
- what time you need them to arrive to be ready to testify—be sure to let them know that they might not be called on time if an earlier witness took longer than expected or the hearing officer breaks early, and
- how long you expect their testimony to take.

iv. Preparing Yourself as a Witness

You will most likely be a witness at the hearing. You have valuable information about your child's history, previous programs, and needs, as well as your worries, your frustrations, and what teachers have said to you about your child.

Your testimony must cover only matters that you know firsthand. At the same time, your testimony doesn't have to cover all aspects of the case. For example, you can testify about the assessment done on your child and what the assessor told you. On the other hand, the assessor is in a better position to give this testimony. In general, then, your testimony should cover the areas in which you are the expert, particularly if no one else will testify on the issue.

You can present your testimony in one of two ways: You can respond to questions (just like you will be asking questions of your witnesses) asked by your spouse, a relative, or close friend, or you can make a statement covering all issues of importance. You can either read your statement or give it from notes. After you're done answering questions or making your statement, the school district representative will cross-examine you.

You want your testimony to be clear, specific, and objective. Break down your points into the following areas, using your mediation statement as a guideline:

- a general description of your child, including age, strengths, and weaknesses (your child profile, discussed in Chapter 10, Section D, can help here)

- your child's disability and the effect of that disability—for example, your child has a learning disability and, as a result, has difficulty with simple computations, reading comprehension, and visual memory

- any secondary difficulties due to the disability —such as emotional problems

- your child's educational history—that is, the current program and class, and previous placements

- the particular issues in dispute and your desired resolution

- your observations at class visits, meetings with teachers and other professionals, and the IEP meeting (for example, "On February 12, 20xx, I visited the second-grade class at Tower School and I observed ....")

- oral statements others have made to you that support your point of view, including your reaction to those oral statements—for instance, "On November 3, 20xx, Mr. Mastin of the school district told me there was no room for my child in the second-grade class at Tower School; I confirmed this conversation in a letter, my Exhibit F, to which Mr. Mastin did not respond."

- your child's specific educational needs and the consequences if they are not met—for example, "Given the assessment by Dr. Pollack, I believe a placement in a program other than the second-grade class at Tower School will have serious emotional and cognitive consequences for my child."

e. Prepare Questions for School Witnesses

Preparing questions for school witnesses is more difficult than preparing for your own witnesses

because you don't know exactly what they'll say. Still, you can develop questions. You can probably guess what many witnesses will say, because you heard their opinions at the IEP meeting.

Start by reviewing your files, the transcript or your notes of the IEP meeting, and the school district's exhibits (you'll get them five days before the hearing). Then make a list of questions to strengthen your case or at least undermine what the school district's witnesses might say.

Example:

Your child's teacher said something very important to you when you visited your child's class. You sent a letter confirming what was said ("Thanks for talking to me today. I was glad to hear that you agreed Jake should remain in a regular class with the help of an aide"). The teacher never objected to your confirming letter, but you now believe she will say the opposite at the hearing. Be ready to point out the discrepancy—for instance, "Ms. Jenkins, you testified this morning that you feel Jake should be placed in a special education class. Do you recall when we met on October 15th, and you told me that Jake was doing well in the regular class but needed an aide to keep up? You don't recall that meeting? Please look at Exhibit B, my November 1st letter to you."

Rules of Evidence

You may have heard of something called the "rules of evidence." These formal rules, which are very specific and sometimes quite arcane, are used in courts to guide judges in deciding what evidence can be included and what must be excluded. These rules don't have to be followed at fair hearings, but the hearing officer can use them as appropriate.

For example, some rules relate to hearsay evidence—information that a witness did not hear or receive directly. "I saw Jack hit Frank" is not hearsay; "Jack told me that Frank hit Bill" is. Hearsay evidence can be excluded at a fair hearing.

Don't worry too much about formal rules of evidence. If the other side objects to a question you ask because it violates a rule of evidence, ask the hearing officer to explain the rule, and then rephrase your question or move on.

f.   Exchange Witness Lists and Evidence

Remember, you must submit a list of your witnesses and copies of written exhibits at least five days before the hearing begins. (34 C.F.R. §§ 300.509 (a)(3), (b)(1).) Once you have your exhibits (organized in binders) and your list of witnesses, make two copies. Keep the originals for yourself, send one copy to the fair hearing officer, and send the other copy to the school district representative. To have proof that the others received the items at least five days before the hearing, send them *certified mail, return receipt requested*.

5. The Fair Hearing

The fair hearing normally proceeds as follows:
1. The hearing officer opens the hearing and explains the process. The hearing officer will usually identify and confirm the written testimony or exhibits that you and the school district submitted. Finally, the officer will set up the tape recorder and make sure the parties are ready.
2. The parties introduce themselves.
3. The hearing officer turns on the tape recorder, and the formal hearing begins.
4. You make your opening statement.
5. The school district makes its opening statement.
6. You question (direct examine) your witnesses.
7. The school representative questions (cross-examines) your witnesses.
8. You ask more questions of your witnesses (re-direct) if you want, the school representative cross-examines again (called re-cross) and so on.
9. The school district calls its witnesses with the same pattern of direct examination, cross-examination, re-direct, and re-cross.
10. You call witnesses after the school finishes, if you want. These are called rebuttal witnesses and are used to clarify or contradict testimony raised by the other side. The school district has the same right.
11. You give a closing statement, if you want.
12. The school district gives a closing statement, if it wants.
13. You and the school district submit written briefs discussing the facts presented at the hearing and any applicable law (see Section 6, below).
14. The hearing officer issues a decision within 45 days after you requested due process.

Keeping Track During the Fair Hearing

You want to have an ongoing record of the testimony during the hearing, because you may need to refer back to previous testimony. For example, the district calls a witness who testifies for 45 minutes on various issues. When you cross-examine this witness, you want to refer back to a specific statement he or she made that contradicted other testimony. You need to be able to refer to the earlier statements.

Taking notes is the logical way to keep track; however, it will be difficult for you to do so while also conducting the hearing. Instead, have someone else take notes for you, recording the statements of each witness, while you also take notes on key statements. (You can do this on paper or a laptop computer.) If you had a notetaker at the IEP meeting, consider using the same person, who is probably very familiar with the issues by now. You can tape the hearing, but you won't have time to review taped testimony while the hearing is going on. Also, it is more difficult to try to find an exact statement on a tape than to simply refer to written notes.

How do you use the notes? During your cross-examination you'd say something like "Mr. Adams, you testified that, let me see [look at your notes], and I quote, 'I don't think James needs an aide in class.' Is that correct?" If he concurs, then point out evidence that contradicts him, such as "In her testimony yesterday, Dr. Markham stated that you told her on April 29, 20xx, that James needed an aide. Which statement should we believe?"

a. Make an Opening Statement

You can use the opening statement you prepared for mediation as a starting point, but you will need to modify it for a fair hearing. At mediation, you can say anything. Your aim is to reach a compromise. At a fair hearing, however, your aim is to prove your case. Your opening statement, therefore, should emphasize what you want for your child and how that is supported by evidence. This doesn't mean you shouldn't include items for which your evidence is weak, but it does mean you should carefully think about what you're requesting—and how likely you are to get it. The hearing officer will consider not only your evidence, but your credibility. If you ask for something unsupported by any evidence, your credibility may be affected.

Be sure to include these details in your opening statement:

- basic facts about your child, including age, disability, and current educational program
- a clear statement of your child's needs and the dispute that brought you to the hearing, and
- a brief statement that what you want is supported by evidence, such as "Cheryl needs a full-time aide, as we will clearly show with evidence, including the testimony of several different professionals and exhibits B, D, and M."

Opening statements can be any length, but five to 15 minutes is typical. If you can, don't read a verbatim statement—instead, use notes to guide you in making your points. If you're very nervous, however, it's okay to read the statement. It is important to express your feelings and bring the human element into the hearing. Be careful not to go off on an unfocused monologue or make your argument a personal attack on school district representatives.

b. Questioning Your Witnesses

After opening statements, your witnesses will testify. Think carefully about the order in which you want to present their testimony. You are telling a story, and you need to present the details of the story in an order that will make sense to someone who has little or no prior knowledge of the situation. It's often best to begin with someone (possibly you) who can give general background information about your child. Next, you might want a witness who can present the assessment data, such as your independent assessor.

After that, you want to go to the core of the dispute and make your case. For example, you and the school district disagree on placement and a related service. During the past year, your child was in a regular class, with no assistance. You want your child to stay in that class with an aide; the school district has offered placement in a special day class. Your first witness can give the details of the regular class. The second can talk about why your child needs that class. The third can describe the services offered by the aide. The fourth can explain why your child needs that aide.

Of course, you may have to modify the presentation and go out of order if a witness is available only on a certain day or at a certain time. Or, you may choose a different order to maximize impact. In some instances, the witness who will give the most dramatic and effective testimony should go last, so the hearing officer is left with that impression. Or that person might go first, to set a tone for the rest of the hearing. Only you can decide which strategy will be most effective in your situation.

c.   Questioning Reluctant Witnesses

Question reluctant witnesses with care. You first want to ask the hearing officer to note that the witness is not cooperative. To ensure the person's attendance at the hearing, you should have issued a subpoena. At the hearing, ask something like "Mr. Jones, are you testifying voluntarily?" The response will be something like "No. As you know, I was subpoenaed by you."

Another possibility is to begin your questioning with a statement such as "This witness, Mr. Hobson, the fourth-grade teacher, would not talk to me prior to the hearing. I am calling him as a hostile witness."

Further Suggestions on Questioning Witnesses

No matter how much you prepare, you won't be able to plan exactly how the questioning will go. Be ready to depart from your planned questions. For example, a witness might answer in a way slightly different from what you expected, requiring you to ask follow-up questions. Or the witness may say the opposite of what you expect.

Here are some tips to help you deal with surprises when questioning witnesses:

- Ask for a brief break if you need to gather yourself or consider new questions.
- Keep track of your questions. If you veer off on a line of questioning you had not planned, mark where you are on your list of questions so you can come back to it later.
- Don't ask a question to which you don't know the answer, particularly of a school witness.
- Don't overwhelm the hearing officer with a ton of facts. Parents often try to get everything into the record at the hearing. Know the difference between important facts and minutiae.
- Know when to stop. Stop asking questions when something powerful has been stated. Further questioning will only dilute the impact.
- Don't badger a witness. Ask questions in a firm way, and repeat them if necessary. But don't become hostile, belligerent, or belittling.
- Don't play lawyer. You'll do fine with your own style and language.

d.   How to Use Your Exhibits

Have your exhibits available so you can use them when you question witnesses. For example, "Tell me Dr. Whitland, you said Monroe does not need psychotherapy. Would you please look at Exhibit B, page 4? You reported last year that Monroe had severe emotional difficulties that were interfering with his education. Aren't severe emotional difficulties usually addressed in some kind of psychological therapy?"

e. Closing Statements

After all the evidence has been presented and all witnesses have testified, the hearing officer will likely ask if you want to make closing arguments or submit a written brief.

A closing statement is a summary of each party's key evidence as it relates to the disputed issues. For example, you might say, "Every witness called by us agreed that Michele needs four sessions of speech therapy; not one of the school district's witnesses contradicted that. This is fully consistent with Dr. Hanover's written report, Exhibit L." Your closing statement might also note that the recommended education is consistent with IDEA.

6. Post-Hearing Briefs

If you agree to submit briefs, the parties, with the help of the hearing officer, will set a short time frame (usually no more than one week) to submit the briefs. The purposes of the briefs are to highlight the evidence that supports your case and expand on any legal issues pertinent to your dispute.

To develop your brief, first review your notes, your memory, and the evidence. The written brief should precisely point out the evidence that supports your case and the evidence that contradicts the school district's point of view. If there are legal issues, you should review IDEA and any court cases that support your analysis of the law. (See Chapter 14 for advice on legal research.) You may also want to contact a lawyer or support organization for help.

J. Fair Hearing Decision and Appeals

After the hearing, you're entitled to a written decision, including findings of fact, within 45 days after you first requested due process.

Both you and the school district have the right to appeal the decision to state or federal court, theoretically all the way to the U.S. Supreme Court. (34 C.F.R. § 300.512.) If you lost, several factors will help you decide whether or not to appeal:

- **Strength of your case.** You should already have considered this as part of your decision to pursue due process. For an appeal, you must look at your situation with a more critical eye. Many reviewing courts will defer to the administrative decision and won't want to rehear the evidence anew. Even if you court takes a fresh look at the evidence, remember that a neutral third party has already ruled against you, which suggests that your case has some problems.

- **Costs of an appeal.** There are various costs in appealing a fair hearing decision to court, including filing fees, fees for serving papers on the school district, witness fees, and other trial costs (such as copying exhibits). There's one more cost: potential attorney's fees. While nonattorneys can represent themselves in court, I strongly recommend hiring an attorney for the appeal. At the very least, have an attorney who specializes in IDEA review your case and advise you of your chances on appeal.

- **Time.** State laws vary as to when you must file your appeal (depending on their statute of limitations). And once your case is filed, court workloads may affect how soon your appeal is heard in court. Anticipate a lengthy process, taking many months. Remember, too, that as long as the case is active, your child must stay put. If you want to maintain the status quo, appealing will preserve it longer. Deciding to go to court, however, is a very serious step. Don't do it just to maintain the status quo, particularly if your case is not strong. ■

13

Filing a Complaint for a Legal Violation

As mentioned in Chapter 12, informal negotiation and due process are typically used to resolve factual disputes between you and the school district. But what if your concern isn't over a program, service, or other factual matter—that is, who is right and who is wrong—but, rather, that the school district has violated a legal requirement under IDEA? For legal disputes, IDEA provides a complaint process. (34 C.F.R. §§ 300.660-662; see Appendix 1.)

A. When to File a Complaint

IDEA statutes and regulations set out the school district's legal obligations. Excerpts of key sections of IDEA are contained in Appendix 1. Here are some common school district actions (or inactions) that violate IDEA:

- failing to provide a child's records
- failing to do assessments
- failing to meet assessment and IEP timelines
- failing to hold an IEP meeting
- failing to allow parents to effectively represent their child in the IEP meeting— for example, by limiting who can attend or by intimidating the parent
- failing to follow required procedures before suspending or expelling a special education student (see Chapter 2, Section A)
- failing to discuss all elements in an IEP meeting—goals and objectives, placement, related services, transition plans
- failing to implement an agreed-to IEP—for example, if your child's IEP calls for three sessions of speech therapy and the school district provides only one session, and
- failing to give notice before changing, or refusing to change, a child's IEP. Your district cannot change your child's IEP without giving you notice of that change and holding an IEP meeting, nor can it refuse you the right to have an IEP meeting if you want a change.

Collective Complaints: There's Strength in Numbers

If your school district is violating the law in a way that affects a group of children, consider filing a complaint together. A complaint filed by more than one family can be more effective. Your state department of education has a legal duty under IDEA to monitor all school districts to make sure they are following the law—and to take any necessary steps to force a recalcitrant district to shape up. States are usually more sensitive to what may be a pattern of IDEA violations rather than a one-time incident. If you are able to show that many children are being hurt by the district's failure to follow the law, your state department of education may be quicker to step in and take action. And it's much less costly for a group of parents to hire one attorney to draft and submit a complaint than for each family to hire its own lawyer.

B. Where to File a Complaint

Section A, above, lists common violations of IDEA, but it is not an exhaustive list. If you believe your school district has violated IDEA or any state special education law, contact your state department of education (or a locally designated agency), or the U.S. Department of Education, Office for Civil Rights (OCR). Contact information for both is in Appendix 2.

You can file a complaint with either the state or federal education agency. Both handle violations of IDEA, state law, or Section 504 of the Rehabilitation Act of 1973.

See Chapter 7, Section F, for a brief description of Section 504, which prohibits schools from denying access to children with disabilities.

State departments of education are primarily geared toward investigating IDEA violations, but they will also look into complaints regarding Section 504. In contrast, the federal OCR is primarily concerned with Section 504 or discrimination violations, but will also investigate IDEA complaints.

Before deciding where to file a complaint, contact your state department of education and the regional office of the OCR and ask the following questions:

- What kinds of complaints do they investigate?
- What is the deadline for filing a complaint? Section 504 complaints must be filed within 180 days of the last alleged act of discrimination against your child. IDEA complaints must be filed within the time established in your state statute of limitations (discussed in Chapter 12, Section A).
- How do they handle complaints? In some states, an IDEA or Section 504 complaint is investigated initially by the school district. If you have a choice, opt for an investigator who is not associated with your school district.
- What are their timelines for investigating complaints?
- What remedies are available, such as reimbursement for attorney's fees or the cost of related services?

Notifying the U.S. Department of Education, Office of Special Education and Rehabilitation Services

In addition to filing a complaint, you can notify the U.S. Department of Education, Office of Special Education and Rehabilitation Services, Office of Special Education Programs (OSEP). OSEP will neither investigate the problem nor issue a decision. But OSEP has overall responsibility for monitoring how states implement IDEA and might consider your comments when conducting its annual review of the programs in your state. Contact information is in Appendix 2.

C. What to Include in a Complaint

Your state department of education may have a complaint form for you to use. OCR has one, but you aren't required to use it. Whether you use a form or simply write a letter, include the following information:

- Your name and address (a telephone number where you may be reached during business hours is helpful, but not required).
- Your child's name and school district.
- As precise a description as possible of the violation, including the date, time, and location. If you cite more than one violation or you have very broad concerns, be as specific as possible, describing each violation separately.
- The applicable section of IDEA or any state law, if you know it. Key sections of IDEA are cited throughout this book, and Appendix 1 includes excerpts of IDEA and its regulations. Contact your state department of education (Appendix 2) for state special education laws and regulations.
- The remedy you want, including reimbursement for costs incurred due to the district's violations.

A sample complaint letter is shown below.

Sample Complaint Letter

February 5, 20xx

John Harrington, Director
Compliance Unit
Special Education Division
Department of Education
721 Capitol Mall
Sacramento, CA 95814

Dear Mr. Harrington:

I am formally requesting that you investigate legal violations by the Valley Unified School District, 458 4th Street, Visalia, California. I am making this request pursuant to 34 C.F.R. § 300.660.

The facts in this matter are as follows:

I requested an IEP meeting on October 14, 20xx, just after my child was determined eligible for special education. The school district did not contact us to schedule an IEP meeting until February 2, 20xx, at which time I was told that the meeting would be March 5, 20xx. This violates 34 C.F.R. § 300.343, which provides that an IEP will be held within 30 days of a determination that a child needs special education and related services. I request that an IEP meeting be held within 15 days of the conclusion of your investigation. I also request reimbursement for the cost we incurred to hire a private physical therapist because of the school district's failure to address my child's needs.

Please contact me to confirm receipt of this request, set up times for me to meet with your investigator, and establish timelines for completing the investigation.

Sincerely,

Becky Masteron

Becky Masteron
6004 Green St.
Visalia, CA 95800

D. What Happens When You File a Complaint

After you file your complaint, the investigating agency will most likely meet with you to discuss the case, review evidence and records, meet with the school district, and then issue a decision. IDEA requires that the state issue a decision within 60 days after the complaint is filed. If the district is found to have violated IDEA, the agency will make recommendations that the school district must follow to comply with the law. The decision can be appealed to the U.S. Secretary of Education (contact information is in Appendix 2).

Due Process and Complaints

You can simultaneously go through due process and file a complaint alleging a legal violation. If the district is found to have violated the law, you would certainly want the fair hearing officer to know. Indeed, if timing permits, you may want to file your complaint first so you can submit the decision as an exhibit at the due process hearing.

14

Lawyers and Legal Research

Lawyers can play an important role in special education. While the purpose of this book is to guide you through the IEP process without an attorney, there may be times when you might need to hire or at least consult a lawyer.

This chapter covers:

- how a lawyer can help with the IEP and other IDEA processes
- what to consider when using an attorney in special education
- finding an effective attorney
- how lawyers are paid
- resolving problems with your lawyer, and
- doing your own legal research.

A. How a Lawyer Can Help

Generally speaking, an attorney can help you in one of two ways. A lawyer can provide advice and assistance as needed throughout the IEP process while you do most of the work, or a lawyer can be directly involved as your formal representative.

Here are some of the specific tasks a lawyer can help you with:

- securing your child's school files
- requesting an assessment or an IEP meeting
- preparing for the IEP eligibility meeting
- preparing for the IEP program meeting— including drafting goals and objectives, your child's profile, and program and service descriptions; reviewing supportive evidence and materials; suggesting who should attend and what material will be most effective; and providing pointers about the IEP meeting
- attending an IEP meeting (remember to notify your school district before the meeting if your lawyer will attend)
- reviewing assessments and IEP forms before you sign them
- researching a specific legal issue that applies to your situation
- helping you informally resolve a dispute with the school district

- assessing the strength of your case, if you're considering filing a complaint or pursuing due process
- preparing for and attending mediation and the due process hearing
- writing a post-hearing brief
- preparing a complaint for you to file with the appropriate educational agency, and
- representing you in court.

You may choose to have a lawyer do everything from beginning to end in the IEP process or handle only certain tasks. For example, you might want to attend the IEP meeting yourself, but have an attorney review the IEP document before you sign it.

B. Do You Need an Attorney?

Because lawyers can be expensive—and because hiring a lawyer definitely makes the IEP process more adversarial—you'll want to think carefully before bringing in an attorney. Here are some factors to consider:

- **Complexity of the case.** The more complicated your case is, the more likely it is that you could benefit from some legal advice. A dispute involving complicated placement and service issues, for example, might require the special knowledge and experience of an attorney.
- **Strength of your case.** If you really don't know whether you have a good case against the school district, consider talking to a lawyer. A good attorney should tell you how strong your case looks and, therefore, whether or not your situation justifies hiring him or her.
- **Your time and energy.** If you work full-time, are a single parent, or have a difficult schedule, you may want someone else to take charge. On the other hand, if you have the time and energy to represent yourself and your child, hiring an attorney may not be necessary.

- **Your budget.** Attorneys aren't cheap. Can you afford the help? Are you entitled to reimbursement for your legal costs? (See Section D, below.)
- **Your self-confidence.** The purpose of this book is not only to help you advocate for your child, but also to give you the confidence to be an effective advocate. Still, you may prefer to hire a lawyer rather than wage the fight on your own.
- **Who represents the school district.** If the school district has an attorney, you may want the same protection and leverage.
- **Your relationship with the district.** Hiring a lawyer may change your relationship with the school district. When you involve attorneys, the atmosphere becomes more formal and potentially combative. School personnel will likely be more guarded and may view you as the troublemaker or squeaky wheel. Of course, if you are at the point where you may need an attorney, your relationship with the school district has already changed. Your child's welfare is more important than a cordial relationship with the school district.

C. Finding an Attorney

Special education attorneys are not as numerous as personal injury or business lawyers. It is also unlikely that attorneys working in more standard areas of law—such as wills and estates, criminal law, family matters, or corporation law—will know anything about special education law.

You may be tempted to hire the attorney who did your will, your sister-in-law who just graduated from law school, or the attorney whose ad in the phone book promises the lowest rates. But special education law is highly specialized. Hiring an attorney who does not know the law or have experience in special education will significantly increase your chance of failure, and could ultimately cost you more rather than less. When you

pay an attorney, you are paying for all the time spent on your case, including time spent doing research. You don't want to pay an attorney for on-the-job training.

1. Compile a List of Potential Attorneys

To find the "right" lawyer, compile a list of potential candidates. Here's how:

- Ask other parents in the school district.
- Ask your pediatrician or other health care professionals.
- Ask school district personnel—the district is required to maintain a list of attorneys and other advocacy resources for parents.
- Contact your state special education advisory commission and ask for referrals. IDEA requires each state to have a special education commission, composed of educators and parents, which advises the state about special education. The commissioners should have plenty of special education contacts.
- Contact your state department of education and ask for referrals (see Appendix 2).
- Contact a nearby Parent Training and Information Center (PTI) (see Appendix 3).
- Contact a local disability rights advocacy organization (see Appendix 3).
- Contact a low-cost or free legal clinic, such as legal aid—while most offices focus on common civil issues (such as domestic disputes or evictions), some offices do special education work for low-income people.
- Use your personal network—friends, colleagues, neighbors, or coworkers who know special education lawyers or who know lawyers who can recommend good special education lawyers.

Nonprofit Legal Clinics

There are nonprofit organizations that provide legal assistance in special education, disability rights, or what is generally called "public interest law." Your school district should have a list of disability-specific or special education nonprofit legal clinics in your area. Also see the organizations listed in Appendix 3.

There are advantages and disadvantages to using a nonprofit legal clinic rather than a private attorney. Advantages to using a nonprofit include:

- the attorneys have likely worked in special education and have handled many cases
- nonprofits often do not charge for their services or have significantly reduced rates, and
- nonprofits, particularly disability-focused offices, have special knowledge and often a strong passion about the issues.

But there are disadvantages to using a nonprofit:

- demand is often greater than supply; you may have to wait some time for an appointment, even just to have someone assess your case, and
- nonprofit organizations often have limited resources—some focus on either precedent-setting cases (unusual disputes) or cases that will have an impact on a large number of children—and may not handle individual cases.

How Not to Find a Special Education Lawyer

There are several bad ways to find a special education lawyer. Avoid these traps for the unwary:

- **Heavily advertised legal clinics.** While they may offer low flat rates for routine services such as drafting a will, most make their money on personal injury cases. I am not aware of any such clinics offering special education help.
- **Referral panels set up by local bar associations.** Bar association panels usually do minimal screening before qualifying lawyers as experts in certain areas. While you might get a good referral from these panels, it is highly unlikely that you'll find a special education lawyer listed.
- **Private referral services.** When it comes to services that advertise on TV and billboards, forget it. It is highly unlikely they offer any special education help.

2. Call the Attorneys on Your List

Once you have a list of recommended attorneys, you can either narrow it down to one or two individuals who were enthusiastically recommended or you can make initial contact with everyone on your list.

Try to have a brief phone conversation or ask for a short meeting. Some attorneys will chat with you briefly over the phone to determine the nature of your case and whether or not you need an attorney. Other attorneys may have you speak with an assistant, complete a form describing your case, or make an appointment to come in and talk about the case. Before making an appointment, find out the following information:

- the attorney's fee
- how the attorney will review the case and decide whether or not you should proceed, and
- how much the initial review costs.

3. Meet With the Best Candidates

Make an appointment with those candidates who seem like the best prospects. Naturally, if there is a fee for the initial intake, you may want to see only a few attorneys. Be sure to ask what records the attorney needs to evaluate your case.

When you meet with an attorney, you should ask about your specific case, of course. You also want to ask about the attorney's:

- years of experience
- specific special education experience
- experience with your particular legal issue (such as a due process hearing)
- knowledge of special education law and the IEP process
- experience with your school district
- general style—is the attorney confrontational or cooperative (for example, does he or she like mediation or think it's a waste of time and normally go directly to a fair hearing?)
- references, and
- fees.

Pay attention to the answers. Does the attorney clearly answer your questions about fees, experience, and your specific legal issues? Does the

attorney try to assess your chances in due process? If the lawyer makes you uncomfortable, think carefully about whether his or her expertise and success rate is worth putting up with a difficult style.

Will the attorney provide the type of help you want? Is the attorney willing to advise you now, but hold off on full participation unless and until you need it? If the attorney wants to take over the case but you want only a consultant, you have the wrong attorney.

Will the attorney be accessible? This is important—the most common complaint about lawyers is that they don't return phone calls, respond to faxes or email, or make themselves available when a client calls. Discuss the attorney's response time. While no attorney should be expected to respond instantly, you shouldn't have to wait more than a day or two, except in rare circumstances.

Client's Responsibility in Working With an Attorney

Your attorney should be responsive and courteous, and keep you informed. But the client-attorney relationship is a two-way street. Keep the following in mind:

- Vague questions are likely to receive vague responses; be clear and specific when you discuss matters or ask questions.
- No matter how good an attorney is, the quality of the case—that is, the strength of the evidence—is the key to success. Your attorney cannot transform a bad case into a good one.
- You have some of the responsibility for controlling your legal bill. Be especially aware of time. If you talk to your lawyer for 30 minutes, you will be billed for 30 minutes, even if you feel you were "just chatting."
- You cannot call up an attorney, chat for five minutes, and have your problem resolved. I frequently receive phone calls that go something like this:

  "Hello. I have a question about special education. Do you know special education law?"

  "Yes."

  "My daughter has an IEP on Thursday. She is learning disabled, and I want her placed in a private school. The school district has offered a special day class. What do you recommend?"

  Any attorney who tries to answer that question is doing a disservice to himself and the caller. And the caller is being unfair. Many lawyers will try to answer simple questions over the phone from first-time callers—such as, "Can you tell me if a school has to do an assessment of a child before the child enters special education?"—but most questions are more complicated than that. It is unfair to assume that an attorney can either provide a simple answer to a complex question or provide free advice.

4. Ask for a Case Evaluation

A good attorney will evaluate the evidence before giving you any advice. After reviewing your case materials, a good attorney should be able to:

- tell you the strength of your case
- explain the process
- evaluate your documents and potential witnesses
- tell you if additional supportive material is needed
- estimate the cost of hiring an attorney for due process or beyond
- estimate how long your case may take
- provide insights into school district personnel, particularly if the attorney has worked with the district before, and
- provide a cost-benefit analysis of hiring the attorney to represent you versus using the attorney as an advisor only.

5. A Word on an Attorney's Style

Some attorneys are pleasant, patient, and good listeners. Others are unpleasant, impatient, and bad listeners. Although you may want the former, you may get the latter. Whatever the style of your attorney, make it clear that you know the attorney is busy, but you expect to be treated courteously, explain matters, kept fully posted about what is happening, and included as an active partner in the process. An effective professional relationship must be based on mutual respect.

Furthermore, the attorney should contact you regarding any decision to be made, whether scheduling a meeting, deciding on tactics, reviewing a key issue, or considering a possible resolution of the dispute.

If at any time you don't understand what your attorney has said, requested, or planned, ask for clarification. If the answer isn't clear, ask again. Although you hired the attorney because of his or her professional expertise and knowledge—and therefore have relinquished a certain amount of control—it does not mean you should be kept in the dark.

D. How Attorneys Are Paid

How you pay your lawyer depends on the type of legal services you need and the amount of legal work involved. Once you choose a lawyer, ask for a written agreement explaining how fees and costs will be billed and paid. In some states, a written agreement is required by law; even if it isn't, always ask for one. A good attorney will provide you with a written contract (whether you ask or not). Be sure to tell the lawyer how much you are able (and willing) to spend—if you and the lawyer agree on a cap or limit on legal fees, that should also be in your fee agreement.

As your case progresses, you'll want to make sure you receive a bill or statement at least once a month. A lawyer's time adds up quickly. If your lawyer will be delegating some of the work to a less experienced associate, paralegal, or secretary, the delegated work should be billed at a lower hourly rate. Make sure this is stated in your written fee agreement.

1. Lawyers' Billing Methods

Lawyers charge for their services in three different ways:

Hourly rate. Most special education attorneys charge by the hour. In most parts of the U.S., you can secure competent representation for $100 to $250 an hour. Many clients prefer an hourly rate to a flat fee (discussed next) because you pay only for the attorney's actual time spent on your case. Comparison shopping among lawyers can help you avoid overpaying, but only if you compare lawyers with similar expertise. A highly experienced special education attorney (who has a higher hourly rate) may be cheaper in the long run than a general practitioner (at a lower rate). The special education attorney won't have to

research routine questions and should be able to evaluate your case quickly.

Legal Time

How much time your attorney will spend on your case depends on the nature of your dispute. The following can serve as a general guideline for the amount of time required for common legal tasks:

- initial review of your records and interview with you .... 2-3 hours
- help you with the IEP process— developing a blueprint, contacting assessors and school personnel; drafting goals and objectives .... 2-5 hours
- attend the IEP meeting .... 2-4 hours (per meeting)
- prepare for and attend mediation session .... 3-8 hours
- prepare for and attend fair hearing .... 10-35 hours

---

Flat rate. A flat rate is a single fee that will cover all the work the lawyer has agreed to do— for example, the amount the attorney will charge you to prepare for and attend the IEP meeting or prepare for and conduct the fair hearing. You are obligated to pay the flat fee no matter how many hours the lawyer spends on your case. A flat fee can be quite economical if the fee is reasonable and you anticipate a lot of work. On the other hand, if the case is resolved early in the process, you may end up paying much more than you would have paid in hourly fees. Most special education attorneys charge by the hour and may be unwilling to work on a flat fee.

Contingency fee. Contingency fee arrangements are rarely used in special education cases. A contingency fee is a percentage of whatever money the party wins; if you don't win anything, the attorney doesn't earn anything. Because almost all successful special education cases involve providing a program or service rather than an award of money, don't expect a special education attorney to work on a contingency.

Legal Costs

In addition to the fees they charge for their time, lawyers bill for a variety of items. These costs can add up quickly and may include charges for:

- photocopies
- faxes
- postage
- overnight mail
- messenger services
- expert witness fees
- court filing fees
- long-distance phone calls
- process servers
- work by investigators
- work by legal assistants or paralegals
- deposition transcripts
- online legal research, and
- travel.

Some lawyers absorb the cost of photocopies, faxes, and local phone calls as normal office overhead, but that's not always the case. When working out the fee arrangement, ask for a list of costs you'll be expected to pay. If the lawyer seems intent on nickel-and-diming you or hitting you with a $3-per-page fax charge, you should talk about it. While this may not reflect the attorney's skills or ability to win a case, it may raise red flags about how he or she does business.

---

2. Reimbursement for Legal Fees and Costs

If you hire an attorney and pay for his or her services, *and* you prevail at mediation or the fair hearing, you are entitled to be reimbursed by your school district for your attorney's fees and other due process costs. (20 U.S.C. § 1415(i)(3); 34 C.F.R. § 300.513.)

But your right to reimbursement can be limited. First, you are not entitled to reimbursement for the fees you paid an attorney to attend the IEP meeting, unless the meeting was required as part of due process. This might happen if the fair hearing officer orders a second IEP meeting to discuss matters that were improperly omitted in the first meeting.

Second, you are not entitled to reimbursement if the school district makes a settlement offer ten days before the due process hearing, you reject the offer, *and* the hearing officer finds that what you actually won in due process is no better than the school district's settlement offer. If the hearing officer finds that you were substantially justified in rejecting the settlement offer, however, you are entitled to full reimbursement. What constitutes "substantially justified" is not defined in IDEA.

Third, the hearing officer can reduce the amount of attorney's fees to which you are entitled if the officer finds that any of the following are true:

- you unreasonably protracted or extended the final resolution of the controversy
- the attorney's fees unreasonably exceed hourly rates others in the community charge for similar services
- the time and services provided by the attorney were excessive, or
- the attorney failed to provide certain information required by law. (34 C.F.R. § 300.513 (c)(4).)

You should discuss these reimbursement issues carefully with your attorney before you evaluate any settlement offers or decide whether to request a fair hearing.

3. Reducing Legal Fees

There are several ways to control legal fees.

Be organized. Especially when you are paying by the hour, it's important to gather important documents, write a short chronology of events, and explain a problem concisely to your lawyer. Keep a copy of everything you give to your lawyer.

Be prepared before you meet your lawyer. Whenever possible, put your questions in writing and mail, fax, or deliver them to your lawyer before all meetings or phone conversations. Early preparation also helps focus the meeting so there is less chance of digressing (at your expense) into unrelated topics.

Carefully review lawyer bills. Like everyone else, lawyers make mistakes. For example, .1 of an hour (six minutes) may be transposed into a 1. (one hour) when the data is entered into the billing system. That's $200 instead of $20 if your lawyer charges $200 per hour. Don't hesitate to question your bill. You have the right to a clear explanation of costs.

Ask your lawyer what work you can do. There are some things you can do to save time. For example, you could go through the school's record and highlight key statements. Or you could talk with important witnesses to find out their attitudes about key issues in the case. Some attorneys may be comfortable with you doing substantial work; others will not be. Be sure to discuss this ahead of time.

E. Resolving Problems With a Lawyer

If you see a problem emerging with your lawyer, don't just sit back and fume. Call or write your lawyer. Whatever it is that rankles—a too-high bill, a missed deadline, or a strategic move you don't understand—have an honest discussion about your feelings.

If you can't discuss these matters frankly with your lawyer or you are unsatisfied with the outcome of any discussion, it's time to consider finding another attorney. If you don't, you may waste money on unnecessary legal fees and risk having matters turn out badly.

If you decide to change lawyers, be sure to end the first professional relationship before you hire a new attorney. If you don't, you could find yourself being billed by two lawyers at the same time. Also, be sure all important legal documents are returned to you. Tell your new lawyer what your old one has done to date and pass on the file.

Here are some tips on resolving specific problems:

- If you have a dispute over fees, the local bar association may be able to mediate it for you.
- If a lawyer has violated legal ethics—for example, had a conflict of interest, overbilled you, or didn't represent you zealously—the state agency that licenses lawyers may discipline the lawyer.
- Where a major mistake has been made—for example, a lawyer missed the fair hearing deadline for submitting the witness list and exhibits—you might even consider suing for malpractice. Many lawyers carry malpractice insurance.

Remember, while there will be times when you question your attorney's tactics, you have hired someone because of his or her expertise and experience. Before confronting the attorney, ask yourself whether the attorney misfired or you are overreacting.

> ### Your Rights as a Client
>
> As a client, you have the right to expect the following:
> - courteous treatment by your lawyer and staff members
> - an itemized statement of services rendered and a full advance explanation of billing practices
> - charges for agreed-upon fees and nothing more
> - prompt responses to phone calls and letters
> - confidential legal conferences, free from unwarranted interruptions
> - up-to-date information on the status of your case
> - diligent and competent legal representation, and
> - clear answers to all questions.

A final word on attorneys: We live in a time when public attitudes about attorneys are negative, to some degree rightfully so. There are, of course, many conscientious attorneys, particularly in special education, where you will actually find a high percentage of compassionate, able, and decent professionals.

F. Doing Your Own Legal Research

Using this book is a good way to educate yourself about the laws that affect your rights as a parent of a special education child. Chapter 2 has already provided you with much of the key legal language of IDEA. But because the laws and court decisions of 50 states are involved, no one book can give you all the information you need.

There's a lot you can do on your own, once you understand a few basics about law libraries, statute books, court opinions, and the general reference books that lawyers use to learn about

issues. Some basic legal research skills can help you determine how strong your case is and the best and most effective way to go forward. Whether the issue is private school placement, the type or amount of a related service, an assessment question, or an eligibility issue, IDEA and judicial decisions can help you judge the strength of your case.

> ### Using the Library
>
> Look for a law library that is open to the public—there may be one in your main county or city courthouse or state capitol. Law librarians, who often have experience working with nonlawyers, can help you find the appropriate resources. Publicly funded law schools generally permit the public to use their libraries, and some private law schools also grant access to the public, sometimes for a modest fee.
>
> If you can't find an accessible law library, don't overlook the public library. Many large public libraries have sizable legal reference collections, including state and federal statutes. If you are working with a lawyer, you might also ask about using the research materials at the lawyer's office.

Examples:
- You want your child in a private school that has an identical program to the one available in your school district. Legal research should lead you to the conclusion that your position isn't a winning one. The law is clear—there is no right to a private school in this situation.
- Your child is deaf and you want her to have an American Sign Language (ASL) interpreter in her mainstreamed class. You do some research and find that IDEA does not require a specific language or

methodology in the class. You realize that you will have to prove that without ASL your child cannot benefit from her education.

- You want your child who has some autistic behaviors to be mainstreamed with an aide. You visit a law library and discover that in the case of *Board of Education v. Holland,* 4F.3d 1398 (9th Circuit, 1994), the court established guidelines for determining when a child is entitled to be mainstreamed, including an analysis of:
  - ▲ the academic and nonacademic benefits to the child
  - ▲ the effect of the placement on the teacher and other students, and
  - ▲ the cost of the aids and services needed to mainstream.

The materials you can research include the following:

- IDEA statutes and regulations (excerpts are in Appendix 1)
- state statutes
- court cases interpreting IDEA and other relevant statutes
- explanatory documents, such as the U.S. Department of Education policy guidelines and correspondence (these documents do not have the authority of a statute or court case, but they reflect the Department's analysis of the law)
- fair hearing decisions (available through your state department of education and the *Individuals with Disabilities Education Law Reporter,* discussed below)—although these are binding only on the parties to that specific hearing, they may be of value to you in showing how hearing officers make decisions in your state, and
- law review and other articles about IDEA and special education issues.

1. Individuals With Disabilities Education Act (IDEA): Where to Find It

Like all federal laws, IDEA is found in a multi-volume series of books called the United States Code (U.S.C.), which is available in most libraries and online. The U.S.C. consists of separate numbered titles, each covering a specific subject matter. IDEA is found in Title 20, beginning with Section 1400. Appendix 1 includes a copy of key sections of the IDEA statute and regulations.

You can find annotated versions of the U.S.C., which include not only the text of IDEA, but also summaries of cases that interpret IDEA and a reference to where each case can be found. Annotated codes also list articles that discuss IDEA. Annotated codes have comprehensive indexes by topic, and are kept up to date with paperback supplements (called pocket parts) found inside the back cover of each volume or in a separate paperback volume. Supplements include changes to IDEA and recent cases.

Your school district is required to provide you with copies of federal law—that is, the statutes and regulations of IDEA. Your school district, however, is not required to inform you of any changes to IDEA made by Congress or of any legal decisions on IDEA. One source of up-to-date information, including policy guidelines on the IDEA, is the U.S. Department of Education (see Appendix 2). But that's not the only source.

Special newsletters provide extensive detail about most fields of law. Special education has one such publication called the *Individuals with Disabilities Education Law Reporter* (IDELR), published by LRP Publications (contact information is in Appendix 3). IDELR issues a bimonthly highlights newsletter, along with the written decisions of IDEA court rulings, fair hearing decisions, Department of Education policy, and other publications. IDELR has a subject index, making it easy to locate the specific cases you want to review. At a current cost of $890 per year, IDELR is aimed at special education lawyers and school districts.

Some law libraries subscribe to IDELR—call the nearest law libraries and ask. Some school districts also subscribe. If this fails, contact a local nonprofit special education or disability organization in your area and ask if they receive IDELR.

2. State Statutes

As noted in Chapter 2, each state has passed a law that parallels IDEA. States are allowed to develop laws that provide students with greater rights than those provided in IDEA. You should take a look at your state's special education laws, which are available in many public libraries and all law libraries.

Many states also make their statutes available online (see Section G, below). In some states, statutes are organized by subject matter, with each title, chapter, or code covering a particular legal area—for example, the vehicle code or the corporations code. Most states have some kind of education code. In some states, statutes are simply numbered sequentially without regard to subject matter, meaning you'll have to use the index to find what you need. State codes are like the federal U.S.C., with annotated volumes, indexes, and pocket parts.

Some states have their own regulations implementing special education laws; check your state department of education for information about these regulations.

 Appendix 2 includes addresses, phone numbers, and websites of state departments of education.

3. Court Decisions

When Congress passes a law, it cannot address every possible situation or clarify what each section of the law means. It is the job of a court—federal or state—to interpret the applicable laws and apply them to particular facts. The court will often explain, clarify, and even expand or limit what actually appears in a statute. These court decisions are often referred to as "case law."

Court decisions are published in state or federal reporters. Each decision has a name and a citation, indicating the volume, name, and page of the reporter in which it appears, the court that issued the decision, and the year of the decision. With the citation, you can locate the printed decision.

Example:

The first special education case to reach the U.S. Supreme Court was *Rowley v. Board of Education*. It concerned a deaf child who wanted a sign language interpreter in her regular classroom. The U.S. Supreme Court said she didn't need one.

The case was first decided by a federal trial court: The case citation is 483 F. Supp. 536 (S.D.N.Y. 1980). This means that the case can be found in volume 483 of a reporter called the Federal Supplement, starting at page 536. The court that issued the decision was the federal court for the Southern District of New York. The case was decided in 1980.

That decision was appealed, and the case citation of the appeal court's decision is 623 F.2d 945 (2d Cir. 1980). This means that the decision can be found in volume 623 of the Federal Reporter (2d Series), starting at page 945. The court that ruled on the appeal was the Second Circuit Court of Appeals. The appeal was decided in 1980.

The citation of the U.S. Supreme Court decision is 102 S.Ct 3034 (1982). The decision can be found in volume 102 of the Supreme Court Reports, starting at page 3034. The court decided the case in 1982.

Most cases involving a federal law such as IDEA are decided by the federal courts. IDEA also gives you or the school district the option of appealing the due process decision to a state court, however. Each state has a unique reporting system, but decisions are usually found in regional reporters. For example, in the case of *State of Connecticut v. Bruno*, 673 A.2d 1117 (Conn. 1996), the decision was published in volume 673 of the regional law reporter called the Atlantic Second Series and begins on page 1117. The case comes from the state of Connecticut (not surprising given the name of the case) and was decided in 1996.

4. Finding Cases on Special Education

Every decision that a court issues is specific to the facts of that case. Even though a case addresses the same underlying legal concepts as yours, it might be very different, factually, from your child's situation. A court case decides whether IDEA procedures and rules were followed in the context of one particular factual situation, for one particular child.

Every once in a while, a court will issue a broader decision that applies more generally. For example, in a famous case in 1986, a federal court ruled that IQ tests were not valid for determining whether African-American students have learning disabilities. (*Larry P. v. Riles*, 793 F.2d 969 (9th Cir. 1984).) It is very unusual, however, for a court to make this kind of blanket ruling.

You can find cases that interpret every aspect of IDEA, including assessment, educational methodology, eligibility, placement, services, suspension, and expulsion. One great way to find cases is through IDELR (see Section 1, above). IDELR has a set of books called *Topical Index/Current Decisions*. Each book covers cases reprinted in particular volumes of IDELR. The topics are arranged alphabetically. You can use the index to look up topics that apply to your situation.

IDELR reprints not only court decisions, but also decisions made by fair hearing officers (usually referred to as SEA, or state educational agency, decisions) and the Office of Civil Rights (which investigations Section 504 complaints). IDELR also includes IDEA policy analysis by the U.S. Department of Education, Office of Special Education Programs (OSEP). These materials can be of real value to your child, because they indicate how these departments and agencies interpret IDEA's legal requirements.

Further Reading on Legal Research. *Legal Research: How to Find & Understand the Law*, by Stephen Elias and Susan Levinkind (Nolo), gives easy-to-use, step-by-step instructions on how to find legal information.

When you research cases, be sure the case you find has not been overturned or replaced by a more recent court decision. You can do this with a set of books known as Shepard's. A friendly law librarian might have the time and patience to guide you, but if not, Nolo's book *Legal Research* has an easy-to-follow explanation of how to use the Shepard's system to expand and update your research.

When you find a court decision, there will be a short synopsis of the decision at the beginning. This synopsis not only will help you determine whether the case is relevant to your situation, but also will tell you what the court decided. After the case synopsis, there will be a list of numbered items, each item followed by a short summary. The numbers (1, 2, 3, and so on) refer to the location in the written decision where that legal issue is discussed.

Keep in mind that your situation may or may not relate exactly to a particular court decision. It will depend on the similarity of the facts and whether your situation and the legal decision involve the same sections of IDEA. The more alike the facts and pertinent parts of IDEA, the more you can use the decision to your advantage. But the existence of a case that supports your position does not mean that the school district has to apply or even abide by that decision. It is certainly a very persuasive precedent, but it is just an example of how one court has ruled in a similar situation.

If the decision was reached by the U.S. Supreme Court, the federal court of appeals covering your state, your federal district court, or your state supreme court, the case represents the law in your area. Decisions in other federal circuits can be useful as long as there is not a different legal standard in your circuit.

If you find a case that is similar to yours and the decision is a good one, think about writing to your school district, explaining why you think you'll prevail in due process.

⚠ Do legal research with care. Analyzing case law and the meaning and reach of legal statutes can be complicated. Make sure you know what you're talking about before you cite the law. While you can learn a good deal, becoming expert at legal research requires care, time, and training. Proceed carefully, and use what you learn with real caution.

Letter Encouraging School Board Settlement

Date: April 20, 20xx

To: Howard Yankolon, Superintendent
Eugene School District
15578 South Main
Eugene, OR 97412

Re: Clara Centler, student in Westside School, fifth-grade

I appreciated your efforts at the April 14, 20xx, IEP meeting; as you know, we are in disagreement about Clara's need for a one-to-one aide so she can be mainstreamed.

I have requested a fair hearing. I have also done some research on this matter and determined that the facts and the law in the U.S. Supreme Court's decision in *Board of Education v. Holland* are almost identical to our dispute. I strongly believe that with the Supreme Court's direction in that case, it would be a real waste of time and district money to go to due process.

I am therefore requesting that you consider this and meet with me to discuss a possible settlement of our differences.

Sincerely,

Stuart Centler

Stuart Centler
78 Pine Ave.
Eugene, OR 97412
Phones: 555-5543 (home); 555-0933 (work)

G. Online Legal Research

Every day, a growing number of basic legal resources are available online through the Internet. There are a number of different ways to use the Internet to search for material, but by far the most important and common tool for doing research on the Internet is the World Wide Web. The Web provides links among documents and makes it easy to jump from one resource to another. Each resource is organized graphically like a book, allowing you to skip from topic to topic.

In addition, a wide variety of secondary sources intended for both lawyers and the general public have been posted on the Internet by law schools and firms. If you are on the Web, for example, a good way to find these sources is to visit any of the following websites, each of which provides links to legal information by specific subject:

- **www.nolo.com.** Nolo's Internet site contains helpful articles, information about new legislation, and a legal research center you can use to find state and federal statutes.

- **www.law.cornell.edu.** This site is maintained by Cornell Law School. You can find the text of the U.S. Code, federal court decisions, and some state court decisions. You can also search for material by topic.

- **www.law.indiana.edu/v-lib.** This site is maintained by Indiana University's School of Law at Bloomington. You can search by organization, including the U.S. government, state governments, and law journals, or by topic.

- **www.access.gpo.gov/nara/cfr/.** This site provides the entire Federal Code of Regulations.

- **www.statelocalgov.net/index.cfm.** This comprehensive site provides links to state and local government websites. Look here to find a link to your state's department of education, your county government's website, and perhaps even a website for your city or town.

In addition, Appendix 3 includes a section entitled "Legal Resources for Parents of a Special Education Child." These resources include websites that offer a wealth of legal and practical materials on special education. ■

15

Parent Organizations and Special Education

The first word in IDEA is "Individuals." Special education law, philosophy, and approach is based on the individual child, which makes it somewhat difficult to approach special education from a collective or group perspective. Each IEP is different, which is why this book has focused on strategies and procedures for parents acting alone.

There are, however, situations in which a group of parents working together can have a tremendous impact on a school district and the programs available for children with disabilities. When a group of parents approaches a school to recommend changes, the school is more likely to take notice. A parent group can also serve as an invaluable resource for information and support as you go through the special education process.

A. Join a Parent Organization

There are many ways to find an existing parent group. You can start by getting in touch with the local PTA. In addition, most school districts have a parent advisory committee (sometimes called community advisory committees, or CACs) specifically formed for special education matters. If you haven't already done so, contact your school district to find out about that committee. It is likely composed of special education professionals and other parents. If you can't find information on a local group, try the state level. Appendix 3 contains a state-by-state list of Parent Training and Information Centers (PTIs). PTIs are parent-to-parent organizations that can provide advice, training, and even advocacy help.

A parent organization can help you in several ways:

- There is strength in numbers. School districts often pay more attention to two parents than one, four parents than two, ten parents than five.
- A parent group can provide you with all kinds of important information about the school administrator, staff (including teach-

ers who are not afraid to be frank), existing classes, the local IEP process, and outside support professionals, such as independent assessors, private service providers, private schools, and attorneys.

- A parent group can suggest successful educational strategies, methodologies geared for your child, and even sophisticated knowledge about IDEA and its legal mandates.
- A parent group can provide the emotional support and advice you will need to navigate the special education process and reinforce the important feeling that you are not alone.

⚠ **Community advisory committees may include school district representatives.** School personnel regularly attend meetings of these committees, so parents may find it difficult to speak frankly. This is not to say that you shouldn't trust or include school personnel, but you should recognize that there may be times when the presence of school personnel inhibits honest discussion of certain issues. If this is the only organization in your area, consider forming an independent parent organization.

B. Form a Parent Organization

If your community doesn't have a parent organization, the existing group is too tied to or influenced by the school district, or the existing group doesn't meet your needs, you can organize a new group. How do you begin?

First, consider how wide or narrow you want your focus to be. If your numbers can support such a group, you may want to form an organization of parents whose children have similar disabling conditions. You don't need a lot of people. Three or four parents can be quite effective. There is certainly nothing wrong with forming a cross-disability group, and the parents in your area may prefer it. The strength that comes from a large group can often offset the challenges that come with a diversity of concerns.

Sometimes a few simple phone calls will lead to very useful recommendations. Here's how to get started and prepare for your first meeting:

- Invite all possible parents who fit within your chosen scope.
- Ask them for agenda ideas, focusing on common issues and concerns.
- Ask them for the names of other parents to invite.
- Ask your child's teacher or pediatrician to mention the meeting to other parents who might be interested.
- Ask the PTA and your school district to announce the meeting or to include information on it in any mailings.
- Place an announcement in your local newspaper.
- Contact local disability organizations. They may be able to connect you with other parent support groups in your state. They may also be able to advise you if you encounter problems.

At your first meeting, you can decide how formal you want to be and what issues you want to focus on. If you take the formal route, you'll need to select a name, elect officers, decide whether to charge dues (and if so, how much), collect those dues, and establish regular meetings.

No matter how formal or informal you are, you need to spend some time discussing your purpose and what you hope to accomplish. Do you simply want to establish better ties with the school administration? Do you want to address specific concerns, such as the quality of a particular class, intimidation by school personnel during the IEP process, or certain procedures that you find unfair? Once you decide which issues you want to tackle, you can figure out how to formally contact the district and raise your concerns.

At later meetings, consider inviting guests, such as representatives of the school district or a local special education attorney. The attorney will probably charge for his or her time. Your dues or an additional contribution from each family can cover the cost. Also, consider developing a newsletter (online is easiest) to maintain communication with other parents in your area.

Get Involved With the School District

Whether you work alone or with a group, there are many ways to improve your child's educational program through direct involvement with the school district. Volunteer at school or in the administrative office, run for school board, or assist in school fundraisers. Generally, this kind of activity gets you involved, opens doors, and allows you to meet the people in charge. This often can foster a good relationship with school personnel, making it easier for you to pick up the phone and call about—and resolve—a problem.

The same advice goes for your parent group. You should meet with the district on a somewhat regular basis, to find out how you can help the school. Build a relationship between your group and the school. Ultimately, you and the school district really do have the same goal (if unfortunately not the necessary budget or time): to help your child grow into an effective, productive, and happy adult.

Appendix 1

Special Education Law and Regulations

Individuals with Disabilities Education Act (Key Sections)

Sec. 1401. Definitions

Except as otherwise provided, as used in this chapter:

(1) Assistive technology device. The term "assistive technology device" means any item, piece of equipment, or product system, whether acquired commercially off the shelf, modified, or customized, that is used to increase, maintain, or improve functional capabilities of a child with a disability.

(2) Assistive technology service. The term "assistive technology service" means any service that directly assists a child with a disability in the selection, acquisition, or use of an assistive technology device. Such term includes:

(A) the evaluation of the needs of such child, including a functional evaluation of the child in the child's customary environment;

(B) purchasing, leasing, or otherwise providing for the acquisition of assistive technology devices by such child;

(C) selecting, designing, fitting, customizing, adapting, applying, maintaining, repairing, or replacing of assistive technology devices;

(D) coordinating and using other therapies, interventions, or services with assistive technology devices, such as those associated with existing education and rehabilitation plans and programs;

(E) training or technical assistance for such child, or, where appropriate, the family of such child; and

(F) training or technical assistance for professionals (including individuals providing education and rehabilitation services), employers, or other individuals who provide services to, employ, or are otherwise substantially involved in the major life functions of such child.

(3) Child with a disability

(A) *In general.* The term "child with a disability" means a child:

(i) with mental retardation, hearing impairments (including deafness), speech or language impairments, visual impairments (including blindness), serious emotional disturbance (hereinafter referred to as "emotional disturbance"), orthopedic impairments, autism, traumatic brain injury, other health impairments, or specific learning disabilities; and

(ii) who, by reason thereof, needs special education and related services.

(B) *Child aged 3 through 9.* The term "child with a disability" for a child aged 3 through 9 may, at the discretion of the State and the local educational agency, include a child:

(i) experiencing developmental delays, as defined by the State and as measured by appropriate diagnostic instruments and procedures, in one or more of the following areas: physical development, cognitive development, communication development, social or emotional development, or adaptive development; and

(ii) who, by reason thereof, needs special education and related services.

(4) Educational service agency. The term "educational service agency":

(A) means a regional public multiservice agency:

(i) authorized by State law to develop, manage, and provide services or programs to local educational agencies; and

(ii) recognized as an administrative agency for purposes of the provision of special education and related services provided within public elementary and secondary schools of the State; and

(B) includes any other public institution or agency having administrative control and direction over a public elementary or secondary school.

(5) Elementary school. The term "elementary school" means a nonprofit institutional day or residential school that provides elementary education, as determined under State law.

(6) Equipment. The term "equipment" includes:

(A) machinery, utilities, and built-in equipment and any necessary enclosures or structures to house such machinery, utilities, or equipment; and

(B) all other items necessary for the functioning of a particular facility as a facility for the provision of educational services, including items such as instructional equipment and necessary furniture; printed, published, and audio-visual instructional materials; telecommunications, sensory, and other technological aids and devices; and books, periodicals, documents, and other related materials.

(7) Excess costs. The term "excess costs" means those costs that are in excess of the average annual per-student expenditure in a local educational agency during the preceding school year for an elementary or secondary school student, as may be appropriate, and which shall be computed after deducting:

(A) amounts received:

(i) under subchapter II of this chapter;

(ii) under part A of title I of the Elementary and Secondary Education Act of 1965 (20 U.S.C. 6311 et seq.); or

(iii) under part A of title VII of that Act (20 U.S.C. 7401 et seq.); and

(B) any State or local funds expended for programs that would qualify for assistance under any of those parts.

(8) Free appropriate public education. The term "free appropriate public education" means special education and related services that:

(A) have been provided at public expense, under public supervision and direction, and without charge;

(B) meet the standards of the State educational agency;

(C) include an appropriate preschool, elementary, or secondary school education in the State involved; and

(D) are provided in conformity with the individualized education program required under section 1414(d) of this title.

(9) Indian. The term "Indian" means an individual who is a member of an Indian tribe.

(10) Indian tribe. The term "Indian tribe" means any Federal or State Indian tribe, band, rancheria, pueblo, colony, or community, including any Alaska Native village or regional village corporation (as defined in or established under the Alaska Native Claims Settlement Act (43 U.S.C. 1601 et seq.)).

(11) Individualized education program. The term "individualized education program" or "IEP" means a written statement for each child with a disability that is developed, reviewed, and revised in accordance with section 1414(d) of this title.

(12) Individualized family service plan. The term "individualized family service plan" has the meaning given such term in section 1436 of this title.

(13) Infant or toddler with a disability. The term "infant or toddler with a disability" has the meaning given such term in section 1432 of this title.

(14) Institution of higher education. The term "institution of higher education":

(A) has the meaning given that term in section 1141(a) of this title; and

(B) also includes any community college receiving funding from the Secretary of the Interior under the Tribally Controlled Community College Assistance Act of 1978 (25 U.S.C. 1801 et seq.).

(15) Local educational agency

(A) The term "local educational agency" means a public board of education or other public authority legally constituted within a State for either administrative control or direction of, or to perform a service function for, public elementary or secondary schools in a city, county, township, school district, or other political subdivision of a State, or for such combination of school districts or counties as are recognized in a State as an administrative agency for its public elementary or secondary schools.

(B) The term includes:

(i) an educational service agency, as defined in paragraph (4); and

(ii) any other public institution or agency having administrative control and direction of a public elementary or secondary school.

(C) The term includes an elementary or secondary school funded by the Bureau of Indian Affairs, but only to the extent that such inclusion makes the school eligible for programs for which specific eligibility is not provided to the school in another provision of law and the school does not have a student population that is smaller than the student population of the local educational agency receiving assistance under this chapter with the smallest student population, except that the school shall not be subject to the jurisdiction of any State educational agency other than the Bureau of Indian Affairs.

(16) Native language. The term "native language", when used with reference to an individual of limited English proficiency, means the language normally used by the individual, or in the case of a child, the language normally used by the parents of the child.

(17) Nonprofit. The term "nonprofit", as applied to a school, agency, organization, or institution, means a school, agency, organization, or institution owned and operated by one or more nonprofit corporations or associations no part of the net earnings of which inures, or may lawfully inure, to the benefit of any private shareholder or individual.

(18) Outlying area. The term "outlying area" means the United States Virgin Islands, Guam, American Samoa, and the Commonwealth of the Northern Mariana Islands.

(19) Parent. The term "parent":

(A) includes a legal guardian; and

(B) except as used in sections 1415(b)(2) and 1439(a)(5) of this title, includes an individual assigned under either of those sections to be a surrogate parent.

(20) Parent organization. The term "parent organization" has the meaning given that term in section 1482(g) of this title.

(21) Parent training and information center. The term "parent training and information center" means a center assisted under section 1482 or 1483 of this title.

(22) Related services. The term "related services" means transportation, and such developmental, corrective, and other supportive services (including speech-language pathology and audiology services, psychological services, physical and occupational therapy, recreation, including therapeutic recreation, social work services, counseling services, including rehabilitation counseling, orientation and mobility services, and medical services, except that such medical services shall be for diagnostic and evaluation purposes only) as may be required to assist a child with a disability to benefit from special education, and includes the early identification and assessment of disabling conditions in children.

(23) Secondary school. The term "secondary school" means a nonprofit institutional day or residential school that provides secondary education, as determined under State law, except that it does not include any education beyond grade 12.

(24) Secretary. The term "Secretary" means the Secretary of Education.

(25) Special education. The term "special education" means specially designed instruction, at no cost to parents, to meet the unique needs of a child with a disability, including:

(A) instruction conducted in the classroom, in the home, in hospitals and institutions, and in other settings; and

(B) instruction in physical education.

(26) Specific learning disability

(A) *In general.* The term "specific learning disability" means a disorder in one or more of the basic psychological processes involved in understanding or in using language, spoken or written, which disorder may manifest itself in imperfect ability to listen, think, speak, read, write, spell, or do mathematical calculations.

(B) *Disorders included.* Such term includes such conditions as perceptual disabilities, brain injury, minimal brain dysfunction, dyslexia, and developmental aphasia.

(C) *Disorders not included.* Such term does not include a learning problem that is primarily the result of visual, hearing, or motor disabilities, of mental retardation, of emotional disturbance, or of environmental, cultural, or economic disadvantage.

(27) State. The term "State" means each of the 50 States, the District of Columbia, the Commonwealth of Puerto Rico, and each of the outlying areas.

(28) State educational agency. The term "State educational agency" means the State board of education or other agency or officer primarily responsible for the State supervision of public elementary and secondary schools, or, if there is no such officer or agency, an officer or agency designated by the Governor or by State law.

(29) Supplementary aids and services. The term "supplementary aids and services" means aids, services, and other supports that are provided in regular education classes or other education-related settings to enable children with disabilities to be educated with nondisabled children to the maximum extent appropriate in accordance with section 1412(a)(5) of this title.

(30) Transition services. The term "transition services" means a coordinated set of activities for a student with a disability that:

(A) is designed within an outcome-oriented process, which promotes movement from school to post-school activities, including post-secondary education, vocational training, integrated employment (including supported employment), continuing and adult education, adult services, independent living, or community participation;

(B) is based upon the individual student's needs, taking into account the student's preferences and interests; and includes instruction, related services, community experiences, the development of employment and other post-school adult living objectives, and, when appropriate, acquisition of daily living skills and functional vocational evaluation.

Sec. 1412. State eligibility

(a) In general. A State is eligible for assistance under this subchapter for a fiscal year if the State demonstrates to the satisfaction of the Secretary that the State has in effect policies and procedures to ensure that it meets each of the following conditions:

(1) *Free appropriate public education*

(A) *In general.* A free appropriate public education is available to all children with disabilities residing in the State between the ages of 3 and 21, inclusive, including children with disabilities who have been suspended or expelled from school.

(B) *Limitation.* The obligation to make a free appropriate public education available to all children with disabilities does not apply with respect to children:

(i) aged 3 through 5 and 18 through 21 in a State to the extent that its application to those children would be inconsistent with State law or practice, or the order of any court, respecting the provision of public education to children in those age ranges; and

(ii) aged 18 through 21 to the extent that State law does not require that special education and related services under this subchapter be provided to children with disabilities who, in the educational placement prior to their incarceration in an adult correctional facility:

(I) were not actually identified as being a child with a disability under section 1401(3) of this title; or

(II) did not have an individualized education program under this subchapter.

(2) *Full educational opportunity goal.* The State has established a goal of providing full educational opportunity to all children with disabilities and a detailed timetable for accomplishing that goal.

(3) *Child find*

(A) *In general.* All children with disabilities residing in the State, including children with disabilities attending private schools, regardless of the severity of their disabilities, and who are in need of special education and related services, are identified, located, and evaluated and a practical method is developed and implemented to determine which children with disabilities are currently receiving needed special education and related services.

(B) *Construction.* Nothing in this chapter requires that children be classified by their disability so long as each child who has a disability listed in section 1401 of this title and who, by reason of that disability, needs special education and related services is regarded as a child with a disability under this subchapter.

(4) *Individualized education program.* An individualized education program, or an individualized family service plan that meets the requirements of section 1436(d) of this title, is developed, reviewed, and revised for each child with a disability in accordance with section 1414(d) of this title.

(5) *Least restrictive environment*

(A) *In general.* To the maximum extent appropriate, children with disabilities, including children in public or private institutions or other care facilities, are educated with children who are not disabled, and special classes, separate schooling, or other removal of children with disabilities from the regular educational environment occurs only when the nature or severity of the disability of a child is such that education in regular classes with the use of supplementary aids and services cannot be achieved satisfactorily.

(B) *Additional requirement*

(i) In general. If the State uses a funding mechanism by which the State distributes State funds on the basis of the type of setting in which a child is served, the funding mechanism does not result in placements that violate the requirements of subparagraph (A).

(ii) Assurance. If the State does not have policies and procedures to ensure compliance with clause (i), the State shall provide the Secretary an assurance that it will revise the funding mechanism as soon as feasible to ensure that such mechanism does not result in such placements.

(6) *Procedural safeguards*

(A) *In general.* Children with disabilities and their parents are afforded the procedural safeguards required by section 1415 of this title.

(B) *Additional procedural safeguards.* Procedures to ensure that testing and evaluation materials and procedures utilized for the purposes of evaluation and placement of children with disabilities will be selected and administered so as not to be racially or culturally discriminatory. Such materials or procedures shall be provided and administered in the child's native language or mode of communication, unless it clearly is not feasible to do so, and no single procedure shall be the sole criterion for determining an appropriate educational program for a child.

(7) *Evaluation.* Children with disabilities are evaluated in accordance with subsections (a) through (c) of section 1414 of this title.

(8) *Confidentiality.* Agencies in the State comply with section 1417(c) of this title (relating to the confidentiality of records and information).

(9) *Transition from subchapter III to preschool programs.* Children participating in early-intervention programs assisted under subchapter III of this chapter, and who will participate in preschool programs assisted under this subchapter, experience a smooth and effective transition to those preschool programs in a manner consistent with section 1437(a)(8) of this title. By the third birthday of such a child, an individualized education program or, if consistent with sections 1414(d)(2)(B) and 1436(d) of this title, an individualized family service plan, has been developed and is being implemented for the child. The local educational agency will participate in transition planning conferences arranged by the designated lead agency under section 1437(a)(8) of this title.

(10) *Children in private schools*

(A) Children enrolled in private schools by their parents

(i) In general. To the extent consistent with the number and location of children with disabilities in the State who are enrolled by their parents in private elementary and secondary schools, provision is made for the participation of those children in the program assisted or carried out under this subchapter by providing for such children special education and related services in accordance with the following requirements, unless the Secretary has arranged for services to those children under subsection (f) of this section:

(I) Amounts expended for the provision of those services by a local educational agency shall be equal to a proportionate amount of Federal funds made available under this subchapter.

(II) Such services may be provided to children with disabilities on the premises of private, including parochial, schools, to the extent consistent with law.

(ii) Child-find requirement. The requirements of paragraph (3) of this subsection (relating to child find) shall apply with respect to children with disabilities in the State who are enrolled in private, including parochial, elementary and secondary schools.

(B) Children placed in, or referred to, private schools by public agencies

(i) In general. Children with disabilities in private schools and facilities are provided special education and related services, in accordance with an individualized education program, at no cost to their parents, if such children are placed in, or referred to, such schools or facilities by the State or appropriate local educational agency as the means of carrying out the requirements of this subchapter or any other applicable law requiring the provision of special education and related services to all children with disabilities within such State.

(ii) *Standards.* In all cases described in clause (i), the State educational agency shall determine whether such schools and facilities meet standards that apply to State and local educational agencies and that children so served have all the rights they would have if served by such agencies.

(C) Payment for education of children enrolled in private schools without consent of or referral by the public agency

(i) *In general.* Subject to subparagraph (A), this subchapter does not require a local educational agency to pay for the cost of education, including special education and related services, of a child with a disability at a private school or facility if that agency made a free appropriate public education available to the child and the parents elected to place the child in such private school or facility.

(ii) Reimbursement for private school placement. If the parents of a child with a disability, who previously received special education and related services under the authority of a public agency, enroll the child in a private elementary or secondary school without the consent of or referral by the public agency, a court or a hearing officer may require the agency to reimburse the parents for the cost of that enrollment if the court or hearing officer finds that the agency had not made a free appropriate public education available to the child in a timely manner prior to that enrollment.

(iii) Limitation on reimbursement. The cost of reimbursement described in clause (ii) may be reduced or denied:

(I) if:

(aa) at the most recent IEP meeting that the parents attended prior to removal of the child from the public school, the parents did not inform the IEP Team that they were rejecting the placement proposed by the public agency to provide a free appropriate public education to their child, including stating their concerns and their intent to enroll their child in a private school at public expense; or

(bb) 10 business days (including any holidays that occur on a business day) prior to the removal of the child from the public school, the parents did not give written notice to the public agency of the information described in division (aa);

(II) if, prior to the parents' removal of the child from the public school, the public agency informed the parents, through the notice requirements described in section 1415(b)(7) of this title, of its intent to evaluate the child (including a statement of the purpose of the evaluation that was appropriate and reasonable), but the parents did not make the child available for such evaluation; or

(III) upon a judicial finding of unreasonableness with respect to actions taken by the parents.

(iv) *Exception.* Notwithstanding the notice requirement in clause (iii)(I), the cost of reimbursement may not be reduced or denied for failure to provide such notice if:

(I) the parent is illiterate and cannot write in English;

(II) compliance with clause (iii)(I) would likely result in physical or serious emotional harm to the child;

(III) the school prevented the parent from providing such notice; or

(IV) the parents had not received notice, pursuant to section 1415 of this title, of the notice requirement in clause (iii)(I).

(11) *State educational agency responsible for general supervision*

(A) *In general.* The State educational agency is responsible for ensuring that:

(i) the requirements of this subchapter are met; and

(ii) all educational programs for children with disabilities in the State, including all such programs administered by any other State or local agency:

(I) are under the general supervision of individuals in the State who are responsible for educational programs for children with disabilities; and

(II) meet the educational standards of the State educational agency.

(B) Limitation Subparagraph (A) shall not limit the responsibility of agencies in the State other than the State educational agency to provide, or pay for some or all of the costs of, a free appropriate public education for any child with a disability in the State.

(C) *Exception.* Notwithstanding subparagraphs (A) and (B), the Governor (or another individual pursuant to State law), consistent with State law, may assign to any public agency in the State the responsibility of ensuring that the requirements of this subchapter are met with respect to children with disabilities who are convicted as adults under State law and incarcerated in adult prisons.

(12) *Obligations related to and methods of ensuring services*

(A) *Establishing responsibility for services.* The Chief Executive Officer or designee of the officer shall ensure that an interagency agreement or other mechanism for interagency coordination is in effect between each public agency described in subparagraph (B) and the State educational agency, in order to ensure that all services described in subparagraph (B)(i) that are needed to ensure a free appropriate public education are provided, including the provision of such services during the pendency of any dispute under clause (iii). Such agreement or mechanism shall include the following:

(i) Agency financial responsibility. An identification of, or a method for defining, the financial responsibility of each agency for providing services described in subparagraph (B)(i) to ensure a free appropriate public education to children with disabilities, provided that the financial responsibility of each public agency described in subparagraph (B), including the State Medicaid agency and other public insurers of children with disabilities, shall precede the financial responsibility of the local educational agency (or the State agency responsible for developing the child's IEP).

(ii) Conditions and terms of reimbursement. The conditions, terms, and procedures under which a local educational agency shall be reimbursed by other agencies.

(iii) Interagency disputes. Procedures for resolving interagency disputes (including procedures under which local educational agencies may initiate proceedings) under the agreement or other mechanism to secure reimbursement from other agencies or otherwise implement the provisions of the agreement or mechanism.

(iv) Coordination of services procedures. Policies and procedures for agencies to determine and identify the interagency coordination responsibilities of each agency to promote the coordination and timely and appropriate delivery of services described in subparagraph (B)(i).

(B) *Obligation of public agency*

(i) *In general.* If any public agency other than an educational agency is otherwise obligated under Federal or State law, or assigned responsibility under State policy or pursuant to subparagraph (A), to provide or pay for any services that are also considered special education or related services (such as,

but not limited to, services described in sections 1401(1) relating to assistive technology devices, 1401(2) relating to assistive technology services, 1401(22) relating to related services, 1401(29) relating to supplementary aids and services, and 1401(30) of this title relating to transition services) that are necessary for ensuring a free appropriate public education to children with disabilities within the State, such public agency shall fulfill that obligation or responsibility, either directly or through contract or other arrangement.

(ii) Reimbursement for services by public agency. If a public agency other than an educational agency fails to provide or pay for the special education and related services described in clause (i), the local educational agency (or State agency responsible for developing the child's IEP) shall provide or pay for such services to the child. Such local educational agency or State agency may then claim reimbursement for the services from the public agency that failed to provide or pay for such services and such public agency shall reimburse the local educational agency or State agency pursuant to the terms of the interagency agreement or other mechanism described in subparagraph (A)(i) according to the procedures established in such agreement pursuant to subparagraph (A)(ii).

(C) *Special rule.* The requirements of subparagraph (A) may be met through:

(i) state statute or regulation;

(ii) signed agreements between respective agency officials that clearly identify the responsibilities of each agency relating to the provision of services; or

(iii) other appropriate written methods as determined by the Chief Executive Officer of the State or designee of the officer.

(13) *Procedural requirements relating to local educational agency eligibility.* The State educational agency will not make a final determination that a local educational agency is not eligible for assistance under this subchapter without first affording that agency reasonable notice and an opportunity for a hearing.

(14) *Comprehensive system of personnel development.* The State has in effect, consistent with the purposes of this chapter and with section 1435(a)(8) of this title, a comprehensive system of personnel development that is designed to ensure an adequate supply of qualified special education, regular education, and related services personnel that meets the requirements for a State improvement plan relating to personnel development in subsections (b)(2)(B) and (c)(3)(D) of section 1453 of this title.

(15) *Personnel standards*

(A) *In general.* The State educational agency has established and maintains standards to ensure that personnel necessary to carry out this subchapter are appropriately and adequately prepared and trained.

(B) *Standards described.* Such standards shall:

(i) be consistent with any State-approved or State-recognized certification, licensing, registration, or other comparable requirements that apply to the professional discipline in which those personnel are providing special education or related services;

(ii) to the extent the standards described in subparagraph (A) are not based on the highest requirements in the State applicable to a specific profession or discipline, the State is taking steps to require retraining or hiring of personnel that meet appropriate professional requirements in the State; and

(iii) allow paraprofessionals and assistants who are appropriately trained and supervised, in accordance with State law, regulations, or written policy, in meeting the requirements of this subchapter to be used to assist in the provision of special education and related services to children with disabilities under this subchapter.

(C) *Policy*. In implementing this paragraph, a State may adopt a policy that includes a requirement that local educational agencies in the State make an ongoing good-faith effort to recruit and hire appropriately and adequately trained personnel to provide special education and related services to children with disabilities, including, in a geographic area of the State where there is a shortage of such personnel, the most qualified individuals available who are making satisfactory progress toward completing applicable course work necessary to meet the standards described in subparagraph (B)(i), consistent with State law, and the steps described in subparagraph (B)(ii) within three years.

(16) *Performance goals and indicators*. The State:

(A) has established goals for the performance of children with disabilities in the State that:

(i) will promote the purposes of this chapter, as stated in section 1400(d) of this title; and

(ii) are consistent, to the maximum extent appropriate, with other goals and standards for children established by the State;

(B) has established performance indicators the State will use to assess progress toward achieving those goals that, at a minimum, address the performance of children with disabilities on assessments, drop-out rates, and graduation rates;

(C) will, every two years, report to the Secretary and the public on the progress of the State, and of children with disabilities in the State, toward meeting the goals established under subparagraph (A); and

(D) based on its assessment of that progress, will revise its State improvement plan under part A of subchapter IV of this chapter as may be needed to improve its performance, if the State receives assistance under that part.

(17) *Participation in assessments*

(A) *In general*. Children with disabilities are included in general State and district-wide assessment programs, with appropriate accommodations, where necessary. As appropriate, the State or local educational agency:

(i) develops guidelines for the participation of children with disabilities in alternate assessments for those children who cannot participate in State and district-wide assessment programs; and

(ii) develops and, beginning not later than July 1, 2000, conducts those alternate assessments.

(B) *Reports*. The State educational agency makes available to the public, and reports to the public with the same frequency and in the same detail as it reports on the assessment of non-disabled children, the following:

(i) The number of children with disabilities participating in regular assessments.

(ii) The number of those children participating in alternate assessments.

(iii)

(I) The performance of those children on regular assessments (beginning not later than July 1, 1998) and on alternate assessments (not later than July 1, 2000), if doing so would be statistically sound and would not result in the disclosure of performance results identifiable to individual children.

(II) Data relating to the performance of children described under subclause (I) shall be disaggregated:

(aa) for assessments conducted after July 1, 1998; and

(bb) for assessments conducted before July 1, 1998, if the State is required to disaggregate such data prior to July 1, 1998.

(18) *Supplementation of State, local, and other Federal funds*

(A) *Expenditures*. Funds paid to a State under this subchapter will be expended in accordance with all the provisions of this subchapter.

(B) *Prohibition against commingling*. Funds paid to a State under this subchapter will not be commingled with State funds.

(C) *Prohibition against supplantation and conditions for waiver by Secretary*. Except as provided in section 1413 of this title, funds paid to a State under this subchapter will be used to supplement the level of Federal, State, and local funds (including funds that are not under the direct control of State or local educational agencies) expended for special education and related services provided to children with disabilities under this subchapter and in no case to supplant such Federal, State, and local funds, except that, where the State provides clear and convincing evidence that all children with disabilities have available to them a free appropriate public education, the Secretary may waive, in whole or in part, the requirements of this subparagraph if the Secretary concurs with the evidence provided by the State.

(19) *Maintenance of State financial support*

(A) *In general*. The State does not reduce the amount of State financial support for special education and related services for children with disabilities, or otherwise made available because of the excess costs of educating those children, below the amount of that support for the preceding fiscal year.

(B) *Reduction of funds for failure to maintain support*. The Secretary shall reduce the allocation of funds under section 1411 of this title for any fiscal year following the fiscal year in which the State fails to comply with the requirement of subparagraph (A) by the same amount by which the State fails to meet the requirement.

(C) *Waivers for exceptional or uncontrollable circumstances*. The Secretary may waive the requirement of subparagraph (A) for a State, for one fiscal year at a time, if the Secretary determines that:

(i) granting a waiver would be equitable due to exceptional or uncontrollable circumstances such as a natural disaster or a precipitous and unforeseen decline in the financial resources of the State; or

(ii) the State meets the standard in paragraph (18)(C) of this section for a waiver of the requirement to supplement, and not to supplant, funds received under this subchapter.

(D) *Subsequent years.* If, for any year, a State fails to meet the requirement of subparagraph (A), including any year for which the State is granted a waiver under subparagraph (C), the financial support required of the State in future years under subparagraph (A) shall be the amount that would have been required in the absence of that failure and not the reduced level of the State's support.

(E) *Regulations*

(i) The Secretary shall, by regulation, establish procedures (including objective criteria and consideration of the results of compliance reviews of the State conducted by the Secretary) for determining whether to grant a waiver under subparagraph (C)(ii).

(ii) The Secretary shall publish proposed regulations under clause (i) not later than 6 months after June 4, 1997, and shall issue final regulations under clause (i) not later than 1 year after June 4, 1997.

(20) *Public participation.* Prior to the adoption of any policies and procedures needed to comply with this section (including any amendments to such policies and procedures), the State ensures that there are public hearings, adequate notice of the hearings, and an opportunity for comment available to the general public, including individuals with disabilities and parents of children with disabilities.

(21) *State advisory panel*

(A) *In general.* The State has established and maintains an advisory panel for the purpose of providing policy guidance with respect to special education and related services for children with disabilities in the State.

(B) *Membership.* Such advisory panel shall consist of members appointed by the Governor, or any other official authorized under State law to make such appointments, that is representative of the State population and that is composed of individuals involved in, or concerned with, the education of children with disabilities, including:

(i) parents of children with disabilities;

(ii) individuals with disabilities;

(iii) teachers;

(iv) representatives of institutions of higher education that prepare special education and related services personnel;

(v) State and local education officials;

(vi) administrators of programs for children with disabilities;

(vii) representatives of other State agencies involved in the financing or delivery of related services to children with disabilities;

(viii) representatives of private schools and public charter schools;

(ix) at least one representative of a vocational, community, or business organization concerned with the provision of transition services to children with disabilities; and

(x) representatives from the State juvenile and adult corrections agencies.

(C) *Special rule.* A majority of the members of the panel shall be individuals with disabilities or parents of children with disabilities.

(D) *Duties.* The advisory panel shall:

(i) advise the State educational agency of unmet needs within the State in the education of children with disabilities;

(ii) comment publicly on any rules or regulations proposed by the State regarding the education of children with disabilities;

(iii) advise the State educational agency in developing evaluations and reporting on data to the Secretary under section 1418 of this title;

(iv) advise the State educational agency in developing corrective action plans to address findings identified in Federal monitoring reports under this subchapter; and

(v) advise the State educational agency in developing and implementing policies relating to the coordination of services for children with disabilities.

(22) *Suspension and expulsion rates*

(A) *In general.* The State educational agency examines data to determine if significant discrepancies are occurring in the rate of long-term suspensions and expulsions of children with disabilities:

(i) among local educational agencies in the State; or

(ii) compared to such rates for nondisabled children within such agencies.

(B) *Review and revision of policies.* If such discrepancies are occurring, the State educational agency reviews and, if appropriate, revises (or requires the affected State or local educational agency to revise) its policies, procedures, and practices relating to the development and implementation of IEPs, the use of behavioral interventions, and procedural safeguards, to ensure that such policies, procedures, and practices comply with this chapter.

(b) State educational agency as provider of free appropriate public education or direct services. If the State educational agency provides free appropriate public education to children with disabilities, or provides direct services to such children, such agency:

(1) shall comply with any additional requirements of section 1413(a) of this title, as if such agency were a local educational agency; and

(2) may use amounts that are otherwise available to such agency under this subchapter to serve those children without regard to section 1413(a)(2)(A)(i) of this title (relating to excess costs).

(c) Exception for prior State plans

(1) *In general.* If a State has on file with the Secretary policies and procedures that demonstrate that such State meets any requirement of subsection (a) of this section, including any policies and procedures filed under this subchapter as in effect before the effective date of the Individuals with Disabilities Education Act Amendments of 1997, the Secretary shall consider such State to have met such requirement for purposes of receiving a grant under this subchapter.

(2) *Modifications made by State.* Subject to paragraph (3), an application submitted by a State in accordance with this section shall remain in effect until the State submits to the Secretary such modifications as the State deems necessary. This section shall apply to a modification to an application to

the same extent and in the same manner as this section applies to the original plan.

(3) *Modifications required by Secretary.* If, after the effective date of the Individuals with Disabilities Education Act Amendments of 1997, the provisions of this chapter are amended (or the regulations developed to carry out this chapter are amended), or there is a new interpretation of this chapter by a Federal court or a State's highest court, or there is an official finding of noncompliance with Federal law or regulations, the Secretary may require a State to modify its application only to the extent necessary to ensure the State's compliance with this subchapter.

(d) Approval by Secretary

(1) *In general.* If the Secretary determines that a State is eligible to receive a grant under this subchapter, the Secretary shall notify the State of that determination.

(2) *Notice and hearing.* The Secretary shall not make a final determination that a State is not eligible to receive a grant under this subchapter until after providing the State:

(A) with reasonable notice; and

(B) with an opportunity for a hearing.

(e) Assistance under other Federal programs. Nothing in this chapter permits a State to reduce medical and other assistance available, or to alter eligibility, under titles V and XIX of the Social Security Act (42 U.S.C. 701 et seq., 1396 et seq.) with respect to the provision of a free appropriate public education for children with disabilities in the State.

(f) By-pass for children in private schools

(1) *In general.* If, on December 2, 1983, a State educational agency is prohibited by law from providing for the participation in special programs of children with disabilities enrolled in private elementary and secondary schools as required by subsection (a)(10)(A) of this section, the Secretary shall, notwithstanding such provision of law, arrange for the provision of services to such children through arrangements which shall be subject to the requirements of such subsection.

(2) *Payments*

(A) *Determination of amounts.* If the Secretary arranges for services pursuant to this subsection, the Secretary, after consultation with the appropriate public and private school officials, shall pay to the provider of such services for a fiscal year an amount per child that does not exceed the amount determined by dividing:

(i) the total amount received by the State under this subchapter for such fiscal year; by

(ii) the number of children with disabilities served in the prior year, as reported to the Secretary by the State under section 1418 of this title.

(B) Withholding of certain amounts. Pending final resolution of any investigation or complaint that could result in a determination under this subsection, the Secretary may withhold from the allocation of the affected State educational agency the amount the Secretary estimates would be necessary to pay the cost of services described in subparagraph (A).

(C) *Period of payments.* The period under which payments are made under subparagraph (A) shall continue until the Secretary determines that there will no longer be any failure or inability on the part of the State educational agency to meet the requirements of subsection (a)(10)(A) of this section.

(3) *Notice and hearing*

(A) *In general.* The Secretary shall not take any final action under this subsection until the State educational agency affected by such action has had an opportunity, for at least 45 days after receiving written notice thereof, to submit written objections and to appear before the Secretary or the Secretary's designee to show cause why such action should not be taken.

(B) *Review of action.* If a State educational agency is dissatisfied with the Secretary's final action after a proceeding under subparagraph (A), such agency may, not later than 60 days after notice of such action, file with the United States court of appeals for the circuit in which such State is located a petition for review of that action. A copy of the petition shall be forthwith transmitted by the clerk of the court to the Secretary. The Secretary thereupon shall file in the court the record of the proceedings on which the Secretary based the Secretary's action, as provided in section 2112 of title 28.

(C) *Review of findings of fact.* The findings of fact by the Secretary, if supported by substantial evidence, shall be conclusive, but the court, for good cause shown, may remand the case to the Secretary to take further evidence, and the Secretary may thereupon make new or modified findings of fact and may modify the Secretary's previous action, and shall file in the court the record of the further proceedings. Such new or modified findings of fact shall likewise be conclusive if supported by substantial evidence.

(D) *Jurisdiction of court of appeals; review by United States Supreme Court.* Upon the filing of a petition under subparagraph (B), the United States court of appeals shall have jurisdiction to affirm the action of the Secretary or to set it aside, in whole or in part. The judgment of the court shall be subject to review by the Supreme Court of the United States upon certiorari or certification as provided in section 1254 of title 28.

Sec. 1414. Evaluations, eligibility determinations, individualized education programs, and educational placements

(a) Evaluations and reevaluations

(1) *Initial evaluations*

(A) *In general.* A State educational agency, other State agency, or local educational agency shall conduct a full and individual initial evaluation, in accordance with this paragraph and subsection (b) of this section, before the initial provision of special education and related services to a child with a disability under this subchapter.

(B) *Procedures.* Such initial evaluation shall consist of procedures:

(i) to determine whether a child is a child with a disability (as defined in section 1401(3) of this title); and

(ii) to determine the educational needs of such child.

(C) *Parental consent*

(i) *In general.* The agency proposing to conduct an initial evaluation to determine if the child qualifies as a child with a disability as defined in section 1401(3)(A) or 1401(3)(B) of this title shall obtain an informed consent from the parent of such child before the evaluation is conducted. Parental consent for evaluation shall not be construed as consent for placement for receipt of special education and related services.

(ii) *Refusal.* If the parents of such child refuse consent for the evaluation, the agency may continue to pursue an evaluation by utilizing the mediation and due process procedures under section 1415 of this title, except to the extent inconsistent with State law relating to parental consent.

(2) *Reevaluations.* A local educational agency shall ensure that a reevaluation of each child with a disability is conducted:

(A) if conditions warrant a reevaluation or if the child's parent or teacher requests a reevaluation, but at least once every 3 years; and

(B) in accordance with subsections (b) and (c) of this section.

(b) Evaluation procedures

(1) *Notice.* The local educational agency shall provide notice to the parents of a child with a disability, in accordance with subsections (b)(3), (b)(4), and (c) of section 1415 of this title, that describes any evaluation procedures such agency proposes to conduct.

(2) *Conduct of evaluation.* In conducting the evaluation, the local educational agency shall:

(A) use a variety of assessment tools and strategies to gather relevant functional and developmental information, including information provided by the parent, that may assist in determining whether the child is a child with a disability and the content of the child's individualized education program, including information related to enabling the child to be involved in and progress in the general curriculum or, for preschool children, to participate in appropriate activities;

(B) not use any single procedure as the sole criterion for determining whether a child is a child with a disability or determining an appropriate educational program for the child; and

(C) use technically sound instruments that may assess the relative contribution of cognitive and behavioral factors, in addition to physical or developmental factors.

(3) *Additional requirements.* Each local educational agency shall ensure that:

(A) tests and other evaluation materials used to assess a child under this section:

(i) are selected and administered so as not to be discriminatory on a racial or cultural basis; and

(ii) are provided and administered in the child's native language or other mode of communication, unless it is clearly not feasible to do so; and

(B) any standardized tests that are given to the child:

(i) have been validated for the specific purpose for which they are used;

(ii) are administered by trained and knowledgeable personnel; and

(iii) are administered in accordance with any instructions provided by the producer of such tests;

(C) the child is assessed in all areas of suspected disability; and

(D) assessment tools and strategies that provide relevant information that directly assists persons in determining the educational needs of the child are provided.

(4) *Determination of eligibility.* Upon completion of administration of tests and other evaluation materials:

(A) the determination of whether the child is a child with a disability as defined in section 1401(3) of this title shall be made by a team of qualified professionals and the parent of the child in accordance with paragraph (5); and

(B) a copy of the evaluation report and the documentation of determination of eligibility will be given to the parent.

(5) *Special rule for eligibility determination.* In making a determination of eligibility under paragraph (4)(A), a child shall not be determined to be a child with a disability if the determinant factor for such determination is lack of instruction in reading or math or limited English proficiency.

(c) Additional requirements for evaluation and reevaluations

(1) *Review of existing evaluation data.* As part of an initial evaluation (if appropriate) and as part of any reevaluation under this section, the IEP Team described in subsection (d)(1)(B) of this section and other qualified professionals, as appropriate, shall:

(A) review existing evaluation data on the child, including evaluations and information provided by the parents of the child, current classroom-based assessments and observations, and teacher and related services providers observation; and

(B) on the basis of that review, and input from the child's parents, identify what additional data, if any, are needed to determine:

(i) whether the child has a particular category of disability, as described in section 1401 (3) of this title, or, in case of a reevaluation of a child, whether the child continues to have such a disability;

(ii) the present levels of performance and educational needs of the child;

(iii) whether the child needs special education and related services, or in the case of a reevaluation of a child, whether the child continues to need special education and related services; and

(iv) whether any additions or modifications to the special education and related services are needed to enable the child to meet the measurable annual goals set out in the individualized education program of the child and to participate, as appropriate, in the general curriculum.

(2) *Source of data.* The local educational agency shall administer such tests and other evaluation materials as may be needed to produce the data identified by the IEP Team under paragraph (1)(B).

(3) *Parental consent.* Each local educational agency shall obtain informed parental consent, in accordance with subsection (a)(1)(C) of this section, prior to conducting any reevaluation of a child with a disability, except that such informed parent consent need not be obtained if the local educational agency can demonstrate that it had taken reasonable measures to obtain such consent and the child's parent has failed to respond.

(4) *Requirements if additional data are not needed.* If the IEP Team and other qualified professionals, as appropriate, determine that no additional data are needed to determine whether the child continues to be a child with a disability, the local educational agency:

(A) shall notify the child's parents of:

(i) that determination and the reasons for it; and

(ii) the right of such parents to request an assessment to determine whether the child continues to be a child with a disability; and

(B) shall not be required to conduct such an assessment unless requested to by the child's parents.

(5) *Evaluations before change in eligibility.* A local educational agency shall evaluate a child with a disability in accordance with this section before determining that the child is no longer a child with a disability.

(d) Individualized education programs.

(1) *Definitions*

As used in this chapter:

(A) *Individualized education program.* The term "individualized education program" or "IEP" means a written statement for each child with a disability that is developed, reviewed, and revised in accordance with this section and that includes:

(i) a statement of the child's present levels of educational performance, including:

(I) how the child's disability affects the child's involvement and progress in the general curriculum; or

(II) for preschool children, as appropriate, how the disability affects the child's participation in appropriate activities;

(ii) a statement of measurable annual goals, including benchmarks or short-term objectives, related to:

(I) meeting the child's needs that result from the child's disability to enable the child to be involved in and progress in the general curriculum; and

(II) meeting each of the child's other educational needs that result from the child's disability;

(iii) a statement of the special education and related services and supplementary aids and services to be provided to the child, or on behalf of the child, and a statement of the program modifications or supports for school personnel that will be provided for the child:

(I) to advance appropriately toward attaining the annual goals;

(II) to be involved and progress in the general curriculum in accordance with clause (i) and to participate in extracurricular and other nonacademic activities; and

(III) to be educated and participate with other children with disabilities and nondisabled children in the activities described in this paragraph;

(iv) an explanation of the extent, if any, to which the child will not participate with nondisabled children in the regular class and in the activities described in clause (iii);

(v)

(I) a statement of any individual modifications in the administration of State or districtwide assessments of student achievement that are needed in order for the child to participate in such assessment; and

(II) if the IEP Team determines that the child will not participate in a particular State or districtwide assessment of student achievement (or part of such an assessment), a statement of:

(aa) why that assessment is not appropriate for the child; and

(bb) how the child will be assessed;

(vi) the projected date for the beginning of the services and modifications described in clause (iii), and the anticipated frequency, location, and duration of those services and modifications;

(vii) a statement of:

(I) beginning at age 14, and updated annually, a statement of the transition service needs of the child under the applicable components of the child's IEP that focuses on the child's courses of study (such as participation in advanced-placement courses or a vocational education program);

(II) beginning at age 16 (or younger, if determined appropriate by the IEP Team), a statement of needed transition services for the child, including, when appropriate, a statement of the interagency responsibilities or any needed linkages; and

(III) beginning at least one year before the child reaches the age of majority under State law, a statement that the child has been informed of his or her rights under this chapter, if any, that will transfer to the child on reaching the age of majority under section 1415(m) of this title; and

(viii) a statement of:

(I) how the child's progress toward the annual goals described in clause (ii) will be measured; and

(II) how the child's parents will be regularly informed (by such means as periodic report cards), at least as often as parents are informed of their nondisabled children's progress, of:

(aa) their child's progress toward the annual goals described in clause (ii); and

(bb) the extent to which that progress is sufficient to enable the child to achieve the goals by the end of the year.

(B) *Individualized education program team.* The term "individualized education program team" or "IEP Team" means a group of individuals composed of:

(i) the parents of a child with a disability;

(ii) at least one regular education teacher of such child (if the child is, or may be, participating in the regular education environment);

(iii) at least one special education teacher, or where appropriate, at least one special education provider of such child;

(iv) a representative of the local educational agency who:

(I) is qualified to provide, or supervise the provision of, specially designed instruction to meet the unique needs of children with disabilities;

(II) is knowledgeable about the general curriculum; and

(III) is knowledgeable about the availability of resources of the local educational agency;

(v) an individual who can interpret the instructional implications of evaluation results, who may be a member of the team described in clauses (ii) through (vi);

(vi) at the discretion of the parent or the agency, other individuals who have knowledge or special expertise regarding the child, including related services personnel as appropriate; and

(vii) whenever appropriate, the child with a disability.

(2) *Requirement that program be in effect*

(A) *In general.* At the beginning of each school year, each local educational agency, State educational agency, or other State agency, as the case may be, shall have in effect, for each child with a disability in its jurisdiction, an individualized education program, as defined in paragraph (1)(A).

(B) *Program for child aged 3 through 5.* In the case of a child with a disability aged 3 through 5 (or, at the discretion of the State educational agency, a 2-year-old child with a disability who will turn age 3 during the school year), an individualized family service plan that contains the material described in section 1436 of this title, and that is developed in accordance with this section, may serve as the IEP of the child if using that plan as the IEP is:

(i) consistent with State policy; and

(ii) agreed to by the agency and the child's parents.

(3) *Development of IEP*

(A) *In general.* In developing each child's IEP, the IEP Team, subject to subparagraph (C), shall consider:

(i) the strengths of the child and the concerns of the parents for enhancing the education of their child; and

(ii) the results of the initial evaluation or most recent evaluation of the child.

(B) *Consideration of special factors.* The IEP Team shall:

(i) in the case of a child whose behavior impedes his or her learning or that of others, consider, when appropriate, strategies, including positive behavioral interventions, strategies, and supports to address that behavior;

(ii) in the case of a child with limited English proficiency, consider the language needs of the child as such needs relate to the child's IEP;

(iii) in the case of a child who is blind or visually impaired, provide for instruction in Braille and the use of Braille unless the IEP Team determines, after an evaluation of the child's reading and writing skills, needs, and appropriate reading and writing media (including an evaluation of the child's future needs for instruction in Braille or the use of Braille), that instruction in Braille or the use of Braille is not appropriate for the child;

(iv) consider the communication needs of the child, and in the case of a child who is deaf or hard of hearing, consider the child's language and communication needs, opportunities for direct communications with peers and professional personnel in the child's language and communication mode, academic level, and full range of needs, including opportunities for direct instruction in the child's language and communication mode; and

(v) consider whether the child requires assistive technology devices and services.

(C) *Requirement with respect to regular education teacher.* The regular education teacher of the child, as a member of the IEP Team, shall, to the extent appropriate, participate in the development of the IEP of the child, including the determination of appropriate positive behavioral interventions and strategies and the determination of supplementary aids and services, program modifications, and support for school personnel consistent with paragraph (1)(A)(iii).

(4) *Review and revision of IEP*

(A) *In general.* The local educational agency shall ensure that, subject to subparagraph (B), the IEP Team:

(i) reviews the child's IEP periodically, but not less than annually to determine whether the annual goals for the child are being achieved; and

(ii) revises the IEP as appropriate to address:

(I) any lack of expected progress toward the annual goals and in the general curriculum, where appropriate;

(II) the results of any reevaluation conducted under this section;

(III) information about the child provided to, or by, the parents, as described in subsection (c)(1)(B) of this section;

(IV) the child's anticipated needs; or

(V) other matters.

(B) *Requirement with respect to regular education teacher.* The regular education teacher of the child, as a member of the IEP Team, shall, to the extent appropriate, participate in the review and revision of the IEP of the child.

(5) *Failure to meet transition objectives.* If a participating agency, other than the local educational agency, fails to provide the transition services described in the IEP in accordance with paragraph (1)(A)(vii), the local educational agency shall reconvene the IEP Team to identify alternative strategies to meet the transition objectives for the child set out in that program.

(6) *Children with disabilities in adult prisons*

(A) *In general.* The following requirements do not apply to children with disabilities who are convicted as adults under State law and incarcerated in adult prisons:

(i) The requirements contained in section 1412(a)(17) of this title and paragraph (1)(A)(v) of this subsection (relating to participation of children with disabilities in general assessments).

(ii) The requirements of subclauses (I) and (II) of paragraph (1)(A)(vii) of this subsection (relating to transition planning and transition services), do not apply with respect to such children whose eligibility under this subchapter will end, because of their age, before they will be released from prison.

(B) *Additional requirement.* If a child with a disability is convicted as an adult under State law and incarcerated in an adult prison, the child's IEP Team may modify the child's IEP or placement notwithstanding the requirements of section 1412 (a)(5)(A) of this title and subsection (d)(1)(A) of this section if the State has demonstrated a bona fide security or compelling penological interest that cannot otherwise be accommodated.

(e) Construction. Team to include information under one component of a child's IEP that is already contained under another component of such IEP.

(f) Educational placements. Each local educational agency or State educational agency shall ensure that the parents of each child with a disability are members of any group that makes decisions on the educational placement of their child.

Sec. 1415. Procedural safeguards

(a) Establishment of procedures. Any State educational agency, State agency, or local educational agency that receives assistance under this subchapter shall establish and maintain procedures in accordance with this section to ensure that children with disabilities and their parents are guaranteed procedural safeguards with respect to the provision of free appropriate public education by such agencies.

(b) Types of procedures. The procedures required by this section shall include:

(1) an opportunity for the parents of a child with a disability to examine all records relating to such child and to participate in meetings with respect to the identification, evaluation, and educational placement of the child, and the provision of a free appropriate public education to such child, and to obtain an independent educational evaluation of the child;

(2) procedures to protect the rights of the child whenever the parents of the child are not known, the agency cannot, after reasonable efforts, locate the parents, or the child is a ward of the State, including the assignment of an individual (who shall not be an employee of the State educational agency, the local educational agency, or any other agency that is involved in the education or care of the child) to act as a surrogate for the parents;

(3) written prior notice to the parents of the child whenever such agency:

(A) proposes to initiate or change; or

(B) refuses to initiate or change; the identification, evaluation, or educational placement of the child, in accordance with subsection (c) of this section, or the provision of a free appropriate public education to the child;

(4) procedures designed to ensure that the notice required by paragraph (3) is in the native language of the parents, unless it clearly is not feasible to do so;

(5) an opportunity for mediation in accordance with subsection (e) of this section;

(6) an opportunity to present complaints with respect to any matter relating to the identification, evaluation, or educational placement of the child, or the provision of a free appropriate public education to such child;

(7) procedures that require the parent of a child with a disability, or the attorney representing the child, to provide notice (which shall remain confidential):

(A) to the State educational agency or local educational agency, as the case may be, in the complaint filed under paragraph (6); and

(B) that shall include:

(i) the name of the child, the address of the residence of the child, and the name of the school the child is attending;

(ii) a description of the nature of the problem of the child relating to such proposed initiation or change, including facts relating to such problem; and

(iii) a proposed resolution of the problem to the extent known and available to the parents at the time; and

(8) procedures that require the State educational agency to develop a model form to assist parents in filing a complaint in accordance with paragraph (7).

(c) Content of prior written notice. The notice required by subsection (b)(3) of this section shall include:

(1) a description of the action proposed or refused by the agency;

(2) an explanation of why the agency proposes or refuses to take the action;

(3) a description of any other options that the agency considered and the reasons why those options were rejected;

(4) a description of each evaluation procedure, test, record, or report the agency used as a basis for the proposed or refused action;

(5) a description of any other factors that are relevant to the agency's proposal or refusal;

(6) a statement that the parents of a child with a disability have protection under the procedural safeguards of this subchapter and, if this notice is not an initial referral for evaluation, the means by which a copy of a description of the procedural safeguards can be obtained; and

(7) sources for parents to contact to obtain assistance in understanding the provisions of this subchapter.

(d) Procedural safeguards notice

(1) *In general.* A copy of the procedural safeguards available to the parents of a child with a disability shall be given to the parents, at a minimum:

(A) upon initial referral for evaluation;

(B) upon each notification of an individualized education program meeting and upon reevaluation of the child; and

(C) upon registration of a complaint under subsection (b)(6) of this section.

(2) *Contents.* The procedural safeguards notice shall include a full explanation of the procedural safeguards, written in the native language of the parents, unless it clearly is not feasible to do so, and written in an easily understandable manner, available under this section and under regulations promulgated by the Secretary relating to:

(A) independent educational evaluation;

(B) prior written notice;

(C) parental consent;

(D) access to educational records;

(E) opportunity to present complaints;

(F) the child's placement during pendency of due process proceedings;

(G) procedures for students who are subject to placement in an interim alternative educational setting;

(H) requirements for unilateral placement by parents of children in private schools at public expense;

(I) mediation;

(J) due process hearings, including requirements for disclosure of evaluation results and recommendations;

(K) State-level appeals (if applicable in that State);

(L) civil actions; and

(M) attorneys' fees.

(e) Mediation

(1) *In general.* Any State educational agency or local educational agency that receives assistance under this subchapter shall ensure that procedures are established and implemented to allow parties to disputes involving any matter described in subsection (b)(6) of this section to resolve such disputes through a mediation process which, at a minimum, shall be available whenever a hearing is requested under subsection (f) or (k) of this section.

(2) *Requirements.* Such procedures shall meet the following requirements:

(A) The procedures shall ensure that the mediation process:

(i) is voluntary on the part of the parties;

(ii) is not used to deny or delay a parent's right to a due process hearing under subsection (f) of this section, or to deny any other rights afforded under this subchapter; and

(iii) is conducted by a qualified and impartial mediator who is trained in effective mediation techniques.

(B) A local educational agency or a State agency may establish procedures to require parents who choose not to use the mediation process to meet, at a time and location convenient to the parents, with a disinterested party who is under contract with:

(i) a parent training and information center or community parent resource center in the State established under section 1482 or 1483 of this title; or

(ii) an appropriate alternative dispute resolution entity; to encourage the use, and explain the benefits, of the mediation process to the parents.

(C) The State shall maintain a list of individuals who are qualified mediators and knowledgeable in laws and regulations relating to the provision of special education and related services.

(D) The State shall bear the cost of the mediation process, including the costs of meetings described in subparagraph (B).

(E) Each session in the mediation process shall be scheduled in a timely manner and shall be held in a location that is convenient to the parties to the dispute.

(F) An agreement reached by the parties to the dispute in the mediation process shall be set forth in a written mediation agreement.

(G) Discussions that occur during the mediation process shall be confidential and may not be used as evidence in any subsequent due process hearings or civil proceedings and the parties to the mediation process may be required to sign a confidentiality pledge prior to the commencement of such process.

(f) Impartial due process hearing

(1) *In general.* Whenever a complaint has been received under subsection (b)(6) or (k) of this section, the parents involved in such complaint shall have an opportunity for an impartial due process hearing, which shall be conducted by the State educational agency or by the local educational agency, as determined by State law or by the State educational agency.

(2) *Disclosure of evaluations and recommendations*

(A) *In general.* At least 5 business days prior to a hearing conducted pursuant to paragraph (1), each party shall disclose to all other parties all evaluations completed by that date and recommendations based on the offering party's evaluations that the party intends to use at the hearing.

(B) *Failure to disclose.* A hearing officer may bar any party that fails to comply with subparagraph (A) from introducing the relevant evaluation or recommendation at the hearing without the consent of the other party.

(3) *Limitation on conduct of hearing.* A hearing conducted pursuant to paragraph (1) may not be conducted by an employee of the State educational agency or the local educational agency involved in the education or care of the child.

(g) Appeal. If the hearing required by subsection (f) of this section is conducted by a local educational agency, any party aggrieved by the findings and decision rendered in such a hearing may appeal such findings and decision to the State educational agency. Such agency shall conduct an impartial review of such decision. The officer conducting such review shall make an independent decision upon completion of such review.

(h) Safeguards. Any party to a hearing conducted pursuant to subsection (f) or (k) of this section, or an appeal conducted pursuant to subsection (g) of this section, shall be accorded:

(1) the right to be accompanied and advised by counsel and by individuals with special knowledge or training with respect to the problems of children with disabilities;

(2) the right to present evidence and confront, cross-examine, and compel the attendance of witnesses;

(3) the right to a written, or, at the option of the parents, electronic verbatim record of such hearing; and

(4) the right to written, or, at the option of the parents, electronic findings of fact and decisions (which findings and decisions shall be made available to the public consistent with the requirements of section 1417(c) of this title (relating to the confidentiality of data, information, and records) and shall also be transmitted to the advisory panel established pursuant to section 141 (a)(21) of this title).

(i) Administrative procedures

(1) *In general*

(A) *Decision made in hearing.* A decision made in a hearing conducted pursuant to subsection (f) or (k) of this section shall be final, except that any party involved in such hearing may appeal such decision under the provisions of subsection (g) of this section and paragraph (2) of this subsection.

(B) *Decision made at appeal.* A decision made under subsection (g) of this section shall be final, except that any party may bring an action under paragraph (2) of this subsection.

(2) *Right to bring civil action*

(A) *In general.* Any party aggrieved by the findings and decision made under subsection (f) or (k) of this section who does not have the right to an appeal under subsection (g) of this section, and any party aggrieved by the findings and decision under this subsection, shall have the right to bring a civil action with respect to the complaint presented pursuant to this section, which action may be brought in any State court of competent jurisdiction or in a district court of the United States without regard to the amount in controversy.

(B) *Additional requirements.* In any action brought under this paragraph, the court:

(i) shall receive the records of the administrative proceedings;

(ii) shall hear additional evidence at the request of a party; and

(iii) basing its decision on the preponderance of the evidence, shall grant such relief as the court determines is appropriate.

(3) *Jurisdiction of district courts; attorneys' fees*

(A) *In general.* The district courts of the United States shall have jurisdiction of actions brought under this section without regard to the amount in controversy.

(B) *Award of attorneys' fees.* In any action or proceeding brought under this section, the court, in its discretion, may award reasonable attorneys' fees as part of the costs to the parents of a child with a disability who is the prevailing party.

(C) *Determination of amount of attorneys' fees.* Fees awarded under this paragraph shall be based on rates prevailing in the community in which the action or proceeding arose for the kind and quality of services furnished. No bonus or multiplier may be used in calculating the fees awarded under this subsection.

(D) *Prohibition of attorneys' fees and related costs for certain services*

(i) Attorneys' fees may not be awarded and related costs may not be reimbursed in any action or proceeding under this section for services performed subsequent to the time of a written offer of settlement to a parent if:

(I) the offer is made within the time prescribed by Rule 68 of the Federal Rules of Civil Procedure or, in the case of an administrative proceeding, at any time more than 10 days before the proceeding begins;

(II) the offer is not accepted within 10 days; and

(III) the court or administrative hearing officer finds that the relief finally obtained by the parents is not more favorable to the parents than the offer of settlement.

(ii) Attorneys' fees may not be awarded relating to any meeting of the IEP Team unless such meeting is convened as a result of an administrative proceeding or judicial action, or, at the discretion of the State, for a mediation described in subsection (e) of this section that is conducted prior to the filing of a complaint under subsection (b)(6) or (k) of this section.

(E) *Exception to prohibition on attorneys' fees and related costs.* Notwithstanding subparagraph (D), an award of attorneys' fees and related costs may be made to a parent who is the prevailing party and who was substantially justified in rejecting the settlement offer.

(F) *Reduction in amount of attorneys' fees.* Except as provided in subparagraph (G), whenever the court finds that:

(i) the parent, during the course of the action or proceeding, unreasonably protracted the final resolution of the controversy;

(ii) the amount of the attorneys' fees otherwise authorized to be awarded unreasonably exceeds the hourly rate prevailing in the community for similar services by attorneys of reasonably comparable skill, reputation, and experience;

(iii) the time spent and legal services furnished were excessive considering the nature of the action or proceeding; or

(iv) the attorney representing the parent did not provide to the school district the appropriate information in the due process complaint in accordance with subsection (b)(7) of this section; the court shall reduce, accordingly, the amount of the attorneys' fees awarded under this section.

(G) *Exception to reduction in amount of attorneys' fees.* The provisions of subparagraph (F) shall not apply in any action or proceeding if the court finds that the State or local educational agency unreasonably protracted the final resolution of the action or proceeding or there was a violation of this section.

(j) Maintenance of current educational placement. Except as provided in subsection (k)(7) of this section, during the pendency of any proceedings conducted pursuant to this section, unless the State or local educational agency and the parents otherwise agree, the child shall remain in the then-current educational placement of such child, or, if applying for initial admission to a public school, shall, with the consent of the parents, be placed in the public school program until all such proceedings have been completed.

(k) Placement in alternative educational setting

(1) *Authority of school personnel*

(A) School personnel under this section may order a change in the placement of a child with a disability:

(i) to an appropriate interim alternative educational setting, another setting, or suspension, for not more than 10 school days (to the extent such alternatives would be applied to children without disabilities); and

(ii) to an appropriate interim alternative educational setting for the same amount of time that a child without a disability would be subject to discipline, but for not more than 45 days if:

(I) the child carries a weapon to school or to a school function under the jurisdiction of a State or a local educational agency; or

(II) the child knowingly possesses or uses illegal drugs or sells or solicits the sale of a controlled substance while at school or a school function under the jurisdiction of a State or local educational agency.

(B) Either before or not later than 10 days after taking a disciplinary action described in subparagraph (A):

(i) if the local educational agency did not conduct a functional behavioral assessment and implement a behavioral intervention plan for such child before the behavior that resulted in the suspension described in subparagraph (A), the agency shall convene an IEP meeting to develop an assessment plan to address that behavior; or

(ii) if the child already has a behavioral intervention plan, the IEP Team shall review the plan and modify it, as necessary, to address the behavior.

(2) *Authority of hearing officer.* A hearing officer under this section may order a change in the placement of a child with a disability to an appropriate interim alternative educational setting for not more than 45 days if the hearing officer:

(A) determines that the public agency has demonstrated by substantial evidence that maintaining the current placement of such child is substantially likely to result in injury to the child or to others;

(B) considers the appropriateness of the child's current placement;

(C) considers whether the public agency has made reasonable efforts to minimize the risk of harm in the child's current placement, including the use of supplementary aids and services; and

(D) determines that the interim alternative educational setting meets the requirements of paragraph (3)(B).

(3) *Determination of setting*

(A) *In general.* The alternative educational setting described in paragraph (1)(A)(ii) shall be determined by the IEP Team.

(B) *Additional requirements.* Any interim alternative educational setting in which a child is placed under paragraph (1) or (2) shall:

(i) be selected so as to enable the child to continue to participate in the general curriculum, although in another setting, and to continue to receive those services and modifications, including those described in the child's current IEP, that will enable the child to meet the goals set out in that IEP; and

(ii) include services and modifications designed to address the behavior described in paragraph (1) or paragraph (2) so that it does not recur.

(4) *Manifestation determination review*

(A) *In general.* If a disciplinary action is contemplated as described in paragraph (1) or paragraph (2) for a behavior of a child with a disability described in either of those paragraphs, or if a disciplinary action involving a change of placement for more than 10 days is contemplated for a child with a disability who has engaged in other behavior that violated any rule or code of conduct of the local educational agency that applies to all children:

(i) not later than the date on which the decision to take that action is made, the parents shall be notified of that decision and of all procedural safeguards accorded under this section; and

(ii) immediately, if possible, but in no case later than 10 school days after the date on which the decision to take that action is made, a review shall be conducted of the relationship between the child's disability and the behavior subject to the disciplinary action.

(B) *Individuals to carry out review.* A review described in subparagraph (A) shall be conducted by the IEP Team and other qualified personnel.

(C) *Conduct of review.* In carrying out a review described in subparagraph (A), the IEP Team may determine that the behavior of the child was not a manifestation of such child's disability only if the IEP Team:

(i) first considers, in terms of the behavior subject to disciplinary action, all relevant information, including:

(I) evaluation and diagnostic results, including such results or other relevant information supplied by the parents of the child;

(II) observations of the child; and

(III) the child's IEP and placement; and

(ii) then determines that:

(I) in relationship to the behavior subject to disciplinary action, the child's IEP and placement were appropriate and the special education services, supplementary aids and services, and behavior intervention strategies were provided consistent with the child's IEP and placement;

(II) the child's disability did not impair the ability of the child to understand the impact and consequences of the behavior subject to disciplinary action; and

(III) the child's disability did not impair the ability of the child to control the behavior subject to disciplinary action.

(5) *Determination that behavior was not manifestation of disability*

(A) *In general.* If the result of the review described in paragraph (4) is a determination, consistent with paragraph (4)(C), that the behavior of the child with a disability was not a manifestation of the child's disability, the relevant disciplinary procedures applicable to children without disabilities may be applied to the child in the same manner in which they would be applied to children without disabilities, except as provided in section 1412(a)(1) of this title.

(B) *Additional requirement.* If the public agency initiates disciplinary procedures applicable to all children, the agency shall ensure that the special education and disciplinary records of the child with a disability are transmitted for consideration by the person or persons making the final determination regarding the disciplinary action.

(6) *Parent appeal*

(A) *In general*

(i) If the child's parent disagrees with a determination that the child's behavior was not a manifestation of the child's disability or with any decision regarding placement, the parent may request a hearing.

(ii) The State or local educational agency shall arrange for an expedited hearing in any case described in this subsection when requested by a parent.

(B) *Review of decision*

(i) In reviewing a decision with respect to the manifestation determination, the hearing officer shall determine whether the public agency has demonstrated that the child's behavior was not a manifestation of such child's disability consistent with the requirements of paragraph (4)(C).

(ii) In reviewing a decision under paragraph (1)(A)(ii) to place the child in an interim alternative educational setting, the hearing officer shall apply the standards set out in paragraph (2).

(7) *Placement during appeals*

(A) *In general.* When a parent requests a hearing regarding a disciplinary action described in paragraph (1)(A)(ii) or paragraph (2) to challenge the interim alternative educational setting or the manifestation determination, the child shall remain in the interim alternative educational setting pending the decision of the hearing officer or until the expiration of the time period provided for in paragraph (1)(A)(ii) or paragraph (2), whichever occurs first, unless the parent and the State or local educational agency agree otherwise.

(B) *Current placement.* If a child is placed in an interim alternative educational setting pursuant to paragraph (1)(A)(ii) or paragraph (2) and school personnel propose to change the child's placement after expiration of the interim alternative placement, during the pendency of any proceeding to challenge the proposed change in placement, the child shall remain in the current placement (the child's placement prior to the interim alternative educational setting), except as provided in subparagraph (C).

(C) *Expedited hearing*

(i) If school personnel maintain that it is dangerous for the child to be in the current placement (placement prior to removal to the interim alternative education setting) during the pendency of the due process proceedings, the local educational agency may request an expedited hearing.

(ii) In determining whether the child may be placed in the alternative educational setting or in another appropriate placement ordered by the hearing officer, the hearing officer shall apply the standards set out in paragraph (2).

(8) *Protections for children not yet eligible for special education and related services*

(A) *In general.* A child who has not been determined to be eligible for special education and related services under this subchapter and who has engaged in behavior that violated any rule or code of conduct of the local educational agency, including any behavior described in paragraph (1), may assert any of the protections provided for in this subchapter if the local educational agency had knowledge (as determined in accordance with this paragraph) that the child was a child with a disability before the behavior that precipitated the disciplinary action occurred.

(B) *Basis of knowledge.* A local educational agency shall be deemed to have knowledge that a child is a child with a disability if:

(i) the parent of the child has expressed concern in writing (unless the parent is illiterate or has a disability that prevents compliance with the requirements contained in this clause) to personnel of the appropriate educational agency that the child is in need of special education and related services;

(ii) the behavior or performance of the child demonstrates the need for such services;

(iii) the parent of the child has requested an evaluation of the child pursuant to section 1414 of this title; or

(iv) the teacher of the child, or other personnel of the local educational agency, has expressed concern about the behavior or performance of the child to the director of special education of such agency or to other personnel of the agency.

(C) *Conditions that apply if no basis of knowledge*

(i) In general. If a local educational agency does not have knowledge that a child is a child with a disability (in accordance with subparagraph (B)) prior to taking disciplinary measures against the child, the child may be subjected to the same disciplinary measures as measures applied to children without disabilities who engaged in comparable behaviors consistent with clause (ii).

(ii) Limitations. If a request is made for an evaluation of a child during the time period in which the child is subjected to disciplinary measures under paragraph (1) or (2), the evaluation shall be conducted in an expedited manner. If the child is determined to be a child with a disability, taking into consideration information from the evaluation conducted by the agency and information provided by the parents, the agency shall provide special education and related services in accordance with the provisions of this subchapter, except that, pending the results of the evaluation, the child shall remain in the educational placement determined by school authorities.

(9) *Referral to and action by law enforcement and judicial authorities*

(A) Nothing in this subchapter shall be construed to prohibit an agency from reporting a crime committed by a child with a disability to appropriate authorities or to prevent State law enforcement and judicial authorities from exercising their responsibilities with regard to the application of Federal and State law to crimes committed by a child with a disability.

(B) An agency reporting a crime committed by a child with a disability shall ensure that copies of the special education and disciplinary records of the child are transmitted for consideration by the appropriate authorities to whom it reports the crime.

(10) *Definitions.* For purposes of this subsection, the following definitions apply:

(A) *Controlled substance.* The term "controlled substance" means a drug or other substance identified under schedules I, II, III, IV, or V in section 20 (c) of the Controlled Substances Act (21 U.S.C. 81 (c)).

(B) *Illegal drug.* The term "illegal drug":

(i) means a controlled substance; but

(ii) does not include such a substance that is legally possessed or used under the supervision of a licensed health-care professional or that is legally possessed or used under any other authority under that Act (21 U.S.C. 801 et seq.) or under any other provision of Federal law.

(C) *Substantial evidence.* The term "substantial evidence" means beyond a preponderance of the evidence.

(D) *Weapon.* The term "weapon" has the meaning given the term "dangerous weapon" under paragraph (2) of the first subsection (g) of section 930 of title 18.

(l) Rule of construction. Nothing in this chapter shall be construed to restrict or limit the rights, procedures, and remedies available under the Constitution, the Americans with Disabilities Act of 1990 (42 U.S.C. 12101 et seq.), title V of the Rehabilitation Act of 1973 (29 U.S.C. 790 et seq.), or other Federal laws protecting the rights of children with disabilities, except that before the filing of a civil action under such laws seeking relief that is also available under this subchapter, the procedures under subsections (f) and (g) of this section shall be exhausted to the same extent as would be required had the action been brought under this subchapter.

(m) Transfer of parental rights at age of majority

(1) *In general.* A State that receives amounts from a grant under this subchapter may provide that, when a child with a disability reaches the age of majority under State law (except for a child with a disability who has been determined to be incompetent under State law):

(A) the public agency shall provide any notice required by this section to both the individual and the parents;

(B) all other rights accorded to parents under this subchapter transfer to the child;

(C) the agency shall notify the individual and the parents of the transfer of rights; and

(D) all rights accorded to parents under this subchapter transfer to children who are incarcerated in an adult or juvenile Federal, State, or local correctional institution.

(2) *Special rule.* If, under State law, a child with a disability who has reached the age of majority under State law, who has not been determined to be incompetent, but who is determined not to have the ability to provide informed consent with respect to the educational program of the child, the State shall establish procedures for appointing the parent of the child, or if the parent is not available, another appropriate individual, to represent the educational interests of the child throughout the period of eligibility of the child under this subchapter.

IDEA Regulations (Key Sections)

These regulations are current as of the publication date of this edition. However, if IDEA is reauthorized, there will likely be new regulations implementing changes to the law. To find out whether these regulations have changed or been updated, check Nolo's website, at www.nolo.com.

Assistance to States for The Education of Children With Disabilities

34 C.F.R. Part 300

Assistance to States for the Education of Children With Disabilities

Subpart A: General Purposes, Applicability, and Regulations That Apply to This Program

Sec. 300.1. Purposes.

The purposes of this part are—

(a) To ensure that all children with disabilities have available to them a free appropriate public education that emphasizes special education and related services designed to meet their unique needs and prepare them for employment and independent living;

(b) To ensure that the rights of children with disabilities and their parents are protected;

(c) To assist States, localities, educational service agencies, and Federal agencies to provide for the education of all children with disabilities; and

(d) To assess and ensure the effectiveness of efforts to educate children with disabilities.

(Authority: 20 U.S.C. 1400 note)

Sec. 300.2 Applicability of this part to State, local, and private agencies.

(a) States. This part applies to each State that receives payments under Part B of the Act.

(b) Public agencies within the State. The provisions of this part—

(1) Apply to all political subdivisions of the State that are involved in the education of children with disabilities, including—

(i) The State educational agency (SEA);

(ii) Local educational agencies (LEAs), educational service agencies (ESAs), and public charter schools that are not otherwise included as LEAs or ESAs and are not a school of an LEA or ESA;

(iii) Other State agencies and schools (such as Departments of Mental Health and Welfare and State schools for children with deafness or children with blindness); and

(iv) State and local juvenile and adult correctional facilities; and

(2) Are binding on each public agency in the State that provides special education and related services to children with disabilities, regardless of whether that agency is receiving funds under Part B.

(c) Private schools and facilities. Each public agency in the State is responsible for ensuring that the rights and protections under Part B of the Act are given to children with disabilities—

(1) Referred to or placed in private schools and facilities by that public agency; or

(2) Placed in private schools by their parents under the provisions of Sec. 300.403(c).

(Authority: 20 U.S.C. 1412)

Sec. 300.3. Regulations that apply.

The following regulations apply to this program:

(a) 34 CFR part 76 (State-Administered Programs) except for Secs. 76.125-76.137 and 76.650-76.662.

(b) 34 CFR part 77 (Definitions).

(c) 34 CFR part 79 (Intergovernmental Review of Department of Education Programs and Activities).

(d) 34 CFR part 80 (Uniform Administrative Requirements for Grants and Cooperative Agreements to State and Local Governments).

(e) 34 CFR part 81 (General Education Provisions Act—Enforcement).

(f) 34 CFR part 82 (New Restrictions on Lobbying).

(g) 34 CFR part 85 (Government-wide Debarment and Suspension (Nonprocurement) and Government-wide Requirements for Drug-Free Workplace (Grants)).

(h) The regulations in this part—34 CFR part 300 (Assistance for Education of Children with Disabilities).

(Authority: 20 U.S.C. 1221e-3(a)(1))

Sec. 300.5. Assistive technology device.

As used in this part, Assistive technology device means any item, piece of equipment, or product system, whether acquired commercially off the shelf, modified, or customized, that is used to increase, maintain, or improve the functional capabilities of a child with a disability.

(Authority: 20 U.S.C. 1401(1))

Sec. 300.6. Assistive technology service.

As used in this part, Assistive technology service means any service that directly assists a child with a disability in the selection, acquisition, or use of an assistive technology device.

The term includes—

(a) The evaluation of the needs of a child with a disability, including a functional evaluation of the child in the child's customary environment;

(b) Purchasing, leasing, or otherwise providing for the acquisition of assistive technology devices by children with disabilities;

(c) Selecting, designing, fitting, customizing, adapting, applying, maintaining, repairing, or replacing assistive technology devices;

(d) Coordinating and using other therapies, interventions, or services with assistive technology devices, such as those associated with existing education and rehabilitation plans and programs;

(e) Training or technical assistance for a child with a disability or, if appropriate, that child's family; and

(f) Training or technical assistance for professionals (including individuals providing education or rehabilitation services), employers, or other individuals who provide services to, employ, or are otherwise substantially involved in the major life functions of that child.

(Authority: 20 U.S.C. 1401(2))

Sec. 300.7. Child with a disability.

(a) General. (1) As used in this part, the term child with a disability means a child evaluated in accordance with Secs. 300.530-300.536 as having mental retardation, a hearing impairment including deafness, a speech or language impairment, a visual impairment including blindness, serious emotional disturbance (hereafter referred to as emotional disturbance), an orthopedic impairment, autism, traumatic brain injury, an other health impairment, a specific learning disability, deaf-blindness, or multiple disabilities, and who, by reason thereof, needs special education and related services.

(2)(i) Subject to paragraph (a)(2)(ii) of this section, if it is determined, through an appropriate evaluation under Secs. 300.530-300.536, that a child has one of the disabilities identified in paragraph (a)(1) of this section, but only needs a related service and not special education, the child is not a child with a disability under this part.

(ii) If, consistent with Sec. 300.26(a)(2), the related service required by the child is considered special education rather than a related service under State standards, the child would be determined to be a child with a disability under paragraph (a)(1) of this section.

(b) Children aged 3 through 9 experiencing developmental delays. The term child with a disability for children aged 3 through 9 may, at the discretion of the State and LEA and in accordance with Sec. 300.313, include a child—

(1) Who is experiencing developmental delays, as defined by the State and as measured by appropriate diagnostic instruments and procedures, in one or more of the following areas: physical development, cognitive development, communication development, social or emotional development, or adaptive development; and

(2) Who, by reason thereof, needs special education and related services.

(c) Definitions of disability terms. The terms used in this definition are defined as follows:

(1)(i) Autism means a developmental disability significantly affecting verbal and nonverbal communication and social interaction, generally evident before age 3, that adversely affects a child's educational performance. Other characteristics often associated with autism are engagement in repetitive activities and stereotyped movements, resistance to environmental change or change in daily routines, and unusual responses to sensory experiences. The term does not apply if a child's educational performance is adversely affected primarily because the child has an emotional disturbance, as defined in paragraph (b)(4) of this section.

(ii) A child who manifests the characteristics of "autism" after age 3 could be diagnosed as having "autism" if the criteria in paragraph (c)(1)(i) of this section are satisfied.

(2) Deaf-blindness means concomitant hearing and visual impairments, the combination of which causes such severe communication and other developmental and educational needs that they cannot be accommodated in special education programs solely for children with deafness or children with blindness.

(3) Deafness means a hearing impairment that is so severe that the child is impaired in processing linguistic information through hearing, with or without amplification, that adversely affects a child's educational performance.

(4) Emotional disturbance is defined as follows:

(i) The term means a condition exhibiting one or more of the following characteristics over a long period of time and to a marked degree that adversely affects a child's educational performance:

(A) An inability to learn that cannot be explained by intellectual, sensory, or health factors.

(B) An inability to build or maintain satisfactory interpersonal relationships with peers and teachers.

(C) Inappropriate types of behavior or feelings under normal circumstances.

(D) A general pervasive mood of unhappiness or depression.

(E) A tendency to develop physical symptoms or fears associated with personal or school problems.

(ii) The term includes schizophrenia. The term does not apply to children who are socially maladjusted, unless it is determined that they have an emotional disturbance.

(5) Hearing impairment means an impairment in hearing, whether permanent or fluctuating, that adversely affects a child's educational performance but that is not included under the definition of deafness in this section.

(6) Mental retardation means significantly subaverage general intellectual functioning, existing concurrently with deficits in adaptive behavior and manifested during the developmental period, that adversely affects a child's educational performance.

(7) Multiple disabilities means concomitant impairments (such as mental retardation-blindness, mental retardation-orthopedic impairment, etc.), the combination of which causes such severe educational needs that they cannot be accommodated in special education programs solely for one of the impairments. The term does not include deaf-blindness.

(8) Orthopedic impairment means a severe orthopedic impairment that adversely affects a child's educational performance. The term includes impairments caused by congenital anomaly (e.g., clubfoot, absence of some member, etc.), impairments caused by disease (e.g., poliomyelitis, bone tuberculosis, etc.), and impairments from other causes (e.g., cerebral palsy, amputations, and fractures or burns that cause contractures).

(9) Other health impairment means having limited strength, vitality or alertness, including a heightened alertness to environmental stimuli, that results in limited alertness with respect to the educational environment, that—

(i) Is due to chronic or acute health problems such as asthma, attention deficit disorder or attention deficit hyperactivity disorder, diabetes, epilepsy, a heart condition, hemophilia, lead poisoning, leukemia, nephritis, rheumatic fever, and sickle cell anemia; and

(ii) Adversely affects a child's educational performance.

(10) Specific learning disability is defined as follows:

(i) General. The term means a disorder in one or more of the basic psychological processes involved in understanding or in using language, spoken or written, that may manifest itself in an imperfect ability to listen, think, speak, read, write, spell, or to do mathematical calculations, including conditions such as perceptual disabilities, brain injury, minimal brain dysfunction, dyslexia, and developmental aphasia.

(ii) Disorders not included. The term does not include learning problems that are primarily the result of visual, hearing, or motor disabilities, of mental retardation, of emotional disturbance, or of environmental, cultural, or economic disadvantage.

(11) Speech or language impairment means a communication disorder, such as stuttering, impaired articulation, a language impairment, or a voice impairment, that adversely affects a child's educational performance.

(12) Traumatic brain injury means an acquired injury to the brain caused by an external physical force, resulting in total or partial functional disability or psychosocial impairment, or both, that adversely affects a child's educational performance. The term applies to open or closed head injuries resulting in impairments in one or more areas, such as cognition; language; memory; attention; reasoning; abstract thinking; judgment; problem-solving; sensory, perceptual, and motor abilities; psychosocial behavior; physical functions; information processing; and speech. The term does not apply to brain injuries that are congenital or degenerative, or to brain injuries induced by birth trauma.

(13) Visual impairment including blindness means an impairment in vision that, even with correction, adversely affects a child's educational performance. The term includes both partial sight and blindness.

(Authority: 20 U.S.C. 1401(3)(A) and (B); 1401(26))

Sec. 300.9. Day; business day; school day.

As used in this part, the term—

(a) Day means calendar day unless otherwise indicated as business day or school day;

(b) Business day means Monday through Friday, except for Federal and State holidays (unless holidays are specifically included in the designation of business day, as in Sec. 300.403(d)(1)(ii)); and

(c)(1) School day means any day, including a partial day, that children are in attendance at school for instructional purposes.

(2) The term school day has the same meaning for all children in school, including children with and without disabilities.

(Authority: 20 U.S.C. 1221e-3)

Sec. 300.10. Educational service agency.

As used in this part, the term educational service agency—

(a) Means a regional public multiservice agency—

(1) Authorized by State law to develop, manage, and provide services or programs to LEAs; and

(2) Recognized as an administrative agency for purposes of the provision of special education and related services provided within public elementary and secondary schools of the State;

(b) Includes any other public institution or agency having administrative control and direction over a public elementary or secondary school; and

(c) Includes entities that meet the definition of intermediate educational unit in section 602(23) of IDEA as in effect prior to June 4, 1997.

(Authority: 20 U.S.C. 1401(4))

Sec. 300.11. Equipment.

As used in this part, the term equipment means—

(a) Machinery, utilities, and built-in equipment and any necessary enclosures or structures to house the machinery, utilities, or equipment; and

(b) All other items necessary for the functioning of a particular facility as a facility for the provision of educational services, including items such as instructional equipment and necessary furniture; printed, published and audio-visual instructional materials; telecommunications, sensory, and other technological aids and devices; and books, periodicals, documents, and other related materials.

(Authority: 20 U.S.C. 1401(6))

Sec. 300.13. Free appropriate public education.

As used in this part, the term free appropriate public education or FAPE means special education and related services that—

(a) Are provided at public expense, under public supervision and direction, and without charge;

(b) Meet the standards of the SEA, including the requirements of this part;

(c) Include preschool, elementary school, or secondary school education in the State; and

(d) Are provided in conformity with an individualized education program (IEP) that meets the requirements of Secs. 300.340-300.350.

(Authority: 20 U.S.C. 1401(8))

Sec. 300.18. Local educational agency.

(a) As used in this part, the term local educational agency means a public board of education or other public authority legally constituted within a State for either administrative control or direction of, or to perform a service function for, public elementary or secondary schools in a city, county, township, school district, or other political subdivision of a State, or for a combination of school districts or

counties as are recognized in a State as an administrative agency for its public elementary or secondary schools.

(b) The term includes—

(1) An educational service agency, as defined in Sec. 300.10;

(2) Any other public institution or agency having administrative control and direction of a public elementary or second-

ary school, including a public charter school that is established as an LEA under State law; and

(3) An elementary or secondary school funded by the Bureau of Indian Affairs, and not subject to the jurisdiction of any SEA other than the Bureau of Indian Affairs, but only to the extent that the inclusion makes the school eligible for programs for which specific eligibility is not provided to the school in another provision of law and the school does not have a student population that is smaller than the student population of the LEA receiving assistance under this Act with the smallest student population.

(Authority: 20 U.S.C. 1401(15))

Sec. 300.19. Native language.

(a) As used in this part, the term native language, if used with reference to an individual of limited English proficiency, means the following:

(1) The language normally used by that individual, or, in the case of a child, the language normally used by the parents of the child, except as provided in paragraph (a)(2) of this section.

(2) In all direct contact with a child (including evaluation of the child), the language normally used by the child in the home or learning environment.

(b) For an individual with deafness or blindness, or for an individual with no written language, the mode of communication is that normally used by the individual (such as sign language, braille, or oral communication).

(Authority: 20 U.S.C. 1401(16))

Sec. 300.20. Parent.

(a) General. As used in this part, the term parent means—

(1) A natural or adoptive parent of a child;

(2) A guardian but not the State if the child is a ward of the State;

(3) A person acting in the place of a parent (such as a grandparent or stepparent with whom the child lives, or a person who is legally responsible for the child's welfare); or

(4) A surrogate parent who has been appointed in accordance with Sec. 300.515.

(b) Foster parent. Unless State law prohibits a foster parent from acting as a parent, a State may allow a foster parent to act as a parent under Part B of the Act if—

(1) The natural parents' authority to make educational decisions on the child's behalf has been extinguished under State law; and

(2) The foster parent—

(i) Has an ongoing, long-term parental relationship with the child;

(ii) Is willing to make the educational decisions required of parents under the Act; and

(iii) Has no interest that would conflict with the interests of the child.

(Authority: 20 U.S.C. 1401(19))

Sec. 300.24. Related services.

(a) General. As used in this part, the term related services means transportation and such developmental, corrective, and other supportive services as are required to assist a child with a disability to benefit from special education, and includes speech-language pathology and audiology services, psychological services, physical and occupational therapy, recreation, including therapeutic recreation, early identification and assessment of disabilities in children, counseling services, including rehabilitation counseling, orientation and mobility services, and medical services for diagnostic or evaluation purposes. The term also includes school health services, social work services in schools, and parent counseling and training.

(b) Individual terms defined. The terms used in this definition are defined as follows:

(1) Audiology includes—

(i) Identification of children with hearing loss;

(ii) Determination of the range, nature, and degree of hearing loss, including referral for medical or other professional attention for the habilitation of hearing;

(iii) Provision of habilitative activities, such as language habilitation, auditory training, speech reading (lip-reading), hearing evaluation, and speech conservation;

(iv) Creation and administration of programs for prevention of hearing loss;

(v) Counseling and guidance of children, parents, and teachers regarding hearing loss; and

(vi) Determination of children's needs for group and individual amplification, selecting and fitting an appropriate aid, and evaluating the effectiveness of amplification.

(2) Counseling services means services provided by qualified social workers, psychologists, guidance counselors, or other qualified personnel.

(3) Early identification and assessment of disabilities in children means the implementation of a formal plan for identifying a disability as early as possible in a child's life.

(4) Medical services means services provided by a licensed physician to determine a child's medically related disability that results in the child's need for special education and related services.

(5) Occupational therapy—

(i) Means services provided by a qualified occupational therapist; and

(ii) Includes—

(A) Improving, developing or restoring functions impaired or lost through illness, injury, or deprivation;

(B) Improving ability to perform tasks for independent functioning if functions are impaired or lost; and

(C) Preventing, through early intervention, initial or further impairment or loss of function.

(6) Orientation and mobility services—

(i) Means services provided to blind or visually impaired students by qualified personnel to enable those students to attain systematic orientation to and safe movement within their environments in school, home, and community; and

(ii) Includes teaching students the following, as appropriate:

(A) Spatial and environmental concepts and use of information received by the senses (such as sound, temperature and vibrations) to establish, maintain, or regain orientation and line of travel (e.g., using sound at a traffic light to cross the street);

(B) To use the long cane to supplement visual travel skills or as a tool for safely negotiating the environment for students with no available travel vision;

(C) To understand and use remaining vision and distance low vision aids; and

(D) Other concepts, techniques, and tools.

(7) Parent counseling and training means—

(i) Assisting parents in understanding the special needs of their child;

(ii) Providing parents with information about child development; and

(iii) Helping parents to acquire the necessary skills that will allow them to support the implementation of their child's IEP or IFSP.

(8) Physical therapy means services provided by a qualified physical therapist.

(9) Psychological services includes—

(i) Administering psychological and educational tests, and other assessment procedures;

(ii) Interpreting assessment results;

(iii) Obtaining, integrating, and interpreting information about child behavior and conditions relating to learning;

(iv) Consulting with other staff members in planning school programs to meet the special needs of children as indicated by psychological tests, interviews, and behavioral evaluations;

(v) Planning and managing a program of psychological services, including psychological counseling for children and parents; and

(vi) Assisting in developing positive behavioral intervention strategies.

(10) Recreation includes—

(i) Assessment of leisure function;

(ii) Therapeutic recreation services;

(iii) Recreation programs in schools and community agencies; and

(iv) Leisure education.

(11) Rehabilitation counseling services means services provided by qualified personnel in individual or group sessions that focus specifically on career development, employment preparation, achieving independence, and integration in the workplace and community of a student with a disability. The term also includes vocational rehabilitation services provided to a student with disabilities by vocational rehabilitation programs funded under the Rehabilitation Act of 1973, as amended.

(12) School health services means services provided by a qualified school nurse or other qualified person.

(13) Social work services in schools includes—

(i) Preparing a social or developmental history on a child with a disability;

(ii) Group and individual counseling with the child and family;

(iii) Working in partnership with parents and others on those problems in a child's living situation (home, school, and community) that affect the child's adjustment in school;

(iv) Mobilizing school and community resources to enable the child to learn as effectively as possible in his or her educational program; and

(v) Assisting in developing positive behavioral intervention strategies.

(14) Speech-language pathology services includes—

(i) Identification of children with speech or language impairments;

(ii) Diagnosis and appraisal of specific speech or language impairments;

(iii) Referral for medical or other professional attention necessary for the habilitation of speech or language impairments;

(iv) Provision of speech and language services for the habilitation or prevention of communicative impairments; and

(v) Counseling and guidance of parents, children, and teachers regarding speech and language impairments.

(15) Transportation includes—

(i) Travel to and from school and between schools;

(ii) Travel in and around school buildings; and

(iii) Specialized equipment (such as special or adapted buses, lifts, and ramps), if required to provide special transportation for a child with a disability.

(Authority: 20 U.S.C. 1401(22))

Sec. 300.26. Special education.

(a) General. (1) As used in this part, the term special education means specially designed instruction, at no cost to the parents, to meet the unique needs of a child with a disability, including—

(i) Instruction conducted in the classroom, in the home, in hospitals and institutions, and in other settings; and

(ii) Instruction in physical education.

(2) The term includes each of the following, if it meets the requirements of paragraph (a)(1) of this section:

(i) Speech-language pathology services, or any other related service, if the service is considered special education rather than a related service under State standards;

(ii) Travel training; and

(iii) Vocational education.

(b) Individual terms defined. The terms in this definition are defined as follows:

(1) At no cost means that all specially-designed instruction is provided without charge, but does not preclude incidental fees that are normally charged to nondisabled students or their parents as a part of the regular education program.

(2) Physical education—

(i) Means the development of—

(A) Physical and motor fitness;

(B) Fundamental motor skills and patterns; and

(C) Skills in aquatics, dance, and individual and group games and sports (including intramural and lifetime sports); and

(ii) Includes special physical education, adapted physical education, movement education, and motor development.

(3) Specially-designed instruction means adapting, as appropriate to the needs of an eligible child under this part, the content, methodology, or delivery of instruction—

(i) To address the unique needs of the child that result from the child's disability; and

(ii) To ensure access of the child to the general curriculum, so that he or she can meet the educational standards within the jurisdiction of the public agency that apply to all children.

(4) Travel training means providing instruction, as appropriate, to children with significant cognitive disabilities, and any other children with disabilities who require this instruction, to enable them to—

(i) Develop an awareness of the environment in which they live; and

(ii) Learn the skills necessary to move effectively and safely from place to place within that environment (e.g., in school, in the home, at work, and in the community).

(5) Vocational education means organized educational programs that are directly related to the preparation of individuals for paid or unpaid employment, or for additional preparation for a career requiring other than a baccalaureate or advanced degree.

(Authority: 20 U.S.C. 1401(25))

Sec. 300.28. Supplementary aids and services.

As used in this part, the term supplementary aids and services means, aids, services, and other supports that are provided in regular education classes or other education-related settings to enable children with disabilities to be educated with nondisabled children to the maximum extent appropriate in accordance with Secs. 300.550-300.556.

(Authority: 20 U.S.C. 1401(29))

Sec. 300.29. Transition services.

(a) As used in this part, transition services means a coordinated set of activities for a student with a disability that—

(1) Is designed within an outcome-oriented process, that promotes movement from school to post-school activities, including postsecondary education, vocational training, integrated employment (including supported employment), continuing and adult education, adult services, independent living, or community participation;

(2) Is based on the individual student's needs, taking into account the student's preferences and interests; and

(3) Includes—

(i) Instruction;

(ii) Related services;

(iii) Community experiences;

(iv) The development of employment and other post-school adult living objectives; and

(v) If appropriate, acquisition of daily living skills and functional vocational evaluation.

(b) Transition services for students with disabilities may be special education, if provided as specially designed instruction, or related services, if required to assist a student with a disability to benefit from special education.

(Authority: 20 U.S.C. 1401(30))

Subpart B—

State and Local Eligibility

Sec. 300.125. Child find.

(a) General requirement. (1) The State must have in effect policies and procedures to ensure that—

(i) All children with disabilities residing in the State, including children with disabilities attending private schools, regardless of the severity of their disability, and who are in need of special education and related services, are identified, located, and evaluated; and

(ii) A practical method is developed and implemented to determine which children are currently receiving needed special education and related services.

(2) The requirements of paragraph (a)(1) of this section apply to—

(i) Highly mobile children with disabilities (such as migrant and homeless children); and

(ii) Children who are suspected of being a child with a disability under Sec. 300.7 and in need of special education, even though they are advancing from grade to grade.

(b) Documents relating to child find. The State must have on file with the Secretary the policies and procedures described in paragraph (a) of this section, including—

(1) The name of the State agency (if other than the SEA) responsible for coordinating the planning and implementation of the policies and procedures under paragraph (a) of this section;

(2) The name of each agency that participates in the planning and implementation of the child find activities and a description of the nature and extent of its participation;

(3) A description of how the policies and procedures under paragraph (a) of this section will be monitored to ensure that the SEA obtains—

(i) The number of children with disabilities within each disability category that have been identified, located, and evaluated; and

(ii) Information adequate to evaluate the effectiveness of those policies and procedures; and

(4) A description of the method the State uses to determine which children are currently receiving special education and related services.

(c) Child find for children from birth through age 2 when the SEA and lead agency for the Part C program are different. (1) In States where the SEA and the State's lead agency for the Part C program are different and the Part C lead agency will be participating in the child find activities described in paragraph (a) of this section, a description of the nature and extent of the Part C lead agency's participation must be included under paragraph (b)(2) of this section.

(2) With the SEA's agreement, the Part C lead agency's participation may include the actual implementation of child find activities for infants and toddlers with disabilities.

(3) The use of an interagency agreement or other mechanism for providing for the Part C lead agency's participation does not alter or diminish the responsibility of the SEA to ensure compliance with the requirements of this section.

(d) Construction. Nothing in the Act requires that children be classified by their disability so long as each child who has a disability listed in Sec. 300.7 and who, by reason of that disability, needs special education and related services is regarded as a child with a disability under Part B of the Act.

(e) Confidentiality of child find data. The collection and use of data to meet the requirements of this section are subject to the confidentiality requirements of Secs. 300.560-300.577.

(Authority: 20 U.S.C. 1412 (a)(3)(A) and (B))

Sec. 300.136. Personnel standards.

(a) Definitions. As used in this part—

(1) Appropriate professional requirements in the State means entry level requirements that—

(i) Are based on the highest requirements in the State applicable to the profession or discipline in which a person is providing special education or related services; and

(ii) Establish suitable qualifications for personnel providing special education and related services under Part B of the Act to children with disabilities who are served by State, local, and private agencies (see Sec. 300.2);

(2) Highest requirements in the State applicable to a specific profession or discipline means the highest entry-level academic degree needed for any State-approved or -recognized certification, licensing, registration, or other comparable requirements that apply to that profession or discipline;

(3) Profession or discipline means a specific occupational category that—

(i) Provides special education and related services to children with disabilities under Part B of the Act;

(ii) Has been established or designated by the State;

(iii) Has a required scope of responsibility and degree of supervision; and

(iv) Is not limited to traditional occupational categories; and

(4) State-approved or -recognized certification, licensing, registration, or other comparable requirements means the requirements that a State legislature either has enacted or has authorized a State agency to promulgate through rules to establish the entry-level standards for employment in a specific profession or discipline in that State.

(b) Policies and procedures. (1)(i) The State must have on file with the Secretary policies and procedures relating to the establishment and maintenance of standards to ensure that personnel necessary to carry out the purposes of this part are appropriately and adequately prepared and trained.

(ii) The policies and procedures required in paragraph (b)(1)(i) of this section must provide for the establishment and maintenance of standards that are consistent with any State-approved or -recognized certification, licensing, registration, or other comparable requirements that apply to the profession or discipline in which a person is providing special education or related services.

(2) Each State may—

(i) Determine the specific occupational categories required to provide special education and related services within the State; and

(ii) Revise or expand those categories as needed.

(3) Nothing in this part requires a State to establish a specified training standard (e.g., a masters degree) for personnel who provide special education and related services under Part B of the Act.

(4) A State with only one entry-level academic degree for employment of personnel in a specific profession or discipline may modify that standard as necessary to ensure the provision of FAPE to all children with disabilities in the State without violating the requirements of this section.

(c) Steps for retraining or hiring personnel. To the extent that a State's standards for a profession or discipline, including standards for temporary or emergency certification, are not based on the highest requirements in the State applicable to a specific profession or discipline, the State must provide the steps the State is taking and the procedures for notifying public agencies and personnel of those steps and the timelines it has established for the retraining or hiring of personnel to meet appropriate professional requirements in the State.

(d) Status of personnel standards in the State. (1) In meeting the requirements in paragraphs (b) and (c) of this section, a determination must be made about the status of personnel standards in the State. That determination must be based on current information that accurately describes, for each profession or discipline in which personnel are providing special education or related services, whether the applicable standards are consistent with the highest requirements in the State for that profession or discipline.

(2) The information required in paragraph (d)(1) of this section must be on file in the SEA and available to the public.

(e) Applicability of State statutes and agency rules. In identifying the highest requirements in the State for purposes of this section, the requirements of all State statutes and the rules of all State agencies applicable to serving children with disabilities must be considered.

(f) Use of paraprofessionals and assistants. A State may allow paraprofessionals and assistants who are appropriately trained and supervised, in accordance with State law, regulations, or written policy, in meeting the requirements of this part to be used to assist in the provision of special education and related services to children with disabilities under Part B of the Act.

(g) Policy to address shortage of personnel.

(1) In implementing this section, a State may adopt a policy that includes a requirement that LEAs in the State make an ongoing good faith effort to recruit and hire appropriately and adequately trained personnel to provide special education and related services to children with disabilities, including, in a geographic area of the State where there is a shortage of personnel that meet these qualifications, the most qualified individuals available who are making satisfactory progress toward completing applicable course work necessary to meet the standards described in paragraph (b)(2) of this section, consistent with State law and the steps described in paragraph (c) of this section, within three years.

(2) If a State has reached its established date under paragraph (c) of this section, the State may still exercise the option

under paragraph (g)(1) of this section for training or hiring all personnel in a specific profession or discipline to meet appropriate professional requirements in the State.

(3)(i) Each State must have a mechanism for serving children with disabilities if instructional needs exceed available personnel who meet appropriate professional requirements in the State for a specific profession or discipline.

(ii) A State that continues to experience shortages of qualified personnel must address those shortages in its comprehensive system of personnel development under Sec. 300.135.

(Authority: 20 U.S.C. 1412(a)(15))

Sec. 300.245. School-based improvement plan.

(a) General. Each LEA may, in accordance with paragraph (b) of this section, use funds made available under Part B of the Act to permit a public school within the jurisdiction of the LEA to design, implement, and evaluate a school-based improvement plan that—

(1) Is consistent with the purposes described in section 651(b) of the Act; and

(2) Is designed to improve educational and transitional results for all children with disabilities and, as appropriate, for other children consistent with Sec. 300.235(a) and (b) in that public school.

(b) Authority. (1) General. An SEA may grant authority to an LEA to permit a public school described in Sec. 300.245 (through a school-based standing panel established under Sec. 300.247(b)) to design, implement, and evaluate a school-based improvement plan described in Sec. 300.245 for a period not to exceed 3 years.

(2) Responsibility of LEA. If an SEA grants the authority described in paragraph (b)(1) of this section, an LEA that is granted this authority must have the sole responsibility of oversight of all activities relating to the design, implementation, and evaluation of any school-based improvement plan that a public school is permitted to design under this section.

(Authority: 20 U.S.C. 1413(g)(1) and (g)(2)).

Sec. 300.246. Plan requirements.

A school-based improvement plan described in Sec. 300.245 must—

(a) Be designed to be consistent with the purposes described in section 651(b) of the Act and to improve educational and transitional results for all children with disabilities and, as appropriate, for other children consistent with Sec. 300.235(a) and (b), who attend the school for which the plan is designed and implemented;

(b) Be designed, evaluated, and, as appropriate, implemented by a school-based standing panel established in accordance with Sec. 300.247(b);

(c) Include goals and measurable indicators to assess the progress of the public school in meeting these goals; and

(d) Ensure that all children with disabilities receive the services described in their IEPs.

(Authority: 20 U.S.C. 1413(g)(3))

Sec. 300.247. Responsibilities of the LEA.

An LEA that is granted authority under Sec. 300.245(b) to permit a public school to design, implement, and evaluate a school-based improvement plan shall—

(a) Select each school under the jurisdiction of the agency that is eligible to design, implement, and evaluate the plan;

(b) Require each school selected under paragraph (a) of this section, in accordance with criteria established by the LEA under paragraph (c) of this section, to establish a school-based standing panel to carry out the duties described in Sec. 300.246(b);

(c) Establish—

(1) Criteria that must be used by the LEA in the selection of an eligible school under paragraph (a) of this section;

(2) Criteria that must be used by a public school selected under paragraph (a) of this section in the establishment of a school-based standing panel to carry out the duties described in Sec. 300.246(b) and that ensure that the membership of the panel reflects the diversity of the community in which the public school is located and includes, at a minimum—

(i) Parents of children with disabilities who attend a public school, including parents of children with disabilities from unserved and underserved populations, as appropriate;

(ii) Special education and general education teachers of public schools;

(iii) Special education and general education administrators, or the designee of those administrators, of those public schools; and

(iv) Related services providers who are responsible for providing services to the children with disabilities who attend those public schools; and

(3) Criteria that must be used by the LEA with respect to the distribution of funds under Part B of the Act to carry out this section;

(d) Disseminate the criteria established under paragraph (c) of this section to local school district personnel and local parent organizations within the jurisdiction of the LEA;

(e) Require a public school that desires to design, implement, and evaluate a school-based improvement plan to submit an application at the time, in the manner and accompanied by the information, that the LEA shall reasonably require; and

(f) Establish procedures for approval by the LEA of a school-based improvement plan designed under Part B of the Act.

(Authority:1413(g)(4))

Sec. 300.280. Public hearings before adopting State policies and procedures.

Prior to its adoption of State policies and procedures related to this part, the SEA shall—

(a) Make the policies and procedures available to the general public;

(b) Hold public hearings; and

(c) Provide an opportunity for comment by the general public on the policies and procedures.

(Authority: 20 U.S.C. 1412(a)(20))

Subpart C—

Services

Sec. 300.300. Provision of FAPE.

(a) General. (1) Subject to paragraphs (b) and (c) of this section and Sec. 300.311, each State receiving assistance under this part shall ensure that FAPE is available to all children with disabilities, aged 3 through 21, residing in the State, including children with disabilities who have been suspended or expelled from school.

(2) As a part of its obligation under paragraph (a)(1) of this section, each State must ensure that the requirements of Sec. 300.125 (to identify, locate, and evaluate all children with disabilities) are implemented by public agencies throughout the State.

(3)(i) The services provided to the child under this part address all of the child's identified special education and related services needs described in paragraph (a) of this section.

(ii) The services and placement needed by each child with a disability to receive FAPE must be based on the child's unique needs and not on the child's disability.

(b) Exception for age ranges 3-5 and 18-21. This paragraph provides the rules for applying the requirements in paragraph (a) of this section to children with disabilities aged 3, 4, 5, 18, 19, 20, and 21 within the State:

(1) If State law or a court order requires the State to provide education for children with disabilities in any disability category in any of these age groups, the State must make FAPE available to all children with disabilities of the same age who have that disability.

(2) If a public agency provides education to nondisabled children in any of these age groups, it must make FAPE available to at least a proportionate number of children with disabilities of the same age.

(3) If a public agency provides education to 50 percent or more of its children with disabilities in any disability category in any of these age groups, it must make FAPE available to all its children with disabilities of the same age who have that disability. This provision does not apply to children aged 3 through 5 for any fiscal year for which the State receives a grant under section 619(a)(1) of the Act.

(4) If a public agency provides education to a child with a disability in any of these age groups, it must make FAPE available to that child and provide that child and his or her parents all of the rights under Part B of the Act and this part.

(5) A State is not required to make FAPE available to a child with a disability in one of these age groups if—

(i) State law expressly prohibits, or does not authorize, the expenditure of public funds to provide education to nondisabled children in that age group; or

(ii) The requirement is inconsistent with a court order that governs the provision of free public education to children with disabilities in that State.

(c) Children aged 3 through 21 on Indian reservations. With the exception of children identified in Sec. 300.715(b) and (c), the SEA shall ensure that all of the requirements of Part B of the Act are implemented for all children with disabilities aged 3 through 21 on reservations.

(Authority: 20 U.S.C. 1412(a)(1), 1411(i)(1)(C), S. Rep. No. 94—168, p. 19 (1975))

Sec. 300.302. Residential placement.

If placement in a public or private residential program is necessary to provide special education and related services to a child with a disability, the program, including non-medical care and room and board, must be at no cost to the parents of the child.

(Authority: 20 U.S.C. 1412(a)(1), 1412(a)(10)(B))

Sec. 300.303. Proper functioning of hearing aids.

Each public agency shall ensure that the hearing aids worn in school by children with hearing impairments, including deafness, are functioning properly.

(Authority: 20 U.S.C. 1412(a)(1))

Sec. 300.304. Full educational opportunity goal.

Each SEA shall ensure that each public agency establishes and implements a goal of providing full educational opportunity to all children with disabilities in the area served by the public agency.

(Authority: 20 U.S.C. 1412(a)(2)

Sec. 300.305. Program options.

Each public agency shall take steps to ensure that its children with disabilities have available to them the variety of educational programs and services available to nondisabled children in the area served by the agency, including art, music, industrial arts, consumer and homemaking education, and vocational education.

(Authority: 20 U.S.C. 1412(a)(2), 1413(a)(1))

Sec. 300.306. Nonacademic services.

(a) Each public agency shall take steps to provide nonacademic and extracurricular services and activities in the manner necessary to afford children with disabilities an equal opportunity for participation in those services and activities.

(b) Nonacademic and extracurricular services and activities may include counseling services, athletics, transportation, health services, recreational activities, special interest groups or clubs sponsored by the public agency, referrals to agencies that provide assistance to individuals with disabilities, and employment of students, including both employment by the public agency and assistance in making outside employment available.

(Authority: 20 U.S.C. 1412(a)(1))

Sec. 300.307. Physical education.

(a) General. Physical education services, specially designed if necessary, must be made available to every child with a disability receiving FAPE.

(b) Regular physical education. Each child with a disability must be afforded the opportunity to participate in the regular physical education program available to nondisabled children unless—

(1) The child is enrolled full time in a separate facility; or

(2) The child needs specially designed physical education, as prescribed in the child's IEP.

(c) Special physical education. If specially designed physical education is prescribed in a child's IEP, the public agency responsible for the education of that child shall provide the services directly or make arrangements for those services to be provided through other public or private programs.

(d) Education in separate facilities. The public agency responsible for the education of a child with a disability who is enrolled in a separate facility shall ensure that the child receives appropriate physical education services in compliance with paragraphs (a) and (c) of this section.

(Authority: 20 U.S.C. 1412(a)(25), 1412(a)(5)(A))

Sec. 300.308. Assistive technology.

(a) Each public agency shall ensure that assistive technology devices or assistive technology services, or both, as those terms are defined in Secs. 300.5-300.6, are made available to a child with a disability if required as a part of the child's—

(1) Special education under Sec. 300.26;

(2) Related services under Sec. 300.24; or

(3) Supplementary aids and services under Secs. 300.28 and 300.550(b)(2).

(b) On a case-by-case basis, the use of school-purchased assistive technology devices in a child's home or in other settings is required if the child's IEP team determines that the child needs access to those devices in order to receive FAPE.

(Authority: 20 U.S.C. 1412(a)(12)(B)(i))

Sec. 300.309. Extended school year services.

(a) General. (1) Each public agency shall ensure that extended school year services are available as necessary to provide FAPE, consistent with paragraph (a)(2) of this section.

(2) Extended school year services must be provided only if a child's IEP team determines, on an individual basis, in accordance with Secs. 300.340-300.350, that the services are necessary for the provision of FAPE to the child.

(3) In implementing the requirements of this section, a public agency may not—

(i) Limit extended school year services to particular categories of disability; or

(ii) Unilaterally limit the type, amount, or duration of those services.

(b) Definition. As used in this section, the term extended school year services means special education and related services that—

(1) Are provided to a child with a disability—

(i) Beyond the normal school year of the public agency;

(ii) In accordance with the child's IEP; and

(iii) At no cost to the parents of the child; and

(2) Meet the standards of the SEA.

(Authority: 20 U.S.C. 1412(a)(1))

Sec. 300.311 FAPE requirements for students with disabilities in adult prisons.

(a) Exception to FAPE for certain students. Except as provided in Sec. 300.122(a)(2)(ii), the obligation to make FAPE available to all children with disabilities does not apply with respect to students aged 18 through 21 to the extent that State law does not require that special education and related services under Part B of the Act be provided to students with disabilities who, in the last educational placement prior to their incarceration in an adult correctional facility—

(1) Were not actually identified as being a child with a disability under Sec. 300.7; and

(2) Did not have an IEP under Part B of the Act.

(b) Requirements that do not apply. The following requirements do not apply to students with disabilities who are convicted as adults under State law and incarcerated in adult prisons:

(1) The requirements contained in Sec. 300.138 and Sec. 300.347(a)(5)(i) (relating to participation of children with disabilities in general assessments).

(2) The requirements in Sec. 300.347(b) (relating to transition planning and transition services), with respect to the students whose eligibility under Part B of the Act will end, because of their age, before they will be eligible to be released from prison based on consideration of their sentence and eligibility for early release.

(c) Modifications of IEP or placement.

(1) Subject to paragraph (c)(2) of this section, the IEP team of a student with a disability, who is convicted as an adult under State law and incarcerated in an adult prison, may modify the student's IEP or placement if the State has demonstrated a bona fide security or compelling penological interest that cannot otherwise be accommodated.

(2) The requirements of Secs. 300.340(a) and 300.347(a) relating to IEPs, and 300.550(b) relating to LRE, do not apply with respect to the modifications described in paragraph (c)(1) of this section.

(Authority: 20 U.S.C. 1412(a)(1), 1414(d)(6))

Sec. 300.312 Children with disabilities in public charter schools.

(a) Children with disabilities who attend public charter schools and their parents retain all rights under this part.

(b) If the public charter school is an LEA, consistent with Sec. 300.17, that receives funding under Secs. 300.711-300.714, that charter school is responsible for ensuring that the requirements of this part are met, unless State law assigns that responsibility to some other entity.

(c) If the public charter school is a school of an LEA that receives funding under Secs. 300.711-300.714 and includes other public schools—

(1) The LEA is responsible for ensuring that the requirements of this part are met, unless State law assigns that responsibility to some other entity; and

(2) The LEA must meet the requirements of Sec. 300.241.

(d)(1) If the public charter school is not an LEA receiving funding under Secs. 300.711-300.714, or a school that is part of an LEA receiving funding under Secs. 300.711-300.714, the SEA is responsible for ensuring that the requirements of this part are met.

(2) Paragraph (d)(1) of this section does not preclude a State from assigning initial responsibility for ensuring the re-

quirements of this part are met to another entity; however, the SEA must maintain the ultimate responsibility for ensuring compliance with this part, consistent with Sec. 300.600.

(Authority: 20 U.S.C. 1413(a)(5))

Sec. 300.313 Children experiencing developmental delays.

(a) Use of term developmental delay.

(1) A State that adopts the term developmental delay under Sec. 300.7(b) determines whether it applies to children aged 3 through 9, or to a subset of that age range (e.g., ages 3 through 5).

(2) A State may not require an LEA to adopt and use the term developmental delay for any children within its jurisdiction.

(3) If an LEA uses the term developmental delay for children described in Sec. 300.7(b), the LEA must conform to both the State's definition of that term and to the age range that has been adopted by the State.

(4) If a State does not adopt the term developmental delay, an LEA may not independently use that term as a basis for establishing a child's eligibility under this part.

(b) Use of individual disability categories.

(1) Any State or LEA that elects to use the term developmental delay for children aged 3 through 9 may also use one or more of the disability categories described in Sec. 300.7 for any child within that age range if it is determined, through the evaluation conducted under Secs. 300.530-300.536, that the child has an impairment described in Sec. 300.7, and because of that impairment needs special education and related services.

(2) The State or LEA shall ensure that all of the child's special education and related services needs that have been identified through the evaluation described in paragraph (b)(1) of this section are appropriately addressed.

(c) Common definition of developmental delay. A State may adopt a common definition of developmental delay for use in programs under Parts B and C of the Act.

(Authority: 20 U.S.C. 1401(3)(A) and (B))

Evaluations and Reevaluations

Sec. 300.320 Initial evaluations.

(a) Each public agency shall ensure that a full and individual evaluation is conducted for each child being considered for special education and related services under Part B of the Act—

(1) To determine if the child is a "child with a disability" under Sec. 300.7; and

(2) To determine the educational needs of the child.

(b) In implementing the requirements of paragraph (a) of this section, the public agency shall ensure that—

(1) The evaluation is conducted in accordance with the procedures described in Secs. 300.530-300.535; and

(2) The results of the evaluation are used by the child's IEP team in meeting the requirements of Secs. 300.340-300.350.

(Authority: 20 U.S.C. 1414(a), (b), and (c))

Sec. 300.340 Definitions related to IEPs.

(a) Individualized education program. As used in this part, the term individualized education program or IEP means a written statement for a child with a disability that is developed, reviewed, and revised in a meeting in accordance with Secs. 300.341-300.350.

(b) Participating agency. As used in Sec. 300.348, participating agency means a State or local agency, other than the public agency responsible for a student's education, that is financially and legally responsible for providing transition services to the student.

(Authority: 20 U.S.C. 1401(11), 1412(a)(10)(B))

Sec. 300.341 Responsibility of SEA and other public agencies for IEPs.

(a) The SEA shall ensure that each public agency—

(1) Except as provided in Secs. 300.450-300.462, develops and implements an IEP for each child with a disability served by that agency; and

(2) Ensures that an IEP is developed and implemented for each eligible child placed in or referred to a private school or facility by the public agency.

(b) Paragraph (a) of this section applies to—

(1) The SEA, if it is involved in providing direct services to children with disabilities, in accordance with Sec. 300.370(a) and (b)(1); and

(2) Except as provided in Sec. 300.600(d), the other public agencies described in Sec. 300.2, including LEAs and other State agencies that provide special education and related services either directly, by contract, or through other arrangements.

(Authority: 20 U.S.C. 1412(a)(4), (a)(10)(B))

Sec. 300.342 When IEPs must be in effect.

(a) General. At the beginning of each school year, each public agency shall have an IEP in effect for each child with a disability within its jurisdiction.

(b) Implementation of IEPs. Each public agency shall ensure that—

(1) An IEP—

(i) Is in effect before special education and related services are provided to an eligible child under this part; and

(ii) Is implemented as soon as possible following the meetings described under Sec. 300.343;

(2) The child's IEP is accessible to each regular education teacher, special education teacher, related service provider, and other service provider who is responsible for its implementation; and

(3) Each teacher and provider described in paragraph (b)(2) of this section is informed of—

(i) His or her specific responsibilities related to implementing the child's IEP; and

(ii) The specific accommodations, modifications, and supports that must be provided for the child in accordance with the IEP.

(c) IEP or IFSP for children aged 3 through 5.

(1) In the case of a child with a disability aged 3 through 5 (or, at the discretion of the SEA a 2-year-old child with a dis-

ability who will turn age 3 during the school year), an IFSP that contains the material described in section 636 of the Act, and that is developed in accordance with Secs. 300.341-300.346 and Secs. 300.349-300.350, may serve as the IEP of the child if using that plan as the IEP is—

(i) Consistent with State policy; and

(ii) Agreed to by the agency and the child's parents.

(2) In implementing the requirements of paragraph (c)(1) of this section, the public agency shall—

(i) Provide to the child's parents a detailed explanation of the differences between an IFSP and an IEP; and

(ii) If the parents choose an IFSP, obtain written informed consent from the parents.

(d) Effective date for new requirements. All IEPs developed, reviewed, or revised on or after July 1, 1998 must meet the requirements of Secs. 300.340-300.350.

(Authority: 20 U.S.C. 1414(d)(2)(A) and (B), Pub. L. 105-17, sec. 201(a)(2)(A), (C)

Sec. 300.343 IEP meetings.

(a) General. Each public agency is responsible for initiating and conducting meetings for the purpose of developing, reviewing, and revising the IEP of a child with a disability (or, if consistent with Sec. 300.342(c), an IFSP).

(b) Initial IEPs; provision of services.

(1) Each public agency shall ensure that within a reasonable period of time following the agency's receipt of parent consent to an initial evaluation of a child—

(i) The child is evaluated; and

(ii) If determined eligible under this part, special education and related services are made available to the child in accordance with an IEP.

(2) In meeting the requirement in paragraph (b)(1) of this section, a meeting to develop an IEP for the child must be conducted within 30-days of a determination that the child needs special education and related services.

(c) Review and revision of IEPs. Each public agency shall ensure that the IEP team—

(1) Reviews the child's IEP periodically, but not less than annually, to determine whether the annual goals for the child are being achieved; and

(2) Revises the IEP as appropriate to address—

(i) Any lack of expected progress toward the annual goals described in Sec. 300.347(a), and in the general curriculum, if appropriate;

(ii) The results of any reevaluation conducted under Sec. 300.536;

(iii) Information about the child provided to, or by, the parents, as described in Sec. 300.533(a)(1);

(iv) The child's anticipated needs; or

(v) Other matters.

(Authority: 20 U.S.C. 1413(a)(1), 1414(d)(4)(A)

Sec. 300.344 IEP team.

(a) General. The public agency shall ensure that the IEP team for each child with a disability includes—

(1) The parents of the child;

(2) At least one regular education teacher of the child (if the child is, or may be, participating in the regular education environment);

(3) At least one special education teacher of the child, or if appropriate, at least one special education provider of the child;

(4) A representative of the public agency who—

(i) Is qualified to provide, or supervise the provision of, specially designed instruction to meet the unique needs of children with disabilities;

(ii) Is knowledgeable about the general curriculum; and

(iii) Is knowledgeable about the availability of resources of the public agency;

(5) An individual who can interpret the instructional implications of evaluation results, who may be a member of the team described in paragraphs (a)(2) through (6) of this section;

(6) At the discretion of the parent or the agency, other individuals who have knowledge or special expertise regarding the child, including related services personnel as appropriate; and

(7) If appropriate, the child.

(b) Transition services participants.

(1) Under paragraph (a)(7) of this section, the public agency shall invite a student with a disability of any age to attend his or her IEP meeting if a purpose of the meeting will be the consideration of—

(i) The student's transition services needs under Sec. 300.347(b)(1);

(ii) The needed transition services for the student under Sec. 300.347(b)(2); or

(iii) Both.

(2) If the student does not attend the IEP meeting, the public agency shall take other steps to ensure that the student's preferences and interests are considered.

(3)(i) In implementing the requirements of Sec. 300.347(b)(2), the public agency also shall invite a representative of any other agency that is likely to be responsible for providing or paying for transition services.

(ii) If an agency invited to send a representative to a meeting does not do so, the public agency shall take other steps to obtain participation of the other agency in the planning of any transition services.

(c) Determination of knowledge and special expertise. The determination of the knowledge or special expertise of any individual described in paragraph (a)(6) of this section shall be made by the party (parents or public agency) who invited the individual to be a member of the IEP.

(d) Designating a public agency representative. A public agency may designate another public agency member of the IEP team to also serve as the agency representative, if the criteria in paragraph (a)(4) of this section are satisfied.

(Authority: 20 U.S.C. 1401(30), 1414(d)(1)(A)(7), (B))

Sec. 300.345 Parent participation.

(a) Public agency responsibility—general. Each public agency shall take steps to ensure that one or both of the parents of a child with a disability are present at each IEP meeting or are afforded the opportunity to participate, including—

(1) Notifying parents of the meeting early enough to ensure that they will have an opportunity to attend; and

(2) Scheduling the meeting at a mutually agreed on time and place.

(b) Information provided to parents.

(1) The notice required under paragraph (a)(1) of this section must—

(i) Indicate the purpose, time, and location of the meeting and who will be in attendance; and

(ii) Inform the parents of the provisions in Sec. 300.344(a)(6) and (c) (relating to the participation of other individuals on the IEP team who have knowledge or special expertise about the child).

(2) For a student with a disability beginning at age 14, or younger, if appropriate, the notice must also—

(i) Indicate that a purpose of the meeting will be the development of a statement of the transition services needs of the student required in Sec. 300.347(b)(1); and

(ii) Indicate that the agency will invite the student.

(3) For a student with a disability beginning at age 16, or younger, if appropriate, the notice must—

(i) Indicate that a purpose of the meeting is the consideration of needed transition services for the student required in Sec. 300.347(b)(2);

(ii) Indicate that the agency will invite the student; and

(iii) Identify any other agency that will be invited to send a representative.

(c) Other methods to ensure parent participation. If neither parent can attend, the public agency shall use other methods to ensure parent participation, including individual or conference telephone calls.

(d) Conducting an IEP meeting without a parent in attendance. A meeting may be conducted without a parent in attendance if the public agency is unable to convince the parents that they should attend. In this case the public agency must have a record of its attempts to arrange a mutually agreed on time and place, such as—

(1) Detailed records of telephone calls made or attempted and the results of those calls;

(2) Copies of correspondence sent to the parents and any responses received; and

(3) Detailed records of visits made to the parent's home or place of employment and the results of those visits.

(e) Use of interpreters or other action, as appropriate. The public agency shall take whatever action is necessary to ensure that the parent understands the proceedings at the IEP meeting, including arranging for an interpreter for parents with deafness or whose native language is other than English.

(f) Parent copy of child's IEP. The public agency shall give the parent a copy of the child's IEP at no cost to the parent.

(Authority: 20 U.S.C. 1414(d)(1)(B)(i))

Sec. 300.346 Development, review, and revision of IEP.

(a) Development of IEP.

(1) General. In developing each child's IEP, the IEP team, shall consider—

(i) The strengths of the child and the concerns of the parents for enhancing the education of their child;

(ii) The results of the initial or most recent evaluation of the child; and

(iii) As appropriate, the results of the child's performance on any general State or district-wide assessment programs.

(2) Consideration of special factors. The IEP team also shall—

(i) In the case of a child whose behavior impedes his or her learning or that of others, consider, if appropriate, strategies, including positive behavioral interventions, strategies, and supports to address that behavior;

(ii) In the case of a child with limited English proficiency, consider the language needs of the child as those needs relate to the child's IEP;

(iii) In the case of a child who is blind or visually impaired, provide for instruction in Braille and the use of Braille unless the IEP team determines, after an evaluation of the child's reading and writing skills, needs, and appropriate reading and writing media (including an evaluation of the child's future needs for instruction in Braille or the use of Braille), that instruction in Braille or the use of Braille is not appropriate for the child;

(iv) Consider the communication needs of the child, and in the case of a child who is deaf or hard of hearing, consider the child's language and communication needs, opportunities for direct communications with peers and professional personnel in the child's language and communication mode, academic level, and full range of needs, including opportunities for direct instruction in the child's language and communication mode; and

(v) Consider whether the child requires assistive technology devices and services.

(b) Review and Revision of IEP. In conducting a meeting to review, and, if appropriate, revise a child's IEP, the IEP team shall consider the factors described in paragraph (a) of this section.

(c) Statement in IEP. If, in considering the special factors described in paragraphs (a)(1) and (2) of this section, the IEP team determines that a child needs a particular device or service (including an intervention, accommodation, or other program modification) in order for the child to receive FAPE, the IEP team must include a statement to that effect in the child's IEP.

(d) Requirement with respect to regular education teacher. The regular education teacher of a child with a disability, as a member of the IEP team, must, to the extent appropriate, participate in the development, review, and revision of the child's IEP, including assisting in the determination of—

(1) Appropriate positive behavioral interventions and strategies for the child; and

(2) Supplementary aids and services, program modifications or supports for school personnel that will be provided for the child, consistent with Sec. 300.347(a)(3).

(e) Construction. Nothing in this section shall be construed to require the IEP team to include information under one component of a child's IEP that is already contained under another component of the child's IEP.

(Authority: 20 U.S.C. 1414(d)(3) and (4)(B) and (e))

Sec. 300.347 Content of IEP.

(a) General. The IEP for each child with a disability must include—

(1) A statement of the child's present levels of educational performance, including—

(i) How the child's disability affects the child's involvement and progress in the general curriculum (i.e., the same curriculum as for nondisabled children); or

(ii) For preschool children, as appropriate, how the disability affects the child's participation in appropriate activities;

(2) A statement of measurable annual goals, including benchmarks or short-term objectives, related to—

(i) Meeting the child's needs that result from the child's disability to enable the child to be involved in and progress in the general curriculum (i.e., the same curriculum as for nondisabled children), or for preschool children, as appropriate, to participate in appropriate activities; and

(ii) Meeting each of the child's other educational needs that result from the child's disability;

(3) A statement of the special education and related services and supplementary aids and services to be provided to the child, or on behalf of the child, and a statement of the program modifications or supports for school personnel that will be provided for the child—

(i) To advance appropriately toward attaining the annual goals;

(ii) To be involved and progress in the general curriculum in accordance with paragraph (a)(1) of this section and to participate in extracurricular and other nonacademic activities; and

(iii) To be educated and participate with other children with disabilities and nondisabled children in the activities described in this section;

(4) An explanation of the extent, if any, to which the child will not participate with nondisabled children in the regular class and in the activities described in paragraph (a)(3) of this section;

(5)(i) A statement of any individual modifications in the administration of State or district-wide assessments of student achievement that are needed in order for the child to participate in the assessment; and

(ii) If the IEP team determines that the child will not participate in a particular State or district-wide assessment of student achievement (or part of an assessment), a statement of—

(A) Why that assessment is not appropriate for the child; and

(B) How the child will be assessed;

(6) The projected date for the beginning of the services and modifications described in paragraph (a)(3) of this section, and the anticipated frequency, location, and duration of those services and modifications; and

(7) A statement of—

(i) How the child's progress toward the annual goals described in paragraph (a)(2) of this section will be measured; and

(ii) How the child's parents will be regularly informed (through such means as periodic report cards), at least as of-

ten as parents are informed of their nondisabled children's progress, of—

(A) Their child's progress toward the annual goals; and

(B) The extent to which that progress is sufficient to enable the child to achieve the goals by the end of the year.

(b) Transition services. The IEP must include—

(1) For each student with a disability beginning at age 14 (or younger, if determined appropriate by the IEP team), and updated annually, a statement of the transition service needs of the student under the applicable components of the student's IEP that focuses on the student's courses of study (such as participation in advanced-placement courses or a vocational education program); and

(2) For each student beginning at age 16 (or younger, if determined appropriate by the IEP team), a statement of needed transition services for the student, including, if appropriate, a statement of the interagency responsibilities or any needed linkages.

(c) Transfer of rights. In a State that transfers rights at the age majority, beginning at least one year before a student reaches the age of majority under State law, the student's IEP must include a statement that the student has been informed of his or her rights under Part B of the Act, if any, that will transfer to the student on reaching the age of majority, consistent with Sec. 300.517.

(d) Students with disabilities convicted as adults and incarcerated in adult prisons. Special rules concerning the content of IEPs for students with disabilities convicted as adults and incarcerated in adult prisons are contained in Sec. 300.311(b) and (c).

(Authority: 20 U.S.C. 1414(d)(1)(A) and (d)(6)(A)(ii))

Sec. 300.348 Agency responsibilities for transition services.

(a) If a participating agency, other than the public agency, fails to provide the transition services described in the IEP in accordance with Sec. 300.347(b)(1), the public agency shall reconvene the IEP team to identify alternative strategies to meet the transition objectives for the student set out in the IEP.

(b) Nothing in this part relieves any participating agency, including a State vocational rehabilitation agency, of the responsibility to provide or pay for any transition service that the agency would otherwise provide to students with disabilities who meet the eligibility criteria of that agency.

(Authority: 20 U.S.C. 1414(d)(5); 1414(d)(1)(A)(vii))

Sec. 300.349 Private school placements by public agencies.

(a) Developing IEPs.

(1) Before a public agency places a child with a disability in, or refers a child to, a private school or facility, the agency shall initiate and conduct a meeting to develop an IEP for the child in accordance with Secs. 300.346 and 300.347.

(2) The agency shall ensure that a representative of the private school or facility attends the meeting. If the representative cannot attend, the agency shall use other methods to en-

sure participation by the private school or facility, including individual or conference telephone calls.

(b) Reviewing and revising IEPs.

(1) After a child with a disability enters a private school or facility, any meetings to review and revise the child's IEP may be initiated and conducted by the private school or facility at the discretion of the public agency.

(2) If the private school or facility initiates and conducts these meetings, the public agency shall ensure that the parents and an agency representative—

(i) Are involved in any decision about the child's IEP; and

(ii) Agree to any proposed changes in the IEP before those changes are implemented.

(c) Responsibility. Even if a private school or facility implements a child's IEP, responsibility for compliance with this part remains with the public agency and the SEA.

(Authority: 20 U.S.C. 1412(a)(10)(B))

Sec. 300.350 IEP—accountability.

(a) Provision of services. Subject to paragraph (b) of this section, each public agency must—

(1) Provide special education and related services to a child with a disability in accordance with the child's IEP; and

(2) Make a good faith effort to assist the child to achieve the goals and objectives or benchmarks listed in the IEP.

(b) Accountability. Part B of the Act does not require that any agency, teacher, or other person be held accountable if a child does not achieve the growth projected in the annual goals and benchmarks or objectives. However, the Act does not prohibit a State or public agency from establishing its own accountability systems regarding teacher, school, or agency performance.

(c) Construction—parent rights. Nothing in this section limits a parent's right to ask for revisions of the child's IEP or to invoke due process procedures if the parent feels that the efforts required in paragraph (a) of this section are not being made.

(Authority: 20 U.S.C. 1414(d))

Subpart D—

Children in Private Schools

Sec. 300.400 Applicability of Secs. 300.400-300.402. Children With Disabilities in Private Schools Placed or Referred byPublic Agencies

Sections 300.401-300.402 apply only to children with disabilities who are or have been placed in or referred to a private school or facility by a public agency as a means of providing special education and related services.

(Authority: 20 U.S.C. 1412(a)(10)(B))

Sec. 300.401 Responsibility of State educational agency.

Each SEA shall ensure that a child with a disability who is placed in or referred to a private school or facility by a public agency—

(a) Is provided special education and related services—

(1) In conformance with an IEP that meets the requirements of Secs. 300.340-300.350; and

(2) At no cost to the parents;

(b) Is provided an education that meets the standards that apply to education provided by the SEA and LEAs (including the requirements of this part); and

(c) Has all of the rights of a child with a disability who is served by a public agency.

(Authority: 20 U.S.C. 1412(a)(10)(B))

Sec. 300.402 Implementation by State educational agency.

In implementing Sec. 300.401, the SEA shall—

(a) Monitor compliance through procedures such as written reports, on-site visits, and parent questionnaires;

(b) Disseminate copies of applicable standards to each private school and facility to which a public agency has referred or placed a child with a disability; and

(c) Provide an opportunity for those private schools and facilities to participate in the development and revision of State standards that apply to them.

(Authority: 20 U.S.C. 1412(a)(10)(B))

Sec. 300.403 Placement of children by parents if FAPE is at issue.

(a) General. This part does not require an LEA to pay for the cost of education, including special education and related services, of a child with a disability at a private school or facility if that agency made FAPE available to the child and the parents elected to place the child in a private school or facility. However, the public agency shall include that child in the population whose needs are addressed consistent with Secs. 300.450-300.462.

(b) Disagreements about FAPE. Disagreements between a parent and a public agency regarding the availability of a program appropriate for the child, and the question of financial responsibility, are subject to the due process procedures of Secs. 300.500-300.517.

(c) Reimbursement for private school placement. If the parents of a child with a disability, who previously received special education and related services under the authority of a public agency, enroll the child in a private preschool, elementary, or secondary school without the consent of or referral by the public agency, a court or a hearing officer may require the agency to reimburse the parents for the cost of that enrollment if the court or hearing officer finds that the agency had not made FAPE available to the child in a timely manner prior to that enrollment and that the private placement is appropriate. A parental placement may be found to be appropriate by a hearing officer or a court even if it does not meet the State standards that apply to education provided by the SEA and LEAs.

(d) Limitation on reimbursement. The cost of reimbursement described in paragraph (c) of this section may be reduced or denied—

(1) If—

(i) At the most recent IEP meeting that the parents attended prior to removal of the child from the public school, the parents did not inform the IEP team that they were rejecting the placement proposed by the public agency to provide FAPE to their child, including stating their concerns and their intent to enroll their child in a private school at public expense; or

(ii) At least ten (10) business days (including any holidays that occur on a business day) prior to the removal of the child from the public school, the parents did not give written notice to the public agency of the information described in paragraph (d)(1)(i) of this section;

(2) If, prior to the parents' removal of the child from the public school, the public agency informed the parents, through the notice requirements described in Sec. 300.503(a)(1), of its intent to evaluate the child (including a statement of the purpose of the evaluation that was appropriate and reasonable), but the parents did not make the child available for the evaluation; or

(3) Upon a judicial finding of unreasonableness with respect to actions taken by the parents.

(e) Exception. Notwithstanding the notice requirement in paragraph (d)(1) of this section, the cost of reimbursement may not be reduced or denied for failure to provide the notice if—

(1) The parent is illiterate and cannot write in English;

(2) Compliance with paragraph (d)(1) of this section would likely result in physical or serious emotional harm to the child;

(3) The school prevented the parent from providing the notice; or

(4) The parents had not received notice, pursuant to section 615 of the Act, of the notice requirement in paragraph (d)(1) of this section.

(Authority: 20 U.S.C. 1412(a)(10)(C))

Sec. 300.450 Definition of "private school children with disabilities."

As used in this part, private school children with disabilities means children with disabilities enrolled by their parents in private schools or facilities other than children with disabilities covered under Secs. 300.400-300.402.

(Authority: 20 U.S.C. 1412(a)(10)(A))

Sec. 300.451 Child find for private school children with disabilities.

(a) Each LEA shall locate, identify, and evaluate all private school children with disabilities, including religious-school children residing in the jurisdiction of the LEA, in accordance with Secs. 300.125 and 300.220. The activities undertaken to carry out this responsibility for private school children with disabilities must be comparable to activities undertaken for children with disabilities in public schools.

(b) Each LEA shall consult with appropriate representatives of private school children with disabilities on how to carry out the activities described in paragraph (a) of this section.

(Authority: 20 U.S.C. 1412(a)(10)(A)(ii))

Sec. 300.452 Provision of services—basic requirement.

(a) General. To the extent consistent with their number and location in the State, provision must be made for the participation of private school children with disabilities in the program assisted or carried out under Part B of the Act by providing them with special education and related services in accordance with Secs. 300.453-300.462.

(b) SEA Responsibility—services plan. Each SEA shall ensure that, in accordance with paragraph (a) of this section and Secs. 300.454- 300.456, a services plan is developed and implemented for each private school child with a disability who has been designated to receive special education and related services under this part.

(Authority: 20 U.S.C. 1412(a)(10)(A)(i))

Sec. 300.453 Expenditures.

(a) Formula. To meet the requirement of Sec. 300.452(a), each LEA must spend on providing special education and related services to private school children with disabilities—

(1) For children aged 3 through 21, an amount that is the same proportion of the LEA's total subgrant under section 611(g) of the Act as the number of private school children with disabilities aged 3 through 21 residing in its jurisdiction is to the total number of children with disabilities in its jurisdiction aged 3 through 21; and

(2) For children aged 3 through 5, an amount that is the same proportion of the LEA's total subgrant under section 619(g) of the Act as the number of private school children with disabilities aged 3 through 5 residing in its jurisdiction is to the total number of children with disabilities in its jurisdiction aged 3 through 5.

(b) Child count.

(1) Each LEA shall—

(i) Consult with representatives of private school children in deciding how to conduct the annual count of the number of private school children with disabilities; and

(ii) Ensure that the count is conducted on December 1 or the last Friday of October of each year.

(2) The child count must be used to determine the amount that the LEA must spend on providing special education and related services to private school children with disabilities in the next subsequent fiscal year.

(c) Expenditures for child find may not be considered. Expenditures for child find activities described in Sec. 300.451 may not be considered in determining whether the LEA has met the requirements of paragraph (a) of this section.

(d) Additional services permissible. State and local educational agencies are not prohibited from providing services to private school children with disabilities in excess of those required by this part, consistent with State law or local policy.

(Authority: 20 U.S.C. 1412(a)(10)(A))

Sec. 300.454 Services determined.

(a) No individual right to special education and related services.

(1) No private school child with a disability has an individual right to receive some or all of the special education and related services that the child would receive if enrolled in a public school.

(2) Decisions about the services that will be provided to private school children with disabilities under Secs. 300.452-

300.462, must be made in accordance with paragraphs (b), and (c) of this section.

(b) Consultation with representatives of private school children with disabilities.

(1) General. Each LEA shall consult, in a timely and meaningful way, with appropriate representatives of private school children with disabilities in light of the funding under Sec. 300.453, the number of private school children with disabilities, the needs of private school children with disabilities, and their location to decide—

(i) Which children will receive services under Sec. 300.452;

(ii) What services will be provided;

(iii) How and where the services will be provided; and

(iv) How the services provided will be evaluated.

(2) Genuine opportunity. Each LEA shall give appropriate representatives of private school children with disabilities a genuine opportunity to express their views regarding each matter that is subject to the consultation requirements in this section.

(3) Timing. The consultation required by paragraph (b)(1) of this section must occur before the LEA makes any decision that affects the opportunities of private school children with disabilities to participate in services under Secs. 300.452-300.462.

(4) Decisions. The LEA shall make the final decisions with respect to the services to be provided to eligible private school children.

(c) Services plan for each child served under Secs. 300.450-300.462. If a child with a disability is enrolled in a religious or other private school and will receive special education or related services from an LEA, the LEA shall—

(1) Initiate and conduct meetings to develop, review, and revise a services plan for the child, in accordance with Sec. 300.455(b); and

(2) Ensure that a representative of the religious or other private school attends each meeting. If the representative cannot attend, the LEA shall use other methods to ensure participation by the private school, including individual or conference telephone calls.

(Authority: 1412(a)(10)(A))

Sec. 300.455 Services provided.

(a) General.

(1) The services provided to private school children with disabilities must be provided by personnel meeting the same standards as personnel providing services in the public schools.

(2) Private school children with disabilities may receive a different amount of services than children with disabilities in public schools.

(3) No private school child with a disability is entitled to any service or to any amount of a service the child would receive if enrolled in a public school.

(b) Services provided in accordance with a services plan.

(1) Each private school child with a disability who has been designated to receive services under Sec. 300.452 must have a services plan that describes the specific special education and

related services that the LEA will provide to the child in light of the services that the LEA has determined, through the process described in Secs. 300.453-300.454, it will make available to private school children with disabilities.

(2) The services plan must, to the extent appropriate—

(i) Meet the requirements of Sec. 300.347, with respect to the services provided; and

(ii) Be developed, reviewed, and revised consistent with Secs. 300.342-300.346.

(Authority: 20 U.S.C. 1412(a)(10)(A))

Sec. 300.456 Location of services; transportation.

(a) On-site. Services provided to private school children with disabilities may be provided on-site at a child's private school, including a religious school, to the extent consistent with law.

(b) Transportation.

(1) General.

(i) If necessary for the child to benefit from or participate in the services provided under this part, a private school child with a disability must be provided transportation—

(A) From the child's school or the child's home to a site other than the private school; and

(B) From the service site to the private school, or to the child's home, depending on the timing of the services.

(ii) LEAs are not required to provide transportation from the child's home to the private school.

(2) Cost of transportation. The cost of the transportation described in paragraph (b)(1)(i) of this section may be included in calculating whether the LEA has met the requirement of Sec. 300.453.

(Authority: 20 U.S.C. 1412(a)(10)(A))

Sec. 300.457 Complaints.

(a) Due process inapplicable. The procedures in Secs. 300.504- 300.515 do not apply to complaints that an LEA has failed to meet the requirements of Secs. 300.452-300.462, including the provision of services indicated on the child's services plan.

(b) Due process applicable. The procedures in Secs. 300.504-300.515 do apply to complaints that an LEA has failed to meet the requirements of Sec. 300.451, including the requirements of Secs. 300.530-300.543.

(c) State complaints. Complaints that an SEA or LEA has failed to meet the requirements of Secs. 300.451-300.462 may be filed under the procedures in Secs. 300.660-300.662.

(Authority: 20 U.S.C. 1412(a)(10)(A))

Sec. 300.458 Separate classes prohibited.

An LEA may not use funds available under section 611 or 619 of the Act for classes that are organized separately on the basis of school enrollment or religion of the students if—

(a) The classes are at the same site; and

(b) The classes include students enrolled in public schools and students enrolled in private schools.

(Authority: 20 U.S.C. 1412(a)(10)(A))

Sec. 300.459 Requirement that funds not benefit a private school.

(a) An LEA may not use funds provided under section 611 or 619 of the Act to finance the existing level of instruction in a private school or to otherwise benefit the private school.

(b) The LEA shall use funds provided under Part B of the Act to meet the special education and related services needs of students enrolled in private schools, but not for—

(1) The needs of a private school; or

(2) The general needs of the students enrolled in the private school.

(Authority: 20 U.S.C. 1412(a)(10)(A))

Sec. 300.460 Use of public school personnel.

An LEA may use funds available under sections 611 and 619 of the Act to make public school personnel available in other than public facilities—

(a) To the extent necessary to provide services under Secs. 300.450- 300.462 for private school children with disabilities; and

(b) If those services are not normally provided by the private school.

(Authority: 20 U.S.C. 1412(a)(10)(A))

Sec. 300.461 Use of private school personnel.

An LEA may use funds available under section 611 or 619 of the Act to pay for the services of an employee of a private school to provide services under Secs. 300.450-300.462 if—

(a) The employee performs the services outside of his or her regular hours of duty; and

(b) The employee performs the services under public supervision and control.

(Authority: 20 U.S.C. 1412(a)(10)(A))

Sec. 300.462 Requirements concerning property, equipment, and supplies for the benefit of private school children with disabilities.

(a) A public agency must keep title to and exercise continuing administrative control of all property, equipment, and supplies that the public agency acquires with funds under section 611 or 619 of the Act for the benefit of private school children with disabilities.

(b) The public agency may place equipment and supplies in a private school for the period of time needed for the program.

(c) The public agency shall ensure that the equipment and supplies placed in a private school—

(1) Are used only for Part B purposes; and

(2) Can be removed from the private school without remodeling the private school facility.

(d) The public agency shall remove equipment and supplies from a private school if—

(1) The equipment and supplies are no longer needed for Part B purposes; or

(2) Removal is necessary to avoid unauthorized use of the equipment and supplies for other than Part B purposes.

(e) No funds under Part B of the Act may be used for repairs, minor remodeling, or construction of private school facilities.

(Authority: 20 U.S.C. 1412(a)(10)(A))

Subpart E—

Procedural Safeguards

Sec. 300.500 General responsibility of public agencies; definitions.

Due Process Procedures for Parents and Children

(a) Responsibility of SEA and other public agencies. Each SEA shall ensure that each public agency establishes, maintains, and implements procedural safeguards that meet the requirements of Secs. 300.500- 300.529.

(b) Definitions of "consent," "evaluation," and "personally identifiable." As used in this part —

(1) Consent means that —

(i) The parent has been fully informed of all information relevant to the activity for which consent is sought, in his or her native language, or other mode of communication;

(ii) The parent understands and agrees in writing to the carrying out of the activity for which his or her consent is sought, and the consent describes that activity and lists the records (if any) that will be released and to whom; and

(iii)(A) The parent understands that the granting of consent is voluntary on the part of the parent and may be revoked at anytime.

(B) If a parent revokes consent, that revocation is not retroactive (i.e., it does not negate an action that has occurred after the consent was given and before the consent was revoked).

(2) Evaluation means procedures used in accordance with Secs. 300.530-300.536 to determine whether a child has a disability and the nature and extent of the special education and related services that the child needs; and

(3) Personally identifiable means that information includes—

(i) The name of the child, the child's parent, or other family member;

(ii) The address of the child;

(iii) A personal identifier, such as the child's social security number or student number; or

(iv) A list of personal characteristics or other information that would make it possible to identify the child with reasonable certainty.

(Authority: 20 U.S.C. 1415(a))

Sec. 300.501 Opportunity to examine records; parent participation in meetings.

(a) General. The parents of a child with a disability must be afforded, in accordance with the procedures of Secs. 300.562- 300.569, an opportunity to—

(1) Inspect and review all education records with respect to—

(i) The identification, evaluation, and educational placement of the child; and

(ii) The provision of FAPE to the child; and

(2) Participate in meetings with respect to —

(i) The identification, evaluation, and educational placement of the child; and

(ii) The provision of FAPE to the child.

(b) Parent participation in meetings.

(1) Each public agency shall provide notice consistent with Sec. 300.345(a)(1) and (b)(1) to ensure that parents of children with disabilities have the opportunity to participate in meetings described in paragraph (a)(2) of this section.

(2) A meeting does not include informal or unscheduled conversations involving public agency personnel and conversations on issues such as teaching methodology, lesson plans, or coordination of service provision if those issues are not addressed in the child's IEP. A meeting also does not include preparatory activities that public agency personnel engage in to develop a proposal or response to a parent proposal that will be discussed at a later meeting.

(c) Parent involvement in placement decisions.

(1) Each public agency shall ensure that the parents of each child with a disability are members of any group that makes decisions on the educational placement of their child.

(2) In implementing the requirements of paragraph (c)(1) of this section, the public agency shall use procedures consistent with the procedures described in Sec. 300.345(a) through (b)(1).

(3) If neither parent can participate in a meeting in which a decision is to be made relating to the educational placement of their child, the public agency shall use other methods to ensure their participation, including individual or conference telephone calls, or video conferencing.

(4) A placement decision may be made by a group without the involvement of the parents, if the public agency is unable to obtain the parents' participation in the decision. In this case, the public agency must have a record of its attempt to ensure their involvement, including information that is consistent with the requirements of Sec. 300.345(d).

(5) The public agency shall make reasonable efforts to ensure that the parents understand, and are able to participate in, any group discussions relating to the educational placement of their child, including arranging for an interpreter for parents with deafness, or whose native language is other than English.

(Authority: 20 U.S.C. 1414(f), 1415(b)(1))

Sec. 300.502 Independent educational evaluation.

(a) General.

(1) The parents of a child with a disability have the right under this part to obtain an independent educational evaluation of the child, subject to paragraphs (b) through (e) of this section.

(2) Each public agency shall provide to parents, upon request for an independent educational evaluation, information about where an independent educational evaluation may be obtained, and the agency criteria applicable for independent educational evaluations as set forth in paragraph (e) of this section.

(3) For the purposes of this part—

(i) Independent educational evaluation means an evaluation conducted by a qualified examiner who is not employed by the public agency responsible for the education of the child in question; and

(ii) Public expense means that the public agency either pays for the full cost of the evaluation or ensures that the evaluation is otherwise provided at no cost to the parent, consistent with Sec. 300.301.

(b) Parent right to evaluation at public expense.

(1) A parent has the right to an independent educational evaluation at public expense if the parent disagrees with an evaluation obtained by the public agency.

(2) If a parent requests an independent educational evaluation at public expense, the public agency must, without unnecessary delay, either—

(i) Initiate a hearing under Sec. 300.507 to show that its evaluation is appropriate; or

(ii) Ensure that an independent educational evaluation is provided at public expense, unless the agency demonstrates in a hearing under Sec. 300.507 that the evaluation obtained by the parent did not meet agency criteria.

(3) If the public agency initiates a hearing and the final decision is that the agency's evaluation is appropriate, the parent still has the right to an independent educational evaluation, but not at public expense.

(4) If a parent requests an independent educational evaluation, the public agency may ask for the parent's reason why he or she objects to the public evaluation. However, the explanation by the parent may not be required and the public agency may not unreasonably delay either providing the independent educational evaluation at public expense or initiating a due process hearing to defend the public evaluation.

(c) Parent-initiated evaluations. If the parent obtains an independent educational evaluation at private expense, the results of the evaluation—

(1) Must be considered by the public agency, if it meets agency criteria, in any decision made with respect to the provision of FAPE to the child; and

(2) May be presented as evidence at a hearing under this subpart regarding that child.

(d) Requests for evaluations by hearing officers. If a hearing officer requests an independent educational evaluation as part of a hearing, the cost of the evaluation must be at public expense.

(e) Agency criteria.

(1) If an independent educational evaluation is at public expense, the criteria under which the evaluation is obtained, including the location of the evaluation and the qualifications of the examiner, must be the same as the criteria that the public agency uses when it initiates an evaluation, to the extent those criteria are consistent with the parent's right to an independent educational evaluation.

(2) Except for the criteria described in paragraph (e)(1) of this section, a public agency may not impose conditions or timelines related to obtaining an independent educational evaluation at public expense.

(Authority: 20 U.S.C. 1415(b)(1))

Sec. 300.503 Prior notice by the public agency; content of notice.

(a) Notice.

(1) Written notice that meets the requirements of paragraph (b) of this section must be given to the parents of a child with a disability a reasonable time before the public agency—

(i) Proposes to initiate or change the identification, evaluation, or educational placement of the child or the provision of FAPE to the child; or

(ii) Refuses to initiate or change the identification, evaluation, or educational placement of the child or the provision of FAPE to the child.

(2) If the notice described under paragraph (a)(1) of this section relates to an action proposed by the public agency that also requires parental consent under Sec. 300.505, the agency may give notice at the same time it requests parent consent.

(b) Content of notice. The notice required under paragraph (a) of this section must include—

(1) A description of the action proposed or refused by the agency;

(2) An explanation of why the agency proposes or refuses to take the action;

(3) A description of any other options that the agency considered and the reasons why those options were rejected;

(4) A description of each evaluation procedure, test, record, or report the agency used as a basis for the proposed or refused action;

(5) A description of any other factors that are relevant to the agency's proposal or refusal;

(6) A statement that the parents of a child with a disability have protection under the procedural safeguards of this part and, if this notice is not an initial referral for evaluation, the means by which a copy of a description of the procedural safeguards can be obtained; and

(7) Sources for parents to contact to obtain assistance in understanding the provisions of this part.

(c) Notice in understandable language.

(1) The notice required under paragraph (a) of this section must be—

(i) Written in language understandable to the general public; and

(ii) Provided in the native language of the parent or other mode of communication used by the parent, unless it is clearly not feasible to do so.

(2) If the native language or other mode of communication of the parent is not a written language, the public agency shall take steps to ensure—

(i) That the notice is translated orally or by other means to the parent in his or her native language or other mode of communication;

(ii) That the parent understands the content of the notice; and

(iii) That there is written evidence that the requirements in paragraphs (c)(2) (i) and (ii) of this section have been met.

(Authority: 20 U.S.C. 1415(b)(3), (4) and (c), 1414(b)(1))

Sec. 300.504 Procedural safeguards notice.

(a) General. A copy of the procedural safeguards available to the parents of a child with a disability must be given to the parents, at a minimum—

(1) Upon initial referral for evaluation;

(2) Upon each notification of an IEP meeting;

(3) Upon reevaluation of the child; and

(4) Upon receipt of a request for due process under Sec. 300.507.

(b) Contents. The procedural safeguards notice must include a full explanation of all of the procedural safeguards available under Secs. 300.403, 300.500-300.529, and 300.560-300.577, and the State complaint procedures available under Secs. 300.660-300.662 relating to—

(1) Independent educational evaluation;

(2) Prior written notice;

(3) Parental consent;

(4) Access to educational records;

(5) Opportunity to present complaints to initiate due process hearings;

(6) The child's placement during pendency of due process proceedings;

(7) Procedures for students who are subject to placement in an interim alternative educational setting;

(8) Requirements for unilateral placement by parents of children in private schools at public expense;

(9) Mediation;

(10) Due process hearings, including requirements for disclosure of evaluation results and recommendations;

(11) State-level appeals (if applicable in that State);

(12) Civil actions;

(13) Attorneys' fees; and

(14) The State complaint procedures under Secs. 300.660-300.662, including a description of how to file a complaint and the timelines under those procedures.

(c) Notice in understandable language. The notice required under paragraph (a) of this section must meet the requirements of Sec. 300.503(c).

(Authority: 20 U.S.C. 1415(d))

Sec. 300.505 Parental consent.

(a) General. (1) Subject to paragraphs (a)(3), (b) and (c) of this section, informed parent consent must be obtained before—

(i) Conducting an initial evaluation or reevaluation; and

(ii) Initial provision of special education and related services to a child with a disability.

(2) Consent for initial evaluation may not be construed as consent for initial placement described in paragraph (a)(1)(ii) of this section.

(3) Parental consent is not required before—

(i) Reviewing existing data as part of an evaluation or a reevaluation; or

(ii) Administering a test or other evaluation that is administered to all children unless, before administration of that test or evaluation, consent is required of parents of all children.

(b) Refusal. If the parents of a child with a disability refuse consent for initial evaluation or a reevaluation, the agency may continue to pursue those evaluations by using the due process procedures under Secs. 300.507-300.509, or the mediation procedures under Sec. 300.506 if appropriate, except to the extent inconsistent with State law relating to parental consent.

(c) Failure to respond to request for reevaluation.

(1) Informed parental consent need not be obtained for reevaluation if the public agency can demonstrate that it has taken reasonable measures to obtain that consent, and the child's parent has failed to respond.

(2) To meet the reasonable measures requirement in paragraph (c)(1) of this section, the public agency must use procedures consistent with those in Sec. 300.345(d).

(d) Additional State consent requirements. In addition to the parental consent requirements described in paragraph (a) of this section, a State may require parental consent for other services and activities under this part if it ensures that each public agency in the State establishes and implements effective procedures to ensure that a parent's refusal to consent does not result in a failure to provide the child with FAPE.

(e) Limitation. A public agency may not use a parent's refusal to consent to one service or activity under paragraphs (a) and (d) of this section to deny the parent or child any other service, benefit, or activity of the public agency, except as required by this part.

(Authority: 20 U.S.C. 1415(b)(3); 1414(a)(1)(C) and (c)(3))

Sec. 300.506 Mediation.

(a) General. Each public agency shall ensure that procedures are established and implemented to allow parties to disputes involving any matter described in Sec. 300.503(a)(1) to resolve the disputes through a mediation process that, at a minimum, must be available whenever a hearing is requested under Secs. 300.507 or 300.520-300.528.

(b) Requirements. The procedures must meet the following requirements:

(1) The procedures must ensure that the mediation process—

(i) Is voluntary on the part of the parties;

(ii) Is not used to deny or delay a parent's right to a due process hearing under Sec. 300.507, or to deny any other rights afforded under Part B of the Act; and

(iii) Is conducted by a qualified and impartial mediator who is trained in effective mediation techniques.

(2)(i) The State shall maintain a list of individuals who are qualified mediators and knowledgeable in laws and regulations relating to the provision of special education and related services.

(ii) If a mediator is not selected on a random (e.g., a rotation) basis from the list described in paragraph (b)(2)(i) of this section, both parties must be involved in selecting the mediator and agree with the selection of the individual who will mediate.

(3) The State shall bear the cost of the mediation process, including the costs of meetings described in paragraph (d) of this section.

(4) Each session in the mediation process must be scheduled in a timely manner and must be held in a location that is convenient to the parties to the dispute.

(5) An agreement reached by the parties to the dispute in the mediation process must be set forth in a written mediation agreement.

(6) Discussions that occur during the mediation process must be confidential and may not be used as evidence in any subsequent due process hearings or civil proceedings, and the parties to the mediation process may be required to sign a confidentiality pledge prior to the commencement of the process.

(c) Impartiality of mediator.

(1) An individual who serves as a mediator under this part—

(i) May not be an employee of—

(A) Any LEA or any State agency described under Sec. 300.194; or

(B) An SEA that is providing direct services to a child who is the subject of the mediation process; and

(ii) Must not have a personal or professional conflict of interest.

(2) A person who otherwise qualifies as a mediator is not an employee of an LEA or State agency described under Sec. 300.194 solely because he or she is paid by the agency to serve as a mediator.

(d) Meeting to encourage mediation. (1) A public agency may establish procedures to require parents who elect not to use the mediation process to meet, at a time and location convenient to the parents, with a disinterested party—

(i) Who is under contract with a parent training and information center or community parent resource center in

the State established under section 682 or 683 of the Act, or an appropriate alternative dispute resolution entity; and

(ii) Who would explain the benefits of the mediation process, and encourage the parents to use the process.

(2) A public agency may not deny or delay a parent's right to a due process hearing under Sec. 300.507 if the parent fails to participate in the meeting described in paragraph (d)(1) of this section.

(Authority: 20 U.S.C. 1415(e))

Sec. 300.507 Impartial due process hearing; parent notice.

(a) General.

(1) A parent or a public agency may initiate a hearing on any of the matters described in Sec. 300.503(a)(1) and (2) (relating to the identification, evaluation or educational placement of a child with a disability, or the provision of FAPE to the child).

(2) When a hearing is initiated under paragraph (a)(1) of this section, the public agency shall inform the parents of the availability of mediation described in Sec. 300.506.

(3) The public agency shall inform the parent of any free or low- cost legal and other relevant services available in the area if—

(i) The parent requests the information; or

(ii) The parent or the agency initiates a hearing under this section.

(b) Agency responsible for conducting hearing. The hearing described in paragraph (a) of this section must be conducted by the SEA or the public agency directly responsible for the education of the child, as determined under State statute, State regulation, or a written policy of the SEA.

(c) Parent notice to the public agency. (1) General. The public agency must have procedures that require the parent of a child with a disability or the attorney representing the child, to provide notice (which must remain confidential) to the public agency in a request for a hearing under paragraph (a)(1) of this section.

(2) Content of parent notice. The notice required in paragraph (c)(1) of this section must include—

(i) The name of the child;

(ii) The address of the residence of the child;

(iii) The name of the school the child is attending;

(iv) A description of the nature of the problem of the child relating to the proposed or refused initiation or change, including facts relating to the problem; and

(v) A proposed resolution of the problem to the extent known and available to the parents at the time.

(3) Model form to assist parents. Each SEA shall develop a model form to assist parents in filing a request for due process that includes the information required in paragraphs (c)(1) and (2) of this section.

(4) Right to due process hearing. A public agency may not deny or delay a parent's right to a due process hearing for failure to provide the notice required in paragraphs (c)(1) and (2) of this section.

(Authority: 20 U.S.C. 1415(b)(5), (b)(6), (b)(7), (b)(8), (e)(1) and (f)(1))

Sec. 300.508 Impartial hearing officer.

(a) A hearing may not be conducted—

(1) By a person who is an employee of the State agency or the LEA that is involved in the education or care of the child; or

(2) By any person having a personal or professional interest that would conflict with his or her objectivity in the hearing.

(b) A person who otherwise qualifies to conduct a hearing under paragraph (a) of this section is not an employee of the agency solely because he or she is paid by the agency to serve as a hearing officer.

(c) Each public agency shall keep a list of the persons who serve as hearing officers. The list must include a statement of the qualifications of each of those persons.

(Authority: 20 U.S.C. 1415(f)(3))

Sec. 300.509 Hearing rights.

(a) General. Any party to a hearing conducted pursuant to Secs. 300.507 or 300.520-300.528, or an appeal conducted pursuant to Sec. 300.510, has the right to—

(1) Be accompanied and advised by counsel and by individuals with special knowledge or training with respect to the problems of children with disabilities;

(2) Present evidence and confront, cross-examine, and compel the attendance of witnesses;

(3) Prohibit the introduction of any evidence at the hearing that has not been disclosed to that party at least 5 business days before the hearing;

(4) Obtain a written, or, at the option of the parents, electronic, verbatim record of the hearing; and

(5) Obtain written, or, at the option of the parents, electronic findings of fact and decisions.

(b) Additional disclosure of information. (1) At least 5 business days prior to a hearing conducted pursuant to Sec. 300.507(a), each party shall disclose to all other parties all evaluations completed by that date and recommendations based on the offering party's evaluations that the party intends to use at the hearing.

(2) A hearing officer may bar any party that fails to comply with paragraph (b)(1) of this section from introducing the relevant evaluation or recommendation at the hearing without the consent of the other party.

(c) Parental rights at hearings.

(1) Parents involved in hearings must be given the right to—

(i) Have the child who is the subject of the hearing present; and

(ii) Open the hearing to the public.

(2) The record of the hearing and the findings of fact and decisions described in paragraphs (a)(4) and (a)(5) of this section must be provided at no cost to parents.

(d) Findings and decision to advisory panel and general public. The public agency, after deleting any personally identifiable information, shall —

(1) Transmit the findings and decisions referred to in paragraph (a)(5) of this section to the State advisory panel established under Sec. 300.650; and

(2) Make those findings and decisions available to the public.

(Authority: 20 U.S.C. 1415(f)(2) and (h))

Sec. 300.510 Finality of decision; appeal; impartial review.

(a) Finality of decision. A decision made in a hearing conducted pursuant to Secs. 300.507 or 300.520-300.528 is final, except that any party involved in the hearing may appeal the decision under the provisions of paragraph (b) of this section and Sec. 300.512.

(Authority: 20 U.S.C. 1415(i)(1)(A))

(b) Appeal of decisions; impartial review.

(1) General. If the hearing required by Sec. 300.507 is conducted by a public agency other than the SEA, any party aggrieved by the findings and decision in the hearing may appeal to the SEA.

(2) SEA responsibility for review. If there is an appeal, the SEA shall conduct an impartial review of the hearing. The official conducting the review shall—

(i) Examine the entire hearing record;

(ii) Ensure that the procedures at the hearing were consistent with the requirements of due process;

(iii) Seek additional evidence if necessary. If a hearing is held to receive additional evidence, the rights in Sec. 300.509 apply;

(iv) Afford the parties an opportunity for oral or written argument, or both, at the discretion of the reviewing official;

(v) Make an independent decision on completion of the review; and

(vi) Give a copy of the written, or, at the option of the parents, electronic findings of fact and decisions to the parties.

(c) Findings and decision to advisory panel and general public. The SEA, after deleting any personally identifiable information, shall—

(1) Transmit the findings and decisions referred to in paragraph (b)(2)(vi) of this section to the State advisory panel established under Sec. 300.650; and

(2) Make those findings and decisions available to the public.

(d) Finality of review decision. The decision made by the reviewing official is final unless a party brings a civil action under Sec. 300.512.

(Authority: 20 U.S.C. 1415(g); H. R. Rep. No. 94-664, at p. 49 (1975))

Sec. 300.511 Timelines and convenience of hearings and reviews.

(a) The public agency shall ensure that not later than 45 days after the receipt of a request for a hearing—

(1) A final decision is reached in the hearing; and

(2) A copy of the decision is mailed to each of the parties.

(b) The SEA shall ensure that not later than 30 days after the receipt of a request for a review—

(1) A final decision is reached in the review; and

(2) A copy of the decision is mailed to each of the parties.

(c) A hearing or reviewing officer may grant specific extensions of time beyond the periods set out in paragraphs (a) and (b) of this section at the request of either party.

(d) Each hearing and each review involving oral arguments must be conducted at a time and place that is reasonably convenient to the parents and child involved.

(Authority: 20 U.S.C. 1415)

Sec. 300.512 Civil action.

(a) General. Any party aggrieved by the findings and decision made under Secs. 300.507 or 300.520-300.528 who does not have the right to an appeal under Sec. 300.510(b), and any party aggrieved by the findings and decision under Sec. 300.510(b), has the right to bring a civil action with respect to the complaint presented pursuant to Sec. 300.507. The action may be brought in any State court of competent jurisdiction or in a district court of the United States without regard to the amount in controversy.

(b) Additional requirements. In any action brought under paragraph (a) of this section, the court—

(1) Shall receive the records of the administrative proceedings;

(2) Shall hear additional evidence at the request of a party; and

(3) Basing its decision on the preponderance of the evidence, shall grant the relief that the court determines to be appropriate.

(c) Jurisdiction of district courts. The district courts of the United States have jurisdiction of actions brought under section 615 of the Act without regard to the amount in controversy.

(d) Rule of construction. Nothing in this part restricts or limits the rights, procedures, and remedies available under the Constitution, the Americans with Disabilities Act of 1990, title V of the Rehabilitation Act of 1973, or other Federal laws protecting the rights of children with disabilities, except that before the filing of a civil action under these laws seeking relief that is also available under section 615 of the Act, the procedures under Secs. 300.507 and 300.510 must be exhausted to the same extent as would be required had the action been brought under section 615 of the Act.

(Authority: 20 U.S.C. 1415(i)(2), (i)(3)(A), and 1415(l))

Sec. 300.513 Attorneys' fees.

(a) In any action or proceeding brought under section 615 of the Act, the court, in its discretion, may award reasonable attorneys' fees as part of the costs to the parents of a child with a disability who is the prevailing party.

(b)(1) Funds under Part B of the Act may not be used to pay attorneys' fees or costs of a party related to an action or proceeding under section 615 of the Act and subpart E of this part.

(2) Paragraph (b)(1) of this section does not preclude a public agency from using funds under Part B of the Act for conducting an action or proceeding under section 615 of the Act.

(c) A court awards reasonable attorney's fees under section 615(i)(3) of the Act consistent with the following:

(1) Determination of amount of attorneys' fees. Fees awarded under section 615(i)(3) of the Act must be based on rates prevailing in the community in which the action or proceeding arose for the kind and quality of services furnished. No bonus or multiplier may be used in calculating the fees awarded under this subsection.

(2) Prohibition of attorneys' fees and related costs for certain services. (i) Attorneys' fees may not be awarded and related costs may not be reimbursed in any action or proceeding under section 615 of the Act for services performed subsequent to the time of a written offer of settlement to a parent if—

(A) The offer is made within the time prescribed by Rule 68 of the Federal Rules of Civil Procedure or, in the case of an administrative proceeding, at any time more than 10 days before the proceeding begins;

(B) The offer is not accepted within 10 days; and

(C) The court or administrative hearing officer finds that the relief finally obtained by the parents is not more favorable to the parents than the offer of settlement.

(ii) Attorneys' fees may not be awarded relating to any meeting of the IEP team unless the meeting is convened as a result of an administrative proceeding or judicial action, or at the discretion of the State, for a mediation described in Sec. 300.506 that is conducted prior to the filing of a request for due process under Secs. 300.507 or 300.520-300.528.

(3) Exception to prohibition on attorneys' fees and related costs. Notwithstanding paragraph (c)(2) of this section, an award of attorneys' fees and related costs may be made to a parent who is the prevailing party and who was substantially justified in rejecting the settlement offer.

(4) Reduction of amount of attorneys' fees. Except as provided in paragraph (c)(5) of this section, the court reduces, accordingly, the amount of the attorneys' fees awarded under section 615 of the Act, if the court finds that—

(i) The parent, during the course of the action or proceeding, unreasonably protracted the final resolution of the controversy;

(ii) The amount of the attorneys' fees otherwise authorized to be awarded unreasonably exceeds the hourly rate prevailing in the community for similar services by attorneys of reasonably comparable skill, reputation, and experience;

(iii) The time spent and legal services furnished were excessive considering the nature of the action or proceeding; or

(iv) The attorney representing the parent did not provide to the school district the appropriate information in the due process complaint in accordance with Sec. 300.507(c).

(5) Exception to reduction in amount of attorneys' fees. The provisions of paragraph (c)(4) of this section do not apply in any action or proceeding if the court finds that the State or local agency unreasonably protracted the final resolution of the action or proceeding or there was a violation of section 615 of the Act.

(Authority: 20 U.S.C. 1415(i)(3)(B)-(G))

Sec. 300.514 Child's status during proceedings.

(a) Except as provided in Sec. 300.526, during the pendency of any administrative or judicial proceeding regarding a complaint under Sec. 300.507, unless the State or local agency and the parents of the child agree otherwise, the child involved in the complaint must remain in his or her current educational placement.

(b) If the complaint involves an application for initial admission to public school, the child, with the consent of the parents, must be placed in the public school until the completion of all the proceedings.

(c) If the decision of a hearing officer in a due process hearing conducted by the SEA or a State review official in an administrative appeal agrees with the child's parents that a change of placement is appropriate, that placement must be treated as an agreement between the State or local agency and the parents for purposes of paragraph (a) of this section.

(Authority: 20 U.S.C. 1415(j))

Sec. 300.515 Surrogate parents.

(a) General. Each public agency shall ensure that the rights of a child are protected if—

(1) No parent (as defined in Sec. 300.20) can be identified;

(2) The public agency, after reasonable efforts, cannot discover the whereabouts of a parent; or

(3) The child is a ward of the State under the laws of that State.

(b) Duty of public agency. The duty of a public agency under paragraph (a) of this section includes the assignment of an individual to act as a surrogate for the parents. This must include a method—

(1) For determining whether a child needs a surrogate parent; and

(2) For assigning a surrogate parent to the child.

(c) Criteria for selection of surrogates. (1) The public agency may select a surrogate parent in any way permitted under State law.

(2) Except as provided in paragraph (c)(3) of this section, public agencies shall ensure that a person selected as a surrogate—

(i) Is not an employee of the SEA, the LEA, or any other agency that is involved in the education or care of the child;

(ii) Has no interest that conflicts with the interest of the child he or she represents; and

(iii) Has knowledge and skills that ensure adequate representation of the child.

(3) A public agency may select as a surrogate a person who is an employee of a nonpublic agency that only provides noneducational care for the child and who meets the standards in paragraphs (c)(2)(ii) and (iii) of this section.

(d) Non-employee requirement; compensation. A person who otherwise qualifies to be a surrogate parent under paragraph (c) of this section is not an employee of the agency solely because he or she is paid by the agency to serve as a surrogate parent.

(e) Responsibilities. The surrogate parent may represent the child in all matters relating to—

(1) The identification, evaluation, and educational placement of the child; and

(2) The provision of FAPE to the child.

(Authority: 20 U.S.C. 1415(b)(2))

Sec. 300.517 Transfer of parental rights at age of majority.

(a) General. A State may provide that, when a student with a disability reaches the age of majority under State law that applies to all students (except for a student with a disability who has been determined to be incompetent under State law)—

(1)(i) The public agency shall provide any notice required by this part to both the individual and the parents; and

(ii) All other rights accorded to parents under Part B of the Act transfer to the student; and

(2) All rights accorded to parents under Part B of the Act transfer to students who are incarcerated in an adult or juvenile, State or local correctional institution.

(3) Whenever a State transfers rights under this part pursuant to paragraph (a)(1) or (a)(2) of this section, the agency shall notify the individual and the parents of the transfer of rights.

(b) Special rule. If, under State law, a State has a mechanism to determine that a student with a disability, who has reached the age of majority under State law that applies to all children and has not been determined incompetent under State law, does not have the ability to provide informed consent with respect to his or her educational program, the State shall establish procedures for appointing the parent, or, if the parent is not available another appropriate individual, to represent the educational interests of the student throughout the student's eligibility under Part B of the Act.

(Authority: 20 U.S.C. 1415(m))

Discipline Procedures

Sec. 300.519 Change of placement for disciplinary removals.

For purposes of removals of a child with a disability from the child's current educational placement under Secs. 300.520-300.529, a change of placement occurs if—

(a) The removal is for more than 10 consecutive school days; or

(b) The child is subjected to a series of removals that constitute a pattern because they cumulate to more than 10 school days in a school year, and because of factors such as the length of each removal, the total amount of time the child is removed, and the proximity of the removals to one another.

(Authority: 20 U.S.C. 1415(k))

Sec. 300.520 Authority of school personnel.

(a) School personnel may order—

(1)(i) To the extent removal would be applied to children without disabilities, the removal of a child with a disability from the child's current placement for not more than 10 consecutive school days for any violation of school rules, and additional removals of not more than 10 consecutive school days in that same school year for separate incidents of misconduct (as long as those removals do not constitute a change of placement under Sec. 300.519(b));

(ii) After a child with a disability has been removed from his or her current placement for more than 10 school days in the same school year, during any subsequent days of removal the public agency must provide services to the extent required under Sec. 300.121(d); and

(2) A change in placement of a child with a disability to an appropriate interim alternative educational setting for the same amount of time that a child without a disability would be subject to discipline, but for not more than 45 days, if—

(i) The child carries a weapon to school or to a school function under the jurisdiction of a State or a local educational agency; or

(ii) The child knowingly possesses or uses illegal drugs or sells or solicits the sale of a controlled substance while at school or a school function under the jurisdiction of a State or local educational agency.

(b)(1) Either before or not later than 10 business days after either first removing the child for more than 10 school days in a school year or commencing a removal that constitutes a change of placement under Sec. 300.519, including the action described in paragraph (a)(2) of this section—

(i) If the LEA did not conduct a functional behavioral assessment and implement a behavioral intervention plan for the child before the behavior that resulted in the removal described in paragraph (a) of this section, the agency shall convene an IEP meeting to develop an assessment plan.

(ii) If the child already has a behavioral intervention plan, the IEP team shall meet to review the plan and its implementation, and, modify the plan and its implementation as necessary, to address the behavior.

(2) As soon as practicable after developing the plan described in paragraph (b)(1)(i) of this section, and completing the assessments required by the plan, the LEA shall convene an IEP meeting to develop appropriate behavioral interventions to address that behavior and shall implement those interventions.

(c)(1) If subsequently, a child with a disability who has a behavioral intervention plan and who has been removed from the child's current educational placement for more than 10 school days in a school year is subjected to a removal that does not constitute a change of placement under Sec. 300.519, the IEP team members shall review the behavioral intervention plan and its implementation to determine if modifications are necessary.

(2) If one or more of the team members believe that modifications are needed, the team shall meet to modify the plan and its implementation, to the extent the team determines necessary.

(d) For purposes of this section, the following definitions apply:

(1) Controlled substance means a drug or other substance identified under schedules I, II, III, IV, or V in section 202(c) of the Controlled Substances Act (21 U.S.C. 812(c)).

(2) Illegal drug—

(i) Means a controlled substance; but

(ii) Does not include a substance that is legally possessed or used under the supervision of a licensed health-care professional or that is legally possessed or used under any other authority under that Act or under any other provision of Federal law.

(3) Weapon has the meaning given the term "dangerous weapon" under paragraph (2) of the first subsection (g) of section 930 of title 18, United States Code.

(Authority: 20 U.S.C. 1415(k)(1), (10))

Sec. 300.521 Authority of hearing officer.

A hearing officer under section 615 of the Act may order a change in the placement of a child with a disability to an appropriate interim alternative educational setting for not more than 45 days if the hearing officer, in an expedited due process hearing—

(a) Determines that the public agency has demonstrated by substantial evidence that maintaining the current placement of the child is substantially likely to result in injury to the child or to others;

(b) Considers the appropriateness of the child's current placement;

(c) Considers whether the public agency has made reasonable efforts to minimize the risk of harm in the child's current placement, including the use of supplementary aids and services; and

(d) Determines that the interim alternative educational setting that is proposed by school personnel who have consulted with the child's special education teacher, meets the requirements of Sec. 300.522(b).

(e) As used in this section, the term substantial evidence means beyond a preponderance of the evidence.

(Authority: 20 U.S.C. 1415(k)(2), (10))

Sec. 300.522 Determination of setting.

(a) General. The interim alternative educational setting referred to in Sec. 300.520(a)(2) must be determined by the IEP team.

(b) Additional requirements. Any interim alternative educational setting in which a child is placed under Secs. 300.520(a)(2) or 300.521 must—

(1) Be selected so as to enable the child to continue to progress in the general curriculum, although in another setting, and to continue to receive those services and modifications, including those described in the child's current IEP, that will enable the child to meet the goals set out in that IEP; and

(2) Include services and modifications to address the behavior described in Secs. 300.520(a)(2) or 300.521, that are designed to prevent the behavior from recurring.

(Authority: 20 U.S.C. 1415(k)(3))

Sec. 300.523 Manifestation determination review.

(a) General. If an action is contemplated regarding behavior described in Secs. 300.520(a)(2) or 300.521, or involving a removal that constitutes a change of placement under Sec. 300.519 for a child with a disability who has engaged in other behavior that violated any rule or code of conduct of the LEA that applies to all children—

(1) Not later than the date on which the decision to take that action is made, the parents must be notified of that decision and provided the procedural safeguards notice described in Sec. 300.504; and

(2) Immediately, if possible, but in no case later than 10 school days after the date on which the decision to take that action is made, a review must be conducted of the relationship between the child's disability and the behavior subject to the disciplinary action.

(b) Individuals to carry out review. A review described in paragraph (a) of this section must be conducted by the IEP team and other qualified personnel in a meeting.

(c) Conduct of review. In carrying out a review described in paragraph (a) of this section, the IEP team and other qualified personnel may determine that the behavior of the child was not a manifestation of the child's disability only if the IEP team and other qualified personnel—

(1) First consider, in terms of the behavior subject to disciplinary action, all relevant information, including —

(i) Evaluation and diagnostic results, including the results or other relevant information supplied by the parents of the child;

(ii) Observations of the child; and

(iii) The child's IEP and placement; and

(2) Then determine that—

(i) In relationship to the behavior subject to disciplinary action, the child's IEP and placement were appropriate and the special education services, supplementary aids and services, and behavior intervention strategies were provided consistent with the child's IEP and placement;

(ii) The child's disability did not impair the ability of the child to understand the impact and consequences of the behavior subject to disciplinary action; and

(iii) The child's disability did not impair the ability of the child to control the behavior subject to disciplinary action.

(d) Decision. If the IEP team and other qualified personnel determine that any of the standards in paragraph (c)(2) of this section were not met, the behavior must be considered a manifestation of the child's disability.

(e) Meeting. The review described in paragraph (a) of this section may be conducted at the same IEP meeting that is convened under Sec. 300.520(b).

(f) Deficiencies in IEP or placement. If, in the review in paragraphs (b) and (c) of this section, a public agency identifies deficiencies in the child's IEP or placement or in their implementation, it must take immediate steps to remedy those deficiencies.

(Authority: 20 U.S.C. 1415(k)(4))

Sec. 300.524 Determination that behavior was not manifestation of disability.

(a) General. If the result of the review described in Sec. 300.523 is a determination, consistent with Sec. 300.523(d), that the behavior of the child with a disability was not a manifestation of the child's disability, the relevant disciplinary procedures applicable to children without disabilities may be applied to the child in the same manner in which they would be applied to children without disabilities, except as provided in Sec. 300.121(d).

(b) Additional requirement. If the public agency initiates disciplinary procedures applicable to all children, the agency shall ensure that the special education and disciplinary records of the child with a disability are transmitted for consideration by the person or persons making the final determination regarding the disciplinary action.

(c) Child's status during due process proceedings. Except as provided in Sec. 300.526, Sec. 300.514 applies if a parent requests a hearing to challenge a determination, made through the review described in Sec. 300.523, that the behavior of the child was not a manifestation of the child's disability.

(Authority: 20 U.S.C. 1415(k)(5))

Sec. 300.525 Parent appeal.

(a) General.

(1) If the child's parent disagrees with a determination that the child's behavior was not a manifestation of the child's disability or with any decision regarding placement under Secs. 300.520-300.528, the parent may request a hearing.

(2) The State or local educational agency shall arrange for an expedited hearing in any case described in paragraph (a)(1) of this section if a hearing is requested by a parent.

(b) Review of decision. (1) In reviewing a decision with respect to the manifestation determination, the hearing officer shall determine whether the public agency has demonstrated that the child's behavior was not a manifestation of the child's disability consistent with the requirements of Sec. 300.523(d).

(2) In reviewing a decision under Sec. 300.520(a)(2) to place the child in an interim alternative educational setting, the hearing officer shall apply the standards in Sec. 300.521.

(Authority: 20 U.S.C. 1415(k)(6))

Sec. 300.526 Placement during appeals.

(a) General. If a parent requests a hearing or an appeal regarding a disciplinary action described in Sec. 300.520(a)(2) or 300.521 to challenge the interim alternative educational setting or the manifestation determination, the child must remain in the interim alternative educational setting pending the decision of the hearing officer or until the expiration of the time period provided for in Sec. 300.520(a)(2) or 300.521, whichever occurs first, unless the parent and the State agency or local educational agency agree otherwise.

(b) Current placement. If a child is placed in an interim alternative educational setting pursuant to Sec. 300.520(a)(2) or 300.521 and school personnel propose to change the child's placement after expiration of the interim alternative placement, during the pendency of any proceeding to challenge the proposed change in placement the child must remain in the current placement (the child's placement prior to the interim alternative educational setting), except as provided in paragraph (c) of this section.

(c) Expedited hearing.

(1) If school personnel maintain that it is dangerous for the child to be in the current placement (placement prior to removal to the interim alternative education setting) during the pendency of the due process proceedings, the LEA may request an expedited due process hearing.

(2) In determining whether the child may be placed in the alternative educational setting or in another appropriate placement ordered by the hearing officer, the hearing officer shall apply the standards in Sec. 300.521.

(3) A placement ordered pursuant to paragraph (c)(2) of this section may not be longer than 45 days.

(4) The procedure in paragraph (c) of this section may be repeated, as necessary.

(Authority: 20 U.S.C. 1415(k)(7))

Sec. 300.527 Protections for children not yet eligible for special education and related services.

(a) General. A child who has not been determined to be eligible for special education and related services under this part and who has engaged in behavior that violated any rule or code of conduct of the local educational agency, including any behavior described in Secs. 300.520 or 300.521, may assert any of the protections provided for in this part if the LEA had knowledge (as determined in accordance with paragraph (b) of this section) that the child was a child with a disability before the behavior that precipitated the disciplinary action occurred.

(b) Basis of knowledge. An LEA must be deemed to have knowledge that a child is a child with a disability if—

(1) The parent of the child has expressed concern in writing (or orally if the parent does not know how to write or has a disability that prevents a written statement) to personnel of the appropriate educational agency that the child is in need of special education and related services;

(2) The behavior or performance of the child demonstrates the need for these services, in accordance with Sec. 300.7;

(3) The parent of the child has requested an evaluation of the child pursuant to Secs. 300.530-300.536; or

(4) The teacher of the child, or other personnel of the local educational agency, has expressed concern about the behavior or performance of the child to the director of special education of the agency or to other personnel in accordance with the agency's established child find or special education referral system.

(c) Exception. A public agency would not be deemed to have knowledge under paragraph (b) of this section if, as a result of receiving the information specified in that paragraph, the agency—

(1) Either—

(i) Conducted an evaluation under Secs. 300.530-300.536, and determined that the child was not a child with a disability under this part; or

(ii) Determined that an evaluation was not necessary; and

(2) Provided notice to the child's parents of its determination under paragraph (c)(1) of this section, consistent with Sec. 300.503.

(d) Conditions that apply if no basis of knowledge.

(1) General. If an LEA does not have knowledge that a child is a child with a disability (in accordance with paragraphs (b) and (c) of this section) prior to taking disciplinary measures against the child, the child may be subjected to the same disciplinary measures as measures applied to children without disabilities who engaged in comparable behaviors consistent with paragraph (d)(2) of this section.

(2) Limitations.

(i) If a request is made for an evaluation of a child during the time period in which the child is subjected to disciplinary measures under Sec. 300.520 or 300.521, the evaluation must be conducted in an expedited manner.

(ii) Until the evaluation is completed, the child remains in the educational placement determined by school authorities, which can include suspension or expulsion without educational services.

(iii) If the child is determined to be a child with a disability, taking into consideration information from the evaluation conducted by the agency and information provided by the parents, the agency shall provide special education and related services in accordance with the provisions of this part, including the requirements of Secs. 300.520- 300.529 and section 612(a)(1)(A) of the Act.

(Authority: 20 U.S.C. 1415(k)(8))

Sec. 300.528 Expedited due process hearings.

(a) Expedited due process hearings under Secs. 300.521-300.526 must—

(1) Meet the requirements of Sec. 300.509, except that a State may provide that the time periods identified in Secs. 300.509(a)(3) and Sec. 300.509(b) for purposes of expedited due process hearings under Secs. 300.521-300.526 are not less than two business days; and

(2) Be conducted by a due process hearing officer who satisfies the requirements of Sec. 300.508.

(b)(1) Each State shall establish a timeline for expedited due process hearings that results in a written decision being mailed to the parties within 45 days of the public agency's receipt of the request for the hearing, without exceptions or extensions.

(2) The timeline established under paragraph (b)(1) of this section must be the same for hearings requested by parents or public agencies.

(c) A State may establish different procedural rules for expedited hearings under Secs. 300.521-300.526 than it has established for due process hearings under Sec. 300.507.

(d) The decisions on expedited due process hearings are appealable consistent with Sec. 300.510.

(Authority: 20 U.S.C. 1415(k)(2), (6), (7))

Sec. 300.529 Referral to and action by law enforcement and judicial authorities.

(a) Nothing in this part prohibits an agency from reporting a crime committed by a child with a disability to appropriate authorities or to prevent State law enforcement and judicial authorities from exercising their responsibilities with regard to the application of Federal and State law to crimes committed by a child with a disability.

(b)(1) An agency reporting a crime committed by a child with a disability shall ensure that copies of the special education and disciplinary records of the child are transmitted for consideration by the appropriate authorities to whom it reports the crime.

(2) An agency reporting a crime under this section may transmit copies of the child's special education and disciplinary records only to the extent that the transmission is permitted by the Family Educational Rights and Privacy Act.

(Authority: 20 U.S.C. 1415(k)(9))

Procedures for Evaluation and Determination of Eligibility

Sec. 300.530 General.

Each SEA shall ensure that each public agency establishes and implements procedures that meet the requirements of Secs. 300.531-300.536.

(Authority: 20 U.S.C. 1414(b)(3); 1412(a)(7))

Sec. 300.531 Initial evaluation.

Each public agency shall conduct a full and individual initial evaluation, in accordance with Secs. 300.532 and 300.533, before the initial provision of special education and related services to a child with a disability under Part B of the Act.

(Authority: 20 U.S.C. 1414(a)(1))

Sec. 300.532 Evaluation procedures.

Each public agency shall ensure, at a minimum, that the following requirements are met:

(a)(1) Tests and other evaluation materials used to assess a child under Part B of the Act—

(i) Are selected and administered so as not to be discriminatory on a racial or cultural basis; and

(ii) Are provided and administered in the child's native language or other mode of communication, unless it is clearly not feasible to do so; and

(2) Materials and procedures used to assess a child with limited English proficiency are selected and administered to ensure that they measure the extent to which the child has a disability and needs special education, rather than measuring the child's English language skills.

(b) A variety of assessment tools and strategies are used to gather relevant functional and developmental information about the child, including information provided by the parent, and information related to enabling the child to be involved in and progress in the general curriculum (or for a preschool child, to participate in appropriate activities), that may assist in determining—

(1) Whether the child is a child with a disability under Sec. 300.7;and

(2) The content of the child's IEP.

(c)(1) Any standardized tests that are given to a child—

(i) Have been validated for the specific purpose for which they are used; and

(ii) Are administered by trained and knowledgeable personnel in accordance with any instructions provided by the producer of the tests.

(2) If an assessment is not conducted under standard conditions, a description of the extent to which it varied from standard conditions (e.g., the qualifications of the person administering the test, or the method of test administration) must be included in the evaluation report.

(d) Tests and other evaluation materials include those tailored to assess specific areas of educational need and not merely those that are designed to provide a single general intelligence quotient.

(e) Tests are selected and administered so as best to ensure that if a test is administered to a child with impaired sensory, manual, or speaking skills, the test results accurately reflect the child's aptitude or achievement level or whatever other factors the test purports to measure, rather than reflecting the child's impaired sensory, manual, or speaking skills (unless those skills are the factors that the test purports to measure).

(f) No single procedure is used as the sole criterion for determining whether a child is a child with a disability and for determining an appropriate educational program for the child.

(g) The child is assessed in all areas related to the suspected disability, including, if appropriate, health, vision, hearing, social and emotional status, general intelligence, academic performance, communicative status, and motor abilities.

(h) In evaluating each child with a disability under Secs. 300.531-300.536, the evaluation is sufficiently comprehensive to identify all of the child's special education and related services needs, whether or not commonly linked to the disability category in which the child has been classified.

(i) The public agency uses technically sound instruments that may assess the relative contribution of cognitive and behavioral factors, in addition to physical or developmental factors.

(j) The public agency uses assessment tools and strategies that provide relevant information that directly assists persons in determining the educational needs of the child.

(Authority: 20 U.S.C. 1412(a)(6)(B), 1414(b)(2) and (3))

Sec. 300.533 Determination of needed evaluation data.

(a) Review of existing evaluation data.

As part of an initial evaluation (if appropriate) and as part of any reevaluation under Part B of the Act, a group that includes the individuals described in Sec. 300.344, and other qualified professionals, as appropriate, shall—

(1) Review existing evaluation data on the child, including—

(i) Evaluations and information provided by the parents of the child;

(ii) Current classroom-based assessments and observations; and

(iii) Observations by teachers and related services providers; and

(2) On the basis of that review, and input from the child's parents, identify what additional data, if any, are needed to determine—

(i) Whether the child has a particular category of disability, as described in Sec. 300.7, or, in case of a reevaluation of a child, whether the child continues to have such a disability;

(ii) The present levels of performance and educational needs of the child;

(iii) Whether the child needs special education and related services, or in the case of a reevaluation of a child, whether the child continues to need special education and related services; and

(iv) Whether any additions or modifications to the special education and related services are needed to enable the child to meet the measurable annual goals set out in the IEP of the child and to participate, as appropriate, in the general curriculum.

(b) Conduct of review. The group described in paragraph (a) of this section may conduct its review without a meeting.

(c) Need for additional data. The public agency shall administer tests and other evaluation materials as may be needed to produce the data identified under paragraph (a) of this section.

(d) Requirements if additional data are not needed.

(1) If the determination under paragraph (a) of this section is that no additional data are needed to determine whether the child continues to be a child with a disability, the public agency shall notify the child's parents—

(i) Of that determination and the reasons for it; and

(ii) Of the right of the parents to request an assessment to determine whether, for purposes of services under this part, the child continues to be a child with a disability.

(2) The public agency is not required to conduct the assessment described in paragraph (d)(1)(ii) of this section unless requested to do so by the child's parents.

(Authority: 20 U.S.C. 1414(c)(1), (2) and (4))

Sec. 300.534 Determination of eligibility.

(a) Upon completing the administration of tests and other evaluation materials—

(1) A group of qualified professionals and the parent of the child must determine whether the child is a child with a disability, as defined in Sec. 300.7; and

(2) The public agency must provide a copy of the evaluation report and the documentation of determination of eligibility to the parent.

(b) A child may not be determined to be eligible under this part if—

(1) The determinant factor for that eligibility determination is—

(i) Lack of instruction in reading or math; or

(ii) Limited English proficiency; and

(2) The child does not otherwise meet the eligibility criteria under Sec. 300.7(a).

(c)(1) A public agency must evaluate a child with a disability in accordance with Secs. 300.532 and 300.533 before determining that the child is no longer a child with a disability.

(2) The evaluation described in paragraph (c)(1) of this section is not required before the termination of a student's eligibility under Part B of the Act due to graduation with a regular high school diploma, or exceeding the age eligibility for FAPE under State law.

(Authority: 20 U.S.C. 1414(b)(4) and (5), (c)(5))

Sec. 300.535 Procedures for determining eligibility and placement.

(a) In interpreting evaluation data for the purpose of determining if a child is a child with a disability under Sec. 300.7, and the educational needs of the child, each public agency shall—

(1) Draw upon information from a variety of sources, including aptitude and achievement tests, parent input, teacher recommendations, physical condition, social or cultural background, and adaptive behavior; and

(2) Ensure that information obtained from all of these sources is documented and carefully considered.

(b) If a determination is made that a child has a disability and needs special education and related services, an IEP must be developed for the child in accordance with Secs. 300.340-300.350.

(Authority: 20 U.S.C. 1412(a)(6), 1414(b)(4))

Sec. 300.536 Reevaluation.

Each public agency shall ensure—

(a) That the IEP of each child with a disability is reviewed in accordance with Secs. 300.340-300.350; and

(b) That a reevaluation of each child, in accordance with Secs. 300.532-300.535, is conducted if conditions warrant an evaluation, or if the child's parent or teacher requests an evaluation, but at least once every three years.

(Authority: 20 U.S.C. 1414(a)(2))

Additional Procedures for Evaluating Children With Specific Learning Disabilities

Sec. 300.540 Additional team members.

The determination of whether a child suspected of having a specific learning disability is a child with a disability as defined in Sec. 300.7, must be made by the child's parents and a team of qualified professionals which must include—

(a)(1) The child's regular teacher; or

(2) If the child does not have a regular teacher, a regular classroom teacher qualified to teach a child of his or her age; or

(3) For a child of less than school age, an individual qualified by the SEA to teach a child of his or her age; and

(b) At least one person qualified to conduct individual diagnostic examinations of children, such as a school psychologist, speech-language pathologist, or remedial reading teacher.

(Authority: Sec. 5(b), Pub. L. 94-142)

Sec. 300.541 Criteria for determining the existence of a specific learning disability.

(a) A team may determine that a child has a specific learning disability if—

(1) The child does not achieve commensurate with his or her age and ability levels in one or more of the areas listed in paragraph (a)(2) of this section, if provided with learning experiences appropriate for the child's age and ability levels; and

(2) The team finds that a child has a severe discrepancy between achievement and intellectual ability in one or more of the following areas:

(i) Oral expression.

(ii) Listening comprehension.

(iii) Written expression.

(iv) Basic reading skill.

(v) Reading comprehension.

(vi) Mathematics calculation.

(vii) Mathematics reasoning.

(b) The team may not identify a child as having a specific learning disability if the severe discrepancy between ability and achievement is primarily the result of—

(1) A visual, hearing, or motor impairment;

(2) Mental retardation;

(3) Emotional disturbance; or

(4) Environmental, cultural or economic disadvantage.

(Authority: Sec. 5(b), Pub. L. 94-142)

Sec. 300.542 Observation.

(a) At least one team member other than the child's regular teacher shall observe the child's academic performance in the regular classroom setting.

(b) In the case of a child of less than school age or out of school, a team member shall observe the child in an environment appropriate for a child of that age.

(Authority: Sec. 5(b), Pub. L. 94-142)

Sec. 300.543 Written report.

(a) For a child suspected of having a specific learning disability, the documentation of the team's determination of eligibility, as required by Sec. 300.534(a)(2), must include a statement of—

(1) Whether the child has a specific learning disability;

(2) The basis for making the determination;

(3) The relevant behavior noted during the observation of the child;

(4) The relationship of that behavior to the child's academic functioning;

(5) The educationally relevant medical findings, if any;

(6) Whether there is a severe discrepancy between achievement and ability that is not correctable without special education and related services; and

(7) The determination of the team concerning the effects of environmental, cultural, or economic disadvantage.

(b) Each team member shall certify in writing whether the report reflects his or her conclusion. If it does not reflect his or her conclusion, the team member must submit a separate statement presenting his or her conclusions.

(Authority: Sec. 5(b), Pub. L. 94-142))

Least Restrictive Environment (LRE)

Sec. 300.550 General LRE requirements.

(a) Except as provided in Sec. 300.311(b) and (c), a State shall demonstrate to the satisfaction of the Secretary that the State has in effect policies and procedures to ensure that it meets the requirements of Secs. 300.550-300.556.

(b) Each public agency shall ensure—

(1) That to the maximum extent appropriate, children with disabilities, including children in public or private institutions or other care facilities, are educated with children who are non disabled; and

(2) That special classes, separate schooling or other removal of children with disabilities from the regular educational environment occurs only if the nature or severity of the disability is such that education in regular classes with the use of supplementary aids and services cannot be achieved satisfactorily.

(Authority: 20 U.S.C. 1412(a)(5))

Sec. 300.551 Continuum of alternative placements.

(a) Each public agency shall ensure that a continuum of alternative placements is available to meet the needs of children with disabilities for special education and related services.

(b) The continuum required in paragraph (a) of this section must—

(1) Include the alternative placements listed in the definition of special education under Sec. 300.26 (instruction in regular classes, special classes, special schools, home instruction, and instruction in hospitals and institutions); and

(2) Make provision for supplementary services (such as resource room or itinerant instruction) to be provided in conjunction with regular class placement.

(Authority: 20 U.S.C. 1412(a)(5))

Sec. 300.552 Placements.

In determining the educational placement of a child with a disability, including a preschool child with a disability, each public agency shall ensure that—

(a) The placement decision—

(1) Is made by a group of persons, including the parents, and other persons knowledgeable about the child, the meaning of the evaluation data, and the placement options; and

(2) Is made in conformity with the LRE provisions of this subpart, including Secs. 300.550-300.554;

(b) The child's placement—

(1) Is determined at least annually;

(2) Is based on the child's IEP; and

(3) Is as close as possible to the child's home;

(c) Unless the IEP of a child with a disability requires some other arrangement, the child is educated in the school that he or she would attend if nondisabled;

(d) In selecting the LRE, consideration is given to any potential harmful effect on the child or on the quality of services that he or she needs; and

(e) A child with a disability is not removed from education in age-appropriate regular classrooms solely because of needed modifications in the general curriculum.

(Authority: 20 U.S.C. 1412(a)(5))

Sec. 300.553 Nonacademic settings.

In providing or arranging for the provision of nonacademic and extracurricular services and activities, including meals, recess periods, and the services and activities set forth in Sec. 300.306, each public agency shall ensure that each child with a disability participates with nondisabled children in those services and activities to the maximum extent appropriate to the needs of that child.

(Authority: 20 U.S.C. 1412(a)(5))

Sec. 300.554 Children in public or private institutions.

Except as provided in Sec. 300.600(d), an SEA must ensure that Sec. 300.550 is effectively implemented, including, if necessary, making arrangements with public and private institutions (such as a memorandum of agreement or special implementation procedures).

(Authority: 20 U.S.C. 1412(a)(5))

Sec. 300.555 Technical assistance and training activities.

Each SEA shall carry out activities to ensure that teachers and administrators in all public agencies—

(a) Are fully informed about their responsibilities for implementing Sec. 300.550; and

(b) Are provided with technical assistance and training necessary to assist them in this effort.

(Authority: 20 U.S.C. 1412(a)(5))

Sec. 300.556 Monitoring activities.

(a) The SEA shall carry out activities to ensure that Sec. 300.550 is implemented by each public agency.

(b) If there is evidence that a public agency makes placements that are inconsistent with Sec. 300.550, the SEA shall—

(1) Review the public agency's justification for its actions; and

(2) Assist in planning and implementing any necessary corrective action.

(Authority: 20 U.S.C. 1412(a)(5))

Confidentiality of Information

Sec. 300.560 Definitions.

As used in Secs. 300.560-300.577—

(a) Destruction means physical destruction or removal of personal identifiers from information so that the information is no longer personally identifiable.

(b) Education records means the type of records covered under the definition of "education records" in 34 CFR part 99 (the regulations implementing the Family Educational Rights and Privacy Act of 1974).

(c) Participating agency means any agency or institution that collects, maintains, or uses personally identifiable information, or from which information is obtained, under Part B of the Act.

(Authority: 20 U.S.C. 1221e-3, 1412(a)(8), 1417(c))

Sec. 300.561 Notice to parents.

(a) The SEA shall give notice that is adequate to fully inform parents about the requirements of Sec. 300.127, including—

(1) A description of the extent that the notice is given in the native languages of the various population groups in the State;

(2) A description of the children on whom personally identifiable information is maintained, the types of information sought, the methods the State intends to use in gathering the information (including the sources from whom information is gathered), and the uses to be made of the information;

(3) A summary of the policies and procedures that participating agencies must follow regarding storage, disclosure to third parties, retention, and destruction of personally identifiable information; and

(4) A description of all of the rights of parents and children regarding this information, including the rights under the Family Educational Rights and Privacy Act of 1974 and implementing regulations in 34 CFR part 99.

(b) Before any major identification, location, or evaluation activity, the notice must be published or announced in newspapers or other media, or both, with circulation adequate to notify parents throughout the State of the activity.

(Authority: 20 U.S.C. 1412(a)(8), 1417(c))

Sec. 300.562 Access rights.

(a) Each participating agency shall permit parents to inspect and review any education records relating to their children that are collected, maintained, or used by the agency under this part. The agency shall comply with a request without unnecessary delay and before any meeting regarding an IEP, or any hearing pursuant to Secs. 300.507 and 300.521-300.528, and in no case more than 45 days after the request has been made.

(b) The right to inspect and review education records under this section includes—

(1) The right to a response from the participating agency to reasonable requests for explanations and interpretations of the records;

(2) The right to request that the agency provide copies of the records containing the information if failure to provide those copies would effectively prevent the parent from exercising the right to inspect and review the records; and

(3) The right to have a representative of the parent inspect and review the records.

(c) An agency may presume that the parent has authority to inspect and review records relating to his or her child unless the agency has been advised that the parent does not have the authority under applicable State law governing such matters as guardianship, separation, and divorce.

(Authority: 20 U.S.C. 1412(a)(8), 1417(c))

Sec. 300.563 Record of access.

Each participating agency shall keep a record of parties obtaining access to education records collected, maintained, or used under Part B of the Act (except access by parents and authorized employees of the participating agency), including the name of the party, the date access was given, and the purpose for which the party is authorized to use the records.

(Authority: 20 U.S.C. 1412(a)(8), 1417(c))

Sec. 300.564 Records on more than one child.

If any education record includes information on more than one child, the parents of those children have the right to inspect and review only the information relating to their child or to be informed of that specific information.

(Authority: 20 U.S.C. 1412(a)(8), 1417(c))

Sec. 300.565 List of types and locations of information.

Each participating agency shall provide parents on request a list of the types and locations of education records collected, maintained, or used by the agency.

(Authority: 20 U.S.C. 1412(a)(8), 1417(c))

Sec. 300.566 Fees.

(a) Each participating agency may charge a fee for copies of records that are made for parents under this part if the fee does not effectively prevent the parents from exercising their right to inspect and review those records.

(b) A participating agency may not charge a fee to search for or to retrieve information under this part.

(Authority: 20 U.S.C. 1412(a)(8), 1417(c))

Sec. 300.567 Amendment of records at parent's request.

(a) A parent who believes that information in the education records collected, maintained, or used under this part is inaccurate or misleading or violates the privacy or other rights of the child may request the participating agency that maintains the information to amend the information.

(b) The agency shall decide whether to amend the information in accordance with the request within a reasonable period of time of receipt of the request.

(c) If the agency decides to refuse to amend the information in accordance with the request, it shall inform the parent of the refusal and advise the parent of the right to a hearing under Sec. 300.568.

(Authority: 20 U.S.C. 1412(a)(8); 1417(c))

Sec. 300.568 Opportunity for a hearing.

The agency shall, on request, provide an opportunity for a hearing to challenge information in education records to ensure that it is not inaccurate, misleading, or otherwise in violation of the privacy or other rights of the child.

(Authority: 20 U.S.C. 1412(a)(8), 1417(c))

Sec. 300.569 Result of hearing.

(a) If, as a result of the hearing, the agency decides that the information is inaccurate, misleading or otherwise in violation of the privacy or other rights of the child, it shall amend the information accordingly and so inform the parent in writing.

(b) If, as a result of the hearing, the agency decides that the information is not inaccurate, misleading, or otherwise in violation of the privacy or other rights of the child, it shall inform the parent of the right to place in the records it maintains on the child a statement commenting on the information or setting forth any reasons for disagreeing with the decision of the agency.

(c) Any explanation placed in the records of the child under this section must—

(1) Be maintained by the agency as part of the records of the child as long as the record or contested portion is maintained by the agency; and

(2) If the records of the child or the contested portion is disclosed by the agency to any party, the explanation must also be disclosed to the party.

(Authority: 20 U.S.C. 1412(a)(8), 1417(c))

Sec. 300.570 Hearing procedures.

A hearing held under Sec. 300.568 must be conducted according to the procedures under 34 CFR 99.22.

(Authority: 20 U.S.C. 1412(a)(8), 1417(c))

Sec. 300.571 Consent.

(a) Except as to disclosures addressed in Sec. 300.529(b) for which parental consent is not required by Part 99, parental consent must be obtained before personally identifiable information is—

(1) Disclosed to anyone other than officials of participating agencies collecting or using the information under this part, subject to paragraph (b) of this section; or

(2) Used for any purpose other than meeting a requirement of this part.

(b) An educational agency or institution subject to 34 CFR part 99 may not release information from education records to participating agencies without parental consent unless authorized to do so under part 99.

(c) The SEA shall provide policies and procedures that are used in the event that a parent refuses to provide consent under this section.

(Authority: 20 U.S.C. 1412(a)(8), 1417(c))

Sec. 300.572 Safeguards.

(a) Each participating agency shall protect the confidentiality of personally identifiable information at collection, storage, disclosure, and destruction stages.

(b) One official at each participating agency shall assume responsibility for ensuring the confidentiality of any personally identifiable information.

(c) All persons collecting or using personally identifiable information must receive training or instruction regarding the State's policies and procedures under Sec. 300.127 and 34 CFR part 99.

(d) Each participating agency shall maintain, for public inspection, a current listing of the names and positions of those employees within the agency who may have access to personally identifiable information.

(Authority: 20 U.S.C. 1412(a)(8), 1417(c))

Sec. 300.573 Destruction of information.

(a) The public agency shall inform parents when personally identifiable information collected, maintained, or used under this part is no longer needed to provide educational services to the child.

(b) The information must be destroyed at the request of the parents. However, a permanent record of a student's name, address, and phone number, his or her grades, attendance record, classes attended, grade level completed, and year completed may be maintained without time limitation.

(Authority: 20 U.S.C. 1412(a)(8), 1417(c))

Sec. 300.574 Children's rights.

(a) The SEA shall provide policies and procedures regarding the extent to which children are afforded rights of privacy similar to those afforded to parents, taking into consideration the age of the child and type or severity of disability.

(b) Under the regulations for the Family Educational Rights and Privacy Act of 1974 (34 CFR 99.5(a)), the rights of parents regarding education records are transferred to the student at age 18.

(c) If the rights accorded to parents under Part B of the Act are transferred to a student who reaches the age of majority, consistent with Sec. 300.517, the rights regarding educational records in Secs. 300.562-300.573 must also be transferred to the student. However, the public agency must provide any notice required under section 615 of the Act to the student and the parents.

(Authority: 20 U.S.C. 1412(a)(8), 1417(c))

Sec. 300.575 Enforcement.

The SEA shall provide the policies and procedures, including sanctions, that the State uses to ensure that its policies and procedures are followed and that the requirements of the Act and the regulations in this part are met.

(Authority: 20 U.S.C. 1412(a)(8), 1417(c))

Sec. 300.576 Disciplinary information.

(a) The State may require that a public agency include in the records of a child with a disability a statement of any current or previous disciplinary action that has been taken against the child and transmit the statement to the same extent that the disciplinary information is included in, and transmitted with, the student records of nondisabled children.

(b) The statement may include a description of any behavior engaged in by the child that required disciplinary action, a description of the disciplinary action taken, and any other information that is relevant to the safety of the child and other individuals involved with the child.

(c) If the State adopts such a policy, and the child transfers from one school to another, the transmission of any of the child's records must include both the child's current individualized education program and any statement of current or previous disciplinary action that has been taken against the child.

(Authority: 20 U.S.C. 1413(j))

Sec. 300.577 Department use of personally identifiable information.

If the Department or its authorized representatives collect any personally identifiable information regarding children with disabilities that is not subject to 5 U.S.C. 552a (the Privacy Act of 1974), the Secretary applies the requirements of 5 U.S.C. 552a (b)(1)-(2), (4)-(11); (c); (d); (e)(1), (2), (3)(A), (B), and (D),(5)-(10); (h); (m); and (n); and the regulations implementing those provisions in 34 CFR part 5b.

(Authority: 20 U.S.C. 1412(a)(8), 1417(c))

Department Procedures

Subpart F—

State Administration

Sec. 300.650 Establishment of advisory panels.

(a) Each State shall establish and maintain, in accordance with Secs. 300.650-300.653, a State advisory panel on the education of children with disabilities.

(b) The advisory panel must be appointed by the Governor or any other official authorized under State law to make those appointments.

(c) If a State has an existing advisory panel that can perform the functions in Sec. 300.652, the State may modify the existing panel so that it fulfills all of the requirements of Secs. 300.650-300.653, instead of establishing a new advisory panel.

(Authority: 20 U.S.C. 1412(a)(21)(A))

Sec. 300.651 Membership.

(a) General. The membership of the State advisory panel must consist of members appointed by the Governor, or any other official authorized under State law to make these appointments, that is representative of the State population and that is composed of individuals involved in, or concerned with the education of children with disabilities, including—

(1) Parents of children with disabilities;

(2) Individuals with disabilities;

(3) Teachers;

(4) Representatives of institutions of higher education that prepare special education and related services personnel;

(5) State and local education officials;

(6) Administrators of programs for children with disabilities;

(7) Representatives of other State agencies involved in the financing or delivery of related services to children with disabilities;

(8) Representatives of private schools and public charter schools;

(9) At least one representative of a vocational, community, or business organization concerned with the provision of transition services to children with disabilities; and

(10) Representatives from the State juvenile and adult corrections agencies.

(b) Special rule. A majority of the members of the panel must be individuals with disabilities or parents of children with disabilities.

(Authority: 20 U.S.C. 1412(a)(21)(B) and (C))

Sec. 300.652 Advisory panel functions.

(a) General. The State advisory panel shall—

(1) Advise the SEA of unmet needs within the State in the education of children with disabilities;

(2) Comment publicly on any rules or regulations proposed by the State regarding the education of children with disabilities;

(3) Advise the SEA in developing evaluations and reporting on data to the Secretary under section 618 of the Act;

(4) Advise the SEA in developing corrective action plans to address findings identified in Federal monitoring reports under Part B of the Act; and

(5) Advise the SEA in developing and implementing policies relating to the coordination of services for children with disabilities.

(b) Advising on eligible students with disabilities in adult prisons. The advisory panel also shall advise on the education of eligible students with disabilities who have been convicted as adults and incarcerated in adult prisons, even if, consistent with Sec. 300.600(d), a State assigns general supervision responsibility for those students to a public agency other than an SEA.

(Authority: 20 U.S.C. 1412(a)(21)(D))

Sec. 300.653 Advisory panel procedures.

(a) The advisory panel shall meet as often as necessary to conduct its business.

(b) By July 1 of each year, the advisory panel shall submit an annual report of panel activities and suggestions to the SEA. This report must be made available to the public in a manner consistent with other public reporting requirements of Part B of the Act.

(c) Official minutes must be kept on all panel meetings and must be made available to the public on request.

(d) All advisory panel meetings and agenda items must be announced enough in advance of the meeting to afford interested parties a reasonable opportunity to attend. Meetings must be open to the public.

(e) Interpreters and other necessary services must be provided at panel meetings for panel members or participants. The State may pay for these services from funds under Sec. 300.620.

(f) The advisory panel shall serve without compensation but the State must reimburse the panel for reasonable and necessary expenses for attending meetings and performing duties. The State may use funds under Sec. 300.620 for this purpose.

(Authority: 20 U.S.C. 1412(a)(21))

State Complaint Procedures

Sec. 300.660 Adoption of State complaint procedures.

(a) General. Each SEA shall adopt written procedures for—

(1) Resolving any complaint, including a complaint filed by an organization or individual from another State, that meets the requirements of Sec. 300.662 by—

(i) Providing for the filing of a complaint with the SEA; and

(ii) At the SEA's discretion, providing for the filing of a complaint with a public agency and the right to have the SEA review the public agency's decision on the complaint; and

(2) Widely disseminating to parents and other interested individuals, including parent training and information centers, protection and advocacy agencies, independent living centers, and other appropriate entities, the State's procedures under Secs. 300.660-300.662.

(b) Remedies for denial of appropriate services. In resolving a complaint in which it has found a failure to provide appropriate services, an SEA, pursuant to its general supervisory authority under Part B of the Act, must address:

(1) How to remediate the denial of those services, including, as appropriate, the awarding of monetary reimbursement or other corrective action appropriate to the needs of the child; and

(2) Appropriate future provision of services for all children with disabilities.

(Authority: 20 U.S.C. 1221e-3)

Sec. 300.661 Minimum State complaint procedures.

(a) Time limit; minimum procedures. Each SEA shall include in its complaint procedures a time limit of 60 days after a complaint is filed under Sec. 300.660(a) to—

(1) Carry out an independent on-site investigation, if the SEA determines that an investigation is necessary;

(2) Give the complainant the opportunity to submit additional information, either orally or in writing, about the allegations in the complaint;

(3) Review all relevant information and make an independent determination as to whether the public agency is violating a requirement of Part B of the Act or of this part; and

(4) Issue a written decision to the complainant that addresses each allegation in the complaint and contains—

(i) Findings of fact and conclusions; and

(ii) The reasons for the SEA's final decision.

(b) Time extension; final decision; implementation. The SEA's procedures described in paragraph (a) of this section also must—

(1) Permit an extension of the time limit under paragraph (a) of this section only if exceptional circumstances exist with respect to a particular complaint; and

(2) Include procedures for effective implementation of the SEA's final decision, if needed, including—

(i) Technical assistance activities;

(ii) Negotiations; and

(iii) Corrective actions to achieve compliance.

(c) Complaints filed under this section, and due process hearings under Secs. 300.507 and 300.520-300.528.

(1) If a written complaint is received that is also the subject of a due process hearing under Sec. 300.507 or Secs. 300.520-300.528, or contains multiple issues, of which one or more are part of that hearing, the State must set aside any part of the complaint that is being addressed in the due process hearing, until the conclusion of the hearing. However, any issue in the complaint that is not a part of the due process action must be resolved using the time limit and procedures described in paragraphs (a) and (b) of this section.

(2) If an issue is raised in a complaint filed under this section that has previously been decided in a due process hearing involving the same parties—

(i) The hearing decision is binding; and

(ii) The SEA must inform the complainant to that effect.

(3) A complaint alleging a public agency's failure to implement a due process decision must be resolved by the SEA.

(Authority: 20 U.S.C. 1221e-3)

Sec. 300.662 Filing a complaint.

(a) An organization or individual may file a signed written complaint under the procedures described in Secs. 300.660-300.661.

(b) The complaint must include—

(1) A statement that a public agency has violated a requirement of Part B of the Act or of this part; and

(2) The facts on which the statement is based.

(c) The complaint must allege a violation that occurred not more than one year prior to the date that the complaint is received in accordance with Sec. 300.660(a) unless a longer period is reasonable because the violation is continuing, or the complainant is requesting compensatory services for a violation that occurred not more than three years prior to the date the complaint is received under Sec. 300.660(a).

(Authority: 20 U.S.C. 1221e-3)

Section 504 of the Rehabilitation Act of 1973 (Key Regulations)

Part 104—Nondiscrimination on the Basis of Handicap in Programs and Activities Receiving Federal Financial Assistance

Sec. 104.1 Purpose

The purpose of this part is to effectuate section 504 of the Rehabilitation Act of 1973, which is designed to eliminate discrimination on the basis of handicap in any program or activity receiving Federal financial assistance.

Sec. 104.2 Application

This part applies to each recipient of Federal financial assistance from the Department of Education and to each program or activity that receives or benefits from such assistance.

Sec. 104.3 Definitions

As used in this part, the term:

(a) The Act means the Rehabilitation Act of 1973, Pub. L. 93-112, as amended by the Rehabilitation Act Amendments of 1974, Pub. L. 93-516, 29 U.S.C. 794.

(b) Section 504 means section 504 of the Act.

(c) Education of the Handicapped Act means that statute as amended by the Education for all Handicapped Children Act of 1975, Pub. L. 94-142, 20 U.S.C. 1401 et seq.

(d) Department means the Department of Education.

(e) Assistant Secretary means the Assistant Secretary for Civil Rights of the Department of Education.

(f) Recipient means any state or its political subdivision, any instrumentality of a state or its political subdivision, any public or private agency, institution, organization, or other entity, or any person to which Federal financial assistance is extended directly or through another recipient, including any successor, assignee, or transferee of a recipient, but excluding the ultimate beneficiary of the assistance.

(g) Applicant for assistance means one who submits an application, request, or plan required to be approved by a Department official or by a recipient as a condition to becoming a recipient.

(h) Federal financial assistance means any grant, loan, contract (other than a procurement contract or a contract of insurance or guaranty), or any other arrangement by which the Department provides or otherwise makes available assistance in the form of:

(1) Funds;

(2) Services of Federal personnel; or

(3) Real and personal property or any interest in or use of such property, including:

(i) Transfers or leases of such property for less than fair market value or for reduced consideration; and

(ii) Proceeds from a subsequent transfer or lease of such property if the Federal share of its fair market value is not returned to the Federal Government.

(i) Facility means all or any portion of buildings, structures, equipment, roads, walks, parking lots, or other real or personal property or interest in such property.

(j) Handicapped person—

(1) Handicapped persons means any person who (i) has a physical or mental impairment which substantially limits one or more major life activities, (ii) has a record of such an impairment, or (iii) is regarded as having such an impairment.

(2) As used in paragraph (j)(1) of this section, the phrase:

(i) Physical or mental impairment means (A) any physiological disorder or condition, cosmetic disfigurement, or anatomical loss affecting one or more of the following body systems: neurological; musculoskeletal; special sense organs; respiratory, including speech organs; cardiovascular; reproductive, digestive, genito-urinary; hemic and lymphatic; skin; and endocrine; or (B) any mental or psychological disorder, such as mental retardation, organic brain syndrome, emotional or mental illness, and specific learning disabilities.

(ii) Major life activities means functions such as caring for one's self, performing manual tasks, walking, seeing, hearing, speaking, breathing, learning, and working.

(iii) Has a record of such an impairment means has a history of, or has been misclassified as having, a mental or physical impairment that substantially limits one or more major life activities.

(iv) Is regarded as having an impairment means (A) has a physical or mental impairment that does not substantially limit major life activities but that is treated by a recipient as constituting such a limitation; (B) has a physical or mental impairment that substantially limits major life activities only as a result of the attitudes of others toward such impairment; or (C) has none of the impairments defined in paragraph (j)(2)(i) of this section but is treated by a recipient as having such an impairment.

(k) Qualified handicapped person means:

(1) With respect to employment, a handicapped person who, with reasonable accommodation, can perform the essential functions of the job in question;

(2) With respect to public preschool elementary, secondary, or adult educational services, a handicappped person (i) of an age during which nonhandicapped persons are provided such services, (ii) of any age during which it is mandatory under state law to provide such services to handicapped persons, or (iii) to whom a state is required to provide a free appropriate public education under section 612 of the Education of the Handicapped Act; and

(3) With respect to postsecondary and vocational education services, a handicapped person who meets the academic and technical standards requisite to admission or participation in the recipient's education program or activity;

(4) With respect to other services, a handicapped person who meets the essential eligibility requirements for the receipt of such services.

(l) Handicap means any condition or characteristic that renders a person a handicapped person as defined in paragraph (j) of this section.

Sec. 104.4 Discrimination prohibited

(a) **General.** No qualified handicapped person shall, on the basis of handicap, be excluded from participation in, be denied the benefits of, or otherwise be subjected to discrimination under any program or activitiy which receives or benefits from Federal financial assistance.

(b) **Discriminatory actions prohibited.** (1) A recipient, in providing any aid, benefit, or service, may not, directly or through contractual, licensing, or other arrangements, on the basis of handicap:

(i) Deny a qualified handicapped person the opportunity to participate in or benefit from the aid, benefit, or service;

(ii) Afford a qualified handicapped person an opportunity to participate in or benefit from the aid, benefit, or service that is not equal to that afforded others;

(iii) Provide a qualified handicapped person with an aid, benefit, or service that is not as effective as that provided to others;

(iv) Provide different or separate aid, benefits, or services to handicapped persons or to any class of handicapped persons unless such action is necessary to provide qualified handicapped persons with aid, benefits, or services that are as effective as those provided to others;

(v) Aid or perpetuate discrimination against a qualified handicapped person by providing significant assistance to an agency, organization, or person that discriminates on the basis of handicap in providing any aid, benefit, or service to beneficiaries of the recipients program;

(vi) Deny a qualified handicapped person the opportunity to participate as a member of planning or advisory boards; or

(vii) Otherwise limit a qualified handicapped person in the enjoyment of any right, privilege, advantage, or opportunity enjoyed by others receiving an aid, benefit, or service.

(2) For purposes of this part, aids, benefits, and services, to be equally effective, are not required to produce the identical result or level of achievement for handicapped and nonhandicapped persons, but must afford handicapped persons equal opportunity to obtain the same result, to gain the same benefit, or to reach the same level of achievement, in the most integrated setting appropriate to the person's needs.

(3) Despite the existence of separate or different programs or activities provided in accordance with this part, a recipient may not deny a qualified handicapped person the opportunity to participate in such programs or activities that are not separate or different.

(4) A recipient may not, directly or through contractual or other arrangements, utilize criteria or methods of administration (i) that have the effect of subjecting qualified handicapped persons to discrimination on the basis of handicap, (ii) that have the purpose or effect of defeating or substantially impairing accomplishment of the objectives of the recipient's program with respect to handicapped persons, or (iii) that perpetuate the discrimination of another recipient if both recipients are subject to common administrative control or are agencies of the same State.

(5) In determining the site or location of a facility, an applicant for assistance or a recipient may not make selections (i)

that have the effect of excluding handicapped persons from, denying them the benefits of, or otherwise subjecting them to discrimination under any program or activity that receives or benefits from Federal financial assistance or (ii) that have the purpose or effect of defeating or substantially impairing the accomplishment of the objectives of the program or activity with respect to handicapped persons.

(6) As used in this section, the aid, benefit, or service provided under a program or activity receiving or benefiting from Federal financial assistance includes any aid, benefit, or service provided in or through a facility that has been constructed, expanded, altered, leased or rented, or otherwise acquired, in whole or in part, with Federal financial assistance.

(c) Programs limited by Federal law. The exclusion of nonhandicapped persons from the benefits of a program limited by Federal statute or executive order to handicapped persons or the exclusion of a specific class of handicapped persons from a program limited by Federal statute or executive order to a different class of handicapped persons is not prohibited by this part.

Sec.104.5 Assurances required

(a) Assurances. An applicant for Federal financial assistance for a program or activity to which this part applies shall submit an assurance, on a form specified by the Assistant Secretary, that the program will be operated in compliance with this part. An applicant may incorporate these assurances by reference in subsequent applications to the Department.

(b) Duration of obligation

(1) In the case of Federal financial assistance extended in the form of real property or to provide real property or structures on the property, the assurance will obligate the recipient or, in the case of a subsequent transfer, the transferee, for the period during which the real property or structures are used for the purpose for which Federal financial assistance is extended or for another purpose involving the provision of similar services or benefits.

(2) In the case of Federal financial assistance extended to provide personal property, the assurance will obligate the recipient for the period during which it retains ownership or possession of the property.

(3) In all other cases the assurance will obligate the recipient for the period during which Federal financial assistance is extended.

(c) Covenants

(1) Where Federal financial assistance is provided in the form of real property or interest in the property from the Department, the instrument effecting or recording this transfer shall contain a covenant running with the land to assure nondiscrimination for the period during which the real property is used for a purpose for which the Federal financial assistance is extended or for another purpose involving the provision of similar services or benefits.

(2) Where no transfer of property is involved but property is purchased or improved with Federal financial assistance, the recipient shall agree to include the covenant described in paragraph (b)(2) of this section in the instrument effecting or recording any subsequent transfer of the property.

(3) Where Federal financial assistance is provided in the form of real property or interest in the property from the Department, the covenant shall also include a condition coupled with a right to be reserved by the Department to revert title to the property in the event of a breach of the covenant. If a transferee of real property proposes to mortgage or otherwise encumber the real property as security for financing construction of new, or improvement of existing, facilities on the property for the purposes for which the property was transferred, the Assistant Secretary may, upon request of the transferee and if necessary to accomplish such financing and upon such conditions as he or she deems appropriate, agree to forbear the exercise of such right to revert title for so long as the lien of such mortgage or other encumbrance remains effective.

Sec.104.21 Discrimination prohibited

No qualified handicapped person shall, because a recipient's facilities are inaccessible to or unusable by handicapped persons, be denied the benefits of, be excluded from participation in, or otherwise be subjected to discrimination under any program or activity to which this part applies.

Sec.104.22 Existing facilities

(a) Program accessibility. A recipient shall operate each program or activity to which this part applies so that the program or activity, when viewed in its entirety, is readily accessible to handicapped persons. This paragraph does not require a recipient to make each of its existing facilities or every part of a facility accessible to and usable by handicapped persons.

(b) Methods. A recipient may comply with the requirements of paragraph (a) of this section through such means as redesign of equipment, reassignment of classes or other services to accessible buildings, assignment of aides to beneficiaries, home visits, delivery of health, welfare, or other social services at alternate accessible sites, alteration of existing facilities and construction of new facilities in conformance with the requirements of Sec. 104.23, or any other methods that result in making its program or activity accessible to handicapped persons. A recipient is not required to make structural changes in existing facilities where other methods are effective in achieving compliance with paragraph (a) of this section. In choosing among available methods for meeting the requirement of paragraph (a) of this section, a recipient shall give priority to those methods that offer programs and activities to handicapped persons in the most integrated setting appropriate.

(c) Small health, welfare, or other social service providers. If a recipient with fewer than fifteen employees that provides health, welfare, or other social services finds, after consultation with a handicapped person seeking its services, that there is no method of complying with paragraph (a) of this section other than making a significant alteration in its existing facilities, the recipient may, as an alternative, refer the handicapped person to other providers of those services that are accessible.

(d) Time period. A recipient shall comply with the requirement of paragraph (a) of this section within sixty days of the effective date of this part except that where structural changes in facilities are necessary, such changes shall be made within three years of the effective date of this part, but in any event as expeditiously as possible.

(e) Transition plan. In the event that structural changes to facilities are necessary to meet the requirement of paragraph (a) of this section, a recipient shall develop, within six months of the effective date of this part, a transition plan setting forth the steps necessary to complete such changes. The plan shall be developed with the assistance of interested persons, including handicapped persons or organizations representing handicapped persons. A copy of the transition plan shall be made available for public inspection. The plan shall, at a minimum:

(1) Identify physical obstacles in the recipient's facilities that limit the accessibility of its program or activity to handicappped persons;

(2) Describe in detail the methods that will be used to make the facilities accessible;

(3) Specify the schedule for taking the steps necessary to achieve full program accessibility and, if the time period of the transition plan is longer than one year, identify the steps of that will be taken during each year of the transition period; and

(4) Indicate the person responsible for implementation of the plan.

(f) Notice. The recipient shall adopt and implement procedures to ensure that interested persons, including persons with impaired vision or hearing, can obtain information as to the existence and location of services, activities, and facilities that are accessible to and usuable by handicapped persons.

Sec.104.23 New construction

(a) Design and construction. Each facility or part of a facility constructed by, on behalf of, or for the use of a recipient shall be designed and constructed in such manner that the facility or part of the facility is readily accessible to and usable by handicapped persons, if the construction was commenced after the effective date of this part.

(b) Alteration. Each facility or part of a facility which is altered by, on behalf of, or for the use of a recipient after the effective date of this part in a manner that affects or could affect the usability of the facility or part of the facility shall, to the maximum extent feasible, be altered in such manner that the altered portion of the facility is readily accessible to and usable by handicapped persons.

(c) Conformance with Uniform Federal Accessibility Standards

(1) Effective as of January 18, 1991, design, construction, or alteration of buildings in conformance with sections 3-8 of the Uniform Federal Accessibility Standards (UFAS) (Appendix A to 41 CFR subpart 101-19.6) shall be deemed to comply with the requirements of this section with respect to those buildings. Departures from particular technical and scoping requirements of UFAS by the use of other methods are permitted where substantially equivalent or greater access to and usability of the building is provided.

(2) For purposes of this section, section 4.1.6(1)(g) of UFAS shall be interpreted to exempt from the requirements of UFAS only mechanical rooms and other spaces that, because of their intended use, will not require accessibility to the public or beneficiaries or result in the employment or residence therein of persons with physical handicaps.

(3) This section does not require recipients to make building alterations that have little likelihood of being accomplished without removing or altering a load-bearing structural member. [45 FR 30936, May 9, 1980; 45 FR 37426, June 3, 1980, as amended at 55 FR 52138, 52141, Dec. 19, 1990]

Subpart D—Preschool, Elementary, and Secondary Education

Sec.104.31 Application of this subpart

Subpart D applies to preschool, elementary, secondary, and adult education programs and activities that receive or benefit from Federal financial assistance and to recipients that operate, or that receive or benefit from Federal financial assistance for the operation of, such programs or activities.

Sec.104.32 Location and notification

A recipient that operates a public elementary or secondary education program shall annually:

(a) Undertake to identify and locate every qualified handicapped person residing in the recipient's jurisdiction who is not receiving a public education; and

(b) Take appropriate steps to notify handicapped persons and their parents or guardians of the recipient's duty under this subpart.

Sec.104.33 Free appropriate public education

(a) General. A recipient that operates a public elementary or secondary education program shall provide a free appropriate public education to each qualified handicapped person who is in the recipient's jurisdiction, regardless of the nature or severity of the person's handicap.

(b) Appropriate education

(1) For the purpose of this subpart, the provision of an appropriate education is the provision of regular or special education and related aids and services that (i) are designed to meet individual educational needs of handicapped persons as adequately as the needs of nonhandicapped persons are met and (ii) are based upon adherence to procedures that satisfy the requirements of Secs. 104.34, 104.35, and 104.36.

(2) Implementation of an individualized education program developed in accordance with the Education of the Handicapped Act is one means of meeting the standard established in paragraph (b)(1)(i) of this section.

(3) A recipient may place a handicapped person in or refer such person to a program other than the the one that it operates as its means of carrying out the requirements of this subpart. If so, the recipient remains responsible for ensuring that the

requirements of this subpart are met with respect to any handicapped person so placed or referred.

(c) Free education—

(1) *General.* For the purpose of this section, the provision of a free education is the provision of educational and related services without cost to the handicapped person or to his or her parents or guardian, except for those fees that are imposed on non-handicapped persons or their parents or guardian. It may consist either of the provision of free services or, if a recipient places a handicapped person in or refers such person to a program not operated by the recipient as its means of carrying out the requirements of this subpart, of payment for the costs of the program. Funds available from any public or private agency may be used to meet the requirements of this subpart. Nothing in this section shall be construed to relieve an insurer or similar third party from an otherwise valid obligation to provide or pay for services provided to a handicapped person.

(2) *Transportation.* If a recipient places a handicapped person in or refers such person to a program not operated by the recipient as its means of carrying out the requirements of this subpart, the recipient shall ensure that adequate transportation to and from the program is provided at no greater cost than would be incurred by the person or his or her parents or guardian if the person were placed in the program operated by the recipient.

(3) *Residential placement.* If placement in a public or private residential program is necessary to provide a free appropriate public education to a handicapped person because of his or her handicap, the program, including non-medical care and room and board, shall be provided at no cost to the person or his or her parents or guardian.

(4) *Placement of handicapped persons by parents.* If a recipient has made available, in conformance with the requirements of this section and Sec. 104.34, a free appropriate public education to a handicapped person and the person's parents or guardian choose to place the person in a private school, the recipient is not required to pay for the person's education in the private school. Disagreements between a parent or guardian and a recipient regarding whether the recipient has made such a program available or otherwise regarding the question of financial responsibility are subject to the due process procedures of Sec. 104.36

(d) Compliance. A recipient may not exclude any qualified handicapped person from a public elementary or secondary education after the effective date of this part. A recipient that is not, on the effective date of this regulation, in full compliance with the other requirements of the preceding paragraphs of this section shall meet such requirements at the earliest practicable time and in no event later than September 1, 1978.

Sec. 104.34 Educational setting

(a) Academic setting. A recipient to which this subpart applies shall educate, or shall provide for the education of, each qualified handicapped person in its jurisdiction with persons who are not handicapped to the maximum extent appropriate to the needs of the handicapped person. A recipient shall place a handicapped person in the regular educational environment operated by the recipient unless it is demonstrated by the recipient that the education of the person in the regular environment with the use of supplementary aids and services cannot be achieved satisfactorily. Whenever a recipient places a person in a setting other than the regular educational environment pursuant to this paragraph, it shall take into account the proximity of the alternate setting to the person's home.

(b) Nonacademic settings. In providing or arranging for the provision of nonacademic and extracurricular services and activities, including meals, recess periods, and the services and activities set forth in Sec. 104.37(a)(2), a recipient shall ensure that handicapped persons participate with nonhandicapped persons in such activities and services to the maximum extent appropriate to the needs of the handicapped person in question.

(c) Comparable facilities. If a recipient, in compliance with paragraph (a) of this section, operates a facility that is identifiable as being for handicapped persons, the recipient shall ensure that the facility and the services and activities provided therein are comparable to the other facilities, services, and activities of the recipient.

Sec. 104.35 Evaluation and placement

(a) Preplacement evaluation. A recipient that operates a public elementary or secondary education program shall conduct an evaluation in accordance with the requirements of paragraph (b) of this section of any person who, because of handicap, needs or is believed to need special education or related services before taking any action with respect to the initial placement of the person in a regular or special education program and any subsequent significant change in placement.

(b) Evaluation procedures. A recipient to which this subpart applies shall establish standards and procedures for the evaluation and placement of persons who, because of handicap, need or are believed to need special education or related services which ensure that:

(1) Tests and other evaluation materials have been validated for the specific purpose for which they are used and are administered by trained personnel in conformance with the instructions provided by their producer;

(2) Tests and other evaluation materials include those tailored to assess specific areas of educational need and not merely those which are designed to provide a single general intelligence quotient; and

(3) Tests are selected and administered so as best to ensure that, when a test is administered to a student with impaired sensory, manual, or speaking skills, the test results accurately reflect the student's aptitude or achievement level or whatever other factor the test purports to measure, rather than reflecting the student's impaired sensory, manual, or speaking skills (except where those skills are the factors that the test purports to measure).

(c) Placement procedures. In interpreting evaluation data and in making placement decisions, a recipient shall (1) draw upon information from a variety of sources, including aptitude and achievement tests, teacher recommendations, physical condition, social or cultural background, and adaptive behavior, (2) establish procedures to ensure that information obtained from all such sources is documented and carefully considered, (3) ensure that the placement decision is made by a group of persons, including persons knowledgeable about the child, the meaning of the evaluation data, and the placement options, and (4) ensure that the placement decision is made in conformity with Sec. 104.34.

(d) Reevaluation. A recipient to which this section applies shall establish procedures, in accordance with paragraph (b) of this section, for periodic reevaluation of students who have been provided special education and related services. A reevaluation procedure consistent with the Education for the Handicapped Act is one means of meeting this requirement.

Sec. 104.36 Procedural safeguards

A recipient that operates a public elementary or secondary education program shall establish and implement, with respect to actions regarding the identification, evaluation, or educational placement of persons who, because of handicap, need or are believed to need special instruction or related services, a system of procedural safeguards that includes notice, an opportunity for the parents or guardian of the person to examine relevant records, an impartial hearing with opportunity for participation by the person's parents or guardian and representation by counsel, and a review procedure. Compliance with the procedural safeguards of section 615 of the Education of the Handicapped Act is one means of meeting this requirement.

Sec. 104.37 Nonacademic services

(a) General

(1) A recipient to which this subpart applies shall provide nonacademic and extracurricular services and activities in such manner as is necessary to afford handicapped students an equal opportunity for participation in such services and activities.

(2) Nonacademic and extracurricular services and activities may include counseling services, physical recreational athletics, transportation, health services, recreational activities, special interest groups or clubs sponsored by the recipients, referrals to agencies which provide assistance to handicapped persons, and employment of students, including both employment by the recipient and assistance in making available outside employment.

(b) Counseling services. A recipient to which this subpart applies that provides personal, academic, or vocational counseling, guidance, or placement services to its students shall provide these services without discrimination on the basis of handicap. The recipient shall ensure that qualified handicapped students are not counseled toward more restrictive career objectives than are nonhandicapped students with similar interests and abilities.

(c) Physical education and athletics

(1) In providing physical education courses and athletics and similar programs and activities to any of its students, a recipient to which this subpart applies may not discriminate on the basis of handicap. A recipient that offers physical education courses or that operates or sponsors interscholastic, club, or intramural athletics shall provide to qualified handicapped students an equal opportunity for participation in these activities.

(2) A recipient may offer to handicapped students physical education and athletic activities that are separate or different from those offered to nonhandicapped students only if separation or differentiation is consistent with the requirements of Sec. 104.34 and only if no qualified handicapped student is denied the opportunity to compete for teams or to participate in courses that are not separate or different.

Sec. 104.38 Preschool and adult education programs

A recipient to which this subpart applies that operates a preschool education or day care program or activity or an adult education program or activity may not, on the basis of handicap, exclude qualified handicapped persons from the program or activity and shall take into account the needs of such persons in determining the aid, benefits, or services to be provided under the program or activity.

Sec.104.39 Private education programs

(a) A recipient that operates a private elementary or secondary education program may not, on the basis of handicap, exclude a qualified handicapped person from such program if the person can, with minor adjustments, be provided an appropriate education, as defined in Sec. 104.33(b)(1), within the recipient's program

(b) A recipient to which this section applies may not charge more for the provision of an appropriate education to handicapped persons than to nonhandicapped persons except to the extent that any additional charge is justified by a substantial increase in cost to the recipient.

(c) A recipient to which this section applies that operates special education programs shall operate such programs in accordance with the provisions of Secs. 104.35 and 104.36. Each recipient to which this section applies is subject to the provisions of Secs. 104.34, 104.37, and 104.38. ∎

Appendix **2**

Federal and State
Departments of Education

Federal Department of Education Offices

The federal Department of Education, Office of Special Education, has the responsibility to ensure that all states meet the requirements of IDEA. For information on IDEA, contact the DOE at:

U.S. Department of Education
Office of Special Education and Rehabilitation
  Services
400 Maryland Avenue, SW
Washington, DC 20202
202-205-5465 (voice)
www.ed.gov/about/offices/list/osers/osep/
  index.html?src=mr

The federal Department of Education, Office for Civil Rights, is one place to file a complaint for IDEA violations. You can contact any of the following OCR offices.

Main Office

U.S. Department of Education
Office for Civil Rights
Mary E. Switzer Building
330 C Street, SW
Washington, DC 20202
800-421-3481 (voice)
877-521-2172 (TDD)
202-205-9862 (fax)
ocr@ed.gov (email)
www.ed.gov/about/offices/list/ocr/index.html

Connecticut, Maine, Massachusetts, New Hampshire, Rhode Island, Vermont

U.S. Department of Education
Office for Civil Rights
J. W. McCormack Post Office and Courthouse
Room 701, 01-0061
Boston, MA 02109-4557
617-223-9662 (voice)
617-223-9695 (TDD)
617-223-9669 (fax)
ocr_boston@ed.gov (email)

New Jersey, New York

U.S. Department of Education
Office for Civil Rights
75 Park Place
New York, NY 10007-2146
212-637-6466 (voice)
212-637-0478 (TDD)
212-264-3803 (fax)
ocr_newyork@ed.gov (email)

Delaware, Kentucky, Maryland, Pennsylvania, West Virginia

U.S. Department of Education
Office for Civil Rights
100 Penn Square East, Suite 515
Philadelphia, PA 19107
215-656-8541 (voice)
215-656-8604 (TDD)
215-656-8605 (fax)
ocr_philadelphia@ed.gov (email)

Alabama, Florida, Georgia, South Carolina, Tennessee

Office for Civil Rights, Atlanta Office
U.S. Department of Education
61 Forsyth Street SW, Suite 19T70
Atlanta, GA 30303-3104
404-562-6350 (voice)
404-331-7236 (TDD)
404-562-6455 (fax)
ocr_atlanta@ed.gov (email)

Arkansas, Louisiana, Mississippi, Oklahoma, Texas

U.S. Department of Education
Office for Civil Rights
1999 Bryan Street, Suite 2600
Dallas, TX 75201
214-880-2459 (voice)
214-880-2456 (TDD)
214-880-3082 (fax)
ocr_dallas@ed.gov (email)

District of Columbia, North Carolina, Virginia

U.S. Department of Education
Office for Civil Rights
1100 Pennsylvania Avenue, NW, Rm. 316
P.O. Box 14620
Washington, DC 20044-4620
202-208-2545 (voice)
202-208-7741 (TDD)
202-208-7797 (fax)
ocr_dc@ed.gov (email)

Illinois, Indiana, Minnesota, Wisconsin

U.S. Department of Education
Office for Civil Rights
111 N. Canal Street, Suite 1053
Chicago, IL 60606-7204
312-886-8434 (voice)
312-353-2540 (TDD)
312-353-4888 (fax)
ocr_chicago@ed.gov (email)

Michigan, Ohio

U.S. Department of Education
Office for Civil Rights
600 Superior Avenue East
Bank One Center, Room 750
Cleveland, OH 44114-2611
216-522-4970 (voice)
216-522-4944 (TDD)
216-522-2573 (fax)
ocr_cleveland@ed.gov (email)

Iowa, Kansas, Missouri, Nebraska, North Dakota, South Dakota

U.S. Department of Education
Office for Civil Rights
8930 Ward Parkway, Suite 2037
Kansas City, MO 64114
816-268-0550 (voice)
800-437-0833 (TDD)
816-823-1404 (fax)
ocr_kansascity@ed.gov (email)

Arizona, Colorado, Montana, New Mexico, Utah, Wyoming

U.S. Department of Education
Office for Civil Rights
Federal Building, Suite 310
1244 Speer Boulevard
Denver, CO 80204-3582
303-844-5695 (voice)
303-844-3417 (TDD)
303-844-4303 (fax)
ocr_denver@ed.gov (email)

California

U.S. Department of Education
Office for Civil Rights
Old Federal Building
50 United Nations Plaza, Room 239
San Francisco, CA 94102-4102
415-556-4275 (voice)
415-437-7786 (TDD)
415-437-7783 (fax)
ocr_sanfrancisco@ed.gov (email)

Alaska, Hawaii, Idaho, Nevada, Oregon, Washington

U.S. Department of Education
Office for Civil Rights
915 Second Avenue, Room 3310
Seattle, WA 98174-1099
206-220-7900 (voice)
206-220-7907 (TDD)
206-220-7887 (fax)
ocr_seattle@ed.gov (email)

State Department of Education Offices

Your state department of education is the place to go to find legislation, curriculum material, or information on state special education programs as well as information about the IDEA and its requirements.

Alabama

Alabama Department of Education
Division of Special Education Services
(Gordon Persons Building)
P.O. Box 302101
Montgomery, AL 36130-2101
334-242-8114 (voice)
334-242-9192 (fax)
www.alsde.edu/html/home.asp

Alaska

Alaska Department of Education
Teaching and Learning Support
801 W. 10th Street, Suite 200
Juneau, AK 99801-1894
907-465-8693 (voice)
907-465-2806 (fax)
www.eed.state.ak.us

Arizona

Arizona Department of Education
Exceptional Student Services
1535 W. Jefferson Street
Phoenix, AZ 85007
602-364-4000 (voice)
602-542-5404 (fax)
www.ade.state.az.us

Arkansas

Arkansas Department of Education
Special Education
Victory Building
1401 W. Capitol, Suite 450
Little Rock, AR 72201-2936
501-682-4221 (voice)
501-682-5159 (fax)
http://arkedu.state.ar.us

California

California Department of Education
Special Education Division
Room 530, 428 J Street
Sacramento, CA 95812-1738
916-445-4602 (voice)
916-327-3706 (fax)
www.cde.ca.gov

Colorado

Colorado Department of Education
Special Education Services Unit
201 E. Colfax Avenue
Denver, CO 80203
303-866-6694 (voice)
303-866-6811 (fax)
www.cde.state.co.us

Connecticut

Connecticut Department of Education
Bureau of Special Education and Pupil Services
25 Industrial Park Road
Middletown, CT 06457
860-807-2025 (voice)
860-807-2047 (fax)
www.state.ct.us/sde

Delaware

Delaware Department of Education
Exceptional Children and Early Childhood
   Education
Townsend Building
P.O. Box 1402
Dover, DE 19903-1402
302-739-5471 (voice)
302-739-2388 (fax)
www.doe.state.de.us

District of Columbia

District of Columbia
Division of Special Education
825 North Capitol Street, NE
Washington, DC 20002
202-442-4800 (voice)
202-442-5117 (fax)
www.K12.dc.us

Florida

Florida Department of Education
Bureau of Instructional Support and Community
    Services
325 W. Gaines Street
Tallahassee, FL 32399-0400
850-488-1570 (voice)
850-921-8246 (fax)
www.firn.edu/doe

Georgia

Georgia Department of Education
Division for Exceptional Students
1870 Twin Towers East
Atlanta, GA 30334
404-656-3963 (voice)
404-651-6457 (fax)
www.doe.k12.ga.us

Hawaii

Hawaii Department of Education
Special Education Section
Building C, Room 102
637 18th Avenue
Honolulu, HI 96816
808-733-4400 (voice)
808-733-4841 (fax)
www.doe.k12.hi.us

Idaho

Idaho Department of Education
Bureau of Special Education
P.O. Box 83720
Boise, ID 83720-0027
208-332-6910 (voice)
208-334-4664 (fax)
www.sde.state.id.us

Illinois

Illinois State Board of Education
Office of Special Education
Mail Code N-253, 100 North First Street
Springfield, IL 62777-0001
217-782-5589 (voice)
217-782-0372 (fax)
www.isbe.state.il.us

Indiana

Indiana Department of Education
Division of Exceptional Learners
Room 229, State House
Indianapolis, IN 46204-2798
317-232-0570 (voice)
317-232-0589 (fax)
http://ideanet.doe.state.in.us

Iowa

Iowa Department of Education
Bureau of Children, Family and Community
    Services
Grimes State Office Building
Des Moines, IA 50319-0146
515-281-3176 (voice)
515-242-6019 (fax)
www.state.ia.us/educate

Kansas

Kansas State Board of Education
Student Support Services
120 SE Tenth Avenue
Topeka, KS 66612-1182
785-291-3097 (voice)
785-296-6715 (fax)
www.ksde.org

Kentucky

Kentucky Department of Education
Division of Exceptional Children Services
500 Mero Street, 8th Floor
Frankfort, KY 40601
502-564-4970 (voice)
502-564-6721 (fax)
www.kde.state.ky.us

Louisiana

Louisiana Department of Education
Division of Special Populations
P.O. Box 94064
Baton Rouge, LA 70804-9064
225-342-3633 (voice)
225-342-6965 (fax)
www.doe.state.la.us

Maine

Maine Department of Education
Office of Special Services
23 State House Station
Augusta, ME 04333-0023
207-624-6650 (voice)
207-624-6651 (fax)
www.state.me.us/education/homepage.htm

Maryland

Maryland State Department of Education
Division of Special Education
200 W. Baltimore Street, 4th Floor
Baltimore, MD 21201
410-767-0238 (voice)
410-333-8165 (fax)
www.msde.state.md.us

Massachusetts

Massachusetts Department of Education
Director of Special Education
350 Main Street
Malden, MA 02148-5023
338-388-3388 (voice)
338-388-3396 (fax)
www.doe.mass.edu

Michigan

Michigan Department of Education
Office of Special Education
608 West Allegan
Lansing, MI 48933
517-373-9433 (voice)
517-373-7504 (fax)
www.michigan.gov/mde

Minnesota

Minnesota Department of Education
Department of Children, Families and Learning
1500 Highway 36 West
Roseville, MN 55113-4266
651-582-8289 (voice)
651-582-8729 (fax)
http://cfl.state.mn.us

Mississippi

Mississippi Department of Education
Office of Special Education
P.O. Box 771
359 North West Street, Suite 335
Jackson, MS 39205-0771
601-359-3498 (voice)
601-359-2198 (fax)
www.mde.k12.ms.us

Missouri

Missouri Department of Elementary and Secondary
  Education
Division of Special Education
P.O. Box 480
Jefferson City, MO 65102
573-751-5739 (voice)
573-526-4404 (fax)
www.dese.state.mo.us

Montana

Montana Office of Public Instruction
Division of Special Education
P.O. Box 202501
Helena, MT 59620-2501
406-444-4429 (voice)
406-444-3924 (fax)
www.opi.state.mt.us

Nebraska

Nebraska Department of Education
Special Populations Office
P.O. Box 94987
301 Centennial Mall South
Lincoln, NE 68509-4987
402-471-2295 (voice)
402-471-5022 (fax)
www.nde.state.ne.us

Nevada

Nevada Department of Education
Office of Special Education
700 E. 5th Street, Suite 113
Carson City, NV 89701
775-687-9171 (voice)
775-687-9123 (fax)
www.nde.state.nv.us

New Hampshire

New Hampshire Department of Education
Bureau for Special Education Services
101 Pleasant Street
Concord, NH 03301-3860
603-271-3741 (voice)
603-271-1953 (fax)
www.ed.state.nh.us

New Jersey

New Jersey Department of Education
Office of Special Education Programs
P.O. Box 500
Trenton, NJ 08625-0500
609-633-6833 (voice)
609-984-8422 (fax)
www.state.nj.us/education

New Mexico

New Mexico Department of Special Education
300 Don Gaspar Avenue
Sante Fe, NM 87501
505-827-6541 (voice)
505-827-6791 (fax)
http://sde.state.nm.us

New York

New York State Education Department
Office of Vocational and Educational Services for
   Individuals With Disabilities
One Commerce Plaza, Room 1606
Albany, NY 12234
518-474-2714 (voice)
518-474-8802 (fax)
www.vesid.nysed.gov

North Carolina

North Carolina Department of Public Instruction
Division of Exceptional Children
6356 Mail Service Center
Raleigh, NC 27699-6356
919-807-3969 (voice)
919-807-3243 (fax)
www.ncpublicschools.org

North Dakota

North Dakota Department of Public Instruction
Office of Special Education
600 E. Boulevard Avenue, Dept. 201
Bismarck, ND 58505-0440
701-328-2277 (voice)
701-328-4149 (fax)
www.dpi.state.nd.us

Ohio

Ohio Department of Education
Office for Exceptional Children
Second Floor, Mail Stop 202
25 S. Front Street
Columbus, OH 43215-4183
614-466-2650 (voice)
614-728-1097 (fax)
www.ode.state.oh.us

Oklahoma

Oklahoma Department of Education
Special Education Services
2500 N. Lincoln Blvd., Suite 411
Oklahoma City, OK 73105-4599
405-521-3351 (voice)
405-522-3503 (fax)
http://sde.state.ok.us

Oregon

Oregon Department of Education
Office of Special Education
255 Capitol Street, NE
Salem, OR 97310-0203
503-378-3600 (voice)
503-378-5156 (fax)
www.ode.state.or.us

Pennsylvania

Pennsylvania Department of Education
Bureau of Special Education
333 Market Street, 7th Floor
Harrisburg, PA 17126-0333
717-783-6913 (voice)
717-783-6139 (fax)
www.pde.state.pa.us

Rhode Island

Rhode Island Department of Education
Office of Special Needs
Shepard Building, 4th Floor
255 Westminster Street
Providence, RI 02903
401-222-4600 (voice)
401-222-6030 (fax)
www.ridoe.net

South Carolina

South Carolina Department of Education
Office of Exceptional Children
1429 Senate Street, Room 808
Columbia, SC 29201-3799
803-734-8806 (voice)
803-734-4824 (fax)
www.myscschools.com

South Dakota

South Dakota Department of Education
Office of Special Education
700 Governors Drive
Pierre, SD 57501-2291
605-773-3678 (voice)
605-773-3782 (fax)
www.state.sd.us/deca

Tennessee

Tennessee Department of Education
Division of Special Education
710 James Robertson Parkway, 5th Floor
Nashville, TN 37243-0380
615-741-2851 (voice)
615-532-9412 (fax)
www.state.tn.us/education

Texas

Texas Education Agency
Division of Special Education
1701 N. Congress Avenue
Austin, TX 78701
512-463-9414 (voice)
512-463-9560 (fax)
www.tea.state.tx.us

Utah

Utah State Office of Education
Services for At-Risk Students
P.O. Box 144200
250 E. 500 South
Salt Lake City, UT 84114-4200
801-538-7711 (voice)
801-538-7991 (fax)
www.usoe.k12.ut.us

Vermont

Vermont Department of Education
Student Support Services Team
State Office Building
120 State Street
Montpelier, VT 05620-2501
802-828-5118 (voice)
802-828-0573 (fax)
www.state.vt.us/educ

Virginia

Virginia Department of Education
Office of Special Education
P.O. Box 2120
Richmond, VA 23218-2120
804-225-2402 (voice)
804-371-8796 (fax)
www.pen.k12.va.us

Washington

Washington Department of Public Instruction
Special Education Section
P.O. Box 47200
600 S. Washington Street
Olympia, WA 98504-7200
360-725-6075 (voice)
360-586-0247 (fax)
www.k12.wa.us

West Virginia

West Virginia Department of Education
Office of Special Education
Building #6
1900 Kanawha Boulevard East, Room 304
Charleston, WV 25305
304-558-2696 (voice)
304-558-3741 (fax)
http://wvde.state.wv.us

Wisconsin

Wisconsin Department of Public Instruction
Division for Learning Support
P.O. Box 7841
125 S. Webster Street
Madison, WI 53707-7841
608-266-1781 (voice)
608-267-3746 (fax)
www.dpi.state.wi.us

Wyoming

Wyoming Department of Education
Special Programs Unit
Hathaway Building
2300 Capitol Avenue, 2nd Floor
Cheyenne, WY 82002-0050
307-777-7417 (voice)
307-777-6221 (fax)
www.k12.wy.us

Appendix 3

Support Groups, Advocacy Organizations, and Other Resources

General Resources on Special Education

Adapted Physical Education National Standards

SUNY Cortland
E224 Park Center
P.O. Box 2000
Cortland, NY 13045
888-APENS-EXAM (voice)
www.cortland.edu/APENS

Ensures that physical education instruction is provided for students with disabilities by qualified physical education instructors. The project has developed national standards for the profession and a national certification examination to measure knowledge of these standards.

American Council on Rural Special Education

Utah State University
2865 Old Main Hill
Logan, UT 84322-2865
435-797-3911 (voice)
acres@cc.usu.edu (email)
http://extension.usu.edu/acres

Provides support and information to families of special education children living in rural America. ACRES publishes a national journal called the *Rural Special Education Quarterly*, and maintains an archive of article abstracts on its website. ACRES also publishes a bimonthly newsletter called "RuraLink."

Disability Resources, Inc.

Four Glatter Lane
Centereach, NY 11720-1032
631-585-0290 (voice/fax)
www.disabilityresources.org

Offers a monthly newsletter and many articles on disabilities. Provides numerous links to other Internet resources.

Education Development Center, Inc.

55 Chapel Street
Newton, MA 02458-1060
617-969-7100 (voice)
617-969-5979 (fax)
617-964-5448 (TTY)
www.edc.org

Promotes the effective use of technology to enhance education for students with sensory, cognitive, physical, and social/emotional disabilities, and offers articles and information on assistive technologies. The Center also has offices in New York and the District of Columbia—check their website for more information.

ERIC Clearinghouse on Disabilities and Gifted Education

1110 North Glebe Road
Arlington, VA 22201-5704
800-328-0272 (voice)
ericec@cec.sped.org (email)
www.ericec.org

Provides a variety of services, research, articles, and products on a broad range of education-related issues. The AskERIC forum is a personalized Internet-based service providing education information to teachers, librarians, counselors, administrators, parents, and others. You can also search ERIC's extensive article database.

Family.com

http://family.go.com

An Internet site affiliated with Disney. Among other things, you can find articles on special education and children with disabilities.

Family Education Network

20 Park Plaza, 12th Floor
Boston, MA 02116
617-542-6500
http://familyeducation.com

Includes information on learning disabilities and children with special needs. Website features include a monthly column by a special education lawyer, "Ask the Expert"—what their expert has to say about learning issues, resources, and special education news.

Federal Resource Center for Special Education

1825 Connecticut Avenue, NW
Washington, DC 20009
202-884-8215 (voice)
202-884-8443 (fax)
202-884-8200 (TTY)
joppenhe@aed.org (email)
www.dssc.org/frc

Supports a nationwide special education technical assistance network (funded by the U.S. Department of Education's Office of Special Education and Rehabilitative Services), plans national meetings of education professionals, and links Regional Resource and Federal Centers with each other and with other technical assistance providers. The website includes the text of certain federal regulations, a list of links to disability organizations, publications (including the RRFC Links Online Newsletter), and proceedings of certain government conferences.

Internet Resources for Special Children

julioc@one.net (email)
www.irsc.org

An Internet site that provides lists of links relating to the needs of children with disabilities for parents, family members, caregivers, friends, educators, and medical professionals. Categories are extensive, including almost every possible disability affecting children.

National Early Childhood Technical Assistance Center

Campus Box 8040,UNC-CH
Chapel Hill, NC 27599-8040
919-962-2001 (voice)
919-843-3269 (TDD)
919-966-7463 (fax)
nectac@unc.edu (email)
www.nectac.org

A program of the Child Development Center at the University of North Carolina at Chapel Hill, geared towards younger children (through age five). NECTAC has resources on childhood disabilities, the text of IDEA, and descriptions of programs developed under IDEA.

National Information Center for Children and Youth With Disabilities

P.O. Box 1492
Washington, DC 20013
800-695-0285 (voice/TTY)
202-884-8441 (fax)
nichy@aed.org (email)
www.nichcy.org

Provides information on disabilities and disability-related issues for families, educators, and other professionals. The website contains contact information for local disability organizations, lists of disability organizations and government agencies by state, publications, and information on various disability topics, including how to prepare children with disabilities to make the transition from high school to the adult world.

Parent Soup

www.parentsoup.com

An Internet resource that includes an Education Central area. Topics include mainstreaming, ADD, ADHD, dyslexia, and IEPs. The site sponsors an expert message board and chat rooms for parents.

School Psychology Resources Online

www.schoolpsychology.net

An Internet site with information on learning disabilities, ADHD, gifted children, autism, adolescence, parenting, psychological assessment, classroom management, and more. You can download handouts aimed at parents and teachers.

Special Education Resources From the Curry School of Education at University of Virginia

P.O. Box 400260
Charlottesville, VA 22904-4260
434-924-3334 (voice)
434-924-0747 (fax)
http://curry.edschool.virginia.edu/sped/projects/ose/
   home.html

This site offers information for parents and teachers on special education, including articles on learning disabilities and links to special education organizations and websites.

Special Education Resources on the Internet

www.seriweb.com

A collection of Internet-accessible information in the field of special education, including material on disabilities (including learning disabilities and ADD), transition resources, technology, and more.

The Association for Persons With Severe Handicaps (TASH)

29 West Susquehanna Avenue, Suite 210
Baltimore, MD 21204
410-828-8274 (voice)
info@tash.org (email)
www.tash.org

Provides information on current trends and issues in the field of disabilities, organizes conferences and workshops, advocates for legislative changes, distributes publications and videos, and disseminates information through electronic media.

Technical Perspectives, Inc.

1411 East Campbell Road, Suite 1900
Richardson, TX 75081
800-594-3779 (voice)
sales@classplus.com (email)
www.classplus.com/classplus

Publishes a software program called Classplus, which you can use to create an Individual Education Plan (IEP). Classplus allows you to develop comprehensive curricula, goals, and objectives for every subject and functional assessments.

On the website, you can see sample reports containing goals and objectives, sample progress reports, and IEP forms.

Parent Training and Information Centers (PTI)

The U.S. Department of Education, Office of Special Education Programs, funds organized parent-to-parent programs. The work is done locally through programs known as Parent Training and Information (PTI) Centers. PTI Centers enable parents to participate more effectively with professionals in meeting the educational needs of children with disabilities. You can contact a local PTI for information; PTI online information is available through the Department of Education's website, www.ed.gov.

Alabama

Special Education Action Committee, Inc.
600 Bel Air Boulevard, Suite 210
P.O. Box 161274
Mobile, AL 36616-2274
334-478-1208 (voice/TTY)
800-222-7322 (voice—Alabama only)
334-473-7877 (fax)
seacofmobile@zebra.net (email)

Alaska

PARENTS, Inc.
4743 E. Northerns Lights Boulevard
Anchorage, AK 99508
907-337-7678 (voice)
800-478-7678 (voice—Alaska only)
907-337-7629 (TTY)
907-337-7671 (fax)
parents@parentsinc.org (email)
www.parentsinc.org

Arizona

Pilot Parents of Southern Arizona
2600 N. Wyatt Drive
Tucson, AZ 85712
520-324-3150 (voice)
877-365-7220 (voice)
520-324-3152 (fax)
ppsa@pilotparents.org (email)
www.pilotparents.org

Raising Special Kids
2400 N. Central Avenue, Suite 200
Phoenix, AZ 85004-9802
602-242-4366 (voice/TTY)
800-237-3007 (voice—Arizona only)
602-242-4306 (fax)
info@raisingspecialkids.org (email)
www.raisingspecialkids.org

Arkansas

Arkansas Disability Coalition
1123 S. University Drive, Suite 225
Little Rock, AR 72204
501-614-7020 (voice/TTY)
800-223-1330 (voice—Arkansas only)
501-614-9082 (fax)
adc@alltel.net (email)
www.adcpti.org

FOCUS, Inc.
305 W. Jefferson Avenue
Jonesboro, AR 72401
870-935-2750 (voice)
877-247-3843 (voice)
870-931-3755 (fax)
focusin_inc2@hotmail.com (email)

California

Central California PTI Center
4440 North First Street
Fresno, CA 93726
559-229-2000 (voice)
559-225-6059 (TTY)
559-229-2956 (fax)
epu1@exceptionalparents.org (email)
www.exceptionalparents.org

Exceptional Family Support, Education, and Advo-
    cacy Center of Northern California, Inc.
6402 Skyway
Paradise, CA 95969
530-876-8321 (voice)
888-263-1311 (voice)
530-876-0346 (fax)
sea@sea-center.org (email)
www.sea-center.org

Matrix: A Parent Network and Resource Center
94 Galli Drive, Suite C
Novato, CA 94949
415-884-3535 (voice)
415-884-3554 (TTY)
415-884-3555 (fax)
matrix@matrixparents.org (email)
www.matrixparents.org

Parents Helping Parents, Inc.
3041 Olcott Street
Santa Clara, CA 95054-3222
408-727-5775 (voice)
866-747-4040 (voice)
408-727-0182 (fax)
general@php.com (email)
www.php.com

Support for Families of Children With Disabilities
2601 Mission Street, Suite 606
San Francisco, CA 94110
415-282-7494 (voice)
415-282-1226 (fax)
info@supportforfamilies.org (email)
www.supportforfamilies.org

Teams of Advocates for Special Kids, Inc. (TASK)
3750 Convoy Street, Suite 303
San Diego, CA 92111-3741
858-874-2386 (voice)
858-874-0123 (fax)
taskca@yahoo.com (email)
www.taskca.org

Teams of Advocates for Special Kids, Inc. (TASK)
100 West Cerritos Avenue
Anaheim, CA 92805
714-533-8275 (voice)
866-828-8275 (voice)
714-533-2533 (fax)
taskca@yahoo.com (email)
www.taskca.org

Colorado

PEAK Parent Center, Inc.
611 North Weber, Suite 200
Colorado Springs, CO 80903
719-531-9400 (voice)
800-284-0251 (voice—Colorado only)
719-531-9403 (TTY)
719-531-9452 (fax)
info@peakparent.org (email)
www.peakparent.org

Connecticut

Connecticut Parent Advocacy Center, Inc.
338 Main Street
Niantic, CT 06357
860-739-3089 (voice)
800-445-2722 (voice—Connecticut only)
860-739-7460 (fax/TTY)
cpac@cpacinc.org (email)
www.cpacinc.org

Delaware

Parent Information Center
700 Barksdale Road, Suite 16
Newark, DE 19711
302-366-0152 (voice)
888-547-4412 (voice—Delaware only)
302-366-0276 (fax)
picofdel@picofdel.org (email)
www.picofdel.org

District of Columbia

Advocates for Justice and Education, Inc.
2041 MLK Avenue, SE, Suite 301
Washington, DC 20020
202-678-8060 (voice)
888-327-8060 (voice)
202-678-8062 (fax)
information@aje-dc.org (email)
www.aje-dc.org

Florida

Family Network on Disabilities
2735 Whitney Road
Clearwater, FL 33760-1610
727-523-1130 (voice)
800-825-5736 (voice—Florida only)
727-523-8687 (fax)
fnd@fndfl.org (email)
http://fndfl.org

Parent to Parent of Miami, Inc.
9040 Sunset Drive, Suite G
Miami, FL 33173
305-271-9797 (voice)
305-271-6628 (fax)
info@ptopmiami.org (email)
www.ptopmiami.org

Georgia

Parent Educating Parents and Professionals
5727 Palazzo Way, Suite B
Douglasville, GA 30134
770-577-7771 (voice)
800-322-7065 (voice—Georgia only)
770-577-7774 (fax)
peppac@peppac.org (email)
www.peppac.org

Hawaii

AWARE (Assisting With Appropriate Rights in Education)
200 North Vineyard Boulevard, Suite 310
Honolulu, HI 96817
808-536-9684 (voice)
800-533-9684 (voice—Hawaii only)
808-536-2280 (TTY)
808-537-6780 (fax)
ldah@ldahawaii.org (email)
www.ldahawaii.org

Idaho

Idaho Parents Unlimited, Inc.
Parent Education Resource Project Center
600 North Curtis, Suite 100
Boise, ID 83706
208-342-5884 (voice/TTY)
800-242-4785 (voice—Idaho only)
208-342-1408 (fax)
parents@ipulidaho.org (email)
www.ipulidaho.org

Illinois

Family Matters
2505 S. Veterans Drive
Effingham, IL 62401
217-347-0880 (voice)
866-436-7842 (voice—Illinois only/TTY)
217-347-5119 (fax)
info@fmptic.org
www.fmptic.org

Family Resource Center on Disabilities
20 East Jackson Boulevard, Room 300
Chicago, IL 60604
312-939-3513 (voice)
800-952-4199 (voice—Illinois only)
312-939-3519 (TDD/TTY)
312-939-7297 (fax)
frcdptiil@ameritech.net (email)
http://frcd.org

Indiana

Indiana Resource Center for Families With Special
  Needs
809 N. Michigan Street
South Bend, IN 46601-1036
219-234-7101 (voice)
800-322-4433 (voice—Indiana only)
219-234-7279 (fax)
insource@insource.org (email)
www.insource.org

Iowa

Access for Special Kids
321 East Sixth Street
Des Moines, IA 50309
515-243-1713 (voice)
800-450-8667 (voice)
515-243-1902 (fax)
PTIIowa@aol.com (email)
www.iowapti.com

Kansas

Families ACT
555 North Woodlawn, Suite 3105
Wichita, KS 67208
316-685-1821 (voice)
316-685-0768 (fax)
nina@mhasck.org (email)
www.mhasck.org

Families Together, Inc.
3340 W. Douglas, Suite 102
Wichita, KS 67203
316-945-7747 (voice)
888-815-6364 (voice—Kansas only)
316-945-7795 (fax)
wichita@familiestogetherinc.org (email)
www.familiestogetherinc.org

Kentucky

Special Parent Involvement Network
10301-B Deering Road
Louisville, KY 40272
502-937-6894 (voice)
800-525-7746 (voice)
502-937-6464 (fax)
spininc@aol.com (email)
www.kyspin.com

Louisiana

Program of Families Helping Families of Greater
   New Orleans: Project PROMPT
4323 Division Street, Suite 110
Metairie, LA 70002-3179
504-888-9111 (voice)
800-766-7736 (voice—Louisiana only)
504-888-0246 (fax)
fhfgno@ix.netcom.com (email)
www.projectprompt.org

Maine

Maine Parent Federation
P.O. Box 2067
Augusta, ME 04338
207-623-2144 (voice/TTY)
800-870-7746 (voice—Maine only)
207-623-2148 (fax)
parentconnect@mpf.org (email)
www.mpf.org

Maryland

Parents Place of Maryland, Inc.
7484 Candlewood Road, Suite S
Hanover, MD 21076-1306
410-859-5300 (voice/TTY)
410-859-5301 (fax)
info@ppmd.org (email)
www.ppmd.org

Massachusetts

Federation for Children With Special Needs
1135 Tremont Street, Suite 420
Boston, MA 02120-2140
617-236-7210 (voice/TTY)
800-331-0688 (voice—Massachusetts only)
617-572-2094 (fax)
fcsninfo@fcsn.org (email)
www.fcsn.org

Michigan

Citizens Alliance to Uphold Special Education
   (CAUSE)
2365 Woodlake Drive, Suite 100
Okemos, MI 48864
517-706-2287 (voice)
800-221-9105 (voice—Michigan only)
517-347-1004 (fax)
info@causeonline.org (email)
www.causeonline.org

Minnesota

PACER Center, Inc.
8161 Normandale Boulevard
Minneapolis, MN 55437
952-838-9000 (voice)
888-248-0822 (voice)
952-838-0190 (TTY)
952-838-0199 (fax)
pacer@pacer.org (email)
www.pacer.org

Mississippi

Parent Partners
Five Old River Place, Suite 101
Jackson, MS 39202
601-354-3302 (voice)
800-366-5707 (voice—Mississippi only)
601-354-2426 (fax)
info@parentpartners.org (email)
www.parentpartners.org

Project Empower
P.O. Box 1733
136 South Poplar Street
Greenville, MS 38701
662-332-4852 (voice)
800-337-4852 (voice)
662-332-1622 (fax)
empower@tecinfo.com (email)

Missouri

Missouri Parents Act (MPACT)
One West Armour, Suite 302
Kansas City, MO 64111
816-531-7070 (voice)
800-743-7634 (voice—Missouri only)
816-531-4777 (fax)
mpact@ptimpact.com (email)
www.ptimpact.com

Montana

Parents Let's Unite for Kids (PLUK)
516 N. 32nd Street
Billings, MT 59101
406-255-0540 (voice)
800-222-7585 (voice—Montana only)
406-255-0540 (TTY)
406-255-0523 (fax)
plukinfo@pluk.org (email)
www.pluk.org

Nebraska

PTI Nebraska
3135 North 93rd Street
Omaha, NE 68134
402-346-0525 (voice)
800-284-8520 (voice—Nebraska only)
402-934-1479 (fax)
info@pti-nebraska.org (email)
www.pti-nebraska.org

Nevada

Nevada PEP
2810 West Charleston, Suite G68
Las Vegas, NV 89102
702-388-8899 (voice)
800-216-5188 (voice)
702-388-2966 (fax)
pepinfo@nvpep.org (email)
www.nvpep.org

New Hampshire

Parent Information Center
P.O. Box 2405
Concord, NH 03302-2405
603-224-7005 (voice/TTY)
800-232-0986 (voice—New Hampshire only)
603-224-4365 (fax)
picnh@aol.com (email)

New Jersey

Statewide Parent Advocacy Network, Inc. (SPAN)
35 Halsey Street, 4th Floor
Newark, NJ 07102
973-642-8100 (voice)
800-654-SPAN (voice—New Jersey only)
973-642-8080 (fax)
SPAN@bellatlantic.net (email)
www.spannj.org

New Mexico

Parents Reaching Out (PRO)
1920B Columbia Drive, SE
Albuquerque, NM 87106
505-247-0192 (voice)
800-524-5176 (voice—New Mexico only)
505-247-1345 (fax)
nmproth@aol.com (email)
www.parentsreachingout.org

New York

Advocacy Center
590 South Avenue
Rochester, NY 14620
585-546-1700 (voice)
800-650-4967 (voice—New York only)
585-546-7069 (fax)
info@advocacycenter.com (email)
www.advocacycenter.com

Advocates for Children of New York
151 W. 30th Street, 5th Floor
New York, NY 10001
212-947-9779 (voice)
212-947-9790 (fax)
info@advocatesforchildren.org (email)
www.advocatesforchildren.org

Resources for Children With Special Needs
116 E. 16th Street, 5th Floor
New York, NY 10003
212-677-4650 (voice)
212-254-4070 (fax)
info@resourcesnyc.org (email)
www.resourcesnyc.org/rcsn.htm

Sinergia/Metropolitan Parent Center
15 W. 65th Street, 6th Floor
New York, NY 10023
212-496-1300 (voice)
212-496-5608 (fax)
sinergia@panix.com (email)
www.sinergiany.org

United We Stand of New York
202 Union Avenue, Suite L
Brooklyn, NY 11211
(718) 302-4313 (voice)
(718) 302-4315 (fax)
uwsofny@aol.com (email)

North Carolina

Exceptional Children's Assistance Center
907 Barra Row, Suites 102 & 103
Davidson, NC 28036
704-892-1321 (voice/TTY)
800-962-6817 (voice—North Carolina only)
704-892-5028 (fax)
ecac@ecacmail.org (email)
www.ECAC-parentcenter.org

North Dakota

Pathfinder Services
1600 Second Avenue, SW, Suite 19
Minot, ND 58701-3459
701-837-7500 (voice)
701-837-7501 (TTY)
701-837-7548 (fax)
ndpath01@minot.ndak.net (email)
www.pathfinder.minot.com

Ohio

Child Advocacy Center
1821 Summit Road, Suite 110
Cincinnati, OH 45237
513-821-2400 (voice/TTY)
888-540-3924 (voice)
513-821-2442 (fax)
cadcenter@aol.com (email)

Ohio Coalition for the Education of Children With
  Disabilities
Bank One Building
165 West Center Street, Suite 302
Marion, OH 43302-3741
740-382-5452 (voice/TTY)
800-374-2806 (voice)
740-383-6421 (fax)
ocecd@gte.net (email)

Oklahoma

Parents Reaching Out in Oklahoma
1917 South Harvard Avenue
Oklahoma City, OK 73128-3049
405-681-9710 (voice)
800-759-4142 (voice)
prook1@aol.com (email)

Oregon

Oregon COPE Project
1745 State Street
Salem, OR 97301
503-581-8156 (voice/TTY)
888-505-COPE (voice—Oregon only)
503-391-0429 (fax)
orcope@open.org (email)
www.open.org/~orpti

Pennsylvania

Hispanics United for Special Needs Children
Buena Vista Plaza
166 West Lehigh Avenue, Suite 400
Philadelphia, PA 19133-3838
215-425-6203 (voice)
215-425-6204 (fax)
huneinc@aol.com (email)

Mentor Parent Program, Inc.
P.O. Box 47
Cole Hill Road
Pittsfield, PA 16340
814-563-3470 (voice)
888-447-1431 (voice—Pennsylvania only)
814-563-3445 (fax)
gwalker@westpa.net (email)
www.mentorparent.org

Parent Education Network
2107 Industrial Highway
York, PA 17402
717-600-0100 (voice)
800-522-5827 (voice—Pennsylvania only/TTY)
717-600-8101 (fax)
pen@parentednet.org (email)

Rhode Island

Rhode Island Parent Information Network
175 Main Street, 1st Floor
Pawtucket, RI 02860
401-727-4144 (voice)
800-464-3399 (voice—Rhode Island only)
401-727-4040 (fax)
ripin@ripin.org (email)
www.ripin.org

South Carolina

Parent Training and Resource Center
   MUSC—College of Health Professions, Research
19 Hagood Avenue, Suite 910
P.O. Box 250882
Charleston, SC 29425
843-792-3025 (voice)
843-792-1107 (fax)
mccartyb@musc.edu (email)

PRO Parents
652 Bush River Road, Suite 218
Columbia, SC 29210
803-772-5688 (voice)
800-759-4776 (voice)
803-772-5341 (fax)
proparents@aol.com (email)

South Dakota

South Dakota Parent Connection
3701 W. 49th Street, Suite 200B
Sioux Falls, SD 57106
605-361-3171 (voice)
800-640-4553 (voice—South Dakota only/TTY)
605-361-2928 (fax)
sdpc@sdparent.org (email)

Tennessee

Support & Training for Exceptional Parents (STEP)
712 Professional Plaza
Greenville, TN 37745
423-639-0125 (voice)
800-280-7837 (voice—Tennessee only)
423-639-8802 (TTY)
423-636-8217 (fax)
tnstep@aol.com (email)
www.tnstep.org

Texas

Arc of Texas in the Rio Grande Valley
   Parents Supporting Parents Network
601 North Texas Boulevard
Weslaco, TX 78596
956-447-8408 (voice)
888-857-8688 (voice)
956-973-9503 (fax)
padillal@earthlink.net (email)
www.thearcoftexas.org

Grassroots Consortium
5055 Bellfort
P.O. Box 266958
Houston, TX 77207-6958
713-734-5355 (voice)
713-643-6291 (fax)
speckids@aol.com (email)

Partners Resource Network, Inc./PATH
1090 Longfellow Drive, Suite B
Beaumont, TX 77706-4819
409-898-4684 (voice)
800-866-4726 (voice—Texas only)
409-898-4816 (TTY)
409-898-4869 (fax)
path@partnerstx.org (email)
www.partnerstx.org

Project PODER
1017 North Main Avenue, Suite 207
San Antonio, TX 78212
210-222-2637 (voice)
800-682-9747 (voice—Texas only)
210-475-9283 (fax)
poder@tfepoder.org (email)
www.tfepoder.org

Utah

Utah Parent Center (UPC)
2290 East, 4500 South, Suite 110
Salt Lake City, UT 84117-4428
801-272-1051 (voice/TTY)
800-468-1160 (voice—Utah only)
801-272-8907 (fax)
helenpo@utahparentcenter.org (email)

Vermont

Vermont Parent Information Center (VPIC)
1 Mill Street, Suite 310
Burlington, VT 05401
802-658-5315 (voice/TTY)
800-639-7170 (voice—Vermont only)
802-658-5395 (fax)
vpic@vtpic.com (email)
www.vtpic.com

Virginia

PADDA, Inc.
813 Forrest Drive, Suite 3
Newport News, VA 23606
757-591-9119 (voice)
888-337-2332 (voice)
757-591-8990 (fax)
webmaster@padda.org (email)
www.padda.org

Parent Educational Advocacy Training Center
6320 Augusta Drive, Suite 1200
Springfield, VA 22150
703-932-0010 (voice/TTY)
800-869-6782 (voice—Virginia only)
703-923-0030 (fax)
partners@peatc.org (email)
www.peatc.org

Washington

Infant Toddler Early Intervention Program
P.O. Box 45201
Olympia, WA 98504-5201
360-902-8488 (voice)
800-322-2588 (voice—Washington only)
360-902-8497 (fax)
360-902-7864 (TTY)
LoercSK@dshs.wa.gov (email)
www.wa.gov/dshs/iteip/iteip.html

Parent to Parent Power (Washington)
1118 South 142nd Street, Suite B
Tacoma, WA 98444
253-531-2022 (voice)
253-538-1126 (fax)
p2ppower@yahoo.com (email)

Washington PAVE
6316 South 12th Street
Tacoma, WA 98465
253-565-2266 (voice/TTY)
800-572-7368 (voice)
253-566-8052 (fax)
wapave9@washingtonpave.com (email)
www.washingtonpave.com

West Virginia

West Virginia PTI
371 Broaddus Avenue
Clarksburg, WV 26301
304-624-1436 (voice/TTY)
800-281-1436 (voice—West Virginia only)
304-624-1438 (fax)
wvpti@aol.com (email)
www.wvpti.org

Wisconsin

Family Assistance Center for Education, Training, and Support
2714 North Martin Luther King Drive
Milwaukee, WI 53212
414-374-4645 (voice)
877-374-4677 (voice)
414-374-4655 (fax)
414-374-4635 (TTY)
wifacets@execpc.com
www.wifacets.org

Native American Family Empowerment Center
Great Lakes Inter-Tribal Council, Inc.
2932 Highway 47 North
P.O. Box 9
Lac du Flambeau, WI 54538
715-588-3324 (voice)
800-472-7207 (voice—Wisconsin only)
715-588-7900 (fax)
drosin@glitc.org (email)
www.glitc.org

Parent Education Project of Wisconsin, Inc. (PEP WI)
2192 South 60th Street
West Allis, WI 53219-1568
414-328-5520 (voice)
414-328-5525 (TTY)
414-328-5530 (fax)
pmcoletti@aol.com (email)

Wyoming

Wyoming PIC
5 North Lobban
Buffalo, WY 82834
307-684-2277 (voice)
800-660-9742 (voice—Wyoming only)
307-684-5314 (fax)
tdawson@wpic.org (email)
www.wpic.org

Legal Resources on Special Education

American Bar Association Commission on Mental and Physical Disability Law

740 15th Street, NW
Washington, DC 20005
202-662-1000 (voice)
www.abanet.org/disability/home.html

Puts out books, reporters, news updates, and other publications to assist lawyers who advocate for the rights of the disabled. The Commission also maintains a library of research materials and provides seminars and workshops.

Bazelon Center

1101 15th Street, NW, Suite 1212
Washington, DC 20005
202-467-5730 (voice)
202-467-4232 (TDD)
202-223-0409 (fax)
webmaster@bazelon.org (email)
www.bazelon.org

A public interest law firm that conducts test case litigation to defend the rights of people with mental disabilities. The Bazelon Center provides legal support to protection and advocacy agencies, legal services offices, and private attorneys, and monitors legislation and regulations.

Center for Law and Education

1875 Connecticut Avenue, NW, Suite 510
Washington, DC 20009
202-986-3000 (voice)
202-986-6648 (fax)
www.cleweb.org

Assists local legal services programs and litigates certain cases in matters concerning education of low-income people. As a national support center, CLE has developed enormous expertise about the legal rights and responsibilities of students and school personnel as well as about key education programs and initiatives, including vocational education programs and special education for students with disabilities.

Children's Defense Fund

25 E Street, NW
Washington, DC 20001
202-628-8787 (voice)
cdfinfo@childrensdefense.org (email)
www.childrensdefense.org

Assesses the adequacy of the screening, diagnosis, and treatment programs for Medicaid-eligible children.

Disability Rights Education and Defense Fund, Inc.

2212 Sixth Street
Berkeley, CA 94710
510-644-2555 (voice/TTY)
510-841-8645 (fax)
dredf@dredf.org (email)
www.dredf.org

Dedicated to protecting and advancing the civil rights of people with disabilities through legislation, litigation, advocacy, technical assistance, and education and training of lawyers, people with disabilities, and parents of children with disabilities.

EDLAW, Inc.

1310 Minor Avenue #207
Seattle, WA 98101
edlaw@edlaw.net (email)
www.edlaw.net

The website includes information on newsletters, books, and conferences; a list of attorneys who specialize in special education; and full texts of special education statutes, regulations, and administrative interpretations. EDLAW also maintains a database of attorneys and advocates through COPAA (the Council of Parent Attorneys and Advocates).

LRP Publications

747 Dresher Road, Suite 500
P.O. Box 980
Horsham, PA 19044
800-341-7874 (voice)
215-784-0860 (voice)
215-784-9639 (fax)
www.lrp.com

Has an extensive library of legal materials, including special education publications. The website includes access to over 65 special education documents, covering assessments, behavior, IDEA, IEPs, Section 504, and much more. LRP also publishes the "Individuals With Disabilities Education Law Reporter."

Wrightslaw

webmaster@wrightslaw.com (email)
www.wrightslaw.com

A website maintained by Pete and Pam Wright. Pete is an attorney who has represented special education children for more than 20 years. Pam is a psychotherapist who has worked with children and families in mental health centers, psychiatric clinics, schools, juvenile detention facilities, hospitals, and homes. Their website includes articles about special education advocacy; statutes, regulations, and cases; information on ordering their advocacy package; information about books, conferences, and other projects; and links to other useful information on the Internet.

Resources Concerning Specific Disabilities

Alexander Graham Bell Association

3417 Volta Place, NW
Washington, DC 20007
202-337-5220 (voice)
202-337-5221 (TTY)
202-337-8314 (fax)
www.agbell.org

Provides hearing-impaired children with information and special education programs, and acts as a support group for parents of deaf children.

American Association of the Deaf-Blind

814 Thayer Avenue
Silver Spring, MD 20910
301-495-4403 (voice)
301-495-4402 (TTY)
301-495-4404 (fax)
info@aadb.org (email)
www.aadb.org

Advocates for people who have combined hearing and vision impairments, and provides technical assistance to families, educators, and service providers of people who are deaf-blind.

American Council of the Blind

1155 15th Street, NW, Suite 1004
Washington, DC 20005
202-467-5081 (voice)
800-424-8666 (voice)
202-467-5085 (fax)
www.acb.org

Advocates for legislative changes, particularly to improve educational and rehabilitation facilities.

American Foundation for the Blind

11 Penn Plaza, Suite 300
New York, NY 10001
212-502-7600 (voice)
212-502-7777 (fax)
afbinfo@afb.net (email)
www.afb.org

Provides information on specialized services in education for sight-impaired children and works to improve the quality of educational services for children and youths with visual impairments.

American Society for Deaf Children

P.O. Box 3355
Gettysburg, PA 17325
717-334-7922 (voice/TTY)
717-334-8808 (fax)
asdc@deafchildren.org (email)
www.deafchildren.org

Advocates for deaf or hard of hearing children's total quality participation in education, including use of signing for enhancing and broadening the social, personal, and educational aspects of deaf and hard of hearing children's lives. ASDC supports flexible, innovative, and effective strategies for facilitating deaf and hard of hearing children's education.

ARC

1010 Wayne Avenue, Suite 650
Silver Spring, MD 20910
301-565-3842 (voice)
301-565-3843 (fax)
info@thearc.org (email)
http://thearc.org

Advocates and provides support for families of people with mental retardation and developmental disabilities.

A-T Children's Project

668 S. Military Trail
Deerfield Beach, FL 33442
800-5-HELP-AT (voice)
954-725-1153 (fax)
info@atcp.org (email)
www.atcp.org

Provides physicians, research scientists, families, and support providers with information about an inherited childhood disease called Ataxia-Telangiectasia.

Attention Deficit Information Network, Inc.

58 Prince Street
Needham, MA 02492
781-455-9895 (voice)
adin@gis.net (email)
www.addinfonetwork.com

Offers support and information to families of children with ADD and provides training programs, conferences, and workshops for parents and professionals who work with individuals with ADD.

Autism Society of America

7910 Woodmont Avenue, Suite 300
Bethesda, MD 20814
301-657-0881 (voice)
800-328-8476 (voice)
301-657-0869 (fax)
www.autism-society.org

Monitors legislation and regulations affecting support, education, training, research, and other services for individuals with autism. ASA also offers referral services.

Blind Childrens' Center

4120 Marathon Street
Los Angeles, CA 90029
323-664-2153 (voice)
800-222-3567 (voice—California only)
800-222-3566 (voice)
213-664-3828 (fax)
info@blindcntr.org (email)
http://blindcntr.org

General information for parents of blind children.

Children and Adults With Attention Deficit Disorder (CHADD)

8181 Professional Place, Suite 201
Landover, MD 20785
301-306-7070 (voice)
301-306-7090 (fax)
www.chadd.org

Provides a network for parents of children with ADD, provides a forum of education for parents of and professionals who work with people with ADD, and works to provide positive educational experiences for children with ADD.

CHADD publishes a quarterly newsletter and educators' manual. The site offers fact sheets, information on IDEA, and scientific research and studies on ADD.

Council for Exceptional Children, Division for Learning Disabilities

1110 N. Glebe Road
Arlington, VA 22201
888-CEC-SPED (voice)
703-264-9494 (fax)
703-264-9446 (TDD)
service@cec.sped.org (email)
www.cec.sped.org

Information and resources for teaching students with learning disabilities. The website includes information on the DLD's publications (*Learning Disabilities Research and Practice Journal*, "Thinking About Inclusion & Learning Disabilities," "Research on Classroom Ecologies and DLD Times Newsletter"), information on upcoming conferences, links to other organizations and government agencies, fact sheets, and detailed articles on particular learning disabilities and instruction techniques.

Council for Learning Disabilities

P.O. Box 4014
Leesburg, VA 20177
571-258-1010 (voice)
571-258-1011 (fax)
www.cldinternational.org

An organization of and for professionals who represent diverse disciplines and who are committed to enhancing the education and life-span development of individuals with learning disabilities. The site offers fact sheets, information on research, and legislative updates.

Epilepsy Foundation of America

4351 Garden City Drive
Landover, MD 20785
800-332-1000 (voice)
301-577-2684 (fax)
www.epilepsyfoundation.org

Promotes research and treatment of epilepsy, disseminates information and educational materials, provides direct services for people with epilepsy, and makes referrals when necessary.

Families of Spinal Muscular Atrophy

P.O. Box 196
Libertyville, IL 60048-0196
847-367-7620 (voice)
800-886-1762 (voice)
847-357-7623 (fax)
www.fsma.org

Promotes and funds research, provides families with the use of an equipment pool to help alleviate the high cost of medical equipment, promotes public awareness, and publishes a quarterly newsletter.

Federation of Families for Children's Mental Health

1101 King Street, Suite 420
Alexandria, VA 22314
703-684-7710 (voice)
703-836-1040 (fax)
ffcmh@ffcmh.org (email)
www.ffcmh.org

Focuses on the needs of children with emotional, behavioral, or mental disorders, by providing information and advocating in several areas including family support, education, and transition services. The website includes publications, IDEA updates, and links to local organizations.

The International Dyslexia Association

The Chester Building, Suite 382
8600 LaSalle Road
Baltimore, MD 21286-2044
410-296-0232 (voice)
800-222-3123 (messages)
410-321-5069 (fax)
info@interdys.org (email)
www.interdys.org

Promotes effective teaching approaches and related clinical educational intervention strategies for people with dyslexia; supports research; and disseminates research through conferences, publications, and local and regional offices.

LD Online

www.ldonline.com

One of my favorites, this site offers lots of detailed articles for parents, teachers, and kids on learning disabilities, assessments, methodologies, IEPs, IDEA, and much more. There's a special area of the site just for kids, as well as bulletin boards and lots of state-by-state links.

Learning Disabilities Association of America

4156 Library Road
Pittsburgh, PA 15234-1349
412-341-1515 (voice)
412-344-0224 (fax)
www.ldaamerica.org

A nonprofit membership organization with state and local affiliates. Members receive a national newsletter along with state and local chapter newsletters and information on advocating for their children, state and federal laws, and support groups. The site offers fact sheets, news, and other resources. Click "State LDA Pages" for links to state and local chapters.

National Aphasia Association

351 Butternut Court
Millersville, MD 21108
800-922-4622 (voice)
www.aphasia.org

Promotes public education, research, rehabilitation, and support services to assist people with aphasia and their families. The site offers information, research, fact sheets, and access to support groups.

National Association of the Deaf

814 Thayer Avenue
Silver Spring, MD 20910-4500
301-587-1788 (voice)
301-587-1789 (TTY)
301-587-1791 (fax)
nadinfo@nad.org (email)
www.nad.org

A consumer advocacy group promoting equal access to communication, education, and employment for people who are deaf or hard of hearing.

National Association of Psychiatric Treatment Centers for Children

1025 Connecticut Avenue, NW, Suite 1012
Washington, DC 20036
202-857-9735 (voice)
202-362-5145 (fax)
naptcc@aol.com (email)

A group whose mission is to promote the availability and delivery of appropriate and relevant services to children and youth with, or at risk of, serious emotional or behavioral disturbances, and their families.

National Brain Injury Association of America

8201 Greensboro Drive, Suite 611
McLean, VA 22102
703-761-0750 (voice)
800-444-6443 (voice)
http://biausa.org

Provides information and support to families of people with brain injuries.

National Center for Learning Disabilities

381 Park Avenue South, Suite 1401
New York, NY 10016
212-545-7510 (voice)
888-575-7373 (voice)
212-545-9665 (fax)
www.ncld.org

Provides information on learning disabilities and resources available in communities nationwide to parents, professionals, and adults with learning disabilities. One of NCLD's areas of primary concern is early identification and intervention, as well as teacher preparation. The website includes links to other LD organizations and school testing organizations, and information on legal issues, gifted/learning disabilities, ADD/ADHD, and home schooling.

National Down Syndrome Congress

1370 Center Drive, Suite 102
Atlanta, GA 30338
770-604-9500 (voice)
800-232-6372 (voice)
info@ndsccenter.org (email)
www.ndsccenter.org

Offers support to parents of children with
Down syndrome through annual seminars, fact
sheets, pamphlets, booklets, newsletter, audio-
tapes, and other educational materials. NDSC
maintains an advocate telephone helpline.

National Down Syndrome Society

666 Broadway, 8th Floor
New York, NY 10012
800-221-4602 (voice)
212-460-9330 (voice)
212-979-2873 (fax)
www.ndss.org

Helps families whose special education needs
concern a child with Down syndrome.

National Federation of the Blind

1800 Johnson Street
Baltimore, MD 21230
410-659-9314 (voice)
410-685-5653 (fax)
nfb@nfb.org (email)
www.nfb.org

Provides referrals and information on adaptive
equipment, advocacy services, protection of
civil rights, development and evaluation of
technology, and support for blind people and
their families. NFB has a special division called
the National Organization of Parents of Blind
Children.

National Fragile X Foundation

P.O. Box 190488
San Francisco, CA 94119
800-688-8765 (voice)
925-938-9315 (fax)
natlfx@fragilex.org (email)
www.fragilex.org

Has information for educators on upcoming
conferences and on support groups for parents
and children, and maintains a family resource
center.

National Spinal Cord Injury Association

6701 Democracy Boulevard, Suite 300-9
Bethesda, MD 20817
800-962-9629 (voice)
301-881-9817 (fax)
www.spinalcord.org

Provides information and support to people
with spinal cord injuries and their families.

National Tourette Syndrome Association, Inc.

42-40 Bell Blvd.
Bayside, NY 11361
718-224-2999 (voice)
www.tsa-usa.org

Has information about TS, its treatment, scientific
research, and consumer services. NTSA publishes a quarterly newsletter, maintains a crisis
hotline, and produces literature for people with
TS and their families, medical professionals,
educators, and legislators.

Schwab Learning

1650 South Amphlett Boulevard, Suite 300
San Mateo, CA 94402
650-655-2410 (voice)
650-655-2411 (fax)
www.schwablearning.org

The Schwab Foundation provides parents and
educators in the San Francisco area quarterly educational programs, information and referrals, and
guidance counseling. The site includes extensive
resources about ADD, assessments, dyslexia,
homework, IEPs, learning disabilities, tutors,
teaching methods, family issues, and much more.

Signing Exact English Center for the Advancement of Deaf Children

P.O. Box 1181
Los Alamitos, CA 90720
562-430-1467 (voice)
562-795-6614 (fax)
www.seecenter.org

Promotes the understanding of signing exact
English to improve English skills for deaf children. SEE Center services include a telephone
information service about deafness, workshops,
videotapes, and a parent information packet
containing questions for parents to ask, especially in the school setting.

Spina Bifida Association of America

4590 MacArthur Blvd., NW, Suite 250
Washington, DC 20007-4226
202-944-3285 (voice)
800-621-3141 (voice)
202-944-3295 (fax)
sbaa@sbaa.org (email)
www.sbaa.org

Offers educational programs and support services for people with spina bifida, their families, and concerned professionals; acts as a clearinghouse on information related to spina bifida; provides referral services; conducts seminars; and monitors legislation and regulations.

United Cerebral Palsy Association

1660 L Street, NW, Suite 700
Washington, DC 20036
800-872-5827 (voice)
202-973-7197 (TTY)
800-776-0414 (fax)
webmaster@ucp.org (email)
www.ucp.org

Assists individuals with cerebral palsy and other developmental disabilities and their families. UCPA provides parent education, early intervention information, family support, respite services, and information on assistive technology.

Williams Syndrome Association

P.O. Box 297
Clawson, MI 48017-0297
800-806-1871 (voice)
248-244-2230 (fax)
info@williams-syndrome.org (email)
www.williams-syndrome.org

Provides information for parents, teachers, and doctors of children with Williams Syndrome, a rare genetic condition that causes medical and developmental problems.

Appendix 4

Sample IEP Form

Every school district, in every state, has its own IEP form. While the forms vary, they must include the same information. We strongly recommend that you request a copy of your school's IEP form early in the process.

To get you familiar with IEP forms, we have included a sample here, reprinted with permission of the Marin County (California) Office of Education. You can also access this form online at www.marinschools.org/selpa.htm.

Individualized Education Program

MARIN SELPA
IEP
Page 1
7/02

Date _____

<table>
<tr><td>Shaded boxes are situational.
All other areas must be addressed.</td></tr>
</table>

IDENTIFYING INFORMATION

Student:_____ Birthdate _____ Age _____ Grade _____ ❑ M ❑ F

❑ LCI
Parent/Guardian _____ ❑ Foster Home _____

Address _____ City _____ Zip _____

Home Phone _____ Work Phone(s) _____ Home Language _____

District of Residence _____ School _____

Student's Language Proficiency ❑ English Only ❑ Fluent English Proficient ❑ Limited English Proficient ❑ Non English Proficient

Determined by _____ Date _____ Primary Language Level _____
                          Name of Test

DATES OF ANTICIPATED MEETINGS

Annual Review _____ AB 3632 6 Month Review _____ 3-yr. Reevaluation _____ Add'l Review _____
         Month/Day/Year   Month/Day/Year   Month/Day/Year   Month/Day/Year

IEP MEETING INFORMATION

Purpose of the meeting: (*Check all that apply*)
❑ Initial ❑ Annual Review ❑ Review Based on 3-yr. Reevaluation ❑ AB3632 6 Month Review ❑ Promotion/Retention
❑ Manifestation Determination   ❑ Transition   ❑ Parent Request   ❑ Amend IEP dated _____
❑ Review assessments   ❑ Determine eligibility   ❑ Develop goals and objectives   ❑ Develop/review behavioral plan
❑ Recommend placement/service(s)   ❑ _____

WHAT CONCERN(S) DOES THE PARENT WANT TO SEE ADDRESSED IN THIS IEP TO ENHANCE THE STUDENT'S EDUCATION?

THE FOLLOWING ASSESSMENT REPORT(S) WERE REVIEWED. REPORT(S) INCLUDE DESCRIPTION(S) OF THE CHILD'S STRENGTHS, GENERAL EDUCATION PERFORMANCE INCLUDING STAR TESTING RESULTS AND REPORT CARDS, AND ACHIEVEMENT TOWARDS GOALS AND OBJECTIVES (*Please list name of report, examiner(s), and date of report*)

Student _____   Date of Meeting _____

MARIN SELPA
IEP
Page 2
10/02

ELIGIBILITY AS AN INDIVIDUAL WITH EXCEPTIONAL NEEDS - Circle primary handicapping condition

1. Meets eligibility criteria as indicated: IEP team previously determined eligibility on _____

❏ Mentally Retarded   ❏ Hard of Hearing   ❏ Visually Impaired   ❏ Orthopedically Impaired

❏ Language or Speech Disorder   ❏ Emotionally Disturbed   ❏ Traumatic Brain Injury   ❏ Deaf/Blind

❏ Autistic-Like Behaviors   ❏ Deaf   ❏ Multi-Handicapped _____

❏ Specific Learning Disability   ❏ Other Health Impaired *Specific Impairment* _____

2. Specific eligibility was unable to be determined. Recommend: _____

3. Does not meet eligibility for handicaps considered: _____

REQUIRED IEP TEAM CONSIDERATIONS - If "yes", indicate where the need is addressed in the IEP

Does the child's behavior impede his or her learning or that of others?   ❏ Yes ❏ No   IEP Page _____

Does the child have limited English proficiency?   ❏ Yes ❏ No   IEP Page _____

Does the child have any special communication needs?   ❏ Yes ❏ No   IEP Page _____

Does the child require any assistive technology devices or services in order to be involved, and
to progress in the general curriculum or to be educated in a less restrictive environment?   ❏ Yes ❏ No   IEP Page _____

If the child is blind or visually impaired, does the evaluation of the child's reading and writing skills,
needs and appropriate reading and writing media (including an evaluation of the child's future need
for instruction in Braille or the use of Braille), indicate the instruction in Braille   ❏ Yes ❏ No
or the use of Braille is appropriate for the child?   ❏ NA   IEP Page _____

If the child is deaf or hard of hearing, does the child have any special language or communication   ❏ Yes ❏ No
needs that affect their education needs?   ❏ NA   IEP Page _____

GOALS AND OBJECTIVES

❏ Draft IEP goals and objectives were reviewed, revised, and are recommended.

❏ IEP goals and objectives were recommended on _____ and are continued.*

❏ In addition to IEP goals and objectives continued from the meeting on _____,* additional goals and
      objectives were reviewed, reivised and are recommended.

   *At or after the Annual Review

PUPIL PROMOTION AND RETENTION (GRADES 2-8)

Promotion from grade _____ to grade _____ shall be based on the following criteria:

❏ District adopted criteria for general education students

❏ IEP Individualized Promotion Standards (specify standards below or on page _____. These promotion standards may
      include grades and achievement of IEP objectives, and level of achievement required for promotion. Grades 2-4
      require reading standards only; grades 5-8 require reading, language arts, and math.)

_____

_____

Is the student at risk of retention? ❏ Yes ❏ No If "yes", the following must be considered by the IEP team:

❏ Yes ❏ No   Is the current IEP for the student's academic, linguistic, social and emotional, and behavioral needs appropriate?

❏ Yes ❏ No   Is the manner of assessment, including any accommodations and modifications, identified in the IEP appropriate?

❏ Yes ❏ No   Were all the services required by the student to make progress in the general education curriculum appropriately identified
                in the student's IEP?

❏ Yes ❏ No   Did the student receive all the services identified in the IEP?

❏ Yes ❏ No   Was the assessment conducted consistent with the IEP?

❏ Yes ❏ No   Was the student's promotion standard appropriate and clarified in the IEP?

See page _____ for IEP Team recommendations

Distribution: White-Permanent File   Canary-Parent   Copies may be made for other team members

Student _____ Date of Meeting _____

MARIN SELPA
IEP
Page 3
6/01

ELIGIBILITY FOR A SPECIFIC LEARNING DISABILITY

I.Presence of a Severe Discrepancy (Select either A or B and then complete items II through IV)
    ❏ A. The IEP Team finds a severe discrepancy (18.5 points or more) between measures of intellectual ability and one
           or more of the following areas of achievement:
         ❏ Oral Expression   ❏ Written Expression   ❏ Listening Comprehension
         ❏ Mathematics Calculation   ❏ Mathematics Reasoning   ❏ Basic Reading Skills
         ❏ Reading Comprehension
         Measure of Intellectual Ability_____ Score(s) _____
         Test(s) of Academic Achievement/Scores(s) _____
         _____
         Discrepancy between Intellectual Ability and Academic Achievement _____

    ❏ B. Standard measures do not reveal a severe discrepancy, but the IEP team finds a severe discrepancy does exist
           based upon the additional documentation provided in the attached report. (Complete and attach "Specific
           Learning Disability Discrepancy" documentation-See page 4)

II. The discrepancy identified in Item 1 (above) is directly related to a processing disorder. ❏ Yes ❏ No
        Check the appropriate area(s):
    ❏ Sensory Motor Skills   ❏ Visual Processing   ❏ Auditory Processing ❏ Attention
    ❏ Cognitive Abilities (including asssociation, conceptualization, and expression)
    Name of Test _____ Score _____

III. If any of the items below (A-E) are checked "Yes", the student may not be identified as having a specific learning
    disability.
    A. The discrepancy is due primarily to limited school experience or poor school attendance.   ❏ Yes ❏ No
    B. The discrepancy is a result of environmental, cultural difference or economic disadvantage.   ❏ Yes ❏ No
    C. The discrepancy is due primarily to mental retardation or emotional disturbance.   ❏ Yes ❏ No
    D. The discrepany is due primarily to a visual, hearing or motor disability   ❏ Yes ❏ No
    E. This discrepancy can be corrected through other regular or categorical services offered within
           the regular instructional program.   ❏ Yes ❏ No

IV. The student has a specific learning disability. ❏ Yes ❏ No

I agree with the conclusions stated above:

_____   _____
Credentialed School Psychologist/Date   Special Ed. Admin./Designee/Date

_____   _____
Resource Specialist/Date   Teacher/Date

_____   _____
Language Speech Specialist/Date   Nurse/Date

_____   _____
Parent/Guardian/Date   Other/Date

_____   _____
Other/Date   Other/Date

My assessment of this student differs from the above report as follows: Statement (attach additional pages as necessary)

_____
Signature and Title/Date
Distribution: White-Permanent File   Canary-Parent   Copies may be made for other team members

Student _____   Date of Meeting _____

**MARIN
SELPA**
IEP
Page 4
6/01

SPECIFIC LEARNING DISABILITY DISCREPANCY DOCUMENTATION REPORT

This form is to be completed in order to document the presence of a Specific Learning Disability in instances when the student does not exhibit a severe discrepancy between ability and achievement as measured by standardized tests. (Ed. Code 3030 (j)(C))

1. Data from assessment instruments (ability and achievement): _____
_____
_____
_____
_____

2. Information provided by parent: _____
_____
_____
_____

3. Information provided by the pupil's present teacher: _____
_____
_____
_____

4. Summary of the pupil's classroom performance:
   a. Observations: _____
   _____
   _____

   b. Work Samples: _____
   _____
   _____

   c. Group Test Scores: _____
   _____
   _____

5. Consideration of the pupil's age: _____
_____
_____
_____

6. Additional Relevant Information _____
_____
_____
_____
_____

Distribution: White-Permanent File   Canary-Parent   Copies may be made for other team members

Student _____ Date of Meeting _____

MARIN SELPA
IEP
Page 5
6/01

ELIGIBILITY FOR LANGUAGE OR SPEECH DISORDER

Must Meet One or More of Criteria 1-5 and Criteria 6 and 7.

❑ 1. **Articulation Disorder -** Such that the pupil's production of speech significantly interferes with communication and attracts adverse attention. Significant interference in communication occurs when the pupil's production of single or multiple speech sounds on a developmental scale of articulation competency is below that expected for his or her chronological age or developmental level.

    Chronological Age or Developmetal Level _____

    Articulation Test _____ Age Equivalent, Standard Score or %ile _____

❑ 2. **Abnormal Voice -** A pupil has an abnormal voice which is characterized by persistent, defective voice quality, pitch or loudness. (Student must have medical clearance for voice therapy.)

❑ 3. **Fluency Disorders -** A pupil has a fluency disorder when the flow of verbal expression including rate and rhythm adversely affects communication between the pupil and listener.

❑ 4. **Language or Speech Disorder -** Which is the result of a hearing loss.

❑ 5. **Language Disorder -** *The pupil has an expressive or receptive language disorder when he or she meets one of the following criteria:*

    ❑ A. The pupil scores at least 1.5 standard deviations (22.5 points) below the mean or below the 7th percentile, for his or her chronological age or developmental level on *two or more* standardized tests in one or more of the following areas of language development. *Check appropriate area(s):*

        ❑ Morphology   ❑ Syntax   ❑ Semantics   ❑ Pragmatics

        Chronological Age or Developmental Level _____

        Standardized Test _____ Discrepancy _____ %ile _____

        Standardized Test _____ Discrepancy _____ %ile _____

    ❑ B. The pupil scores at least 1.5 standard deviations below the mean or the score is below the 7%ile for his or her chrono-logical age or developmental level on one or more standardized tests in one of the areas listed above *AND* displays inappropriate or inadequate usage of expressive or receptive language as measured by a representative spontaneous or elicited language sample of fifty utterances. *Check appropriate area(s):*

        ❑ Morphology   ❑ Syntax   ❑ Semantics   ❑ Pragmatics

        Chronological Age or Developmental Level _____

        Standardized Test: _____ Discrepancy _____ %ile _____

        Language Sample Results _____

❑ 6. **Adversely affects educational performance.**

❑ 7. **Cannot be corrected without special education and related services.**

ELIGIBILITY FOR CHILDREN BETWEEN THE AGES OF THREE AND FIVE YEARS

Must Meet Criteria I and II

I. **Meets eligibility criteria as indicated:**

    ❑ Mentally Retarded   ❑ Hard of Hearing   ❑ Multi-Handicapped   ❑ Visually Impaired

    ❑ Orthopedically Impaired   ❑ Other Health Impaired *Specific Impairment* _____

    ❑ Deaf/Blind   ❑ Autistic-Like Behaviors ❑ Traumatic Brain Injury   ❑ Deaf

    ❑ Specific Learning Disability   ❑ Language or Speech Disorder   ❑ Emotionally Disturbed

    or

    ❑ Has an established medical disability, which is defined as a disabling medical condition or congenital syndrome which the IEP team determines has a high predictability of requiring intensive special education and services.

        *Specify:*_____

II. **If any of the items below (A-D) are checked "Yes", The student may not be eligible for special education and services if his or her educational needs are due primarily to:**

    A. Unfamiliarity with the English Language   ❑ Yes ❑ No

    B. Temporary physical disabilities   ❑ Yes ❑ No

    C. Social maladjustment   ❑ Yes ❑ No

    D. Environmental, cultural or economic factors   ❑ Yes ❑ No

III. **Needs cannot be met with modification of regular environment**   ❑ Yes ❑ No

Distribution: White-Permanent File Canary-Parent   Copies may be made for other team members

Transition Service Needs

Beginning at age 14

Student _____   Date of Meeting _____

Anticipated Date of Graduation or Completion _____

DESIRED POST-SCHOOL OUTCOME STATEMENT - *Long-Range Goals*

Employment/ Post-Secondary Education Outcomes	Domestic	Community Functioning	Transportation	Recreation
Employment ❏ Competitive employment without support ❏ Competitve employment with time-limited support ❏ Competitive employment with long-term support ❏ Supported employment ❏ Sheltered employment ❏ Military ❏ _____ **Education** ❏ Apprenticeship program ❏ Vocational college ❏ Technical institute ❏ Community College ❏ 4-year College ❏ GED Program ❏ _____	**Housing** ❏ Live alone without supports ❏ Live alone with support ❏ Live with family/relative ❏ Live with roommate(s) ❏ Group home-specialized training ❏ Supervised apartment ❏ Residential/nursing facility ❏ Individual services coordinator ❏ Lifetime support/planning ❏ _____ **Income/Resources** ❏ Earned wages ❏ Social Security benefits ❏ Unearned income ❏ Trust/will ❏ Food stamps ❏ _____ **Medicaid Services** ❏ Personal assistive devices ❏ Group insurance ❏ Independent in monitoring medical needs ❏ Requires medical vision/ scheduling ❏ Special therapies and treatments	**Adult Responsibilities** ❏ Voter registration ❏ Registration for selective service ❏ Social Security registration ❏ Self-consumer advocacy ❏ Parenting ❏ Voluteerism ❏ _____ **Support Services** ❏ Guardianship ❏ Family planning ❏ Counseling services ❏ Respite services ❏ Day Activities ❏ _____	**Mode of Transportation** ❏ Self (Driver's License) ❏ Public transportation ❏ Specialized transportation ❏ Family transports ❏ Car pool ❏ _____	**Social and Leisure** ❏ Independent recreation and leisure ❏ Family supported recreation and leisure ❏ Specialized recreation ❏ Community-supported recreation program ❏ Local clubs ❏ Day programs ❏ _____

PROPOSED COURSES RELATED TO DESIRED POST SCHOOL OUTCOMES

8th Grade	9th Grade	10th Grade	11th Grade	12th Grade

Distribution: White-Permanent File   Canary-Parent   Copies may be made for other team members

Transition Services

BEGINNING AT AGE 16 OR YOUNGER, IF DETERMINED APPROPRIATE BY THE IEP TEAM

**MARIN
SELPA**
IEP
Page 7
1/03

Student _____   Date of Meeting _____

❏ If 17 years old, student received a copy of the Procedural Rights _____
                                                                  Student's Signature

SUMMARY OF STUDENT'S NEEDS, INTERESTS, AND PREFERENCES

_____
_____
_____
_____

STATEMENT OF NEEDED SERVICES

Development of Employment/Post-Secondary Education Outcomes

Provide justification if services not needed:

_____
_____
_____

Indicate Outcomes for the Current Year	Semesters	Person or Agency Responsible
❏ Locate sources of occupational and training information		
❏ Classify jobs into occupational categories		
❏ Investigate local occupational and training opportunities		
❏ Submit referral to Department of Rehabilitation		
❏ Make realistic occupational choices		
❏ Identify requirements of appropriate and available jobs		
❏ Identify occupational aptitudes		
❏ Identify major occupational interests		
❏ Plan and make realistic training and job placement decisions		
❏ Develop training plan for occupational choice		
❏ Identify local apprenticeship programs		
❏ Explore enrollment in GED program		
❏ Identify entrance requirements for military services		
❏ Identify entrance requirements for vocational college, technical institute, community college, and/or four year college		
❏ Take the SAT Exam		
❏ Follow directions and observe regulations		
❏ Recognize importance of attendance and punctuality		
❏ Recognize the importance of supervision		
❏ Work with others		
❏ Meet demands for quality and quantity work standards		
❏ Work at a satisfactory rate		
❏ Search for a job		
❏ Apply for a job		
❏ Interview for a job		
❏ _____		

Distribution: White-Permanent File   Canary-Parent   Copies may be made for other team members

Transition Services

BEGINNING AT AGE 16 OR YOUNGER, IF DETERMINED APPROPRIATE BY THE IEP TEAM

MARIN SELPA
IEP
Page 8
1/03

Student _____ Date of Meeting _____

Domestic Skills Outcome for the Current Year

Provide justification if service not needed _____

Indicate Outcomes for the Current Year	Semesters	Person or Agency Responsible
❏ Count money and make correct change		
❏ Keep basic financial records		
❏ Calculate and pay taxes		
❏ Use banking services		
❏ Maintain living environment exterior/interior		
❏ Use basic appliances and tools		
❏ Select adequate housing/personal living space		
❏ Set up household/personal living space		
❏ Exhibit proper grooming and hygiene		
❏ Dress appropriately		
❏ Demonstrate knowledge of common illness, prevention, and treatment		
❏ Practice personal safety and/or basic first aid		
❏ Purchase food		
❏ Demonstrate cleaning food prep area, meal clean-up, and food storage		
❏ Prepare food		
❏ Demonstrate appropriate eating habits		
❏ Plan/eat well balanced meals		
❏ Wash/clean clothing		
❏ Purchase clothing		
❏ Iron, mend, and store clothing		
❏ _____		

Community Functioning Outcomes for the Current Year

Provide justification if services not needed _____

Indicate Outcomes for the Current Year	Semesters	Person or Agency Responsible
❏ Demonstrate knowledge of civil rights and responsibilities		
❏ Identify physical and psychological needs		
❏ Identify interests and abilities		
❏ Express feelings of self-worth and self-confidence		
❏ Accept and give praise/criticism		
❏ Demonstrate listening and responding skills		
❏ Make and maintain friendships		
❏ Demonstrate self-organization		
❏ _____		

Distribution: White-Permanent File   Canary-Parent   Copies may be made for other team members

**MARIN
SELPA**
IEP
Page 9
6/02

Transition Services

BEGINNING AT AGE 16 OR YOUNGER, IF DETERMINED APPROPRIATE BY THE IEP TEAM

Student _____ Date of Meeting _____

Post-Secondary Transportation Outcomes for the Current Year

Provide justification if service not needed _____
_____
_____
_____

Indicate Outcomes for the Current Year	Semesters	Person or Agency Responsible
❑ Demonstrate knowledge of traffic rules and safety		
❑ Demonstrate knowledge and use of various means of transportation		
❑ Find way around community		
❑ Access available transportation		
❑ Study for and take driving test		
❑ Obtain a California Driver's License or ID		
❑ Demonstrate knowledge of car insurance		
❑ _____		

Recreation Outcomes for the Current Year

Provide justification if service not needed
_____
_____
_____
_____

Indicate Outcomes for the Current Year	Semesters	Person or Agency Responsible
❑ Demonstrate knowledge of community leisure/recreational resources		
❑ Choose and plan leisure/recreational activities		
❑ Engage in group and individual leisure/recreational activities		
❑ _____		

DOCUMENTATION OF AGENCY CONTACTS AND LINKAGES

Date	Agency Contacted/ To Be Contacted	Needed Services	Team Member Who Will Make Contact and Follow-Up	Comments
	Department of Rehabilitation	**Client?** ❑ Yes ❑ No		
	Golden Gate Regional Center	**Client?** ❑ Yes ❑ No		
	Social Security Administration	**Client?** ❑ Yes ❑ No		
	Employment Development	**Client?** ❑ Yes ❑ No		
	Community Mental Health	**Client?** ❑ Yes ❑ No		
	Social Services	**Client?** ❑ Yes ❑ No		
		Client? ❑ Yes ❑ No		

Distribution: White-Permanent File   Canary-Parent   Copies may be made for other team members

Behavioral Intervention Plan

**MARIN
SELPA**
IEP
Page 10
6/02

Student _____   Date of Meeting _____

TARGET BEHAVIOR

Describe the behavior that impedes learning. What does it look like?

How often does the behavior occur? With what intensity? How long does it last?

What happens before the behavior occurs? With whom? Where? When? (Most and least likely)

The IEP team believes the behavior occurs because (function/communicative intent):

What is in or missing from the environment, curriculum, or instruction that contributes to this behavior?

TARGET BEHAVIOR PREVENTION PLAN - Based upon antecedent/predictor analysis

What environmental structures and supports need to be changed or introduced to prevent the behavior from occurring?

Behavioral Intervention Plan

MARIN SELPA
IEP
Page 11
6/02

Student _____   Date of Meeting _____

REPLACEMENT BEHAVIOR

What strengths does the student have that will help him/her to be successful in using/learning the replacement behaviors?

What should the student do instead of this behavior? (This should serve the same function/communicatve intent of the target behavior)

Does the student currently have the skills to use the behavior? If "yes", when is it most likey to occur?

Are there goals and objectives related to this plan? ❏ Yes ❏ No If "yes", please indicate page number(s) of goal(s).

REPLACEMENT BEHAVIOR PLAN

Does the replacement behavior identified need reinforcement only?   ❏ Yes ❏ No

Does the replacement behavior need to be taught and reinforced?   ❏ Yes ❏ No
If "yes", describe the teaching strategies needed to help the student master the new behavior:

Are accommodations in curriculum and instruction needed?   ❏ Yes ❏ No
If "yes", see page 18 of the IEP for needed accommodations.

What is the plan for reinforcing the desired replacement behavior when it occurs?

What will the response of staff be if the target behavior occurs?

Distribution: White-Permanent File   Canary-Parent   Copies may be made for other team members

Proposed Behavior Intervention Plan (Hughes Bill)

Student _____ Date of Meeting _____

SUMMARY OF FUNCTIONAL ANALYSIS ASSESSMENT

OBJECTIVE AND MEASURABLE DESCRIPTION OF TARGETED MALADAPTIVE AND REPLACEMENT BEHAVIORS

Targeted maladaptive behavior(s)

Replacement positive behavior(s)

STUDENT'S GOALS AND OBJECTIVES SPECIFIC TO THE BEHAVIORAL INTERVENTION PLAN

DESCRIPTION OF INTERVENTIONS TO BE USED AND CIRCUMSTANCES FOR USE

Distribution: White-Permanent File   Canary-Parent   Copies may be made for other team members

Student _____ Date of Meeting _____

**MARIN
SELPA
IEP
Page 13
6/01**

RECORDING SCHEDULES

Frequency of use of interventions

Frequency of data collection (targeted and replacement behavior(s)

Criteria for discontinuing use of interventions due to lack of effectiveness

Criteria for phasing out or less intense/frequent schedules or techniques

EXTENT TO WHICH INTERVENTIONS WILL BE CARRIED OUT IN OTHER SETTINGS (WORK, COMMUNITY, HOME, ETC.)

DATES FOR PERIODIC REVIEW BY IEP TEAM TO DETERMINE EFFICACY OF PROGRAM

Distribution: White-Permanent File   Canary-Parent   Copies may be made for other team members

Manifestation Determination

Student _____   Date of Present Meeting _____

DESCRIPTION OF BEHAVIOR SUBJECT TO DISCIPLINARY ACTION

THE IEP TEAM CONSIDERED ALL THE RELEVANT INFORMATION INCLUDING:

Evaluation and Diagnostic Results

Information Supplied by the Parents

Observation of the Student

The Student's IEP and Placement

Distribution: White-Permanent File   Canary-Parent   Copies may be made for other team members

MARIN
SELPA
IEP
Page 15
2/03

Student _____ Date of Meeting _____

THE IEP TEAM HAS DETERMINED

In relationship to the behavior subject to the disciplinary action:

❏ Yes ❏ No   Were the student's IEP and placement appropriate?
If "no", specify why the IEP and placement were not appropriate:

❏ Yes ❏ No   Were the special education services, supplementary aids and services, and behavior intervention strategies provided consistent with the student's IEP and placement?

If "no", specify: 1) why the IEP was not implemented and 2) whether the failure to implement the IEP impacted the student's behavior. It may be necessary to review and revise the IEP and placement.

❏ Yes ❏ No   Did the student's disability impair his/her ability to understand the impact and consequences of the behavior subject to disciplinary action.
If "yes", the behavior must be considered a manifestation of the student's disability.

❏ Yes ❏ No   Did the student's disability impair his/her disability to control the behavior subject to disciplinary action.
If "yes", the behavior must be considered a manifestation of the student's disability.

Check the appropriate box:

❏   The student's behavior WAS NOT a manifestation of his/her disability. The relevant disciplinary procedures applicable to students without disabilities may be applied to the student in the same manner in which they are applied to students without disabilities. However, the district must continue to make FAPE available to the student.

❏   The student's behavior WAS a manifestation of his/her disability. The IEP team must review and revise the student's IEP as appropriate, including development or review of a behavioral intervention plan.

Distribution: White-Permanent File   Canary-Parent   Copies may be made for other team members

Student _____   Date of Meeting _____

**MARIN
SELPA**
IEP
Page 16
6/02

DISTRICT JUSTIFICATION FOR EDUCATIONAL PLACEMENT

RECOMMENDED EDUCATIONAL PLACEMENT	CORRESPONDING PLACEMENT
IEP services can be provided solely in the general education classroom	❏ General Education Classroom
Some IEP services should be provided outside the general education classroom	❏ Some services outside the General Education classroom
All IEP services should be provided outside the general education classroom.	❏ Special Day Class
All IEP services should be provided outside the general education classroom and separately from a school that also serves students without disabilities.	❏ Special Day Class on an isolated site ❏ Non Public School - Day Program
IEP services require a 24-hour educational program.	❏ AB 3632 Residential Placement
Home-based IEP services for a student who is 3 to 5 years of age.	❏ Home-based Early Childhood Program
IEP services provided in a program outside of the home for a student who is 3 to 5 years of age.	❏ Center-based Early Childhood Program
A mix of IEP services that are not provided in primarily school-based settings.	❏ Other

JUSTIFICATION FOR NON PARTICIPATION IN GENERAL EDUCATION

Is the student removed from the general education classroom at any time?   ❏ Yes   ❏ No
Percent of time out of general education classroom? _____%
If "yes", why is removal considered critical to the student's program?

1. ❏   Small group instruction is necessary for this student to acquire skills specified in the IEP.
2. ❏   Behavioral intervention plan and/or behavioral goals and objectives recommended in the student's IEP require a degree of structure which cannot be implemented in a large group setting.
3. ❏   The student's needs as addressed in IEP goals and objectives cannot be satisfactorily achieved in the general educational/preschool environment even with the provision of supplemental aids and services.
4. ❏   Student's behavior significantly impairs his/her ability to learn in a large group setting, as well as impairing the learning of other students in a large group setting.
5. ❏   Based upon individual needs and goals and objectives in the student's IEP,
    ❏ the general curriculum/appropriate preschool activities would need to be completely restructured.
    ❏ additional individualized instruction is required to facilitate his/her learning.
    ❏ an intensive behavior management program is required.
6. ❏   A more structured environment is needed than can be provided in the general education classroom.
7. ❏   Student requires utilization of the Severely Handicapped Alternative Curriculum Guide in a highly structured environment to acquire skills specified in their IEP.
8. ❏   _____
    _____

TYPE OF PHYSICAL EDUCATION

❏ Regular Physical Education   ❏ Adapted Physical Education   ❏ Modified Physical Education
❏ Specially Designed Physical Education   ❏ Not Applicable

Distribution: White-Permanent File   Canary-Parent   Copies may be made for other team members

Student _____ Date of Meeting _____

MARIN SELPA
IEP
Page 17
8/02

PLACEMENT, SERVICES, AND EQUIPMENT CONSIDERED AND RECOMMENDED

Considered | IEP Team Recommends

Dates
Unless otherwise specified, services will be for the regular school year.

Location
Please check appropriate box(es) and specify location

___ ❑ Special Day Class From_____ To _____   ❑ Public-Home School _____

___ ❑ Day ❑ Residential ❑ Pursuant to AB 3632   ❑ Public-Other Than Home School* _____
                                                    ❑ Certified Non Public School* _____
                                                    ❑ _____ *

*If not home school, rationale: ❑ Public Preschool ❑ Student would benefit from program available on an isolated site.
❑ Needs cannot be met at home school ❑ Student would benefit from program available at site other than home school

Considered | IEP Team Recommends

Dates (Month/Day/Year)
Services checked below will be provided until the next annual review excluding holidays, non-student days, and all vacations unless otherwise specified.

Frequency

Location
Please identify the specific location(s) of the program(s)/service(s) and indicate
C = Classroom OR
R = Room Other Than Gen. Ed. or SDC

___ ❑ Resource Specialist From_____ To _____ _____ _____ ❑ C ❑ R
                           ❑ Direct   ❑ Consult

___ ❑ Language/Speech From_____ To _____ _____ _____ ❑ C ❑ R
                       ❑ Direct   ❑ Consult

___ ❑ Occupational Tx From_____ To _____ _____ _____ ❑ C ❑ R
                       ❑ Direct   ❑ Consult

___ ❑ CCS Services From_____ To _____ _____ _____
                    ❑ Direct   ❑ Consult   ❑ Monitor ❑ Occupational Therapy ❑ Physical Therapy

___ ❑ Home/Hospital From_____ To _____ _____ _____ ❑ C ❑ R
                     ❑ Direct   ❑ Consult

___ ❑ Add. Classroom From_____ To _____ _____ _____ ❑ C ❑ R
        Support

___ ❑ Community Mental From_____ To _____ _____ _____ ❑ C ❑ R
        Health

___ ❑ _____ From_____ To _____ _____ _____ ❑ C ❑ R
                  ❑ Direct   ❑ Consult

___ ❑ _____ From_____ To _____ _____ _____ ❑ C ❑ R
                  ❑ Direct   ❑ Consult

___ ❑ Transportation _____

___ ❑ Specialized equipment/services _____
     _____

EXTENDED SCHOOL YEAR

❑ Does not require special education and related services in excess of the regular academic year.
❑ Recommended based upon unique or severe needs.

Program/DIS Service	Dates (Month/Day/Year)	Frequency	Location	
❑ Special Day Class	From_____ To _____		_____	
_____	From_____ To _____	_____	_____	❑ C ❑ R
_____	From_____ To _____	_____	_____	❑ C ❑ R
_____	From_____ To _____	_____	_____	❑ C ❑ R
_____	From_____ To _____	_____	_____	❑ C ❑ R
Transportation	From_____ To _____	_____		

MARIN
SELPA
IEP
Page 18
6/02

Student _____   Date of Meeting _____

ACCOMMODATIONS, MODIFICATIONS, AND GRADING

These are to assist the student in attaining the annual goals stated on the IEP as well as increasing the student's involvement and progress in the general curriculum.

Accommodations are adjustments for students with disabilities in instruction or student output that minimize the impact of the disability but do not fundamentally alter or lower course standards or expectations.

Modifications are adjustments for students with disabilities in instruction or student output that minimize the impact of the disability but fundamentally alter or lower course standards or expectations. **Grades** may be modified or a course description may be modified to reflect modified curriculum.

ACCOMMODATION	List specific COURSES	ACCOMMODATION	List specific COURSES
1. Highlighted Texts		13. Preferential Seating	
2. Taped Texts		14. Reduced Paper/Pencil Tasks	
3. Note-Taking Assistance		15. Repeated Review/Drill	
4. Taped Lectures		16. Alternative Materials/Assignments	
5. Peer Buddy		17. Assistive Technology	
6. Peer Tutor		18. Reader Services	
7. Assignment Notebooks		19. Calculator	
8. Extended Time for Completing Assignments		20. Study Sheets	
9. Shortened Assignments		21. Braille	
10. Frequent Breaks		22. Large Type	
11. Directions Given in a Variety of Ways		23. _____	
12. Increased Verbal Response		24. _____	

ACCOMMODATIONS FOR CLASSROOM OR DISTRICT TESTS OTHER THAN STATEWIDE - Specify Course(s)/Tests

1. Extended Time		4. Alternative Tests	
2. Oral Tests		5. Short-Answer Tests	
3. Alternative Setting		6.	

SUPPORTS FOR SCHOOL PERSONNEL

❑ Yes ❑ No   Are supports for school personnel needed for the student to advance appropriately toward attaining the annual goals, participate in the general curriculum, and be educated and participate with others in educational activities? If yes, specify what supports are needed. _____

Distribution: White-Permanent File   Canary-Parent   Copies may be made for other team members

Student _____   Date of Meeting _____

MARIN
SELPA
IEP
Page 19
7/03

MODIFICATIONS - *Use the codes below or use an additional page to describe modifications per course or content area*		
CONTENT AREAS	**CODE**	**DESCRIPTION OF MODIFICATION OF CURRICULUM**
Reading		
Math		
Social Studies/History		
Science		
Language Arts		
Spelling		
Classroom or District Tests Other Than Statewide		

CODES
1. Out of Level Curriculum
2. Partial Curriculum (specify which concepts and standards are covered and which are omitted).
3. Individualized Curriculum, adapting standards to student's ability (attach description of curriculum concepts/ standards to be covered and expectations of student).

GRADES - *Required if grade/course are to be modified*

Which of the courses will result in a modified grade?

How does a modified grade show on the student's report card? On the student's transcript?

Does it affect honor roll or academic awards? ❏ Yes ❏ No   Does it affect class ranking? ❏ Yes ❏ No

Elementary and Middle School Students	**Middle School and High School Students**
Does the modified grade/course affect STAR testing? ❏ Yes ❏ No If "yes", what is the result? ❏ Student participates in STAR Testing with modifications ❏ Student participate in the CAPA	Does the modified grade/course affect credits towards high school graduation? ❏ Yes ❏ No If "yes", what is the result?
Does the modified grade/course affect Promotion/Retention? ❏ Yes ❏ No If "yes", what is the result? ❏ IEP Individualized Promotion Standards ❏	Does the modified grade/course affect ability to pass High School Exit Exam? ❏ Yes ❏ No If "yes", what is the result?

Reason for Modified Curriculum/Grade:
❏ Student requires utilization of SH Modified Alternative Curriculum Guide in a highly structured environment to acquire skills specified in their IEP.
❏ _____

I understand that my son/daughter will receive a modified grade in the subjects/courses listed above and I consent to the modification.
Parent/Guardian Signature _____   Date _____

Distribution: White-Permanent File   Canary-Parent   Copies may be made for other team members

Student _____ Date of Meeting _____

MARIN SELPA
IEP
Page 20a
7/03

PARTICIPATION IN STATEWIDE ASSESSMENT OF STUDENT ACHIEVEMENT - STAR TESTING

STAR Testing - Required for grades 2-11

❏ Student can participate in the statewide achievement testing program without accommodations/modifications.

Eligibility for the CAPA is based on a student's Individualized Education Program (IEP), which reflects an emphasis on functional life skills. To be eligible for participation in alternate assessment, the response to each of the statements below must be "Agree". If the answer to any of these questions is "Disagree", then the IEP team should consider including the student in the state's large-scale assessment.

Circle "Agree" or "Disagree" for each item:

Agree   Disagree   The student requires extensive instruction in multiple settings to acquire, maintain, and generalize skills necessary for application in school, work, home and community environments.

Agree   Disagree   The student demonstrates academic/cognitive ability and adaptive behavior that require substantial adjustments to the general curriculum. That student may participate in man of the same activities as their non-disabled peers; however, their learning objectives and expected outcomes focus on the functional applications of the general curriculum.

Agree   Disagree   The student cannot address the performance level assessed in the statewide assessment, even with extensive accommodations.

Agree   Disagree   The decision to participate in the alternate assessment is not primarily based on excessive or extended absences.

Agree   Disagree   The decision to participate in the alternate assessment is not primarily based on language, cultural or economic differences.

Agree   Disagree   The decision to participate in the alternate assessment is not primarily based deafness, blindness, visual, auditory, and/or motor disabilities.

Agree   Disagree   The decision to participate in the alternate assessment is not primarily based on achievement significantly lower than his or her same age peers.

Agree   Disagree   The decision to participate in the alternate assessment is not primarily based on a specific categorical label.

Agree   Disagree   The decision for alternate assessment is an IEP team decision, rather than an administrative decision.

❏ Student will participate in the California Alternate Performance Assessment (CAPA) at the level corresponding to his/her grade level placement.

❏ Student will participate in the California Alternate Performance Assessment (CAPA) Level 1 because he/she:
- is between the ages of seven and sixteen (grades 2-11) as of December 2
- has severe, pervasive disabilities
- functions at the sensorimotor developmental stage, approximately 24 months or less.

Student _____   Date of Meeting _____   **MARIN SELPA**
IEP
Page 20b
12/02

ACCOMMODATIONS/MODIFICATIONS FOR CALIFORNIA STATEWIDE ASSESSMENTS

❑ Student can participate in the statewide achievement testing program with the following ❑ accommodations ❑ modifications.

Accommodation/Modification	CAT/6	CST	SABE/2	CAHSEE	GSE	CELDT	Physical Fitness
Presentation							
Braille	2	2	2*	2	2	2*	Not Applicable
Large Print	2	2	2	2	2	2	Not Applicable
Use visual magnifying equipment	1	1	1	1	1	1	Not Applicable
Use audio amplication equipment	1	1	1	1	1	1	1
Simplify or clarify test directions	1	1	1	1	1	Not allowed on listening/speaking portion 2 Reading and writing portion	1
Use sign language to translate directions	2	2	2	2	2	2	2
Questions or items read aloud to student/audio presentation.	2 Except reading test 3 Reading test	2 Except ELA Test 3 ELA Test	2	2 Math portion 3** ELA Portion	2 Except reading, writing, and Spanish tests 3 Reading, writing, and Spanish tests	2 Writing portion only	Not Applicable
Use sign language to translate questions or items to student	2 Except reading test 3 Reading test	2 Except ELA Test 3 ELA Test		2 Math portion 3** ELA Portion	2 Except reading, writing, and Spanish tests 3 Reading, writing, and Spanish tests	2 Writing portion only	Not Applicable
Student highlights key words in test booklet	2	2	2	2	2	2	Not Applicable
On task reminders/verbal encouragement	1	1	1	1	1	1	1
Noise buffers	1	1	1	1	1	1	1
Turn pages for student	1	1	1	1	1	1	Not Applicable
Timing/Scheduling							
Extra time within a testing day	2	1	2	1	2	1	1
Test over more than one day (for test expected to be completed within one session)	2	2	2	2 Contact test contractor	2	2	2
Breaks within a subtest (supervised)	2	2	2	2	2	2	2
Administer at time most beneficial to student	2	2	2	2 Contact test contractor	2	2	2
Setting							
Test individually (supervised)	1	1	1	1	1	1	1
Test in small group	1	1	1	1	1	1	1
Provide special lighting	1	1	1	1	1	1	Not Applicable
Use adaptive furniture	1	1	1	1	1	1	Not Applicable
Test in study carrel/study enclosure	1	1	1	1	1	1	Not Applicable
Test at home or in hospital	2	2	2	2	2	2	2

Distribution: White-Permanent File   Canary-Parent   Copies may be made for other team members

Student _____ Date of Meeting _____

ACCOMMODATIONS/MODIFICATIONS FOR CALIFORNIA STATEWIDE ASSESSMENTS - CONTINUED

Accommodation/Modification	CAT/6	CST	SABE/2	CAHSEE	GSE	CELDT	Physical Fitness
Response							
Student marks response in test booklet (adult transfers to answer document)	2	2	2	2	2	2	Not Applicable
Indicate responses to a scribe for selected response items	Not Applicable	2	2	2	2	2	Not Applicable
Indicate responses to a scribe for a writing test (student indicates all spelling and language conventions)	Not Applicable	2	Not Applicable	2	2	2	Not Applicable
Indicate responses to a scribe for a writing test (scribe provides spelling, grammar, and language conventions)	3	3	Not Applicable	3**	3	3	Not Applicable
Use of Aids or Tools							
Use dictionary	3	3	3	3**	3	3	Not Applicable
Use word processing software with spell and grammar check tools turned off	2	2	Not Applicable	2	2	2	Not Applicable
Use spellchecker, grammar checker, or word processing software that checks spelling and grammar	3	3	Not Applicable	3**	3	3	Not Applicable
Use assistive device that does not interfere with the independent work of the student	2	2	2	2	2	2	Not Applicable
Use assistive device that interferes with the independent work of the student	3	3	3	3**	3	3	Not Applicable
Use calculator (program disabled)	3	3	3	3**	3	3	Not Applicable
Use an arithmetic table	3	3	3	3**	3	3	Not Applicable
Use a marker or mask to maintain place	1	1	1	1	1	1	Not Applicable
Use colored overlay	1	1	1	1	1	1	Not Applicable
Other							
Out of Level Testing	Not allowed for grades 2-4 Limited to no more than two grade levels for grades 5 through 11	Not allowed for grades 2-4 Limited to no more than two grade levels for grades 5 through 11	Not allowed for grades 2-4 Limited to no more than two grade levels for grades 5 through 11	Not Applicable	Not Applicable	Not Applicable	Not Applicable
Unlisted accommodation or modification	Check with CDE	Check with CDE	Check with CDE	Check with CDE	Check with CDE	Check with CDE	Check with CDE

*Contact the California Department of Education to find out when a Braille version will be available.

**See waiver policy for the California High School Exit Exam

Category 1 - Testing condition available to students who regularly use it in the classroom

Category 2 - Accommodation available only to students with documentation in IEP or 504 plan

Category 3 - Modification (fundamentally alters what the test measures) available only to students with documentation in IEP or 504 plan

Distribution: White-Permanent File   Canary-Parent   Copies may be made for other team members

Student _____   Date _____

CULMINATION GOAL (FOR SECONDARY STUDENTS)

A student's right to FAPE is terminated upon graduation with a regular high school diploma
Working toward: ❏ Diploma ❏ Certificate of Completion
Anticipated Date of Graduation/Culmination_____
Student has completed _____ units towards graduation.

For students with anticipated dates of graduation before 2003-2004 school year:
1. The District requires proficiency standards ❏ Yes ❏ No

For students with anticipated dates of graduation beginning with the 2003-2004 school year:
1. The High School Exit Exam has been passed: ❏ Math ❏ Reading and Writing
2. The District's prescribed course of study has been completed? ❏ Yes ❏ No
3. The student has demonstrated satisfactory attendance ❏ Yes ❏ No

PLAN TO TRANSITION FROM NPS OR SDC TO GENERAL CLASS PROGRAM

❏ Training for regular ed. teacher and/or other staff.
   Topic:_____
❏ Conference with parents and service providers to talk
   about the special needs of student.
❏ Discussion with students in the regular class.
   Topic:_____
❏ Behavior Plan for use in regular class (See page _____).
❏ Provide regular education assignments to student while
   still in special education class.

❏ Special education teacher, parent, and/or student visit
   the general education/special day class.
❏ General education class routine reviewed with student.
❏ Peer monitor from general education class assigned.
❏ Gradual transition into general education/special day
   class beginning on _____.
❏ _____
  _____

REFERRALS AND ACTIONS REQUIRED FOLLOWING THE IEP

Action	Responsible Personnel and Position	By When
❏ Transportation		
❏ Additional Assessment for _____		
❏ Additional Assessment for _____		
❏ Referral for AB 3632 Assessment		
❏ Copy of IEP to All Service Providers		
❏		
❏		
❏		
❏		
❏		
❏		

Distribution: White-Permanent File   Canary-Parent   Copies may be made for other team members

Student: _____ Date of Meeting _____

MARIN SELPA
IEP
Page 22____
6/01

REFERRALS AND/OR ADDITIONAL RECOMMENDATIONS/COMMENTS

MARIN
SELPA
IEP
Page 23
7/03

Student _____ Date of Meeting _____

This IEP document contains the following pages:

1❑ 2❑ 3❑ 4❑ 5❑ 6❑ 7❑ 8❑ 9❑ 10❑ 11❑ 12❑ 13❑ 14❑ 15❑ 16❑ 17❑ 18❑ 19❑

20a❑ 20b❑ 20c❑ 21❑ 22 ____ to ____ ❑ 23❑ and Goals and Objectives pages _____ through _____.

TEAM MEMBERS - *The following persons affirm that they were in attendance at the IEP Meeeting*

Administrator _____	Parent _____
Administrator _____	Parent _____
Administrator _____	Physical Therapist _____
Agency Rep. _____	Resource Specialist _____
Community Mental Health _____	SDC Teacher _____
CCS _____	Social Worker _____
District Representative _____	Speech/Language Specialist _____
Guidance Counselor _____	Student _____
Hearing Impaired Specialist _____	Teacher for the Visually Impaired _____
Nurse _____	Teacher _____
Psychologist _____	Teacher _____
Occupational Therapist _____	Translator/Interpreter _____
Orientation/Mobility Instructor _____	_____

❑   A copy of Procedural Safeguards was provided to the parent(s) with the notice of the IEP team meeting.
❑   Parent(s) given a copy of the IEP at no cost.
❑   Parent(s) given a copy of the ❑ evaluation report(s) and ❑ eligibility determination, if appropriate, at no cost.

PARENT DECISION/SIGNATURE

❑ I was notified of the IEP meeting and was able to attend; I have reviewed the IEP and consent to it.
❑ I was notified of the IEP meeting and was able to attend; I choose not to make a decision at this time. I have received a
        copy of the IEP and a copy of "Notification of IEP Recommendations".
❑ I agree and give my consent for the above recommendations to be implemented with the exception of:
        ❑ assessment   ❑ eligibility   ❑ goals and objectives   ❑ services   ❑ placement
_____
❑ I acknowledge that my child is not an individual with exceptional needs and thus not eligible for Special Ed. services.
❑ I disagree and wish to schedule: ❑ an IEP meeting   ❑ informal meeting   ❑ local mediation

                        ❑ prehearing mediation conference   ❑ state due process hearing

❑ I decline the services offered.
❑ I agree that the District has offered my child a free appropriate public education. However, I am voluntarily placing my
        child in a private school.
❑ I request a copy of the IEP to be provided in my primary language or alternative format (braille or tape recording).

_____   _____
Signature of Parent/Guardian Signature/Authorized Representative   Date

_____   _____
Signature of Parent/Guardian Signature/Authorized Representative   Date
Distribution: White-Permanent File   Canary-Parent   Copies may be made for other team members

Appendix 5

Tear-Out Forms

Request for Information on Special Education

Request to Begin Special Education Process and Assessment

Request for Child's School File

Request to Amend Child's School File

Special Education Contacts

IEP Journal

Monthly IEP Calendar

IEP Blueprint

Letter Requesting Assessment Report

Request for Joint IEP Eligibility/Program Meeting

Progress Chart

Program Visitation Request Letter

Class Visitation Checklist

Goals and Objectives Chart

IEP Material Organizer Form

IEP Meeting Participants

IEP Meeting Attendance Objection Letter

Letter Confirming Informal Negotiation

Letter Requesting Due Process

Request for Information on Special Education

Date: _____

To: _____

_____

_____

_____

Re: _____

I am writing to you because my child is experiencing difficulties in school. I understand there is a special process for evaluating a child and determining eligibility for special education programs and services. Please send me any written information about that process. Please also send me information about how I can contact other parents and local support groups involved in special education.

Thank you very much for your kind assistance. I look forward to talking with you further about special education.

Sincerely,

_____

_____

_____

_____

_____

Request to Begin Special Education Process and Assessment

Date: _____

To: _____

_____

_____

_____

Re: _____

I am writing to you because my child is experiencing difficulties in school _____

_____

_____

_____

_____

_____ .

I am formally requesting that the school immediately begin its special education process, including initial assessment for eligibility. I understand that you will send me an assessment plan that explains what tests may be given to my child. Because I realize the assessment can take some time, I would appreciate receiving the assessment plan within ten days. Once you receive my approval for the assessment, would you let me know when the assessment will be scheduled?

I would also appreciate any other information regarding the assessment process, how eligibility is determined, and general IEP procedures.

Thank you very much for your kind assistance. I look forward to working with you and your staff.

Sincerely,

_____

_____

_____

_____

_____

Request for Child's School File

Date: _____

To: _____

_____

_____

_____

Re: _____

I would like a copy of my child's file, including all tests, reports, assessments, grades, notes by teachers or other staff members, memoranda, photographs—in short, *everything* in my child's school file. I understand I have a right to these files under _____

_____

_____

_____

_____ .

I would greatly appreciate having these files within the next five days. I would be happy to pick them up. I will call you to discuss how and when I will get copiess.

Thank you for your kind assistance.

Sincerely,

_____

_____

_____

_____

_____

Request to Amend Child's School File

Date: _____

To: _____

_____

_____

_____

Re: _____

I recently reviewed a copy of my child's file and would like to have a portion of the file amended, specifically:

_____

_____

_____

_____

_____

_____

_____ .

IDEA provides that I have the right to request that all information that is "inaccurate or misleading, or violates the privacy of [my] child" be amended. (34 C.F.R. § 300.567.) I feel that this is just such a case. Therefore, I request that you immediately rectify the situation.

Please notify me in writing as soon as possible of your decision regarding this matter. Thank you.

Sincerely,

_____

_____

_____

_____

Special Education Contacts

Name, Address, Phone and Fax Numbers, and Email Address

School Staff

_____

_____

_____

_____

_____

_____

_____

Outside Professionals

_____

_____

_____

_____

_____

Other Parents

_____

_____

_____

_____

_____

Support Groups

_____

_____

State Department of Education

_____

_____

_____

Other

_____

_____

_____

_____

_____

IEP Journal

Date: _____ **Time:** _____ a.m./p.m.

Action: ☐ Phone Call _____ ☐ Meeting _____

☐ Other: _____

Person(s) Contacted: _____

Notes: _____

_____

_____

_____

_____

_____

_____

_____

_____

_____

_____

IEP Journal

Date: _____ **Time:** _____ a.m./p.m.

Action: ☐ Phone Call _____ ☐ Meeting _____

☐ Other: _____

Person(s) Contacted: _____

Notes: _____

_____

_____

_____

_____

_____

_____

_____

_____

_____

Monthly IEP Calendar

Month and Year: _____

1	2	3	4	5	6	7
8	9	10	11	12	13	14
15	16	17	18	19	20	21
22	23	24	25	26	27	28
29	30	31				

NOLO
www.nolo.com

IEP Blueprint

The IEP Blueprint represents the ideal IEP for your child. Use it as a guide to make and record the educational desires you have for your child.

Areas of the IEP	Preferred Situation for Your Child
1. Classroom Setting and Peer Needs— issues to consider:	
☐ regular versus special education class	_____
☐ partially or fully mainstreamed	_____
☐ type of special education class	_____
☐ number of children in the classroom	_____
☐ ages and cognitive ranges of children in class	_____
☐ kinds of students and behaviors that might or might not be appropriate for your child, and	_____
☐ language similarities.	_____
2. Teacher and Staff Needs—issues to consider:	
☐ number of teachers and aides	_____
☐ teacher-pupil ratio	_____
☐ experience, training and expertise of the teacher, and	_____
☐ training and expertise of aides.	_____
3. Curricula and Teaching Methodology— be specific. If you don't know what you *do* want, specify what you *don't* want.	_____

Areas of the IEP	Ideal Situation for Your Child

4. Related Services—issues to consider:

☐ specific needed services

_____

_____

☐ type of services

_____

_____

☐ frequency of services, and

_____

_____

☐ length of services.

_____

_____

5. Identified Programs—specify known programs that you think would work for your child and the school that offers them.

_____

_____

_____

_____

_____

_____

_____

_____

6. Goals and Objectives—goals are long range in nature, while objectives are more short term.

_____

_____

_____

_____

_____

_____

_____

_____

7. Classroom Environment and Other Features—issues to consider:

☐ distance from home

_____

_____

☐ transition plans for mainstreaming

_____

_____

☐ vocational needs

_____

_____

☐ extracurricular and social needs, and

_____

_____

☐ environmental needs.

_____

Letter Requesting Assessment Report

Date: _____

To: _____

      _____

      _____

      _____

Re: _____

I appreciate your involvement in my child's assessment and look forward to your report. Would you please:

1. Send me a copy of a draft of your report before you finalize it. As you can imagine, the process can be overwhelming for parents. It would be most helpful to me to see your report, because the proposed tests are complicated and I need time to evaluate the results.

2. Send me your final report at least four weeks before the IEP meeting.

Again, thank you for your kind assistance.

Sincerely,

_____

_____

_____

_____

_____

Request for Joint IEP Eligibility/Program Meeting

Date: _____

To: _____

_____

_____

_____

Re: _____

I believe there is sufficient information for us to discuss both my child's eligibility for special education and the specifics of my child's IEP at the same meeting. I would appreciate it if you would plan enough time to discuss both those important items at the _____ IEP meeting. I would also like to see any and all reports and other written material that you will be introducing at the IEP meeting, at least two weeks before the meeting.

Thanks in advance for your help. I hope to hear from you soon.

Sincerely,

_____

_____

_____

_____

_____

Progress Chart

Student: _____

Class: _____

Date: _____

Key Goals and Objectives	Current Status	Comments
Math	Progressing appropriately? ☐ yes ☐ no	_____ _____ _____
Reading	Progressing appropriately? ☐ yes ☐ no	_____ _____ _____
Writing	Progressing appropriately? ☐ yes ☐ no	_____ _____ _____
Spelling	Progressing appropriately? ☐ yes ☐ no	_____ _____ _____
Social-behavioral	Progressing appropriately? ☐ yes ☐ no	_____ _____ _____
Language development	Progressing appropriately? ☐ yes ☐ no	_____ _____ _____
Motor development	Progressing appropriately? ☐ yes ☐ no	_____ _____ _____
Other	Progressing appropriately? ☐ yes ☐ no	_____ _____ _____

Program Visitation Request Letter

Date: _____

To: _____

_____

_____

_____

Re: _____

I appreciate the concerns you have, and I realize that you can't know which programs are appropriate for my child until after the IEP meeting. Nonetheless, I think it would be very helpful for me to see existing programs so I can be a more effective member of the IEP team. I do not feel I can make an informed IEP decision without seeing, firsthand, all possible options. I want to assure you that I understand that by giving me the names of existing programs, you are not stating an opinion as to their appropriateness for my child.

I assure you that I will abide by all rules and regulations for parental visits. If those rules and regulations are in writing, please send me a copy.

Thanks in advance for your help. I hope to hear from you soon.

Sincerely,

_____

_____

_____

_____

_____

Class Visitation Checklist

Date: _____ Time: _____ a.m./p.m.

School: _____

Class: _____

Student Description:

Total students: _____ Gender range: _____

Age range: _____

Cognitive range: _____

_____

_____

Language/communication range: _____

_____

_____

_____

Disability range: _____

_____

_____

_____

Behavioral range: _____

_____

_____

_____

Other observations: _____

_____

_____

_____

Staff Description:

Teachers: _____

_____

_____

_____

Aides: _____

_____

_____

_____

Other observations: _____

_____

_____

Curricula/Classroom Strategies:

Curricula: _____

_____

_____

_____

_____

Strategies: _____

_____

_____

_____

_____

Classroom Environment:

Description: _____

_____

_____

_____

_____

_____

Related Services:

_____

_____

_____

Other Comments:

_____

_____

_____

_____

_____

How This Program Relates to IEP Blueprint:

_____

_____

_____

_____

_____

Goals and Objectives Chart

Skill Area	Annual Goal	Short-Term Objective (or Benchmark)	Present Performance Level	How Progress Measured	Date of Completion
Reading					
Math					
Emotional and psychological					

Goals and Objectives Chart

Skill Area	Annual Goal	Short-Term Objective (or Benchmark)	Present Performance Level	How Progress Measured	Date of Completion
Social-behavioral					
Linguistic and communication					
Self-help and independent living skills (transition services)					

Goals and Objectives Chart

IEP Material Organizer Form

Issue: _____

Use this form to track documents and persons that provide support for or opposition to your goals.

Document or Witness* Name(s):	Binder Location (if applicable)	Helps You	Hurts You	Key Supportive or Oppositional Information	Rebuttal Document or Witness Name(s) (If hurts) (If none, what will you say at meeting?)

* A "witness" is someone (teacher, doctor, assessor, tutor, psychologist) who gives an oral or written opinion regarding your child's needs at the IEP meeting.

IEP Meeting Participants

Name	Position/Employer	Purpose for Attending	Point of View

IEP Meeting Attendance Objection Letter

Date: _____

To: _____

_____

_____

_____

Re: _____

I understand that _____ ,

will be at _____ IEP meeting. _____

knows nothing about _____ and appears to have no knowledge that

might be of use to the IEP team. I am formally requesting that _____

not attend, unless there is some clear reason that makes _____

attendance appropriate and necessary for the development of _____

IEP plan. As you know, IEP meetings can be particularly difficult for parents. We are already

anxious about ours and would prefer that you not take action that will heighten our stress

level.

If you insist on _____ attending without any reason, then we

will file a complaint with the state and federal departments of education.

I will call you in a few days to find out your decision on this issue. Thank you for considering

my request.

Sincerely,

_____

_____

_____

_____

_____

Letter Confirming Informal Negotiation

Date: _____

To: _____

_____

_____

_____

Re: _____

I appreciated the chance to meet on _____ and discuss
_____ . I also appreciated your
point of view and the manner in which we solved the problem.

I want to confirm our agreement that _____
_____
_____
_____ .

I greatly appreciate the manner in which you helped solve this problem. _____
_____
_____
_____ .

Thank you.

Sincerely,

_____

_____

_____

_____

_____

Letter Requesting Due Process

Date: _____

To: _____

_____

_____

_____

Re: _____

_____

_____

We are formally requesting due process, beginning with mediation. We believe _____

_____

_____

_____.

We believe an appropriate solution would include, but should not be limited to, the following:

_____

_____

_____

_____

_____.

We understand IDEA (34 C.F.R. § 300.511) requires that a fair hearing decision be rendered within 45 days after you receive this request. We would appreciate it if you would contact us at once to schedule the mediation.

Sincerely,

_____

_____

_____

_____

_____

Index

■

Remember:

Little publishers have big ears.
We really listen to you.

Take 2 Minutes & Give Us Your 2 cents

Your comments make a big difference in the development and revision of Nolo books and software. Please take a few minutes and register your Nolo product—and your comments—with us. Not only will your input make a difference, you'll receive special offers available only to registered owners of Nolo products on our newest books and software. Register now by:

PHONE	**FAX**	**EMAIL**	or **MAIL** us
1-800-728-3555	1-800-645-0895	cs@nolo.com	this registration card

fold here

NOLO

Registration Card

NAME _____ DATE _____

ADDRESS _____

_____

CITY _____ STATE _____ ZIP _____

PHONE _____ E-MAIL _____

WHERE DID YOU HEAR ABOUT THIS PRODUCT? _____

WHERE DID YOU PURCHASE THIS PRODUCT? _____

DID YOU CONSULT A LAWYER? (PLEASE CIRCLE ONE)   YES   NO   NOT APPLICABLE

DID YOU FIND THIS BOOK HELPFUL?   (VERY)   5   4   3   2   1   (NOT AT ALL)

COMMENTS _____

_____

_____

WAS IT EASY TO USE?   (VERY EASY)   5   4   3   2   1   (VERY DIFFICULT)

We occasionally make our mailing list available to carefully selected companies whose products may be of interest to you.

❏ If you do not wish to receive mailings from these companies, please check this box.

❏ You can quote me in future Nolo promotional materials.
    Daytime phone number _____.

IEP 3.0

Nolo *in the* NEWS

"Nolo helps lay people perform legal tasks without the aid—or fees—of lawyers."

—USA TODAY

Nolo books are ..."written in plain language, free of legal mumbo jumbo, and spiced with witty personal observations."

—ASSOCIATED PRESS

"...Nolo publications...guide people simply through the how, when, where and why of law."

—WASHINGTON POST

"Increasingly, people who are not lawyers are performing tasks usually regarded as legal work... And consumers, using books like Nolo's, do routine legal work themselves."

—NEW YORK TIMES

"...All of [Nolo's] books are easy-to-understand, are updated regularly, provide pull-out forms...and are often quite moving in their sense of compassion for the struggles of the lay reader."

—SAN FRANCISCO CHRONICLE

fold here

- -

Place
stamp here

Nolo
950 Parker Street
Berkeley, CA 94710-9867

Attn: IEP 3.0